W9-AXC-575

Agents and Victims
in South China

A fading imprint of Mao Zedong on the wall of an old village house. (1986)

Agents and Victims in South China

Accomplices in Rural Revolution

Helen F. Siu

Yale University Press

New Haven and London

Published with the assistance of the Frederick W.
Hilles Publication Fund of Yale University.

Copyright © 1989 by Yale University. All rights
reserved. This book may not be reproduced, in whole
or in part, including illustrations, in any form (beyond
that copying permitted by Sections 107 and 108 of the
U.S. Copyright Law and except by reviewers for the
public press), without written permission from the
publishers.

Designed by Jo Aerne and set in Meridian type by
The Composing Room of Michigan.
Printed in the United States of America by
Vail-Ballou Press, Binghamton, New York.

Library of Congress Cataloging-in-Publication Data
Siu, Helen F.
    Agents and victims in south China : accomplices in
rural revolution / Helen F. Siu.
        p.   cm.
    Bibliography: p.
    Includes index.
    ISBN 0–300–04465–8 (alk. paper)
    1. Elites (Social sciences)—China.   2. China—
Rural conditions.   3. Local government—China.   4.
China—Politics and government—1949–   I. Title.
HN740.Z9E465   1989   88–26993
307.7'2'0951—dc19   CIP

The paper in this book meets the guidelines for
permanence and durability of the Committee on
Production Guidelines for Book Longevity of the
Council on Library Resources.

10 9 8 7 6 5 4 3 2 1

For my mother,
a most compassionate Chinese woman

Contents

List of Figures and Tables   ix

Acknowledgments   xiii

Prologue: Images   xv

Periods in Chinese History   xxiii

General Administrative Levels, 1958–1983   xxiv

Note on Weights and Measures   xxiv

1   Introduction   1

2   Historical Geography   15

3   Social Cells: Community and Kin   36

4   Cultural Tissues: A Regional Nexus of Power   57

5   The Reign of Local Bosses   88

6   Understanding Revolution: The Language of Class   116

7   Losing Ground: Community Cellularized   143

8   The Leap: Community Bureaucratized   170

9   Complicity and Compliance   189

10   The Paradox of Power   212

11   The Paradox of Self-Reliance   245

12   State Involution   273

13   Agents and Victims   291

Notes   303

References   341

Glossary   365

Index   373

Figures

Photo galleries following pages 56, 142, and 272

2.1	South China: Lingnan	17
2.2	Huicheng and Vicinity before 1949	19
2.3	Xinhui County Boundaries, Kangxi Period, Seventeenth Century	21
2.4	Xinhui County Boundaries, Daoguang Period, Nineteenth Century	22
2.5	The Pearl River Delta	23
7.1	Townships in the Huancheng Area, 1956	145
8.1	Huancheng Commune and Brigades, 1965	172
9.1	The Party Committee in Huancheng Commune, 1970–79	209
9.2	The Revolutionary Committee in Huancheng Commune, 1970–79	210
10.1	Old Waterways in the Huancheng Area	233
10.2	The Plan for the Highway-Dike Project, 1975	234
10.3	The Highway-Dike Project—The Parts Completed	236

Tables

2.1	Sands in the Delta, 1930s	25
5.1	Selected Taxes and Surcharges in Xinhui, 1920s–1940s	92
6.1	Committee Members of the Guangdong Provincial People's Government	120

6.2   Delegates of the First Provincial People's Congress, 1950   122

6.3   Backgrounds of Leading Cadres in the Prefectural,
        Municipal, and County Governments, Guangdong
        Province, 1950   124

6.4   Background of Township and Village Cadres in
        Guangdong and Hunan Provinces, 1952   125

6.5   Class Compositions, Dongjia and Tianlu Xiang   126

7.1   Grain and Citrus Production, Xinhui County, 1949–82   152

8.1   Enterprises in Huancheng Commune, 1958–77   179

8.2   Education and Health Care in Huancheng Commune,
        1961–78   182

8.3   Some Statistics for Huancheng Commune, 1953–65   186

9.1   General Statistics for the Brigades and Teams, 1962–82   194

9.2   General Statistics for the Brigades, 1962–82   196

9.3   Class Differentiations in Selected Brigades, 1964   199

9.4   Class Differences in Savings and Loans, Yuanqing
        Cooperative, Dongjia Brigade, 1962   200

10.1   Leading Cadres in Selected Brigades, 1980   216

10.2   Ages of Leading Brigade Cadres, 1980   217

10.3   Grain Production: Planned Acreage and Output   221

10.4   Grain Production: Actual Acreage and Output   222

10.5   Grain Procurement and Consumption for Huancheng
        Commune   223

10.6   Secondary Crops, Huancheng Commune, 1961–78   224

10.7   Major Crops as a Percentage of Total Cultivated Area,
        1961–82   225

10.8   Grain Quotas for Selected Brigades, 1966–82   227

10.9   Enterprise Performance of Sancun Brigade   241

11.1   The Growth of Commune Enterprises in Huancheng   247

11.2   A Comparison of Commune, Brigade, and Team Output   248

11.3   Industrial Development: Comparisons of Huancheng
        and Other Communes in Xinhui County, 1979   249

11.4   The Background of Leading Cadres in Commune
        Enterprises, 1981   258

11.5   Profiles of Workers in the Huancheng Commune Palm-
        Handicraft Factory, 1978   261

11.6   Profiles of Workers in the Huancheng Commune
        Agricultural Machinery Station, 1978   261

11.7   Profiles of Workers in the Huancheng Commune Paper
        Factory, 1978   262

11.8   Profiles of Workers in the Huancheng Commune
        Agricultural Machinery Factory, 1978   263

11.9   Enterprise Development, Selected Brigades   266

12.1   Cropping Patterns in Dongjia and Tianlu Brigades   275

12.2   Per Capita Team Income of Tianlu Brigade   278

12.3   Per Capita Team Income of Dongjia Brigade   282

Acknowledgments

This project started in 1981 after I finished my dissertation and was unhappy with what I had written. Numerous institutions made this book possible. Some of the data was collected during the time I was a faculty member at the Chinese University of Hong Kong (1976–80), a position that allowed me to use research grants from the Harvard-Yenching Institute and from the Trustees of Lingnan University. As a Culpeper Postdoctoral Fellow at Williams College (1980–82), I continued fieldwork in China during the summers. The Yale Center for International and Area Studies provided supplementary research funds in 1985. In 1986, I received a year-long research grant from the Committee on Scholarly Communication with the People's Republic of China, National Academy of Sciences. Though I focused my research on a neighboring county, I made several short trips back to my old field site to collect comparative data.

I am particularly grateful to colleagues at Yale University in the Department of Anthropology, in the Council of East Asian Studies, and in the Whitney Humanities Center for their support. Special thanks to the past and present members of an informal study group, Jean Agnew, Deborah Davis, Mat Hamabata, William Kelly, Keith Luria, Sarah Morris, Bridgit Murnaghan, James Scott, Susanne Wofford, and Susan Woodward. Our explorations into Renaissance history and literature, social theory, and popular culture have been intellectually exhilarating and socially gratifying. If it were not for them, I would have finished the book four years ago.

I shall always remember three people who contributed to my intellectual commitment but who are no longer with us. Paul Riesman was a most inspiring teacher at Carleton College. Judy Strauch, fellow graduate student at Stanford University, focused my interest on political brokers. Tsui Wei-ying was my first student and research assistant. Her devotion helped us survive the most difficult field trips.

I would like to thank those who have generously given their advice. Peggy Barlett, Myron L. Cohen, Deborah Davis, Nicholas Lardy, Hong Yung Lee, Ann Lindbeck, William Parish, Suzanne Pepper, James Scott, Michael Smith, Jonathan Spence, John Starr, Roger Thompson, Ezra Vogel, Frederic Wakeman, and Arthur Wolf have read and commented on parts or all of the manuscript at different stages of writing.

I am grateful to James Hayes, Ye Xian'en, Liu Zhiwei, and Chen Chunsheng for guiding me through the archives in Hong Kong and Guangzhou. The comradeship of my research assistants, Cheng Man-tsun, Yip Kam-bor, Wen Hing-bo, Wong Chi-ming, and Pong Suet-ling, was essential in the field. The maps have been prepared by Philip Yeung, Too See-lou, and Heidi Fogel. Elizabeth Kyburg converted my statistical tables into works of art. Over the years, Ellen Graham of Yale University Press has encouraged me to persevere with the crucial question: Is the manuscript done? Thanks to Caroline Murphy, production editor, and Emily Booch-ever, manuscript editor, as well as to John Ziemer, for their meticulous attention to the manuscript.

I would like to thank my mother and sisters in Hong Kong, who provided lodging in an otherwise unaffordable city whenever I needed a break from the field. Thanks also to Ching-hwa Tsang and Michael Gaynon, whose phone calls from California have always brought warmth to the chilly New Haven nights.

Last but not least are two friends to whom I owe special intellectual and personal debts. David Faure has rekindled my enthusiasm in the cultural history of the Pearl River delta. I treasure our adventures in the archives and in the field. Both he and Jack Goody have patiently and critically read through the manuscript and have been a constant source of inspiration and humor.

My deepest gratitude of course goes to the people of Huancheng and Huicheng, who have shared with me what was at times politically unthinkable.

Prologue: Images

It was an unusually wet spring in April 1977. I was among ten university teachers from Hong Kong invited by the Chinese authorities to survey various rural communes in the Pearl River delta of Guangdong Province. On the last leg of our journey we reached Huicheng, the county capital of Xinhui, known for its scenic beauty and historical interest at the western edge of the delta. It had rained for three days. I sensed the anxiety behind the civility of our hosts, who arranged for our immediate departure. It seemed that crossing the swollen Xi River (a major tributary of the Pearl River) was quite risky, but being stranded was not a pleasant alternative. Travel facilities were tight, and everyone speculated about when we would reach the provincial capital, Guangzhou (Canton), 110 kilometers away. The atmosphere was tense and uncertain, as were many political careers at the time.[1] When we were ferried across the river, buildings at the pier were half-submerged, and fields that were still quite bare pushed against the currents of the Xi River. Only the lush green fan palms stood out on the dikes against the dismal horizon. We hurried off, but I looked back. For the following ten years I returned to that part of the delta many times to do research. The land and the people with whom I made friends* eventually formed a social landscape that continued to excite my curiosity and capture my imagination. I looked back in time to the history and tradition that elderly villagers relied upon, and I tried to reach beyond present realities to understand their hopes.

It may be helpful to the reader if I explain why I chose to study Huancheng Commune of Xinhui County. In fact, my hosts were often intrigued by the same question. "We are peasants," they said. "What is it that interests you?" I paid my initial visit to rural China in 1974, influenced by ideological preferences to which I hoped to attach academic dignity. I shared the sense of outrage of many modern Chinese intellectuals at how peasants in the first half of the twentieth century had been abused by

---

*The names of most individuals, except for prominent historical figures, have been changed to protect their identity.

xv

successive regimes. Naively assuming that the Communists had come to power with popular support, I began to ask how the party used its ideological and organizational means to build a modern economy and state and to provide a degree of social equality for the vast peasantry. Having been subjects for as long as the Chinese dynasties had been in power, the peasants, I thought, might finally acquire the status of citizens.

I was initially concerned with a central theme in China's development strategy: rural industrialization. Since late 1958, the regime had promoted small-scale enterprises at the commune and brigade levels of administration. These were to provide the communities with income, employment, services for agriculture, and industrial skills. By mobilizing local initiative for self-reliant development, the regime hoped to avoid an exodus from the villages to cities, the social and political consequences of which have continued to plague many agrarian societies in the transition to a modern economy.

What interested me most was the regime's political objectives. These small-scale enterprises were operated by communes and brigades. With their accumulated industrial resources, communes maintained two sets of institutional ties. They contracted with state industries to secure supplies and markets; these economic connections in turn enhanced their leverage over subordinate brigades and teams. In fact, communes were expected to use their resources politically, in a way that narrowed disparities among brigades; the same was expected of brigades in relation to their teams. My political attitudes at the time made me eager to learn how the development of these enterprises facilitated what I believed to be a gradual, benign integration of the vast countryside into a modern socialist state, and how parochial concerns of family and community might eventually be transformed to identifications with party and nation. The Chinese road to socialism, I thought, might become a model for agrarian societies undergoing the pains of modern development.

I chose to study Huancheng Commune because its diversified economy, based on rice, fan palm, fruits, sugarcane, and vegetables, provided ample research materials for my interest in rural enterprises. Historically, the area was known for its palm handicrafts; if one believed that postrevolutionary development bore the stamp of the past, it would be worth examining how the traditional handicrafts and their associated economic arrangements made the transition to new institutional contexts. Looking ahead, the commune's enterprises both meshed with industries at Huicheng at its northern boundary and served agriculture through its 29 brigades comprising 190 production teams. The enterprises were intended to be instrumental in narrowing the disparities among the commune's subordinate units, a step believed to be necessary before the level of accounting could be raised from the team to a higher one within the commune. Both processes were aimed at facilitating the commune's eventual incorporation into the state sector.[2] What better site and moment could there be to indulge my political enthusiasm and academic curiosity?

I began the research for my dissertation in 1977. The political atmosphere was tense as cadres at all levels watched the ambiguous signals from the party center. I was not able to conduct the conventional year-long field research expected of anthropologists. Instead I made do with numerous trips of a few weeks or so.[3] Being an overseas Chinese helped, especially when my mother had a sister in Xinhui County. Such status nonetheless created its own problems. My peasant friends were somewhat offended by the fact that I did not visit my cousins until near the end of my research; my hosts, cadres in the commune, exerted their share of pressure because they generally expected ethnic Chinese to agree with the nation's political priorities. They were quite dismayed that I did not seem to be concerned with my native roots. From the spring of 1977 to the summer of 1980, I paid a series of visits to Huancheng Commune and cities such as Huicheng, Jiangmen, and Guangzhou. I interviewed cadres at various levels of the administration. I visited commune and brigade enterprises and made friends with junior cadres and workers. Over tea and fruit, we exchanged ideas and shared observations until late in the night. Occasionally, I followed them to the villages, sat inside dilapidated ancestral halls then used as administrative headquarters,[4] and listened to elderly peasants reconstruct a history that they felt they had had a part in.[5]

Despite my preoccupation with rural enterprises, I was catching glimpses of another, more disturbing reality in the course of my field research, which would change my views about the nature of modern state-building. The commune and its brigades in fact had little autonomy in what was officially termed self-reliant development. Unlike small-scale industries in Hong Kong or Taiwan, the operations of those in Huancheng Commune fluctuated sharply with national political currents rather than with local or regional market conditions. In the early 1970s, for example, a profitable machine-tool contract with a county factory was revoked by the county administration on the grounds that it would divert the attention of the commune factory from aiding agriculture. Old peasant cadres were chosen to head industrial enterprises not for their technical competence but for their presumed political loyalties. Managers hoarded surplus raw materials so that they could use them for political leverage. A vegetable-processing factory proposed by the commune was abandoned because county-level cadres condemned the project as "capitalistic." A brigade could not build a much needed road because its quota of cement from the county government was small and nothing else was available in rural markets. Accusations of corruption were rampant: cadres had used their leverage to recruit relatives and friends for industrial jobs, which paid higher wages and were sought after by young laborers who wanted to avoid back-breaking work in the fields. Even more alarming were the wasteful projects that the county government obliged the commune to carry out. One such project was the construction of a highway-dike in 1975. To create a set of canals, which later turned out to be an ecological disaster, the commune drained its treasury of funds accumulated over ten years, several brigades in the commune found their valuable farmland reduced in size, and team members lost their fruit trees on the dikes. To top it all, the county government never delivered the water pumps or the electricity that it had promised. When asked why they conducted such a project, cadres in the commune and brigades uniformly replied, "What choice did we have when our county party secretaries wanted to follow the spirit of Dazhai?"[6] Peasants resented the waste but grudgingly complied. Most felt that they had to go along with the cadres. As it was put to me: "Objections were voiced; reports were made to the higher-ups; and we dragged our feet. But we dug the canals, did we not?" Ironically, such fearful paralysis prevailed precisely during the 1970s when socialist ideals were professed most ardently by national party leaders. As a brigade cadre aptly described their predicament, "We may occasionally ride political storms, but we cannot prevent them from coming."

The party has exercised authority in the name of revolution and socialism. How was it held accountable to the people it supposedly served? The mandate of heaven has been changed to a mandate of the people, but to what extent were peasants citizens instead of subjects?[7] Granted that one should treat ideological professions with caution and that China's political tradition could not be expected to change overnight, it is intriguing to explore the predicament of rural society when a regime summoned unprecedented determination to transform it with a different claim to authority.

The commune's apparent lack of political initiative led my attention to rural cadres who were responsible for implementing policies. It is worth comparing their situation with that of the local gentry in imperial China and of political brokers of other state agrarian societies. What is the nature of their power or the lack of it, given the fact that the preeminence of state authority is assumed in Chinese culture and that the postrevolutionary state has amassed a remarkable concentration of economic resources and political leverage?[8] In the course of my research from the mid-1970s to the mid-1980s, I made friends with three of the commune's leading cadres, whose life experiences intertwined to form a continuous political theme in the transformation of the commune, specifically, the step-by-step consolidation of a powerful rural bureaucracy and its inherent paradoxes.

Xu Wenqing was from a family of urban intellectuals. A college graduate working in the provincial government, he responded to the party's call in 1954 to settle in the countryside. His move to Huancheng was a mixed blessing from his point of view. On the one hand, he entertained idealistic notions about his part in the young regime's effort to build socialism; on the other hand, his family's "bourgeois" background made him politically suspect in the eyes of some party leaders. He saw no choice but to make the extra effort to show his commitment. For twenty-five years he lived in a small house in the commune, married a local woman, raised a family, participated in menial work, and helped Huancheng's semiliterate party secretaries handle voluminous documents.

When I met him in 1977, he was director of the office of the commune government, but he did not hold a leadership position in the party committee. A soft-spoken man with a slight build, he was very reserved. However, when I traveled with him to the villages, I was pleasantly surprised by his detailed knowledge of agricultural production. Peasants and brigade cadres greeted him eagerly and pleaded with him to speak for them on various policy matters. He was their "Bao Qing Tian," a legendary official who helped victims of bureaucratic abuse. I once asked him what I could contribute to the commune's effort to modernize, and he answered, "Bring us dictionaries. If we are to face the outside world, we need to start from the basics. The problem with our country is that we have relied too much on faith." I was away when he fell seriously ill in the summer of 1979. Nevertheless, he struggled to instruct my research assistant as to whom I should work with after he was gone. He passed away two days later at the age of fifty-three. It was sadly ironic that his death came at the end of an era of radical politics during which a generation of intellectuals who were eager to construct their country's future were treated with suspicion because of class labels fixed upon them.

Chen Mingfa was the cadre named by Xu Wenqing to help me. They were close friends, though their backgrounds and careers could not have been more different. A peasant activist with a primary school education, Chen was recruited into the party in the early 1950s and had subsequently risen in the party ranks as the area's "peasant theoretician." He spent twenty years in his native village as party secretary until he was transferred to the commune enterprise office in 1971. He admitted later that he hated the job because he felt incompetent and did not adjust easily to industrial

schedules. However, loyalties to his background in the peasant class mattered most at the time, and the commune entrusted him with the task of
preventing the enterprises from neglecting agriculture. He was the head of
the office when I met him in 1977. His dark, weather-beaten complexion
and awkward manners gave him a "peasant" appearance most incongruous with the thick pair of glasses on his face. My respect for him grew
through the years as he revealed the commune economy and officialdom
to me sensitively and sensibly. In an unassuming manner he also exposed
me to the web of social relationships in which he served skillfully as
mediator. To my surprise, he was dismissed from office in 1982 after being
implicated in a corruption case involving one of his subordinates. His
downfall was unexpected among his peers. A sincere man, he was not
disliked by fellow workers. Unfortunately his career paralleled too closely
the reign of Maoist politics. He might have protected his subordinate out of
kindness, but higher officials attuned to party politics were too eager for
political scapegoats at a time of ideological redefinition.

My third contact, Chen Sheyuan, came from the same village as Chen
Mingfa. Also a local activist made party cadre in the 1950s, he had worked
as an accountant and a headmaster of a primary school. He was assigned to
the commune government office in the late 1950s and became its director
after Xu Wenqing's death in 1979. Though he could not live up to Xu's
legacy, he commanded respect in his own way. After all, he was more
"educated" than many of the commune party secretaries. His straightfor-
ward style made him approachable in the eyes of local peasants. I once
watched him jump off our van to remove two 50-catty baskets of grain
blocking the way, embarrassing junior cadres who expected peasants to
respond to our driver's honking. "During the Cultural Revolution, the
tabloids I wrote for the commune would cover all of Huicheng", he often
announced with a broad smile, "but now, economic energies have livened
up to the same degree as politics had then." We met again in March 1986,
and I was not surprised to learn that he had not been forced into retirement
as a matter of policy in the post-Mao era. A low-keyed cadre who toed
ideological lines carefully, he has been a survivor.

Through the maze of human networks introduced by the three cadres, I
came to know many characters—ordinary peasants, team and brigade
cadres, old party secretaries, young workers in the commune and brigade
enterprises. There was the party secretary whom people fearfully referred
to as "the occupant of the gray-brick mansion." Others included brigade
cadres known to have enjoyed "helicopter rides," because they had risen
precipitously during the Cultural Revolution. Between toothless old peasants, who could count every ancestral hall in the village and recalled

details of folk festivals during the lunar year, and young ones, who could only relate to the anti-Confucian campaigns, I experienced the cultural consequence of the revolution. Recent political liberalization has brought with it the revival of popular rituals, and I found that it is no longer uncommon for young people to participate in religious pilgrimages or to subject themselves to the demands of traditional wedding ceremonies. However, when questioned about the wider cultural meanings behind the activities, they responded with perplexed looks that bespoke the problems of a cultural vacuum.

More blatant was the ideological vacuum displayed. I could understand why former landlords and their children held grudges against the regime for having reduced them to a caste of untouchables for more than three decades. However, among a generation of young workers who were relatively literate and articulate, I also detected a disturbing sense of cynicism. Though raised on the socialist ideals promoted by the new regime, they keenly felt the discriminations against their rural status. They also saw careers and hopes shattered by decades of political vicissitudes. The lives of these people were often controlled by political forces quite out of their reach. They collaborated and conflicted to make the best of circumstances. How they perceived their predicaments and pursued their interests and hopes made up the social political dynamics of the commune. They actively used the resources within their means to cope with a state determined to include them. They gave it compliance and, at times, complicity. Yet so many felt victimized by the very structures and processes to which their actions had given significance.

I am not sure when I began to confront my own disillusionment, but my growing unease in the 1980s precipitated an intellectual urge to analyze the source of the problems in the system. Not that I look back to the Maoist days with nostalgia or that I regard the recent reforms as a second liberation. Few of my informants do. Ironically, amidst their anxious efforts to shed their political past and to get ahead economically, a familiar paralysis lurks behind their strategies. It seems to me that despite efforts to reform itself, a weighty bureaucracy representing the party-state continues to reach the most private corners of people's lives. Like the dynasties before it, it is rather self-righteous and arbitrary. Yet unlike many dynasties in the past, it wields tremendous organizational power.

What my peasant friends could not articulate is captured in a novella by Liu Xinwu entitled "Overpass." Though the story develops around bureaucratic bottlenecks that have led to agonizing overcrowding and desperate maneuvering for a family in Beijing, its political and philosophical messages have a wider relevance. In the foreword to an anthology of post-

Mao literature in translation (Siu and Stern 1983, vi), Jonathan Spence writes with regard to "Overpass": "There is extraordinary agreement among these writers about the loss of dignity that afflicts all Chinese denied privacy, in housing as in thought, forced forever to jostle and bargain and plead until the shouts become cries and the cries blows."

In a sense, I went to China with Marxist hopes; but I left with Max Weber's worst fears. Writing this ethnography has been a self-reflective endeavor.

Periods in Chinese History

Late Imperial China

Ming dynasty	1368–1644
Qing dynasty	1644–1911
Reign periods:	
Shunzhi	1644–1661
Kangxi	1662–1722
Yongzheng	1723–1735
Qianlong	1736–1795
Jiaqing	1796–1820
Daoguang	1821–1850
Xianfeng	1851–1861
Tongzhi	1862–1874
Guangxu	1875–1908
Xuantong	1909–1911

Republican China

Warlords	1912–1927
Jiang Jieshi's (Chiang Kai-shek) regime	1927–1949
Japanese occupation	1938–1945
Civil war between the Chinese Communists and the Nationalists	1946–1949

People's Republic of China

Land reform	1949–1952
Collectivization	1953–1957
Great Leap Forward and people's communes	1958–1959
Three bad years	1959–1961
Cultural Revolution	1966–1969
Fall of the "Gang of Four"	1976
Political and economic liberalization	1978–

General Administrative Levels, 1958–1983

Central government
Province (and municipality)
Prefecture (and municipality)
County

} urban environment,
industrial work,
state ownership

Commune
Brigade
Team

} rural environment,
agricultural work,
collective ownership

Note on Weights and Measures

1 li (Chinese mile) = 500 meters
1 jin (catty) = 605 grams
1 dan (picul, 100 catties) = 60.05 kilograms
1 shi (150 catties) = 90.75 kilograms
1 mu = 1/15 hectare
1 qing (100 mu) = 6.66 hectares

Agents and Victims
in South China

CHAPTER 1

Introduction

This ethnography shares with other studies of state agrarian societies a concern for the means by which the ideological and organizational powers of the central government penetrate rural society to exact compliance as well as invoke commitment.[1] In agrarian societies undergoing modern transition, governments engineer changes with a remarkable array of ideologies. Some social institutions are retained, while others are abandoned; some voices prevail, while others are silenced or ignored.

The locality I examine is Huancheng Commune in south China, and for me, the central question is how the dynastic order was replaced by new claims to authority in the twentieth century. Although the late imperial state (the Qing dynasty) increasingly lost its ability to reach rural society, traditional cultural concerns seem to have survived through the Republican period. The question is whether, in the People's Republic, these concerns have been built upon in the creation of a new state.[2]

Peasant China in the last few decades has comprised a curious mixture of "traditional" and "revolutionary" features. At times, the rural social fabric torn by socialist rhetoric has seemed especially vulnerable and exposed, but at other times, concerns for kin and community, entrepreneurship, and popular religion have resurfaced. The recent decade of reforms has triggered an intense upsurge of conventional practices ranging from family enterprises to popular rituals. Even imperial impostors continue to draw an audience (Anagnost 1985). The juxtapositions have been baffling. Have traditional cultural assumptions survived the encounter with the Maoist revolution to come back full circle in the 1980s? Or have processes of modern state-making and nation-building transformed rural society to the extent that what we observe today are mere fragments of tradition reconstituted for coping with contemporary existence, which continues to be shaped by the priorities of the socialist state?

Moreover, even if we can assume that peasant China has hung on to her cultural tradition against the demands of the socialist state, can we be sure that the revolutionary leaders themselves are free of their own cultural past? Both anthropologists and historians will recognize the complexities

of the situation in the following description of the state's major concern by
Stuart Schram (1985, back cover):

> The state was the central power in Chinese society from the start, and exem-
> plary behavior, rites, morality, and indoctrinations have always been consid-
> ered in China as means of government. The continuity between this tradition
> and the principles and practices of the Chinese People's Republic is evident.
> . . . Neither in the realm of organization nor in that of ideology and culture
> would Mao and his successors have striven so hard to promote uniformity if
> the unitary nature of state and society had not been accepted, for the past two
> thousand years, as both natural and right.

The sharing of these assumptions by leaders and masses revealed itself
most clearly during the Cultural Revolution in 1966. When a million
young Red Guards chanted "Chairman Mao lives to ten thousand years,"
they asserted a right for Mao reserved for emperors only.[3] In this case,
traditional notions of moral leadership and of personalized relationships of
dependence were woven into the most "revolutionary" political maneuvers and rhetoric.

While recognizing the intense efforts of the government to use ideological and organizational means to transform rural society, many scholars
doubt that it has succeeded as much as it had hoped. Several kinds of
evidence have been presented to substantiate this argument. First, communal boundaries of villages remain intact despite decades of collectivization aimed at reducing loyalties to them. Second, most scholars would
agree that the Chinese family as a social unit within the community was
never destroyed by the socialist revolution. In fact, some would argue that
the postrevolutionary state had consciously upheld it for purposes of policy
implementation. Family-centered values continue to be felt, and have
often buffered family members against the direct powers of the state.[4]
Third, the functional requisites of rural cadres have often been compared
with those of the traditional gentry (Schurmann 1968). Jean Oi (1985)
observes that policies were implemented through the cadres, who maintained a network of patron-client ties with fellow villagers. Similarly, Vivienne Shue (1988) maintains that the cadres have used traditional communal bases to further their own interests and to shelter villagers from the
intrusions of the party-state, and consequently frustrated its goals.[5] Finally, responses to recent reforms seem to indicate that, once the ideological
lid is lifted, individual entrepreneurship and traditional popular beliefs,
phenomena that the party-state attacked as "feudal practices," have come

back with a vengeance. In sum, one wonders how deeply the socialist state has affected rural society and established its own mandate to rule.[6]

The maneuvers that I observed local people carrying out to cope with life made me realize, though, that the influence of the socialist state was more than superficial. Needless to say, peasants under dynastic rule were subjected to various forms of arbitrary power. Nonetheless, I wondered whether the new state had not replaced the previous political order with a less accessible power structure that created its own arbitrariness. It was not too difficult to see how the postrevolutionary state was able to control a concentrated urban population through the bureaucratic provision of work, housing, and other social services (Whyte and Parish 1984). The urban industrial *danwei* (work unit) acquired tremendous power in defining the scope of people's social life (Henderson and Cohen 1984). However, it was hard for me to understand the presence of the state in rural communities, where the vast peasantry was often left in seemingly isolated villages to rely on its own resources. I was initially skeptical of the idea that as rural collectives were established by the party-state, central direction rather than local initiative shaped the rhythm of life in the rural communities. However, during a stay in south China just after the fall of the Gang of Four, I became quite certain that the state was an entity that the villagers I had come to know had to cope with, and not always successfully. From the general management of the commune economy at the time, I could see that the state had left a strong imprint on rural organization from the 1960s on. When, after a period of hesitant experimentation, decollectivization was thoroughly implemented by the early 1980s, some scholars interpreted the peasants' genuine embrace of the reforms as a revival of local society; but for me, the speed and determination with which the campaigns were pushed indicated the usual imbalance of power between rural society and the party-state. Could the peasants have resisted the reforms even if they had wished to?

The Cellularization of Rural Society

The issues of cultural continuity and change in rural society—and the related questions of whether the socialist state has penetrated it or not and by what means—hinge on a particular analytical point. It has been noted that the rural economy has remained distinctly cellular (Donnithorne 1972). These cellular structures have been seen as concessions on the part of the state to communal loyalties and traditional economic structures

(Skinner 1965). To the protagonists in Michael Frolic's (1980) portrayal of rural transformation, sharing communal resources with outsiders meant "a foot of mud and a pile of shit," an attitude pronounced by both the cadres and the peasants. Richard Madsen (1984) also shows that Confucian morality and entrenched community concerns lurked behind the class-focused political discourse of Chen Village. In rural economic organization (Lardy 1975) and village family life (Parish and Whyte 1978), scholars have observed a distinct "encystment." These observations have political implications. Elizabeth Perry (1985) and Shue (1988) have gone further and described how rural cadres actively encouraged parochial solidarities to create protective shells against the demands of the government. Shue notes in particular that Maoist policies paradoxically helped to preserve rural structures and popular culture, and allowed cadres to maneuver for their own sake as well as for their communities. The reintroduction of market forces in the recent decade has only exposed peasants to less predictable economic conditions in which the central government can intervene more directly. Perry emphasizes that decades of postrevolutionary transformation have strengthened both state and society. Traditional parochialism overlaps with collective interests in the communes to engender unusual strategies of aggression.

However, even if the social cells remain unchanged, the question remains whether they constitute the same cultural tissues. Can one readily assume that local collective actions express local autonomy? Moreover, are the cellular structures remnants of the past that the postrevolutionary regime failed to remove, or are they new creations? To place the inquiry in a historical context, at the turn of the century an economically differentiated but highly integrated rural social landscape dominated the Pearl River delta. At that time, political conditions were more fluid and rural society far less cellular than one is often taught. In that case, when and how did the cellular communities acquire their increased significance in rural life?

Since the mid-Ming period, the delta's varied economy had become increasingly prosperous. Military colonies and subsequent migration into the delta reclaimed vast marshes known as the sands (sha). The development of the sands was paralleled by an increase in population, crop specialization, and the rise of a network of market towns that catered to a highly commercialized agriculture (Ye and Tan 1985a). In time, social relationships in and among the rural communities became very complex. Migrant families grew into powerful groups whose members demonstrated patrilineal descent from a common ancestor. Many held corporately owned properties (zuchang), the income from which went into a trust (tang or zu) to finance lineage activities. The lineages compiled elaborate written genealogies and participated in collective rituals to confirm their membership and status. The trust funds of the larger ones were managed by an elected body of elders and wealthy kinsmen and used to finance rites in the spring and autumn at the ancestral halls and graves. Every male member of a lineage was entitled to a share of its resources, which involved a range of benefits from ceremonial pork to rights of settlement and land tenure. The halls and genealogies expressed the wealth of the lineage as well as the connections of its educated members to the state bureaucracy, which were in themselves sources of prestige and power.

In this part of south China, lineage-based communities of up to several thousand members were not uncommon. Although they were exclusive, they often formed part of higher-order lineages that were based in large market towns and cities and whose trust funds were built on vast estates in the sands. The managerial elites of the higher-order lineages were composed of merchants, landlords, and scholar-officials. These ancestral trusts ritually and instrumentally linked together a large membership spread over a vast area. Managers invested in land reclamations, accumulated rent, dominated the trading of grain and local crops, provided credit for agriculture and commerce, and represented their members in civil and political disputes.[7]

The social landscape was further complicated by merchants who resided in town but controlled interregional trade as well as local agricultural production through credit and trade monopolies. They also contributed to and managed estates held by charity organizations, temples, and academies. Together with the ancestral trusts, these operations created webs of economic interests and overlapping social boundaries in the rural hinterland (Nishikawa 1985; Matsuda 1981).

The political economy was dominated by an alliance of literati and merchants and embodied the creative union of the state and popular cultures in a unitary sociopolitical order that juxtaposed intense social differences and solidarities. In economic terms, the corporate estates (gong chang)[8] commanded intricate mechanisms to extract the resources of the rural areas, but from the peasants' perspective they also provided the necessary means for survival and mobility.

At the turn of the century, peasants in the delta lived in villages, but village life was enriched by affiliations that extended territorially in terms of marketing, defense, and temple networks, and temporally in terms of genealogies and migration histories going back to mythical origins. Peasant life centered upon year-round festivals and lineage rituals that continued to evoke primordial loyalties and demonstrated cultural linkages.[9]

It was not easy for the government to tap local resources in the delta through this maze of social and economic relationships.[10] From the mid-Qing period on, tax officers increasingly relied on established lineages for tax collection (Ye and Tan 1985b; Katayama 1982). However, estate managers and gentry leaders, who sheltered their relatives, also used their power to distribute tax burdens unevenly, to collect high interests from delinquent members, and to pocket the difference. Despite repeated efforts by the Qing and later by the Republican governments, tax officers failed either to secure an accurate estimate of the fields or to extract the taxes due (Qiu 1941). Such historical details warn us against making simplistic comparisons of the texture of rural politics and social life before and after the revolution. To reach rural society, the imperial state worked through a complicated web of social and economic interests.

In contrast to late imperial society, under the postrevolutionary government villages were controlled by state agents who were exceedingly vulnerable to the ideological pressures of the party-state. How could they be the basis of new power structures linking rural communities to the central authorities in a way that might obstruct state penetration? I would like to argue that, paradoxical as it seems, the penetration of the Chinese countryside went hand in hand with the conscious creation of autarkic structures after 1949. With the step-by-step destruction of the traditional networks in land tenure, marketing, and kinship and religious organizations, peasants in the postrevolutionary era found that the world outside their administratively created collectives had shrunk to a minimum. The team, brigade, and commune gradually became their sole source of economic livelihood, social identity, and political status. Instead of having access to multiple centers of political power, peasants were obliged to turn to rural cadres and to the party-state as their sole channels of legitimate political interaction. Traditional sentiments did surface in political dialogues, but they were increasingly structured by the ideological terms defined by a consolidated party-state. Villages might have retained their physical boundaries, but the social meaning of their existence was being changed from within by the Maoist paradigm.

It seems that Mao replaced the traditional community with a peculiar form of organization. It was not a functionally differentiated entity whose organic solidarity was fostered by human activities based on equal, competitive interdependence, as Emile Durkheim envisioned for modern society, nor was it governed by the rational though alienating bureaucratic principles that so concerned Max Weber. Large or small, Mao's organization was to be "all-encompassing" (quan), based on a single, unmediated source of authority and implemented by cadres who were expected to act with moral discretion. The articulation of special interests took place according to principles laid down by the central authority alone.[11]

A closer look at the nature of the authority Mao exercised in the name of socialism shows a paradox. Indeed, scholars have drawn parallels between the philosophical roots of Mao's version of socialism and China's most despotic and Machiavellian rulers—Qin Zheng, Cao Cao, and Zhu Yuanzhang (Yu 1982; Sun 1983). There is a remarkable resemblance, for example, between Mao's ideals for the rural commune and Zhu Yuanzhang's political programs in the early Ming—strict household registration to control mobility, the reliance on an army directly accountable to the emperor and deeply involved with agricultural production, discrimination against commercial activities, state monopoly of ideology through the establishment of academies with rigid curricula, and the operation of comprehensive civil examinations—all considered by historians as bases for imperial despotism (Wu 1948; Grimm 1985). To these scholars, under the veneer of Mao's slogans a personality cult was built that combined populist fervor with the shrewd use of an absolutist tradition. Moreover, Mao's classical Chinese assumptions dovetailed with a Leninist organization to form the basis of a party-state. The product was a system of bureaucratic power that required from its members not only moral activism (Whyte 1974; Schurmann 1968) but also loyalty to a personalized leadership that was counterbalanced by little institutional competition and restraint (Wang 1981; Xu 1987).

I hope to show that this system of power rested precisely on the vast peasant population that it confined in enclosed units of production and administration. The rural party cadres I have come across were vulnerable to the power of that bureaucracy even while forming an important link in its chain of command. Willing accomplices or not, they incorporated into this structure of power the cellularized villages they managed.

Political Brokers and State Agents

Analytical images of hierarchical systems of power quite naturally draw attention to cultural and political brokers and to the nature of the linkages they foster between central governments and local society.[12] The dynamics of these linkages depend on three interlocking factors: the nature of state power as revealed by its ideology and organization; the complex affiliations of kin, community, and class in which peasants find themselves immersed; and the motivations and methods of local leaders who mediate between formal state institutions and the rural populace.

The role of the Chinese gentry as cultural and political brokers for the imperial state is well known. The gentry's influence has led historians to term late imperial China "the gentry society."[13] The relative stability of the Chinese empire is considered to have rested on their brokerage function. Though Janus-faced, the gentry were essential bonding elements in a political order that was neither pluralistic nor absolutist. Instead, it was a system of segmental coordination, with the literati generating a political dialogue to mediate conflicts among themselves and between state and society (Lau 1975).

Historical research on the Pearl River delta shows how local elites were able to act as such political brokers. Through the civil service examinations and the literati culture, they drew upon connections with the imperial state to anchor their influence in the native communities and among their kin; by virtue of their economic power derived from landholding and the social monopoly of education, they also enjoyed the respect of the rural populace. They served as the managers of corporate estates and patronized communal rituals, the local culture that was at once part of and in ambiguous opposition to imperial authority. The state expected them to preach its moral authority and depended on them for important administrative functions. Local society sought their protection against encroachment, official and otherwise.

The multiple bases of affiliation gave local elites room to maneuver. In fact, the imperial order was able to maintain a degree of cultural hegemony precisely because upholding the dominant paradigm was not the exclusive prerogative of the bureaucracy. Instead, local elites actively sought their respective places within the hierarchy by maintaining a constant dialogue with it. What existed in the Pearl River delta by the turn of the century was just such a literati-mediated political economy. Peasants accepted it and depended on it just as much as they suffered under it. A failure to appreciate the delicate balance between autonomy and control in the traditional relationships between state and society makes it easy to overestimate what remains of this structure in the postrevolutionary period.

If one argues that rural economy and society in the Pearl River delta were cellularized by Maoist policies after the revolution, how would that process have changed the nature of political brokerage? Can one justifiably equate the functions of the local gentry with those of rural party cadres, especially if the bases of power in local society as well as the means of legitimation through the central authorities have changed substantially? I accept the view of Shue (1985) that party cadres should not be seen as "mechanical transmission belts ready and willing to convey decisions to the periphery without deviations." However, I would caution that a lack of mechanical compliance on the part of party cadres does little to modify state domination. Nor does it alter the fact that peasants were dependent on cadres to act for them, thus putting themselves at their mercy.[14] Rural cadres were faced with an organized state machinery of which they were a part. They were also part of a greatly transformed rural society. In fact, their very existence has been at the core of that transformation process. In surveying the social and educational background of party cadres, Hong-yung Lee (n.d.) observes how thoroughly the traditionally educated elites were barred from the postrevolutionary leadership at all levels. In the rural areas, the bulk of the cadres remained semiliterate peasants whose sole basis of legitimacy was their class loyalty to the party.[15] Focusing on their predicaments, the study tries to describe how they were recruited by the party-state to construct and manage collectives for agricultural production. In doing so, they not only defined the relationship between the party-state and the rural communities, and between the party and its cadres, but also transformed themselves from poor peasant activists to powerful managers of local society.

As the history of Huancheng will show, when the peasants were increasingly confined to cellular units that defined their social, economic, and political existence, the cadres entrenched themselves further to become an important part of the rural machinery of the party.[16] Conflicts between peasants and cadres intensified as early as the mid-1950s. When alternative channels of social and political mobility were cut by the political campaigns that accompanied collectivization, the peasants grew very anxious over how the collectives were run—for on this their entire livelihood depended. The cadres, however, were keener to conform to the dictates of their party superiors, who had become an unchallenged source of authority.

From time to time peasants tried to influence the cadres by invoking their loyalties to kin and community. Occasionally the cadres colluded with the villagers to resist the demands of the state; they served as patrons to friends and relatives. However, there was little room to maneuver. Though cadres had become indispensable for policy implementation in the countryside, they came to dominate village life when the power of the party was at its height and its ideology most rigid. In fact, their ability to grant political and economic favors depended to a great extent on how solidly they could link up with the party organization. Their power over fellow villagers thus ironically rested on their own political dependence. Through the anxious maneuvers of these cadres, the party-state gained unprecedented organizational power over an increasingly cellularized rural society. What then was the nature of rural leadership? Were local cadres political brokers or state agents? How did they represent state power and authority to the rural populace in everyday social life, and what were the ultimate political and moral consequences?

These questions address the issues raised by Franz Schurmann in his once classic study of ideology and organization in China (1968). Can one claim, as Schurmann did, that the success of the Communist government in penetrating rural society was based on the functional similarity between the party cadres and the traditional Confucian gentry in their relationship to central authority? Or should one focus on the differences in the nature of their brokerage, because the rise of the cadres has been at once the cause and consequence of a drastically changed ideological and social structure?

Cultural Tissues Reconstituted

If we choose to think of villages as social cells, then the rich culture of rural China, much of it expressed in ritual practices, must be the tissue they form. Extending this analogy, one may ask whether mutation took place in the cells after 1949 or, conversely, if the practices introduced by the state were transplants, partly incorporated into the body politic and partly rejected. Before the revolution, peasants practiced religious rituals largely because these were ways of communicating with a hierarchy of supernatural power that interacted with the social institutions to which peasants belonged (Wolf 1974; Ahern 1981). If a deity failed, the believer seldom faulted the authority system the deity symbolized. Appeals to deities expressed faith in the social order. Scholars may point to the revival of popular beliefs and rituals and family enterprises in recent years and claim that the Marxist state did not manage to destroy traditional culture and society. However, a closer look at what is practiced and what meanings practitioners draw from the rituals reveals intriguing political implications.

It is true that popular rituals are observed today no less frequently than in earlier times, though many young practitioners cannot tell one deity from another. Appeals to supernatural powers have taken on an individualistic, competitive, and indiscriminate character. It is also intriguing that the young, previously less involved in religious practices because of their stage in life, are now pursuing them with uncharacteristic fervor.[17] My own fieldwork in the delta in the 1980s reveals that lineage rituals and community celebrations are closely scrutinized by the state authorities and subjected to selective suppression. The censored public rituals stand in sharp contrast to the unusually extravagant practices at domestic altars and for individual pilgrimages and life-cycle rituals of birthdays, weddings, and funerals. The state dominates the public realm of political and symbolic discourse so effectively that ritual outlets seem to have been driven to the privacy of households with greater intensity. Moreover, in communicating with their deities, the practitioners are aware of the fact that their acts are subjected to intervention by a powerful atheistic state. Believers in deities that could not save themselves in political purges must accept limitations on the powers of the objects of their worship.

One therefore wonders whether popular rituals today are revivals or new interpretations of tradition under the powerful influence of the Marxist state. I would argue that they are the latter. In the 1980s, I see the elaborate presence of the party-state making itself felt in social life through individuals who have internalized what state power means and what one needs to do to cope with it. The way popular rituals are "revived" today reminds one not so much of what has been retained, but of how much rural society has been transformed after the revolution.

A parallel situation can be found in economic activities. Despite efforts to liberalize the economy in the last decade, bureaucratic bottlenecks continue to plague the reforms initiated by the party. It would be naive to expect entrenched interests associated with the socialist system to embrace changes that undermine their political capital. It is equally unrealistic to expect initiative from a populace that has participated in the same process of socialist transformation for the past three decades and has given the existing power structure its compliance as well as its complicity. The restraints on independent entrepreneurial strategies are partly self-imposed, because every economic actor has in varying degrees taken the power of the party-state for granted. Structural relations are formed and changed by the interlocking, complementary as well as conflicting actions of human agents faced with choices and dilemmas. The difficulty for the party-state in disengaging itself from the economy and society in the 1980s shows how much its power has been perceived, felt, accepted, and reproduced by those who have both sustained it and been hurt by it.[18] Today one can recognize that the party leaders are liberalizing in earnest, but I would like to show from the experience of Huancheng Commune that the structures of domination are being continuously reproduced and at times improvised on by individuals to produce new cultural forms. The problem I would like to address is this: In the multifaceted political economy of the Huancheng area and its delta vicinity, how did a relationship between state and society, which once thrived on a delicate balance between autonomy and control, come to assume, in the course of this century, a weighty, colorless monotony that defies both Marxist and Weberian definitions?

Human Agency and the Structuring of History

To counter social science analyses that view Chinese rural society as a repository of a cultural tradition mechanically opposed to an external force (that is, the state), I wish to emphasize in this study their interpenetration through time. To do so, I subscribe to the concept of "structuring" in social theory.[19] A common goal of both historians and social scientists is to understand the apparent paradox that human agents are social products at the same time that society is a product of human actions (Berger and Luckman 1967). Instead of taking social groups and institutions as given and then explaining the processes that subsequently arise, I stress their continuous, mutual interaction. A related question involves how one conceptualizes social change without externalizing or reducing to a powerless social decor the structure of meaning that guides human actions (Geertz 1984).

Cultural meaning, the fashioning and informing of a social being, can be lost in a language of market calculations as well as of class and global exploitation.[20] G. William Skinner makes a powerful attempt to analyze Chinese history in terms of cycles of growth and decline in regional economic systems (1985a). Yet his understanding of these vital social units in rural China is based on the calculations of cost-distance by economic maximizers in a given technological and administrative environment. Cultural strategies based on the histories of settlement, community- and lineage-building, and the changing local configurations of power are taken into account only after the marketing cells have been constructed. In contrast, Chinese Marxist literature has indulged in explaining social change in terms of class interests and their contradictions. The human actors remain one-dimensional. This conceptual scheme provides another formalist skeleton imposed on local history. In both cases, it is as if one were describing a forest, yet losing sight of the trees and leaves that give it shape and color.

As a background to my study of recent events, I intend to use the social history of Huancheng Commune in the Pearl River delta to bring out three dimensions of the changes that have taken place in the Chinese countryside during the last eighty years: namely, changes in rural social and economic organizations; changes in the power relationships among the state, the various rural elites, and ordinary peasants; and changes in the world of meanings shared by generations of rural inhabitants, which ultimately crystallized in perceptions of power and authority. The three aspects of this transformation intertwine to form a single but complex structuring process. At the center of the process are human agents who are economically calculating, politically shrewd, and culturally creative. Their perceptions are shaped by self-interested readings of their past as much as by events beyond their control. Both elites and peasants have acted out their moral choices with determination and at times ambivalence. Their separate actions have reproduced and changed institutional structures, which in turn have shaped their options for further action. In the process, new political cultures and economies have been made and shared. My account uses the local history of south China to illustrate how the changing macrostructures encompassing rural communities have affected them through the maneuvers of local elites. Parallel to these changes and often reinforcing them are national ideological currents, in which both elites and peasants have found themselves engulfed, but which they have been able to manipulate occasionally.

In sum, however diverse their intellectual concerns and conclusions are, scholars of state agrarian societies are keenly aware that the lives of peasants and their elites are worlds apart but nonetheless interlocked in many ways. Particular social groups command the means to extract social surplus, and the political economy gives them the material basis from which to exert power over those dependent upon them. They construct dialogues with their subjects out of the cultural repertoire within which they operate. The process turns their power into a system of authority and rights that carries some liabilities, requiring compliance as well as complicity from all concerned.

Such a conceptual framework seems central to a historical anthropology. Social change must be seen as the working and reworking of culture and political economy through the creative, conscious actions of human beings. Human behavior is neither entirely programmed by an infinite variety of cultural rules, nor compelled by externalized political and economic forces. If it were, literature would have great difficulty in sustaining a sense of tragedy.

I begin this study by reconstructing a historical baseline for the Huancheng area in order to show how greatly it was transformed after the revolution. Next I focus on the consolidation of the post-revolutionary state and the emergence of a new bureaucratic structure. The creation of the new political system involved the systematic "stripping down" of rural social institutions and of the cultural meanings associated with them. I compare the multiple bases of authority and autonomy of the traditional elites with the intermediary position of rural cadres, who acted more as state agents than as political brokers.

The national decollectivization programs of the 1980s provoked diverse reactions from the commune population. In this context I will address the question: To what extent can the party-state extricate itself from the economy and more generally the society? Using a historical account, I examine the cumulative sequence of interacting events that created and transformed the Huancheng area, and explore the paradox of state power, the puzzles of human agency, and the conceptual integration of culture and political economy in Chinese anthropology.

In a limited way, I want to address myself to the current debates among scholars of China about the nature of state-society relationships, and particularly those concerning the delicate balance between local autonomy and central control in pre- and postrevolutionary China. By focusing on the dilemmas of political agents who maneuvered within structures that they had helped to create, my account raises a general question in the study of peasants. In complex agrarian societies where distinct hierarchies of power and ideological domination exist, to what extent have peasants contributed to making their world and to shaping its historical process?[21] Were they mere spectators watching political dramas unfold from afar, or were they inevitably drawn into these dramas to become part of their unfolding? What follows are the stories of some Chinese peasants in the twentieth century, who, as Richard Madsen says (1984, 30), have made themselves as they made history.

CHAPTER 2

Historical Geography

Had one visited the southwestern part of the Pearl River delta at the turn of the century, one would have been impressed with the visible signs of wealth, together with the flaunting and the symbolic defense of it. County and township gazetteers as well as genealogies compiled by lineages that settled in the vicinity of Huicheng (the county capital) and a larger city, Jiangmen,[1] describe a varied landscape where large villages clustered upon the slightest indication of a hill. Rows of gray-brick houses some two stories high were built with their backs toward the fields outside. Once the narrow streets were closed off with gates and village guards posted at the watchtowers and entrances, the settlements became virtual fortresses. Clustered at their center were ancestral halls belonging to various lineages, which demonstrated common descent from a founding ancestor. These halls were expensive to build. They had wide entrances with carved stone pillars; the high ceilings of the central and side halls were supported by hardwood beams imported from Indochina. The curved structure on the roofs gave evidence of official recognition, and the elaborate rituals periodically performed symbolized social unity as well as differentiation. The halls and their rituals were financed by income from ancestral estates, some comprising many hectares of polders in the southeastern part of Xinhui County and in the neighboring Xiangshan County (known after 1925 as Zhongshan County). Rich and poor, members of these patrilineal descent groups were characteristically drawn together in south China by their shared historical past and their imposing territorial presence.

However, these village communities were not exclusive. On the contrary, their social and political horizons expanded during periodic market days with the bustling activities of peasants, itinerant traders, wholesale merchants of rice, fruits, and palm, and gentry elites. Nearly every township (*xiang*) in the hinterland of the two cities had one or more markets. For example, *Xinhui xianzhi* (county gazetteer) of 1840 listed forty-six periodic markets and twenty-three daily markets in the county. *Chaolian xiangzhi* (township gazetteer)[2] listed nine (1946, 79–81). The rural communities were linked to one another and to Huicheng and Jiangmen by a

network of ferries and river crossings (*xiangdu*).[3] Such impressions fit the
general picture of the delta's cultural richness and economic vitality, as
described in the colorful account of a foreign traveller up the Xi River in
1903. R. D. Thomas reported that on his boat trip up the river he passed
numerous towns with fortifications and officials, and he saw rice "not by
the acre but by the square mile." There were fruit trees, fish ponds, mulberry shrubs "as far as the eye could see," and silk-filatures. At a flourishing
market town, he spotted colorful "literary poles" erected in front of ancestral halls. On the poles were carved the names of members who had
acquired academic degrees. There were also stone memorial arches and
pagodas built by village communities for the purposes of geomancy and to
glorify traditional virtue. Fortress-like pawnshops served as repositories of
valuables and as local banks. Temples and pilgrimage centers were
thronged with the faithful during festivals (Thomas 1903).

In the Huancheng area, bounded by Huicheng to the north and Jiangmen to the northeast, a large volume of commodities from the rural hinterland was transported through a network of riverways to Huicheng.
Jiangmen handled the extensive interregional trade for the western part of
south China,[4] that moving up and down the Xi River, that connecting to
the Bei River and Dong River via Guangzhou, and that using Jiangmen as a
port for coastal and export trade to Southeast Asia (see figure 2.1).

However, the network of territorial relationships was not limited to the
economic realm. Village alliances centering on community festivals and
temples revealed the aggressive politicking of their gentry and merchant
patrons. Standing beside the Chaolian Hongsheng Temple, for example,
were the headquarters of the township covenant (*xiangyue*) and the community school.[5] On the stone tablets embedded in the walls of the temple
were carved the names of patrons who contributed to the temple's periodic
remodeling from the eighteenth to the twentieth centuries. These patrons—whether local gentry, town merchants, ancestral estates, privately
owned river-crossings, trade guilds and craft associations, or, above them
all, officials of the imperial bureaucracy—revealed the dynamic configurations of power and hidden political aspects of the temple's spiritual community.[6] The etiquette of political discourse and its underlying cultural
values were structured by a world well beyond village horizons.

Huancheng in the Context of the Pearl River Delta

The historical and cultural context is crucial for understanding the perceptions of several generations of peasants and their elites who were drawn

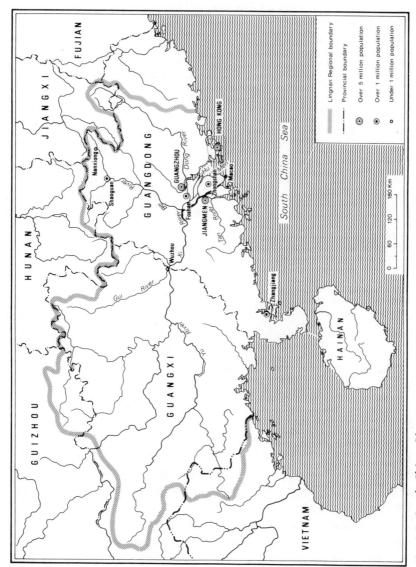

Fig. 2.1. South China: Lingnan

into the revolutionary turmoil of the mid-twentieth century. What were to them "the good old days" or the "bad times"? How did their strategies differ from those of their children, who were taught to treat historical and cultural legacies as ideological artifacts? To the peasants in the first half of the twentieth century, the Huancheng area was a rich, productive place where goods and people were mobile and politics volatile. Peasants and elites were bound by multiple affiliations that extended back in genealogical time and overlapped in social space. Life was by no means comfortable and peaceful; for the majority it was quite capricious. But peasants and their elites habitually perceived in this structure of relationships opportunity as well as constraint, and they devised their strategies accordingly. The following is a description of how generations of Chinese peasants up to the late 1940s transformed an expanding delta into a finely worked but delicate economic system. Underlying this system were social and political institutions whose historical legacy continued to shape livelihoods and confirmed cultural assumptions. However, this local economy was the target of state policies, for the new regime saw economic transformation as the basis of socialism. Through a series of steps, the state imposed its priorities on the local economy.

The administrative boundaries and status of Xinhui County fluctuated in history, but stabilized in the eighteenth century. By the mid-nineteenth century, the county consisted of three periurban districts (*fang*), twelve rural districts (*du*), and 491 villages (*tu, jia*). The three periurban districts were directly administered by the county magistrate, whereas the rural districts were under three subcounty divisions, each headed by a police intendant (*xunjian si*).[7] In the Republican era the administrative boundaries of the districts and villages changed often, reflecting the shifting territorial bases of local strongmen. In 1949, the county consisted of eight districts (*qu*), 2 market towns (*zhen*), 68 large villages and townships (*xiang*), and 1,280 hamlets (*bao*). Seven of the nine townships in the First District and two townships in the Second District fell within the boundary of today's Huancheng area.[8] Figure 2.2 shows the area in relation to Huicheng and Jiangmen.

The physical landscape of the Huancheng area was a varied one. At the turn of the century, if one looked south from Guifeng Mountain behind Huicheng (the county capital), one would have seen extensive rice fields interspersed with dikes where fan palm and fruit trees were grown. The land was bounded by a tributary of the Xi River on its east and the Tan River on its west. At the end of the area, less than ten kilometers away from the city, were two well-known landmarks. The first was a hill on the eastern edge topped with a seven-layer pagoda built by the elites of

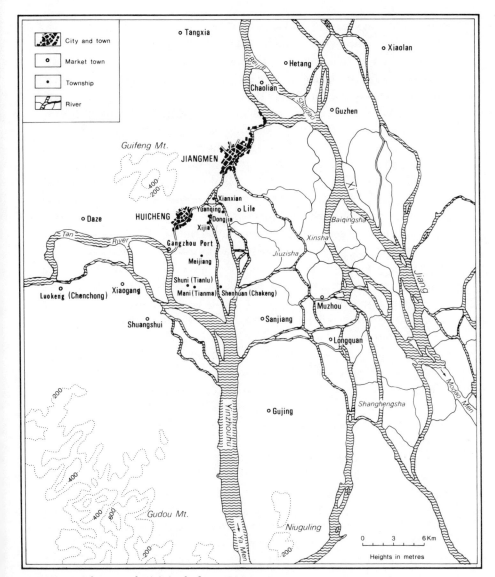

Fig. 2.2. Huicheng and Vicinity before 1949

Huicheng during the reign of Wanli (1573–1619). Another hill, known as Shuni, stood on the western edge, with a smaller pagoda built at its foot. Between the two hills were two mounds named Mani and Changni. Beyond these hills was the confluence of the two rivers. After the rivers joined into one, they wound southward through a narrow river valley known as Yinzhouhu, before reaching the sea via the Ya Men inlet.[9] Xinhui county gazetteers recorded the hills as islands that were eventually joined by marshes formed during the Ming and Qing dynasties (see figures 2.3 and 2.4). Situated at the foot of the hills were three of the district's largest townships, Shenhuan, Tianma, and Tianlu Xiang, each having several thousand residents. A dozen or so smaller communities dotted the alluvial plain between them and Huicheng. An elaborate network of winding waterways linked these villages to one another and to Huicheng and Jiangmen, the area's major commercial and administrative centers.

If one looked farther southeast from the pagoda at Shenhuan Xiang, one would see only a few kilometers away the old market town of Sanjiang and a few smaller settlements radiating from it. To the east of Sanjiang were newly formed alluvial fields known as the sands (*sha*), stretching as far as the eye could see. In the north were Xinsha, Jiuzisha, and Baiqingsha. Around the market town of Muzhou to the south were Dasha and Shanghengsha. These sands, at the western edge of the Pearl River delta, constituted the youngest part of Xinhui County. To put Huancheng's varied landscape in a regional context, what one saw was typical of the Pearl River delta, the largest alluvial plain of south China, measuring 11,300 square kilometers (see figure 2.5). The delta is defined by three points: Sanshui in the north, Shilong in the east, and Ya Men in the southwest. It has grown at a tremendous speed in a southeastern direction, merging with islands and coastal ranges along its path. In the process, it attracted migrant farmers from Taishan and Kaiping counties in the west, from Nanhai and Shunde counties in the northeast, and fishermen (the Dan) along the coast whose ecological niches had shrunk with the delta's expansion. By the late imperial period, many elevated points in the delta had become sites of villages and towns.

The growth of the delta meant that it continued to provide new land of different types for cultivation. The older part of the delta formed by aged alluvial soils was free from flooding. Archaeological evidence permits us to sketch out the shallow prehistoric seabed that extended from Shafu in the southwestern part of Xinhui County through Jiangmen, Hetang, and the county capitals of Shunde (Daliang), Panyu (Shiqiao) and Dongguan (Guancheng) in the eastern part of the delta (*Zhujiang sanjiaozhou nongyezhi* [1976] 1: 26–27; hereafter abbreviated as *Nongyezhi*). Alluvial plains

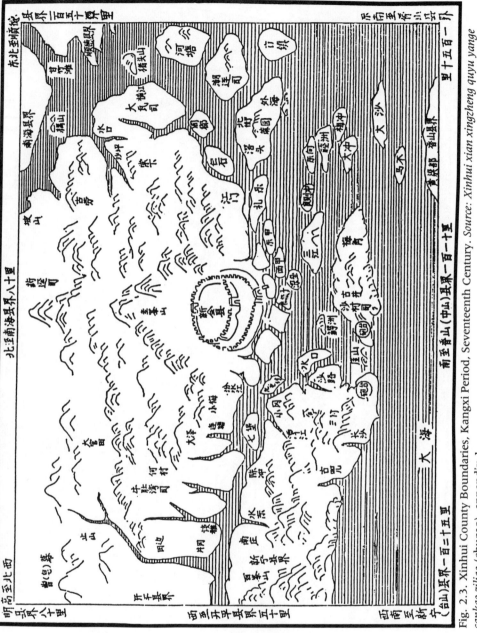

Fig. 2.3. Xinhui County Boundaries, Kangxi Period, Seventeenth Century. *Source: Xinhui xian xingzheng quyu yange cankao ziliao (chugao),* appendix 1.

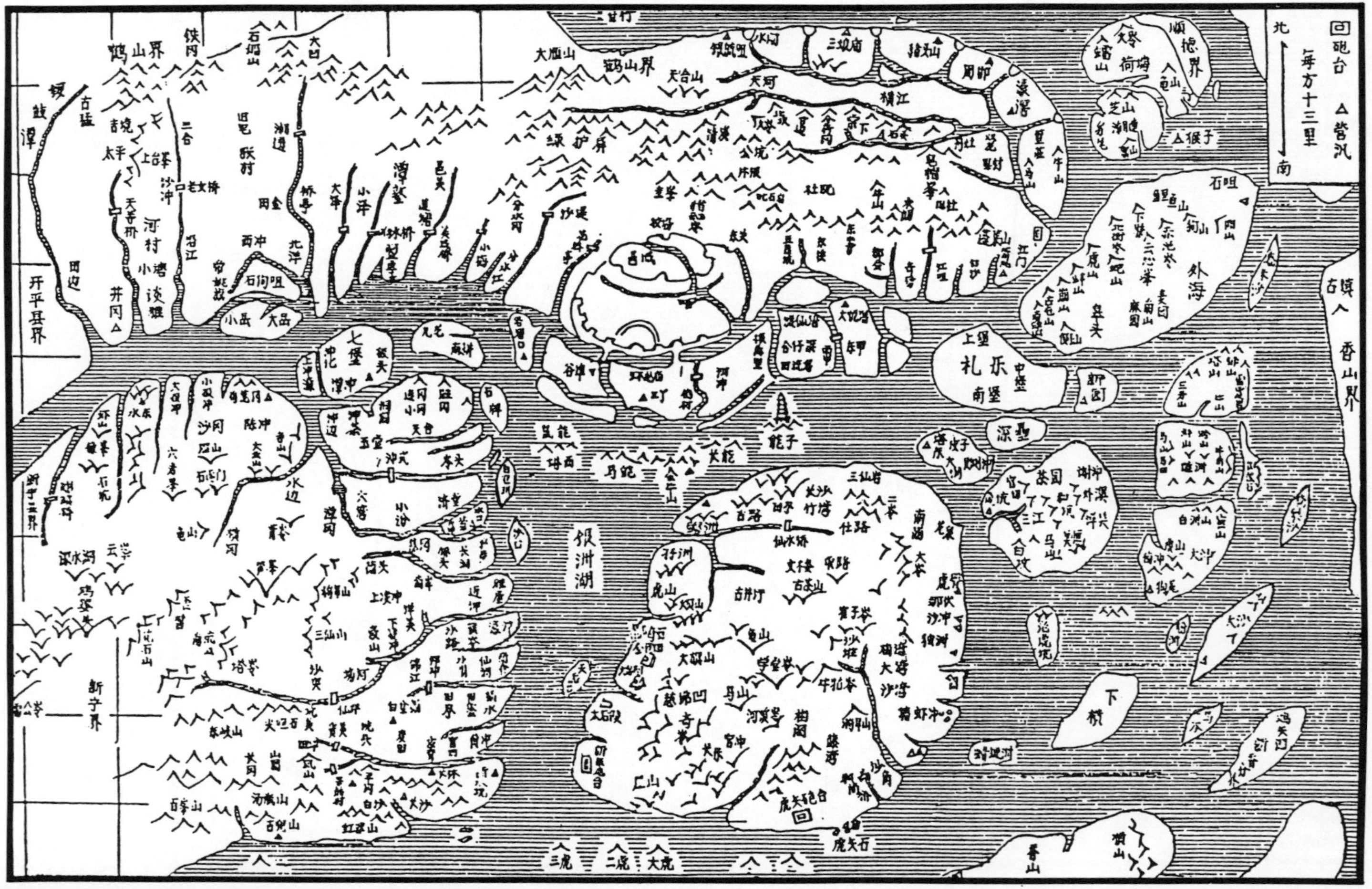

Fig. 2.4 Xinhui County Boundaries, Daoguang Period, Nineteenth Century. *Source: Xinhui xian xingzheng quyu yange cankao ziliao* (chugao)

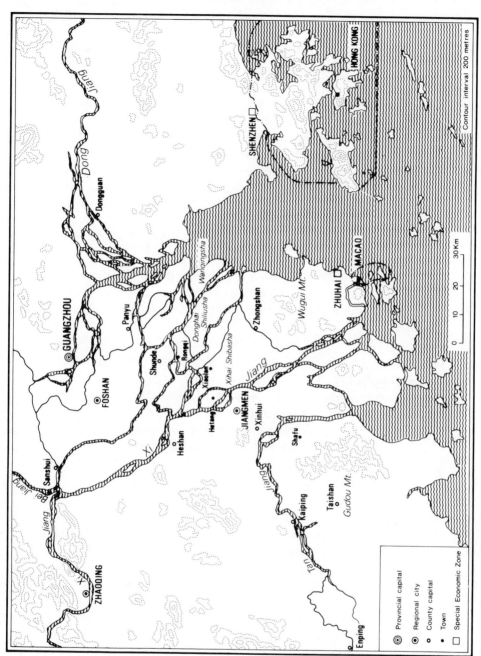

Fig. 2.5. The Pearl River Delta

were formed north of that line owing to a process of sedimentation. The combined efforts of peasants, local elites, and government from the Tang to the Ming dynasties resulted in an elaborate network of dikes (*Nongyezhi* 2). The land was intensively worked by a dense population, and taxed by the imperial government as cultivable land formed by natural sedimentation. This category of land was known as *mintian*.

The part of the delta southeast of the line is composed of recently deposited silt. Settlers continued to reclaim it, but flooding was common, land boundaries unclear, and harvests uncertain. Such an area has been referred to as the sands (*sha* or *shatian*). The older part of the sands, termed *laosha weitian*, consisted of polders of rich silt that had matured over a long period. Protected by a network of dikes built throughout the Ming and Qing dynasties, the area used the flow of river water and the tides for irrigation for up to twenty days a month (*Nongyezhi* 1:7). Blessed with virtually frost-free winters, peasants in the delta had used traditional technology and accumulated wisdom to create a highly productive agricultural system.

A distinct pattern of cultivation emerged in the sands by the late imperial period. There were the newly reclaimed marshes for extensive rice production. At the other end of the scale were peasants engaged in very intensive land use, known as the *sangji yutang* or *guoji yutang*. This was the elaborate but delicate balancing act of growing mulberry or fruit on enlarged dikes built between fish ponds, and using the mulberry leaves in order to raise silkworms to produce silk for regional and world markets. A third type of land use also emerged in time. As the reclaimed marshes aged with diking and cultivation, peasants shifted from extensive rice production to growing two full crops of rice interspersed with fruit, palm, sugarcane, and vegetables.[10] A description of extensive rice cultivation in the sands and of cash crops in the matured polders is relevant here because the Huancheng area saw both types of land use. At its eastern and southern edges, sands such as Dongjia, Xijia, Shenhuan, Tianma, and Tianlu Xiang were at different stages of reclamation. The rest of the land south of Huicheng consisted of polders on which rice, cash crops, and vegetables were grown. They deserve attention because they were tied to the changing markets and sociopolitical institutions in the delta, which in turn provided the basis for a succession of local leaders.

Reclaiming Tidal Marshes for Rice Cultivation

Beginning with the Song dynasty, successive waves of settlement stimulated reclamation efforts along the valleys and in the coastal inlets where marshes had surfaced. For the younger part of the delta, land reclamation accelerated during the Ming. During the first half of the Ming dynasty, efforts were concentrated in the northern part of Xiangshan County, an area known as Xihai Shibasha, and the southeastern part of Xinhui County (*Nongyezhi* 2:4–20). Military colonies were established for reclamation and settlement.[11] After the middle of the Ming period, reclamation efforts spread to marshes in the northeastern part of Xiangshan County, an area known as the Donghai Shiliusha, and southern Panyu, known as Wanqingsha. In the last few centuries, families from the military outposts, migrant farmers from the older parts of the delta, and Dan fishermen formed village communities and towns in the expanding frontier.[12] The ownership of these newer sands, however, was in the hands of estates set up by higher-order lineages, academies, trade guilds, and the like. The owners and managers of these estates had long resided in the market towns and larger cities in the older part of the delta.

A record from 1937 shows a total of 4,000,000 mu of reclaimed land spread over six counties. As shown in table 2.1, the data revealed that Nanhai, Shunde, and Xinhui counties consisted mostly of the matured polders on which were grown two crops of rice and also cash crops. Zhongshan, Dongguan, and Panyu counties, situated in the younger part of the delta, had a larger proportion of undiked sands.

The reclamation involved massive human effort and elaborate financial arrangements. Nishikawa (1985) maintains that this long and expensive process became popular only during the reign of Qianlong (1736–95) and reached its height in the mid-nineteenth century, during the reign of the emperors Daoguang (1821–50) and Xianfeng (1851–61). The complex technical organization involved the government from the very start, as local elites who set up ancestral trusts, charity estates, and academies petitioned county magistrates for areas of 1,000 mu or more at a time (Nishikawa 1985, 20). Reclamation was organized in several stages. Large

Table 2.1.   Sands in the Delta, 1930s (In Hundreds of Mu)

County	Polders (a)	Mulberry Dikes and Fish Ponds (b)	Undiked Marshland (c)	Ratio of Diked to Undiked Land (a + b/c)
Nanhai	2,528.23	4.48	50.99	50:1
Xinhui	5,380.84	—	273.39	20:1
Shunde	3,970.80	627.56	434.64	11:1
Zhongshan	14,999.38	483.36	1,846.15	8:1
Dongguan	3,053.24	0.89	583.99	5:1
Panyu	4,375.50	—	1,527.61	3:1

Source: Qiu Bincun, *Guangdong shatian* (The sands of Guangdong), 3–5.

quantities of stones were deposited in areas where the river flow was slow in order to accelerate sedimentation. When silt accumulated to the level of the stone base, more stones were added. The process was repeated until years or even decades later marshland emerged during low tide. These were areas where "fish could swim, storks could stand." Workers then transported hardened soil from more elevated areas to build a series of dikes on top of the stone bases. Sedimentation took place within the dikes as the high tide continued to submerge the land. Reeds were grown for a few years until the soil was hard enough for a crop of relatively flood-resistant rice. From the beginning of the operations, according to Nishikawa, close supervision of an organized work force and heavy invest-ment were needed. However, the expenses of reclamation were offset by tax exemptions lasting normally up to three years. After that, the govern-ment expected the sands to be registered for taxation. The delta was a productive source of income, and successive governments looked upon it as a widening base of revenue. However, after the reign of Qianlong, the Qing government attempted with little success to register and classify the different grades of sands for taxation.[13] The inability of the governments to collect taxes meant that the wealth of the sands was largely retained by local elites.

From the early Qing, migrant farmers planted one crop of rice for three years and then let the land lie fallow for another three (Qu 1700, vol. 2, no. 57). For the more matured sands, as in the Huancheng area, local farmers practiced a crude double-cropping of rice known as *zhenggao*.[14] Twenty days after transplanting the first crop, peasants planted a second one be-tween the rows of the first. They harvested the first crop in early summer and then treaded down the roots as fertilizer for the second crop, which was harvested in mid-autumn. This method saved peasants the labor of turning over the soil. By planting the second crop early, damage from typhoons in the late summer was reduced. However, *zhenggao* depleted the soil quickly. The peasant households were in a bind: They needed an extensive area of cultivation to meet consumption needs, but at the same time such an extension aggravated the shortage of labor, making it difficult to increase yields by a more refined method of cultivation. They supple-mented their income by catching river shrimp, shellfish, and harvest grubs in the frequently flooded fields.

Accumulating Wealth from the Sands

Wealth was accumulated in several ways. As the process of reclaiming the sands became capitalized over the last two centuries, a stratum of grower-

entrepreneurs, often from the rich and locally influential households, contracted with original claimants to the land to undertake the work. The
reclamation projects resulted in enclosed compounds (*weiguan*), a common sight on the frontier landscape. There were temporary settlements
consisting of straw huts for workmen and migrant farmers, a granary, a
house for the overseers, a watchtower, and often a small crop-watching
force, known as *shafu* (sand guards). The grower-entrepreneurs received
handsome fees as well as guaranteed long-term tenure from their patrons.
Instead of farming the vast estates themselves with the aid of hired laborers, they more often than not parcelled out the land to their own tenant
farmers in return for a share of the crops.

Second, along the open "frontier" the fear of encroachment on land and
harvest necessitated some degree of coordinated crop-watching. In fact,
small sums, known as the *shagu* (skeletal levy) were claimed from tenants
by the owners of the estates for such purposes, and the sums became
symbolic of the landlord's claim on the land. Because of the vast areas
involved, even a small sum per mu became a lucrative source of income
and was fiercely fought for. It was not unusual for entire communities to
feud over the right of collecting the skeletal levy. The disputes over Donghai
Shiliusha between landlords in the county capitals of Xiangshan and
Shunde are typical episodes of this kind.[15] Decades later, the feud between
the Zhao lineage in the township of Sanjiang and an alliance of descent
groups in the township of Longquan over Jiuzisha involved nearly two
thousand heavily armed village guards and complex negotiations with
county and provincial officials.[16]

A third important source of wealth were the harvests. By the late Qing,
managers of the estates in town were exacting cash rents from clients who
contracted tenure for up to twenty years. Such tenures were publicly
auctioned and required large deposits on future rents. These arrangements
were known as *baodian* (tenant-contracting) and were made by resourceful grower-entrepreneurs, who could very well be local bankers, grain
brokers, and wholesale merchants. Areas rented were large, some comprising a diked holding of several hectares. Rent deposits amounting to a
year's rent were common. The value of a year's rent was the cash equivalent of the agreed amount of grain, based on its market price at the time of
auction. A long-term trend of rising grain prices could benefit these contractors more than the owners of the estates. From the 1870s to the early
1930s, grain prices in Guangdong did enjoy a long-term rise (Faure 1985).
Receiving substantial quantities of grain from their own tenant farmers,
large contractors conducted an active trade with brokers in the market
towns and the county capitals.[17]

A description of the grain trade conducted by merchants in Huicheng at the turn of the century reveals its capitalized and competitive nature as well as the multiple checks and balances the town enterprises maintained with the large growers in the rural hinterland (see Huang Fa et al. 1983, 29–40). At the time, there were about 120 grain-trading enterprises. The largest four, Meihe, Yihe, Sanhe, and Dechang, were conveniently situated on the southern bank of the city for the purpose of transporting the large volumes of grain that came under their management. Together they handled 40,000 shi[18] of grain a day, a third of the total trade in the city. Business was competitive. Securing a large and constant supply of grain was crucial, because the larger the supply, the more easily the merchants could maneuver with price fluctuations. Favorable terms were therefore contracted with corporate estates and local strongmen in the townships who had large amounts of rents in kind at their disposal. The large contractors of Tianma Xiang, for example, exclusively patronized the grain mills at Dechang and Wanfeng. They opened storage accounts with the merchants and converted their grain to cash when prices were good. Meanwhile, the merchants used the stored grain to conduct their own trade with the retail shops.

The grain merchants obtained shares in local banks in order to secure credit. They also spread their investments into flour mills, wine-making shops, duck and pig farms, and restaurants. Together with the grain mills, the grain merchants in town organized a *Mihang Gonghui* (association of grain merchants). Its members gathered monthly to exchange market information. They contributed a small percentage of their sales to the association as insurance against accidents, fire, and robbery. The association maintained a management staff to make connections with various power groups in town, to arm the town's defense corps, and to contribute to the festivals of temples and neighborhoods in the rural hinterland.[19]

In sum, by the turn of the century, even the most extensive cultivation of grain in a vast frontier was by no means an isolated and self-sufficient operation. From the very beginning, complex technical, financial, and political maneuvers were required, shaping the fluid market forces and power relationships that extended well beyond village horizons. Though migrant farmers lived in straw huts strung out on the dikes, their immediate concerns of tenure and harvests were set in the context of large-scale land reclamations, grain-price manipulations, and the escorted transport of commodities to the cities, aspects that preoccupied the world of corporate estates and merchants. The exploitation of the sands in the delta supported the development of the region, where tremendous wealth was accumulated through an elaborate organization that spanned the rural-urban nexus.

The Growing of Citrus

If grain production in the sands was commercialized, the cash crops in the periurban areas were even more so. Citrus growing in the vicinity of Huicheng had a long history. The Chen lineage of Waihai (near Jiangmen), for example, noted that as early as the Yuan dynasty, a rent payment was recorded as 10 shi of mandarin oranges (*Nongyezhi* 6:64–69). Orchards replaced many rice fields by the early Qing dynasty. The honey orange of Dongjia Xiang in Huancheng was among the citrus fruits sought after by other provinces. A document of 1840 asserted that "the orange of Xinhui in Guangdong is a fine product of Lingnan. Its skin is thin and tight, the fruit sweet as honey . . . one truly tastes an orange in this variety" (*Nongyezhi* 6:67). Citrus growing continued to increase with the accelerated opening up of south China after the Opium War and peaked during the first quarter of the twentieth century. In 1935 a record of more than 60,000 mu of citrus orchards was distributed among eighty-five settlements in the eastern and southern part of Xinhui County. In the Huancheng area, citrus was grown in the townships of Yuanqing (which included Dongjia), Chengnan, Nantan, Tianlu, and Shenhuan (*Nongyezhi* 6:74–75). The fruit was not only sold in local market towns but also shipped through Jiangmen to cities such as Foshan, Guangzhou, Wuzhou, Shanghai, Macao, Hong Kong, and to Southeast Asia.

Citrus production reflected shrewd calculations of market prices and investment return on the part of growers.

> The price for citrus in the Pearl River delta continued to rise as its market expanded. In 1929, mandarin orange was sold for 10 yuan per picul, tangerine for 4 yuan per picul, and orange for 21 yuan per picul. In 1930, the price of mandarin orange rose to 12 yuan per picul, tangerine to 7 yuan, and orange to 40 yuan. High prices yielded handsome profits. Take the case of Xinhui. Around 1922, the best rice fields yielded an income of 6 taels of silver per mu, compared to three times that much for citrus. After the sixth year of cultivation, each mu of orange orchard could yield an income of 540 taels, ninety times that of rice. A breakdown of the economics of citrus growing shows the following: The first year of an orchard needed a rather large investment because one had to build dikes, to level the fields, to construct irrigation

ditches, and to buy seedlings. From the second year on, taking into account land rent, maintenance [for young alluvial fields] and management fees, income from citrus and others crops yielded a profit three times that of investment. (*Nongyezhi* 6:73)

Trading Orange Peel

Huicheng and the surrounding rural area were known for the production of another valued commodity, the dried peel of mandarin oranges (*chenpi*). Herbal experts acknowledged that aged peel from the county was unmatched by any other. One may roughly estimate from the county gazetteer of Xinhui (1908) that by the turn of the century, 300,000 picul of peel were produced annually for domestic and overseas markets. Considering that only 6 to 8 catties of peel were obtained from a picul of fruit, mandarin oranges must have been widely grown. However, the orchards were not very large, averaging an annual production of a picul of peel. Many rice farmers produced a few catties of peel only as a sideline.[20]

During one of my trips to Huicheng, I was able to discuss the economic history of the region with He Zhuojian, a local historian whose family belonged to the prominent He lineage of Huicheng. Both his grandfather and father had been in the wholesale trade in Huicheng. He ran the Wenming Publication House in the county capital during the 1940s and early 1950s and was very familiar with local historical sources. He informed me that the trade in orange peel was separated into three spheres: a small-scale, grassroots level of collection; a stratum of brokers in the county capital; and the highly capitalized enterprises for long-distance trading. The complexity of their operations matched that of the grain trade. Dried orange peel from growers was collected by itinerant traders whose families operated the business as a sideline. Numbering a hundred or so and residing mostly in the township of Chengnan south of Huicheng, these traders visited markets in the rural hinterland of Huicheng and Jiangmen and ventured into neighboring counties for the commodity.[21] Within a few days of collection, they sold the peel in Huicheng. A network of brokers received dried peel from these itinerant traders and fruit merchants. They then forwarded the collected supplies to the large wholesale merchants who conducted long-distance trade. The role of the brokers was by no means insignificant: One of the largest brokers, for example, traded 200,000 catties of peel a year just before the Japanese occupation in 1938 (He 1965, 115–17).

In the first quarter of the twentieth century, thirty or so wholesale merchants of orange peel clustered to the south of Huicheng. One of the largest wholesale merchants was Lihe Enterprises, owned by a He lineage, which maintained business ties as far away as Shanghai and Chongqing. Disputes among lineage members involving the alleged mismanagement of funds led to its closing in 1934. However, its major competitor, the Liu Yiji enterprise, managed to thrive. Itinerant traders founded this wholesale company in the eighteenth century. The managers of an ancestral trust set up by a lineage segment opened the first shop in Huicheng. The enterprise expanded to Suzhou with a branch shop named Liu Caixing, and conducted the trading of fan palm as well. By the turn of this century, it moved the Suzhou operation to Shanghai and opened more branches in Chongqing, Guangzhou, and Hong Kong. After selling orange peel in the cities, its managers bought back herbs, cotton, and other commodities to be sold in Xinhui. He Zhuojian (1965, 120) estimated that at the height of its operation, the enterprise had a capital of 200,000 yuan of silver.

The fortunes of these large-scale enterprises fluctuated with the financial and political instabilities of Guangdong and China's other major cities, especially in the 1930s and 1940s. The market-sensitive trade suffered a blow during a drastic drop in the prices of citrus in 1933. Peasants responded by converting their orchards to grain fields. The area of citrus cultivation dropped by 17.6 percent in the county. In Dongjia Xiang alone, the orchards shrank 22.6 percent by 1935 (*Nongyezhi* 6:82). Political chaos during the eight years of Japanese occupation between 1938 and 1945 exacerbated the problems. The Japanese troops controlled the major cities in the delta and blockaded the transport routes. Citrus growers shifted to grain production in order to survive. The trend was aggravated by Japanese soldiers who, for fear of guerrilla ambushes, forced growers to cut down the trees. A county document produced after the war estimated that 70 percent of the citrus crops was lost at the time (*Nongyezhi* 6:83). So the trading of peel fluctuated accordingly. He (1965, 113) estimated that before the war the total annual production of peel reached one million catties. During the first three years of the Japanese occupation, it dropped 30 percent. The lowest recorded figure was at the end of the war in 1945, when production was only 30 percent of the prewar level.

The Production and Trading of Fan Palm

Though fan palm in Xinhui was mentioned in historical records as early as the third century A.D., it did not become an important commodity for interregional trade until mid-Ming. Fan palm needs four to five years to mature but continues to produce leaves for another hundred years. They were therefore highly valued for their steady productivity. The usual palm polders (*kuiwei*) were well-drained areas enclosed by dikes. Sometimes fan palms were grown on dikes or hillsides. The leaves were harvested three to four times a year and then dried, graded, and sold to fan-making workshops in Huicheng and Jiangmen. Palm fields were particularly abundant in village settlements immediately south of the two cities, which in the Huancheng area included the townships of Chengnan, Tianlu, and Nantan.[22] Though a somewhat exaggerated account from the eighteenth century claimed that half of the county's population lived on palm production, Guan (1983, 3) estimated that by the late nineteenth century, Xinhui County had roughly 25,000 mu of palm fields. I suspect that fan-palm production peaked between 1911 to 1929, during which time 16 percent of the county's cultivated area was given over to palm fields (*Nongyezhi* 5:48; He 1965b).

Among numerous small growers who owned or rented their fields, there were several larger operations that exercised substantial economic power. At the fall of the Qing, several dozen growers jointly owned over 50 percent of the county's best palm fields, each grower having over 1,000 mu to his name. Guan (1983, 4) listed a He Lunyao who owned about 2,000 mu, a He Rui and Pan Xiting who owned 1,500 mu each, and a Nie Yupai who owned 1,000 mu in the vicinity of Jiangmen and Huicheng. These large growers thrived on related handicraft business. Guan documents that these growers, together with a dozen or so fan-processing enterprises, controlled 90 percent of the county's palm-drying business.[23]

Processed fans went to interregional and overseas markets. There were about twenty medium-size workshops, each producing over one million fans a year for wholesale merchants. The largest seven produced between five to eight million fans, and conducted interregional trade as their major business. Before the war with Japan in the 1930s, 12 to 15 percent of the palm fans were sold in south China. Another 15 percent were exported to Hong Kong via Jiangmen. The rest were distributed by long-distance traders. According to Guan, it was difficult to date the beginning of this long-distance trade. The elders in his family had the impression that merchants from Hankou had sold goods to Foshan and then bought palm fans from Xinhui for sale in the towns along the Yangzi valley. By the Ming dynasty, merchants in Xinhui had started to trade directly with merchants in Hankou. The routes went up through northern Guangdong into Jiangxi by land, at which point the goods were transferred to boats for the Yangzi valley. By the mid-nineteenth century, Xinhui traders had set up various bases of operations in Chongqing, Hankou, Suzhou, and Shanghai. The trading networks centered around native place associations and palm trade guilds, especially in the four major markets.[24] By the turn of the century, there were sixty to seventy long-distance traders with twenty-seven bases of operation in other provinces. Moreover, the opening of coastal trade routes at the end of the Qing boosted the trade and made Jiangmen an important center for export to Shanghai and Hong Kong. As highly capitalized as the orange peel merchants, the palm traders brought back industrial and local goods from other provinces for the local markets (Guan 1983, 5–8).

The production and trading of palm fan required large numbers of workers. During the high season, most farming households in the vicinity of Huicheng would have at least a few members engaged in palm growing, harvesting, drying, transporting, and fan-processing. It is reasonable to assume that since the late Qing the production of fan palm had become an indispensable source of income for households in Huicheng and its rural hinterland.

A Volatile Regional Core

From the descriptions of the various forms of agriculture and associated commodity trade in the area, one may conclude that the Huancheng area shared with the Pearl River delta characteristics of a regional core.[25] The Huancheng area also shared a history of overseas emigration with three other counties to its west.[26] Since the mid-seventeenth century, laborers were recruited by a network of local and overseas contractors to work in the mines and plantations of the Americas and Southeast Asia. Emigration reached its height in the second half of the nineteenth century, depleting the ranks of male laborers and reducing households with women, children, and elderly people to virtual dependence on remittances. Laborers who made enough from their stints abroad often invested in their native communities, setting up ancestral estates, building houses, and contributing to charity and to community defense.

A specialized agriculture, dense population, and overseas connections provided the necessary conditions for the development of local industries. At the turn of the century there were grain mills, oil presses, small sugar refineries, paper-making mills, and textile and food-processing factories in Jiangmen and Huicheng. Some started as small family operations and grew prosperous in a few generations. The Dayou fruit-processing enterprise in Huicheng was one such business.[27] In Huicheng, commercial enterprises predominated. Jiangmen boasted light industries that produced rubber ware, matches, small machine tools, soap, kerosene, glass, and leather goods.[28] As commercial and administrative centers, Jiangmen and Huicheng attracted the aspiring subcounty elites and catered to their consumption needs. By the end of the Qing, the rural hinterland was also covered with small market towns. Known as the *jizhen* or *xu* (periodic markets), the more prosperous ones had populations of four to six thousand. They displayed an array of shops, teahouses, and a village council office, and some even had a small police force.

Linked by easy water transport to Huicheng and Jiangmen, the sizable villages in the Huancheng area did not have periodic markets. Instead, communities such as Shenhuan, Tianma, and Tianlu Xiang supported daily markets. A few shops and teahouses lined the main streets. The center of social and political activities for these settlements was the marketplace where the major temple was situated. In a single surname community such as Tianma, the village council office (known as the *gongsuo* in the Republican period) and temple merged with the Wubentang, the senior ancestral hall for the Chens.[29]

The twentieth century saw a rapid transformation of the regional economy. When large towns and cities in the delta were paralyzed by the chaos of warlord politics and the Japanese occupation in the 1930s and 1940s, small market towns in the regional periphery prospered. The rise of local strongmen in Tianma and Lile during the Japanese occupation is a case in point. In 1939 the Japanese armies had gained control of Guangzhou, Foshan, Shiqi, Jiangmen, and Huicheng and blockaded major transport routes along the coast.[30] The peasants in the area south of Huicheng and Jiangmen shifted to the production of grain and attended the markets farther south to avoid areas of direct conflict. They sought the protection of local militarists who had consolidated their territorial bases. Among these local strongmen was a Zeng Huan of Lile Xiang, who rose to power through war-profiteering and by smuggling supplies behind the Japanese lines. He even printed his own money for circulation and taxed those who attended his market. Because of its sudden change of fortune under Zeng, Lile earned the reputation of "Little Macao."[31] The local strongmen in Tianma sided with the Japanese military in Huicheng, and its residents were regarded by neighbors as exclusive and predatory.

In sum, during the first half of the twentieth century, the delta had a varied economic landscape in which agricultural production was specialized and intensive. Economic operations were capitalized and complex; livelihoods were prosperous yet precarious. The fluid movement of capital, goods, and people, based on shrewd market calculations as well as political maneuvers, meant that the rural communities were very much affected by a larger environment with whose political capriciousness the various social strata had to come to terms. Out of these economic activities arose social affiliations for the average peasant and multiple bases of power for the local elites. How they juggled these resources for survival and advancement shaped their relationships with one another as well as with the highly unstable power of successive regimes. This was the historical baseline of the economy the inhabitants of the region took for granted.[32]

A major focus of the following chapters is the step-by-step transformation of the local economy dictated by the priorities of the socialist state. To implement the changes, the party-state recruited and groomed several generations of local cadres, who replaced the managers of estates in the reclamation of the marshes and in the work of flood prevention. Thousands of peasants from different villages were mobilized by the commune and county governments to embark on very ambitious projects.

The bustling market activities of the prerevolutionary period were restructured by the state's imposition of compulsory sales of grain and of major cash crops.[33] A hierarchy of state-supervised marketing and supply cooperatives took over most of the rural exchange. Tangerine and mandarin oranges, the pride of the area, virtually disappeared from the late 1950s on. The production and sale of fan palm were centralized by the county fan-palm corporation under the department of commerce.

The consequences of state-imposed structures of production and marketing on the region's economy were obvious. During my field trips from the mid-1970s on, there was nothing that resembled the vibrant, bustling, though often precarious economic life that I had gleaned from the historical texts or from the memories of elderly villagers. There was little to sell in the rural markets. Consumers in Huicheng complained about the already limited items of food left unattended in transit. The rice served in the restaurants was stale because it had been improperly stored for too long. Dried orange peel, which according to the elderly villagers was available in abundance up to the 1950s, had become rare, expensive, and also of poor quality. Huicheng and its vicinity, the heart of what was once known as the land of the fan-palm trees and orchards, seemed to have lost its lush green color.

The transformation of the local economy of Huancheng involved one form of encapsulation over another. It raises several interesting sociological questions: How was the economy constructed and maintained in the prerevolutionary era, and what sociopolitical institutions did it sustain? How were changes brought about during almost a century of upheavals? How did the transformations after the Communist revolution affect the fortunes of the various social groups in the local area and shape their interaction with the larger polity? These are the questions to which I now turn.

Social Cells:
Community and Kin

At the turn of the century, the varied agricultural environment of the Huancheng area and its surrounding region supported a complex social structure. From the fringes of the sands inhabited by boat people (Dan),[1] aborigines (Yao), and migrant farmers who acted as bandits, hired hands in the reclamation of the sands, tenant farmers, members of the crop-watching corps, and functionaries of landed estates, to the grower-entrepreneurs who contracted with ancestral and other estates; the wholesale merchants who were members of trade associations and at times assumed the role of tax farmers; and the estate managers and literati who formed a political core at the academies and public bureaus—the social ranks were connected to each other not only through economic interests, but also through kinship and community affiliations, religious alliances, and political patronage.

Easy but unequal access to the productive alluvial plains had enabled local elites to build an array of social institutions in order to communicate with imperial officials. In fact, they took over many of the functions that the state normally performed: tax collection, famine relief and charity, provision of large-scale irrigation and transport facilities, education, maintenance of public security, and community defense. These institutions were built upon affiliations of community and kin, class differentiations, market networks, and practical politics and its ritual guises. They were woven together to form the moral and cultural fabric of the world of peasants and their educated elites. At times human perceptions and social interactions provided a protective shell, room to maneuver, and an arena for contest and resistance; at others, they demanded compliance and induced commitment.[2]

The Political Economy of the Sands

The maturing of the sands in the Ming and the Qing dynasties corresponded with the rise of territorial communities. By the late nineteenth century, the "frontier" of newly reclaimed land had been brought within the reach of entrepreneurial interests in the cities. Elderly villagers in Tianma and Tianlu Xiang, which were founded on reclaimed land at the southern tip of Huancheng, insist that the polders in their communities belonged to the descendants of retainers of the emperor, such as He the Minister and Mo the Eunuch of Huicheng. He the Minister was He Xiong-xiang, whose estate, the He Wenyi ancestral trust, still owned over 6,000 mu of sands at Jiuzisha, bordering the Huancheng area, at the time of the land reform in 1952.[3] Mo the Eunuch was a legendary figure whose power, which derived from his ties to the court, was claimed by the Mo lineage of the "south gate" of Huicheng, which owned vast estates at the time of the land reform. Representatives of the ancestral trusts were influential in gentry institutions in Huicheng and Jiangmen such as the Xi'nan Academy (shuyuan) and the Xinhui Academy, as well as in the local militia body, organized during the 1850s in the northeastern part of the county and known as Dongbei Public Bureau (gongju), all of which held extensive estates in the sands.[4]

The reclamation of the sands in Xinhui contributed to the formation of regional systems in the delta, in which territorial communities, estates, and their managerial elites rose and fell. Drawing from historical documents, Matsuda Yoshiro (1981) notes that local elites affiliated with the government in the older parts of the delta had claimed vast areas of sands in the late Ming and early Qing. Nishikawa Kikuko (1985) further argues that since the mid-Qing, the reclamation process involved elaborate financial arrangements between town-based elites and their functionaries. Increased flooding in the upper reaches of the river had prompted the court in 1772 to forbid reclamation, but grain shortages made the court relax the restrictions. From 1785 to 1835, more than 300,000 mu of new sands were registered (Nishikawa 1985).[5]

Substantial wealth was accumulated because agriculture on the sands was profitable and because tax evasion was common and easy. Katayama (1982), Matsuda (1981), Liu (n.d.), and Ye and Tan (1985b) have all pointed out that during the Ming and Qing dynasties tax officials tried but were unable to decipher the complex lineage and community relationships embodied in tax accounts (hu), and to confront "the locally rich and powerful" (haomen) who accumulated vast fortunes by sheltering their clients and cheating the government over the boundaries of land and their taxability. One outstanding example of delinquency on the sands, albeit from neighboring Dongguan County, was described by Zhang Zhidong, governor-general of Guangdong and Guangxi from 1884 to 1889. He denounced the Mingluntang[6] in 1889 for being difficult regarding taxes on 13,400 mu of the sands under its name. He accused its leaders of tax evasion by falsifying a claim of 100,000 taels of silver as operating expenses, because, as he alleged, it was common knowledge in the province that many groups who had claimed marshes from the government then farmed them out to contractors, who took care of the reclamation. Moreover, the sands in question had been claimed for over thirty years, and Zhang was indignant that tax exemptions had continued for so long (Nishikawa 1985, 14).

For our purpose, the document is significant because it mentions the expenses involved and the contractors who supposedly bore the costs. If estate managers in county capitals were not financing the expensive operations of reclamation, migrant tenant farmers and low-status farmhands could hardly be the likely alternative. In fact, earlier historical documents repeatedly point to a stratum of socially ambiguous middlemen. The 1674 edition of the Xiangshan county gazetteer, for example, claimed that during the early Ming, marshes were seized by powerful families of Shunde, Xinhui, and Panyu counties, who could accumulate "over ten thousand shi of grain" (*Nongyezhi* 2:19–20). Qu Dajun (1630–96) also wrote about the *zongdian* (chief tenants) who reaped handsome profits by parceling out the land they had acquired from subsoil owners to migrant farmers.[7] Not only did they control their own tenants in order to secure part of the harvest, but they also cheated the original claimants. Coercion and outright pillage were not uncommon, a subject on which Qu quoted an official observer at the end of Ming as saying,

> Coastal land in Guangdong emerged continuously, over a few years or decades. Powerful local bosses used the excuse of registering land for taxation to encroach upon matured sands belonging to others. This was known as *zhansha*. As harvests approached, they gathered shiploads of followers and descended upon the disputed areas, brandishing weapons and flags. Casualties were common. This was known as *qiangge*. (Qu 1700, vol. 2, no. 57)

Dealing with the more recently formed marshes farther southeast, Nishikawa (1985, 13) lists documents from the nineteenth century that focus on a stratum of local strongmen similarly categorized in the official historiography as *haomin* or *tuhao*. However, she argues that these were contractors who had secured long-term tenancy over large areas from the numerous original claimants of the land and had then organized their own reclamation. They were not mere secondary landlords who rented out the land in small parcels and lived off the difference between rent paid to them in kind and the cash rent they paid to original owners. Instead, the operations of these local strongmen reflected the increasingly sophisticated processes of technical organization and capital accumulation characteristic of the sands from the mid-nineteenth century on.

Quoting Zhang Zhidong on the diking of Da'nansha in Xiangshan County to the east of Xinhui County, Nishikawa (1985, 18–19) described the experience of a large contractor in the late nineteenth century that illustrates the complications and the scale of investments involved in land reclamation. Da'nansha was made up of over 30,000 mu of marshes, of which 7,000 mu were owned by 289 landlords. In 1887, one Huang Yushu, graduate of the imperial examinations at the provincial level, contracted with these landlords to reclaim their marshes. The landlords had agreed to pay Huang reclamation fees of 2.65 taels of silver per mu, and 6 percent of the land was conceded to him as an area to be taken up by dikes and canals. A dispute erupted between Huang and two of the landlords who had literati backing over the terms of distribution of the reclaimed land. The landlords organized a boatload of Dan fishermen, who descended upon the dikes and threatened their destruction. Subsequent fights and lawsuits revealed not only the power relationships among landlords and large contractors, but also the large sums involved. Huang spent 14,000 taels of silver on the project, but he would have received 20,000 taels as reclamation fees and a surplus of 180 mu of land with a cash value of around 6,000 taels. According to Nishikawa, this kind of diking enterprise was common in the late nineteenth century, and she lists four neighboring polders constructed by similar types of local strongmen.[8]

My own investigations in the sands bordering Xinhui and Xiangshan counties convince me that, in sharp contrast to the towns in which the managers of the estates were located, as long as the sands were recognized as newly reclaimed land, the landlords restricted the rights of their tenants to establish permanent settlement. In the town of Xiaolan, situated in the heart of the sands, there were 393 ancestral halls established by fifty-six surnames (among them three major surnames, each boasting hosts of literati members), and 139 temples and monasteries, among them two Chenghuang temples that only county capitals were expected to build. But on the sands beyond Xiaolan, there was hardly a house of brick or stone. Great disparity existed between the towns and the sands.[9]

Repeated Processes of Social Mobility

A process of social mobility characterized the evolution of a settlement on the sands into a township. On the fringes of land reclamation, the focus of social organization and management was the enclosed compound (*weiguan*). It consisted of straw huts strung out along the dikes and accommodating a large number of farmhands. There were houses for overseers, a granary or two, watchtowers, a fleet of boats for grain transportation, and a crop-watching and rent-collection force.

During the early Ming, Xiaolan seems to have been just a remote outpost similar to the *weiguan* described, the home of migrant farmers and the functionaries of the estates. However, by the late nineteenth century its residents had accumulated independent resources through their direct management of land reclamation and through their control over the grain rents and levies. Local strongmen consolidated their power in the outposts, which they turned into super-centers of wealth. In the process of becoming respectable, they manipulated cultural symbols, such as organizing within ancestral halls to create lineage and community alliances and to differentiate themselves from more recent migrants, and acquired academic degrees and official connections. At the same time, these nouveaux riches of the sands aggressively challenged their former patrons in the county capitals.[10]

The history of Xiaolan and the cases described by Nishikawa and Matsuda are relevant because they provide a profile of the generations of local functionaries who were directly involved in the complex operations of marshland reclamation and who were able to eventually claim a share of wealth and power in the maturing sands. This point clarifies an apparent difference between Matsuda and Nishikawa concerning local elites and land reclamation. Matsuda connects the consolidation of the power of gentry elites to their functions in land reclamation. Nishikawa, on the other hand, focuses on the usurpation of their power by a stratum of functionaries. However, if one sees the role of the middlemen in its proper historical context—that is, paralleling the growth of the delta and within the successive reclamation patterns—the way in which they were transformed from functionaries into respectable elites becomes clearer. The local strongmen of the mid-to-late Ming reaped windfall profits (Qu 1700, vol. 2, no. 57) in the northwestern part of the delta (for example, Xihai Shibasha) and joined ranks with the gentry elites in county capitals of Nanhai, Shunde, Xinhui, and Dongguan by the early Qing. Through official connections, they claimed vast areas in the southeastern part of the delta (Donghai Shiliusha) and engaged a new generation of local strongmen in the capitalized reclamation projects. By the mid-to-late nineteenth century, the residents of the former outposts, now thriving market towns in Xiangshan and Panyu, had ascended to the height of their power and collaborated with their own functionaries for the continued exploitation of the sands farther southeast (Wanqingsha). The step-by-step "colonization" of the delta involved sophisticated reclamation of the marshland, a substantial accumulation of wealth, and a fluid, multitiered power structure among the migrant farmers, the local functionaries, and their gentry patrons in the towns. A nexus of power based on differential access to the wealth of the sands connected the wide-open frontier to entrenched interests in the regional core. The process of social mobility was reenacted by outposts that grew into thriving towns, whose elites in time commanded their own colonizing efforts.[11]

The county capital of Huicheng did not grow from a *weiguan*. It has been a seat of government in this area since the eighth century. The officials stationed at Huicheng granted the recognition for the claimants of the sands in the southeastern part of the county in return for some acceptance of the obligation to pay tax. The more successful among the settlers on the sands rose to elite status by establishing connections to institutions in the city (more on this in the next chapter). It is within this context of regional systems formation that we need to analyze community- and lineage-building in the Huancheng area. The area was rapidly settled during the late Ming and early Qing, when estates in Huicheng accelerated their land reclamation efforts in the southeastern part of the county. The projects attracted large numbers of migrant laborers and Dan fishermen from all directions, who in time turned these outposts with their concentrated resources into large villages of a unique social and cultural configuration. By the turn of the twentieth century, many local strongmen and former functionaries had joined ranks with the elites in Huicheng and Jiangmen and established their own estates, conducting new reclamation projects farther southeast and challenging their former patrons. Residents of territorial communities, many of them associated with a single surname, might appear exclusively cellular in their claims to cultivation rights by tracing their descent from founding ancestors, yet they were intimately tied to the strategies of estates and literati connections in town, and to the opportunities for mobility that the latter exemplified. Subcounty political leadership rested specifically on these connections between town and countryside.

Community-Building

Freedman's lineage paradigm of southeastern China (1958, 1966) has shaped the course of Chinese anthropology for decades.[12] Later research cautions us that a preoccupation with the principles of patrilineal descent and with the functionalist aspects of ancestral trusts for the realization of such principles may easily blind us to other social affiliations that are just as meaningful, culturally and politically, in rural communities.[13] Working in the Pearl River delta and the New Territories of Hong Kong, David Faure argues for the overriding importance of territorial boundaries as delineated by settlement rights traced through descent from the original settlers, maintaining that "lineage was important for territorial control, and that territorial control was at the heart of lineage politics" (1986, 11). Taken together with Emily Ahern's work on lineage segmentation, which shows how preoccupied the keepers of lineage records were with movements of their members in and out of communities, Faure's assertion is a convincing one. The tracing of genealogical ties was essentially a way of keeping track of the inheritance of settlement rights, a major concern of the villagers.[14]

My own survey of the largest villages at the southern end of the Huancheng area shows that genealogical and territorial principles intertwined to produce a curious mixture of communities. I had expected to find highly differentiated and well-endowed lineage segments[15] in these communities because they were situated in a "frontier" area of rice cultivation where large-scale irrigation and defense were important factors that Freedman would have attributed to such a dominant form of internal lineage organization. I would also have expected to find these localized lineages ritually linked to apical ancestral halls (*da zongci*), constructed later in the county capitals and cities and dedicated to remote founding ancestors, which unified large memberships of a single surname spread out in a vast territory.[16] Instead, I found that what villagers referred to as focal ancestral halls (*zuci*) were very common in these rural communities. The halls were not well endowed with property, but they engendered unity among a large membership within a well-defined territory, based on loose affiliations to a common legendary founder. I was intrigued, for example, to find that the focal ancestral hall of the Chens in Tianma Xiang was established with only a little over 3 mu of polders.[17] For this part of the delta, in which the sands were measured in units of qing (100 mu), its endowment was negligible. There was no written record of when the hall in Tianma was established. However, the Chen lineage genealogy described it as containing the tablets of the father and grandfather of the original founder of the lineage in Tianma, who supposedly died during the reign of Zhengde (1506–21) in the Ming. The hall nevertheless assumed a dominant role in the political and economic affairs of the whole community. On a visit in the summer of 1987, I spent an afternoon with six elderly men from the township, in their sixties to eighties, who were considered to be the best informed about local history. Two of them I had interviewed several years before. They made clear to me during our discussions that the majority of the thirty-five segment estates of the Chen lineage in the township emerged only in the turbulent decades of the twentieth century. Before I left, they led me to what they called a new-style ancestral hall built during the Japanese occupation period. It turned out to be an ancestral hall of the "study chamber" type (*shushi*), which was more like an expanded domestic altar where rites for very close kin were performed. The short history of the ancestral estates and halls is confirmed by my reading of the Chen lineage genealogy (1923), compiled by a member of a lineage segment whose founder had moved to Huicheng during the early Qing. As expected, the genealogy emphasized its own segment history. However, in the descriptions of eight earlier generations in Tianma, two ancestral halls were recorded as having been built: the hall built by the segments of the second generation in Tianma, and one built by a segment in the third generation. There was no mention of other ancestral estates or halls.

Searching for an explanation of the importance of the focal ancestral halls, I looked into the history of settlement of these communities. When the Huancheng area was being settled, the "frontier" might have meant something different to its inhabitants. Ancestral trusts and other corporate estates in Huicheng and Jiangmen reached down into the sands, employing considerable capital and creating a multitiered structure of contract tenancy. Formed under the overarching shadow of the town-based trusts, the functional role of large contractors, who could take the form of (1) individual local strongmen, (2) groups centered at community temples, or (3) focal ancestral halls, was vital in formulating community and town interests. The political economy of the sands produced peculiar forms of lineage and community affiliations and provided the basis for a repeated process of social mobility through which local leaders fostered ties with the literati and the merchants in the towns. Data from the Huancheng area illuminates these processes of community-building and shows how migrant outposts grew into single-surname communities that exerted a strong influence in the region.

Lineage Communities in and around the Huancheng Area

Local gazetteers and lineage genealogies trace a steady stream of migration into the area during the Song dynasty. Claiming origin from the central plains of China, the lineages held on to a common myth, that their ancestors first settled in Nanxiong subprefecture of northern Guangdong. Fear of official wrath after a fellow resident sheltered a fugitive courtesan prompted a group of ninety-seven with thirty-five different surnames to migrate south after petitioning the authorities in 1273 to be allowed to do so. They received help from aboriginal populations along the way and finally settled in the open frontier of the delta.[18]

A detailed analysis of the migration myth by Faure (n.d.-2) shows the mechanisms of official registration and taxation to be characteristic of the Ming dynasty rather than the Song. His comparison of this myth with that of the Yao aborigines in Guangdong suggests that the local populations differentiated themselves into Han and Yao identities in response to the impositions of taxes by the Ming court. Evidence that Dan fishermen all along the coast became migrant farmers only complicates the cultural history of the region.[19] Meanwhile the delta continued to be reclaimed in a southeasterly direction. In the initial stages of settlement, neither kin nor community solidarities were evident in the sands. Villages were small and scattered. Migrant farmers lived in straw huts. In time, outposts grew into established lineage communities whose members claimed exclusive rights of settlement by virtue of descent from the original founders of the villages. With expected exaggeration, the *Xinhui xiangtuzhi* (1908, 38) estimated that there was a total of "seven hundred villages populated by numerous surname groups with several thousand members; a dozen or so contain memberships of over tens of thousands."

Exclusive lineage communities could indeed be identified in and around the Huancheng district. Despite the argument by Faure (n.d.-2) that the delta was mostly settled during the Ming, the claims of the Zhaos of Sanjiang that they had settled in the area since the end of the Song were not improbable, because historical evidence shows that during the last days of the southern Song court, the child-emperor Bing and his entourage encamped at the Ya Men inlet farther south before they were overwhelmed by the pursuing Mongol army. The Zhaos claimed rights to vast areas of marshland to the east of Sanjiang.[20] Their tenants claimed that they had migrated from the Shuangshui area in the west during the Qing dynasty and in time established the township of Longquan. By the turn of the century, the Liu, Li, and Zhang surnames of Longquan had become archrivals of the Zhaos for control of the sands and the strategic waterways in the vicinity. Conflicts of interest culminated in a major feud in 1948. Over a thousand village men were involved. The arms accumulated for the feud prompted the intervention of the provincial authorities, who were eager for a part of the spoils.[21] The feuds between Sanjiang and Longquan Xiang show how community and kin interests, economic resources, and political alliances in the sands coalesced in a quest for territorial domination well beyond the boundaries of lineage or village. At the turn of the century, the townships of Shenhuan, Tianma, and Tianlu were prominent features of the rural landscape south of Huicheng. Their histories deserve some attention here. With minor differences they represent examples of how communities and lineages evolved when the sands matured in the shadow of the ancestral trusts and corporate estates based in the county capital.

Chakeng and Shenhuan Xiang

Chakeng was one of the three large villages that made up the township of Shenhuan 10 kilometers southeast of Huicheng. From the supposed founding of the village in the 1620s to the birth of the famous scholar Liang Qichao in 1873, the residents of this single-surname community spanned fifteen generations.[22] The county gazetteer compiled in 1690 describes the hill against which the village was built as an island at the confluence of the Xi and Tan rivers, but as early as the reign of Wanli (1573–1620) in the Ming, elites in Huicheng had erected a seven-story pagoda on top of the hill for purposes of geomancy. Villagers alleged that a kind of legged shellfish had crawled onto land and had poisoned the local inhabitants. The pagoda was erected with the intention of suppressing them.[23] In time migrant farmers reclaimed the marshes that merged with the landmass extending from the south of Huicheng. By the late Qing half of the village polders were devoted to grain, the rest being planted with palm and citrus.

Numbering over two thousand at the turn of the century, the Liang residents claimed that their ancestors came from Kaiping County after a previous sojourn in Nanxiong subprefecture in northern Guangdong. Five ancestral halls stood at the center of the village. The focal ancestral hall, Diecheng Tang, was endowed with 100 mu of land. Two other ancestral halls were built for members of the third generation, and another two for later generations. Judged by the standards of the sands, their estates of 100 mu or so were not large. Moreover, they were not managed by wealthy notables who emerged from the representatives of lineage segments. Instead, their management and income rotated annually among the male members of the component lineage segments, overseen by a council of elders.

A brief description of Liang Qichao's family history will shed some light on the circumstances of an average farmer turned member of the village gentry. As a member of the Liang lineage, Liang's grandfather had the right to build a house in one of the four hamlets of the village. Even after he became its first student scholar (*xiucai*), the grandfather continued to farm several mu of land inherited from his immediate ancestors. Another ancestral trust awarded him a scholarship that he used to buy more than 10 mu of land. As a rich farmer with an education, he was active in community affairs, for example, in the promotion of the *baolianghui,* a village association initiated by the Qing government after the disturbances of the Red Turbans from 1854 to 1856.[24] Liang's father inherited 6 mu of land. He farmed and studied, but never succeeded in passing the examinations. After his son Qichao received the *juren* degree by passing the provincial examinations, the father gained informal status as a member of the village gentry. It was said that he accumulated at least 50 mu of land and rented them out to fellow kinsmen. Meanwhile, he continued to teach and was relied upon to arbitrate disputes in the village. Relatively well off and fairly well educated scholar-cultivators such as Liang Qichao's grandfather were typical of the leaders who represented the lineage and the village to the imperial authorities, and were relied upon by state agents to collect various levies, arbitrate disputes, organize defense, and promote moral education. Their economic interests in fact reinforced their social obligations and political commitments in the communities. Their close ties with community interests, symbolic and otherwise, were shrewdly recognized by the imperial authorities, as illustrated in a case involving Liang Qichao. After the abortive Hundred Days Reforms, imperial wrath against him brought havoc to Chakeng. Qing troops were ordered to march into the village, where they destroyed the ancestral tablets in the halls that symbolized the influence of the Liang lineage.

The two thousand or so residents of the Liang surname in Chakeng made it a populous lineage community in the eyes of the residents of Shenhuan Xiang. The Liang maintained their affiliations with neighboring communities in various ways. On the eighth day of every new year, representatives of lineage segments attended ancestral rites in Tianlu, where descendants of the younger brother of Chakeng's founder had supposedly built an ancestral hall and created an estate in honor of their father. Though the Liang at Chakeng belonged to the senior segment, villagers acknowledged that the Liang lineage of Tianlu had supplied the funds to build the Tianlu hall. On the outskirts of Chakeng were three other communities closely tied to the Liang lineage. The residents of Xiaodong Village consisted of a small branch of the Liang mixed with a few households bearing the Tan and Chen surnames. The latter were referred to by the Liang as *shamin* (residents of the sands) and *xiahu* (mean households). Living "out in the sands" on boats and in straw huts, they did not intermarry with members of the Liang surname. They were referred to as Dan fishermen, who were hired by the Liang lineage to reclaim the sands and who later settled in the area to engage in "menial occupations" such as carrying coffins for the Liang.[25] At the far end of the village were two settlements of a few hundred residents, known respectively as Yuanjiacun and Shierfeng, both inhabited by people bearing the Yuan surname. An origin myth tied the Yuan and Liang surname groups in a peculiar way. It was claimed by the Liang lineage that the focal ancestor of the Yuan surname group, who was a female referred to by the Yuan as the *bopo*, married an ancestor of the Liang. Her brother came with her from Kaiping, but when he died the Liang surname residents would not allow him to be buried on their village land. However, at the hill behind Chakeng, a violent rain caused a landslide that entirely covered the body. Interpreting this as a sign from the heavens, the Liang surname group accepted the Yuan surname residents into the community, even though the two groups could not intermarry. The Yuan group did not have an ancestral hall until the twentieth century.[26] When I visited their only temple, devoted to Tianhou, the empress of heaven, in July 1987, I saw paper flags placed in the front altar, the same types of flags that Dan fishermen put at small altars in the prows of their boats. The myth illuminated a community-building process in Chakeng whereby Dan migrant laborers were eventually accepted as a stratum in the community.

Other social affiliations were maintained through attendance at markets and temples. The three elderly villagers with whom I discussed local history insisted that there had never been a periodic market in Chakeng as long as they could remember. Instead a daily market was attended by itinerant traders from neighboring villages. Usually, the Liang lineage members went to the market at Sanjiang, where they maintained ties with their affines in the Zhao lineage. They also visited the markets in Shuangshui to the southwest and Lile to the northeast. However, they seldom went to Huicheng in the northwest, because, as it was claimed, only the educated members could mingle socially in the cities.

Next to the focal ancestral hall in Chakeng were two major temples, the Beidi and the Kangwang. Annual celebrations at the two temples were held after the harvest of the late crop, around the eleventh month of the lunar year. These temples were attended exclusively by the Liang lineage members, except for a few families of the Yuan surname. The Beidi Temple, which was also the political headquarters of the village, managed a vast area of marshes in the northeast that belonged to the neighboring village of Xijia. When asked how the temple came to manage the lands and collect the rent, villagers recounted that landlords at Xijia had contracted the land to the Liang but were not able to collect rents. The temple, representing the interests of the Liang, was responsible for parceling out the land for cultivation; it collected rent, gave a percentage to the crop-watching forces, and kept the rest. Though the landlords at Xijia nominally had the right to these marshes, in fact they became the property of the temple controlled by the Liang lineage who reclaimed and cultivated them. In essence, the temple served the function of the contractor for the Liang lineage in Chakeng and pocketed the surplus.[27]

The community's third temple, the Sanbao Miao, had a more inclusive following. Built during the reign of Tongzhi (1862–74), it staged an annual *jiao* ceremony of communal exorcism during the seventh lunar month. The procession of the gods reached as far as Xiaodong, the Yuan settlements, and the neighboring community of Dadong, inhabited by a group surnamed Yu, who according to the local people were descendants of the original settlers in the area. The procession of the gods mapped out the social space of Shenhuan Xiang with its multi-surname membership.

Tianlu Xiang

Known locally as Shuni, the township of Tianlu was described by the county gazetteer of 1840 as an island off the tip of the land that extended 6 kilometers southwest from Huicheng. As in Chakeng, centuries of reclamation had turned the shallow marshes into productive polders. The landmass within Tianlu's boundary encompassed eight villages situated closely together. Though five surname groups made up the bulk of the population (Ye, Liang, Huang, Zhang, and Feng), the existence of at least fifteen other surnames suggested that the township had been an open frontier, attracting migrants from a wide area. As in Chakeng, some of these other surnames were referred to by elderly villagers as *xiahu* (mean households). However, in Tianlu Xiang, this group did not consist of the *shamin* (settlers in the sands) who migrated southwards from Jiangmen along the tributary of the Xi River. Instead, villagers described the *xiahu* as poor migrants from the Shuangshui area in the southwest who had no claim to village land and who had attached themselves as hereditary bond servants. Known locally as *dizi* (junior sons), they lived in houses built by their patrons, were given land to cultivate, and were even given ceremonial pork after lineage rituals.

As mentioned earlier in the chapter, villagers in Tianlu today readily point out that most of the land in the township belonged to descendants of He the Minister and Mo the Eunuch. Uncle Ye and Old Liang, the two octogenarian know-it-alls in Tianlu, vividly described how land was acquired "in the days of the dynasties." Officials supposedly obtained the land in the sands by sprinkling grain into the rivers and claiming ownership wherever the grain washed up on shore. To me, the story conveyed the villagers' perception of imperial representatives as distant but arbitrarily powerful figures.

How the land became cultivable involved a long process. Initially, marshes were claimed by ancestral trusts in Huicheng. Laborers were sometimes hired to stack stones along the banks to accelerate sedimentation. When a substantial area of soil had accumulated, the marshes were contracted out to local strongmen who, it was said, "maintained good connections with estate managers and functionaries in town." When a large polder was ready for cultivation, the large contractors called the villagers together and parcelled out the land in public auctions. Tianlu residents paid rent in kind to these local strongmen. With a large amount of grain at their disposal for trading with grain merchants in Huicheng, the local strongmen quickly accumulated resources and acquired their own marshes for reclamation. When some of the polders were converted to the growing of cash crops such as sugarcane, citrus, and fan palm, the strongmen established trading ties with wholesale merchants in town and often had their conflicts arbitrated in trade guilds.

The largest surname, Ye, had seven ancestral halls by the first quarter of the century, with two more added after the 1930s. Of the eight villages, the Ye surnames occupied four. The focal ancestral hall of the Ye, known as Zuluntang, was located in the village of Dongan. The second most powerful surname group, the Liang, resided in the village of Xining and had built a hall for the father of the original founder of the village.[28] Two other halls were added only at the turn of the century. The Huang lineage of Xian Village and the Yu lineage of Xihua Village each had an ancestral hall. The Su lineage, whose elite members had moved into Huicheng, also maintained one. In comparison with the large polders owned by ancestral trusts in Huicheng, estates owned by local segments were relatively small, averaging less than 100 mu each. The estates were auctioned out for cultivation and the income was used for ancestral rituals.

All the surname groups in Tianlu participated in rituals at what they claimed were ancestral graves in the hills north of Huicheng, together with remote kinsmen in Huicheng. It was said that Shushan, the only hill in Tianlu, did not have favorable geomancy for burial, so the ancestors were buried near Huicheng. It was also convenient, according to elderly villagers of the Ye surname, because the rituals meant that "there was pork for distribution." Lineage elites went for political purposes. A fifty-five-year-old villager of the Ye surname alleged that his grandfather, a rather wealthy man, went not only to higher-order ancestral halls and academies in Huicheng where the soul tablets of some of their ancestors were deposited, but also to an apical ancestral hall in Guangzhou during a time of lineage feuds in order to seek possible alliances.

Social cleavages in Tianlu shifted among the different surnames. By the early twentieth century, the Ye and Liang surnames had become the major competitors for the township's best polders. The Liang were envied for their wealth, but no "outsider" would venture to live in Xining Village, which they occupied. In the 1930s a strongman of the Ye surname challenged that exclusiveness. Ye Yi came from humble origins but was able to gather a following of village toughs during a decade of political chaos. Testing the limits, he burnt some crops and boats belonging to the Liang. The Liang were outraged. Feeling outnumbered, they sought help from Liang surname groups in the neighboring townships of Nantan in the north and Qianmu at the southern tip of Xinhui County. A show of force was finally averted through mediation by community elders and notables.

The social boundaries of the eight villages were made explicit by communal participation in popular rituals. Each village in the township had an earth shrine (*she*). Each polder (*wei*) outside the residential area also had an earth shrine. During the celebration of the earth god's birthday, each household under the spiritual jurisdiction of these shrines would contribute money and grain.[29] The township also had four temples: the Wenwu Temple in the village of Xian, the Huaguang Temple, the Chen Kao Temple in the village of Beian, and the Dawang Temple in Dongan. Known also as Yongyou Tang, the Dawang Temple was also the site of the council office of the township.[30] It was situated by the marketplace and was quite obviously the center of activities. Access to the township's common lands, such as dikes, riverways, marshes on the edge of the polders where peasants raised ducks or collected harvest grubs, was auctioned by the council office. The income was used to hire watchmen for the dikes and crops as well as for temple festivals. Apart from the annual celebration of the deity's birthday during the second lunar month, the temple staged a *jiao* ceremony every three years after the harvest of the late crop. As in other temple festivals, the deity was paraded in a prescribed sequence around the communal shrines of the entire township so that the residents of each village could perform the ritual known as *zuosheng* (seating the deity).

Apart from sharing common rituals, residents of Tianlu often mobilized for practical political reasons against the Chen surname group of Tianma Xiang. Both townships were situated in the more recently reclaimed sands. Residents frequently bickered over land boundaries and diking. Rent on land bordering the two townships was cheap because, as I was told, nobody could be sure of who would get the harvest. As we will see in the next chapter, the two townships had a showdown in 1939. Several local strongmen of Tianlu sided with the Nationalist government stationed in Shuang-shui, but those of Tianma sided with the Japanese occupying Huicheng. Because of some alleged rapes, villagers in Tianlu descended upon a group of soldiers supposedly serving the collaborators. The Japanese military retaliated by bombing the township. In the wake of the bombing, local strongmen in Tianma and their followers sacked Tianlu, razed the houses to the ground, dismantled buildings and bridges, and carted the spoils back to Tianma. Lin Qing, the present party secretary of Tianlu, remembered that as a child of eleven he watched the Japanese artillery hit a dozen or so houses in the township; the men went for cover, while women and children hid in their houses. Then he saw "an army of uniformed men" (*dajun*) and village toughs from Tianma coming down the main road. He remembered that a few men and a women of the Ye surname defended themselves with bamboo poles against the invaders under the big tree at the village entrance, while the wounded lay moaning by the roadside. He fled with his family to Shuangshui, a district farther southwest across the river. Some of the villagers never returned. For a decade residents of the two townships did not intermarry or attend each other's markets.

Tianma Xiang

Tianma was a township composed of seven villages clustered at the foot of the Changni, Fengshan, and Mani hills. Numbering over five thousand, the residents of Tianma were considered by neighbors to be exclusive, uncultured, and belligerent. In fact, neighbors called them Dan fishermen, a designation that a majority of those with the Chen surname who lived in five of the villages would reject. Instead, they distinguished themselves from those in the remaining two villages with mixed surnames (such as Deng, Mai, He, Huang). Concentrated at Changni Hill and cultivating the most recent sands, the residents of these two villages were known to wear black cloth (known locally as *Danjia bu*), to live in boats and straw huts, and to engage in fishing during the slack seasons. They were considered *xiahu* and *shamin,* and the Chen surname residents in the other villages did not intermarry with them.

The efforts of the Chen lineage members to distance themselves from Dan associations ironically revealed the contrary. In the preface of the Chen genealogy (1923), where the usual myth of migration from Nan-xiong was described, the author attached another story, which related that fear of persecution in Nanxiong scattered their original ancestors to Guangzhou, Shunde, Xinhui, Nanjing, Kaifeng, and Fujian Province (which were areas where one found Dan settlements). Furthermore, they vowed to "reside by the sand and waters to commemorate their common origins."

How the Chens came to settle in Tianma was the subject of another legend. It was claimed that during the mid-Ming, a woman had married into a Chen family in Shitou of Tangxia Xiang, north of Jiangmen. When her husband was drowned in the Xi River by enemies, she fled to her birthplace near Jiangmen, another place where Dan fisherman congregated, bringing with her a four-year-old son born in the seventh year of the reign of Zhengtong (1443). For fear of further persecution, her family sought the help of a relative, a fisherman by the name of Guo, who lived at Changni.

At the time, the neighboring village of Mani was inhabited by people bearing the Feng surname. It happened that one of them was involved in a killing and had fled the area. The Chen widow was able to buy his house. She settled down to raise her son. He eventually married and had three sons, twelve grandsons, and thirty-five great-grandsons. According to the legend, the Chen surname group competed with the Feng for exclusive rights to settle in the village. Elderly villagers claimed that a rich member of the Feng lineage made a Chen man carry him across the river but was drowned. A lawsuit was brought by the Fengs against the alleged murderer. The thirty-five great-grandsons responded by volunteering to the magistrate as the joint culprits. Observing their unity, the magistrate urged the Feng villagers to leave the area, advice they took. The Chens registered their households with the authorities, paid the taxes, and claimed settlement rights in the area. A member of the seventh generation born in 1650 acquired academic degrees and official honors and then moved to Huicheng. An ancestral hall was built in his name in Huicheng in 1810. Another for his son was built in 1861. Their ancestral trusts maintained land in Tianma and the surrounding sands. In Tianma Xiang, two ancestral halls were built: a focal ancestral hall, Wubentang, built for the founder of the lineage and housing the soul tablets for his father and grandfather, and a Zhigongtang built for one of his grandsons.

The origin myth reveals the Chens' fisherman origins as well as their struggle with the original inhabitants for the right to settle in the area. It was not surprising to find that there were Dan fishermen around. Several hundred years ago, the Tianma area was just an island at the confluence of Xi and Tan rivers and probably served as a shelter for coastal fishermen. The fact that the Chen surname groups continued to visit the grave of "Fisherman Guo" at the New Year and that they worshipped the mother of the original founder as *bopo* in a temple for Chen Kao only added to the unorthodox flavor of their social and cultural background.[31] If the Chen of Tianma were of Dan origin, their presence on the sands since the Ming suggests that they started as hired hands in the reclamation projects.[32] The initial settlements would have taken the form of the *weiguan*. After the sands were reclaimed, these laborers became hired guards carrying out the duties of crop-watching and dike repair, later acquiring settlement rights by driving out less numerous competitors such as the Lin and the Feng. The open sands provided ample opportunities for accumulating resources. The Chen surname groups became respectably Han after a few generations and even built their own ancestral halls and compiled a genealogy.[33]

Elderly villagers insisted that, as in Tianlu, land in the township was predominantly owned by ancestral trusts in Huicheng bearing the He surname. These trusts contracted extensive marshes to local strongmen, who in turn parcelled them out to villagers for reclamation and cultivation. Though Tianma's focal ancestral hall, Wubentang, did not have much land of its own, its council of elders and managers, who were supposedly elected every three years, took care of matters relating to community property such as rights to use riverways, markets, dikes, and wasteland. Rights were auctioned off annually to lineage members, and the sums collected were used for rituals and for charity. The rules of the hall listed generous sums to be contributed to the village elderly as well as to those who had acquired academic degrees and official honors. They also took it upon themselves to maintain public order in the community, threatening with "expulsion from the lineage" those members who committed offenses such as trespassing ancestral graves, committing adultery and gambling, using community boats for piracy and opium smuggling, and, in the case of managers of local estates, delinquency in tax payments. They declared that they would act as guarantors in legal matters and in arbitration, and represented community members faced with official accusations.[34] In addition, the ancestral hall may have served as the contractor for corporate estates in the town, because older villagers insisted that they paid rents to the Wubentang, "which took care of everything, rent, taxes and all."

The community rituals of the Chens were no different from those of their neighbors. Each village had an earth shrine (*she*), as did every polder of more than a few hundred mu. Apart from the Chen Kao Temple, which was regarded more or less as a religious center for the Chens, the township had three other major temples: the Beidi, Guandi and the Tianhou.[35] The communal *jiao* ceremonies took place at the Beidi Temple once every two years. Theatrical troupes were hired from as far away as Foshan and Guangzhou. Unlike a multi-surname community such as Tianlu, ancestral estates in Tianma bore a major part of the ritual costs in the community. In fact, the focal ancestral hall and the Beidi Temple were physically linked by the Chen Kao Temple. They formed the center of social activities and political authority for the Chen lineage in Tianma. It was at this point that the merging of community and kin was most forcefully represented.

Power and Community

The Huancheng area displayed a great variety of community composition. Despite their differences, local residents have consistently stressed their similarities as collective entities whose unity was symbolized by the pre-eminence of focal ancestral halls and of major village temples.[36] Underlying their histories of settlement, one may discern patterns of community-building taking place within an overarching system of land tenure that linked the town and communities on the rural fringes. These settlements seem to have emerged rapidly at the end of the Ming and in the early Qing dynasties. Whether or not the original settlers were freeholders, the an-cestral trusts and merchant and gentry institutions based in town had bought up most of the maturing sands in the county by the late Qing. Reclamation projects brought a mixture of immigrants into the area. Set-tlement rights were subsequently fought out among them, the losers being pushed down to a lower social category. Focal ancestral halls dedicated to remote founders and major community temples were the dominant social affiliations for the villagers. These social and religious institutions more often than not assumed the role of large contractors acting on behalf of the trusts in town.[37] To be able to trace genealogical ties to original settlers meant that one was able to settle in the community, to cultivate its con-tracted land, to be sheltered by the village notables against aggressive neighbors and officials, and to receive charity from the funds of ancestral trusts and community temples. Villagers paid their rents, but tax payments were the business of managers of estates and village notables.

It is true that village life was dominated by local strongmen and rich householders. Some of them might have been bully-like armed guards and functionaries in the reclamation projects who pocketed the crop-watching fees, but many were the shrewd contractors and managers of ancestral trusts and temples. They maintained good relations with patrons in town and were themselves upwardly mobile. However, it was in the interest of the powerful who succeeded in entering elite society to adopt the elite lifestyle and to maintain the cultural traditions that provided a sense of unity to the entire region. The rise of local strongmen was not based solely on brute force, as gentry historiography has portrayed it to be. Successful local strongmen ceased to be illegitimate and became members of the gentry.[38] Their sources of authority and power were embedded in long-established social institutions. At the younger sands, which town estates failed to control, the many easy ways of accumulating wealth had allowed these local strongmen and their descendants to build their own estates, acquire academic degrees, and become respectable by the criteria of the Confucian state culture. They fostered ties with elites in town by participating in the activities higher-order lineages; by contributing sums to town-based ancestral halls where they could place their ancestral tablets; by securing membership in trade guilds and academies as merchants and scholar-officials (more on this in chapter 4). For example, the Chen lineage genealogy of Tianma showed that the tablets of its founding ancestor and of members of several generations were deposited in an apical ancestral hall for the Chen surname in Huicheng. Some were placed in Xi'nan Shuyuan, a powerful academy built in the mid-nineteenth century that included gentry members of different surnames who claimed their origin in the southwestern part of Xinhui County. A directory of Xi'nan Shuyuan compiled in 1922 showed that many members came originally from Chakeng, Tianma, and Tianlu. The academies, as we will see, were institutions that arbitrated political disputes among local elites, and between them and state officials. Though the upwardly mobile local elites were eventually drawn into town, they were still relied upon by their rural associates, especially if they continued to maintain landed interests in the rural communities.[39] Hence the concerns of kin, combined with a broad membership sharing an apical ancestor, produced territorial communities that defended themselves fiercely against outsiders but at the same time actively sought linkages with metropolitan interests.

Thus the process of community-building as described in the Huancheng area adds a historical dimension to Freedman's treatment of lineage communities. It traces how these micro-histories of community-building unfolded and how local residents within them became part of the cultural ethos of the wider region. The local communities, beginning as reclamation settlements, developed within the framework of the lineage and produced successful leaders who climbed up the social ladder and related local customs to the official culture, drawing their own communities into the state structure in the process.

It follows that if one looks at community-building within this wider structure of property and power relationships, one must also examine the town-based corporate estates to appreciate their influence on the rural hinterland. By the time the Huancheng area was settled, Huicheng had already become a sizable economic and political center. As I will show in the next chapter, managerial elites of corporate estates maintained overlapping memberships in ancestral trusts, trade guilds, charity organizations, and academies. They accumulated wealth from the reclamation projects and from trading the resultant grain and cash crops. Both in its genealogical and corporate aspects, the symbolic value of kin ideology operated side by side with shrewd market calculations and political maneuvers. The sophisticated organization and entrepreneurial orientation of the managerial elites enabled them to push the frontier back by relying on a multitiered structure of functionaries and large contractors. Though Freedman may have viewed the powerful lineage organizations as symptoms of the state's loss of control, the economically dominant ancestral trusts in town, which maintained symbiotic relationships with territorially based communities in the rural hinterland, were not antithetical to imperial priorities. In fact, it was precisely during periods of dynastic peace and prosperity that the corporate estates were able to thrive and their leading members to become upwardly mobile. They sought political connections in order to press their interests with representatives of the imperial bureaucracy. These town-based institutions were what the rural communities in the Huancheng area had to come to terms with and at times depended upon.

Fan palm, a major cash crop of Xinhui County. (1982)

The flood plain at the southern tip of the Huancheng area where Tianma, Tianlu, and Shenhuan Xiang are situated. (1980)

The pagoda on the hill behind Chakeng Village, erected by elites in Huicheng during the Ming Dynasty. (1987)

The temple for Chen Kao (named Jingyi Study Chamber). It adjoins the former Beidi temple on the left and Wubentang, the focal ancestral hall of the Chen of Tianma, on the right (not in the picture). (1987)

The focal ancestral hall of Tianma, Wubentang, at the center of the township. (1987)

The focal ancestral hall of the Lu lineage of Chaolian Township, made into a school after the socialist revolution. (1986)

The former cultural and political center of Chaolian Township. On the left once stood the ancestral halls of the Ou; in the middle was the Hongsheng temple; adjoining it on the right were the community public office and school. The temple was renovated in 1985. (1986)

The Hongsheng temple of Chaolian Township. (1986)

One of the two remaining pawnshops in the former merchants' quarters of Jiangmen. Now a workers' hostel. (1986)

The main hall of the former Xinhui Academy in Huicheng, built in the 1920s, now the Xinhui Number One Secondary School. (1987)

Entrance to the former Xinhui Academy. (1987)

CHAPTER 4

Cultural Tissues:
A Regional Nexus of Power

At the northern end of Huicheng, on slightly elevated ground, towered the magistrate's seat, the symbol of imperial power. To its left was the temple of the city god, Chenghuang, representing the bureaucratic powers of the magistrate in the supernatural world. These were flanked by equally imposing buildings of culture and learning. To the right was the Confucian Temple, which was the site of the county's academy, Mingluntang, and bordering on that was the place where a famous scholar of the Ming dynasty, Chen Baisha, had held his academic court. Toward the center of town stood the Gangzhou Academy (*shuyuan*), established in 1752 by a county magistrate and converted to gentry management in 1806. Later it became identified as a public bureau (*gongju*) by the city's literati, who were given the power to organize local defense during the turbulent decades of the mid-nineteenth century.[1] Equally imposing was the Xi'nan Academy nearby, a similarly parapolitical institution established in 1845 by eight degree-holders of different surnames from the southwestern districts of Xinhui. Patrons donated large sums in return for being able to deposit ancestral tablets in the academy, where periodic rituals were performed. Its members took it upon themselves to aid local scholars in the civil service examinations, to build social networks based on particularistic ties in order to arbitrate disputes among lineages and communities, to maintain civil order and defense, and to articulate local grievances against bureaucratic abuse.[2]

Juxtaposed with the parapolitical institutions within the city walls and intimately tied to literati culture were various concrete symbols of lineage prosperity, the most conspicuous being the ornate, official-style ancestral halls. The neighborhood where Xi'nan Academy stood was the stronghold of lineages of the He surname. The area was known as the *Shangshu Fang* (The Neighborhood of the Minister), where descendants of the famous Ming minister, He Xiongxiang, had built ancestral halls for his great-grandfather, his grandfather, the minister himself, his four sons, and three of his grandsons.[3] Three other surname groups, the Mo, Li, and Liu, shared the preeminence of the He lineage. Their ancestral halls lined the southern wall of the city from the eastern to the western end. The larger complexes consisted of three layers of halls with curved roofs, signifying that members had received official honors in the past, and their biannual rituals attracted lineage members from all over the rural hinterland.[4] These halls were endowed with vast estates. There were lineages with lesser estates. In fact, a land reform document in 1952 (*Fan fengjian* 9:1) recorded an initial count of ninety-four ancestral trusts in Huicheng, of which the He had twenty-seven, the Li eight, the Mo three, and the Liu seventeen. The rest were shared by thirteen other surnames. Similar to the academies, these trusts with estates and halls provided an urban base to which upwardly mobile individuals from Huicheng's rural hinterland could attach themselves. The usual path to social advancement was to claim affiliation by contributing to the trusts and depositing the soul tablets of one's own ancestors in these halls, which then enabled one's descendants to participate in the lineage rituals.

Though literati grandeur faded into the bustling world of merchants as one passed through the city's southern gates along the riverbank, commercial and gentry interests were linked by overlapping institutional memberships and shared claims to local power. At the western gate stood the headquarters of the Fan Palm Guild, built in 1842, probably the city's most monopolistic economic institution. An alliance of gentry and merchant leaders flexed their political muscles in order to safeguard the economic contracts of its members, who were spread deep into the palm-growing areas immediately south of Huicheng. A road from the southern gate led directly to Sanyaying, a former post for city guards, where palm-drying and fan-making workshops clustered. The riverbanks between the two gates were lined with wholesale enterprises for purchasing grain and orange peel, the two other major commodities from Huicheng's rural hinterland. In between the two neighborhoods known as the Da Gubu and the Xiao Gubu (grain wharves) was the Dilintang Temple. Though its pantheon of deities represented the power and protocol of the imperial bureaucracy in the supernatural world, merchant groups patronized its ritual activities with fervor. Social groups in the rural hinterland who maintained close ties with the merchants also contributed to the festivities.[5] And the city's chamber of commerce, established in 1907, was conveniently located around the corner. The cultural splendor embodied in these landmarks, though faded in the postrevolutionary decades amid dusty crowds of cyclists and the polluting noise of hand-tractors, was unveiled to me with a touch of nostalgia by two local historians with whom I made friends on visits to Huicheng in 1986 and 1987. However unobstrusive they may have been, the ancestral halls belonging to the Mo and Li lineages along the south side of the city were razed in 1986 to make way for "modern city construction," in the words of a forty-five-year-old manager of the Overseas Chinese Hotel.[6]

Corporate Estates and Land Tenure

Established as an administrative center since the Tang dynasty, Huicheng had become a sizable commercial center by the time of the Qing dynasty. However, the concentration of wealth and power as flaunted in the cultural symbols described above was intimately linked to the development of the sands. Ancestral trusts in town had acquired vast estates that extended from the matured polders south of the city to the rural fringes in the southeastern part of the county. A He Shide trust in Huicheng recorded an accumulation of land from less than 1 mu in 1818 to 2,189 mu in 1891 (Ye and Tan 1985a, 27). During his lifetime, the Ming minister He Xiongxiang in Huicheng accumulated 32,000 mu of land, of which over 5,930 mu was situated in Jiuzisha.[7] To the local way of thinking, He Xiongxiang held a certain aura because of his bureaucratic office and wealth. Not only was the periurban village at the southern bank of the city where he acquired his academic honors renamed "Village of the Rising Star" (Xinkuijiao), but also the part of Huicheng to which he later moved was known as "The Minister's Neighborhood" (*Shangshu Fang*). Furthermore, it was believed that toward the end of his life he specified how his estate was to be divided. When the news of the birth of his ninth child, a son, reached him, he casually allocated him a strip of marshes southeast of Huicheng that he had nearly forgotten. The son died before reaching his first month, but the strip of marshes grew to a landmass of 6,000 mu and subsequently acquired the name of Jiuzisha (Sands for the Ninth Son).[8]

Trade guilds, temple and charity associations, and academies also established corporate estates of various sizes. The Fan Palm Guild and its subguilds, for example, had about 277 mu in their names. After the Japanese occupation, a government effort to confirm and register the landholdings of Dongbei Public Bureau in Jiangmen and of Xi'nan and Xinhui Academies in Huicheng recorded ownership of 1,516 mu, 703 mu, and 1,583 mu, respectively, spread out in the southeastern part of the county (Xinhui Xian Changchan Zhengli Weiyuanhui 1946).

At times, the managers of the corporate estates organized the reclamation of land. More often than not, they auctioned off the tasks to resourceful functionaries, who afterwards enjoyed long-term tenancy. The crucial point was that, due to the relatively remote nature of the landholdings,

town-based estate managers depended entirely on functionaries for buying and selling land, for introducing tenants, and for keeping track of land
boundaries for rent and tax collection.[9] As described in the previous chapter, this stratum of intermediaries ranged from bandit-like local strongmen
out in the sands to managers of temples and focal ancestral halls in villages
and townships, or to entrepreneurial contractors in the cities. How they
interacted with the institutional landlords shaped the power structure that
controlled the fates of both the rural communities and the town-based
estates.

During the late Qing, commercialized corporate estates in Huicheng
sought tenants through public auctions. As with the Dongguan's Mingluntang (Ye 1965), bidders had to pay a security deposit in order to be able to
participate. The security deposit became a rent deposit for the successful
bidder. Deposits were large, amounting often to an entire year's rent. In
fact, a list of the deposits paid to the He Shide trust in Huicheng showed
amounts that came to several times the annual rent.[10] The requirements
for security deposits in the form of rent deposits and advance rent payments in cash virtually excluded the average farmer from the bidding.
Instead, the contractors were mostly grain brokers, local bankers, and
estate managers themselves. They even secured the tenure of land from
several estates within an area of the sands, hired workers to upgrade them
and maintain the irrigation works, and then parcelled out the polders to
tenant farmers for a shared rent of up to 40 percent of the harvest. With a
large amount of rent in kind at their disposal, these contractors were
keenly sought after by grain brokers and wholesale merchants of cash
crops.

If the contractors were town-based, they largely relied on a variety of
intermediaries, such as their own managers, tenancy brokers, and the
hired guards needed for crop-watching and rent collection. The general
problems of the middleman stratum in the delta's sands are well known.[11]
The intermediaries knew the land and the tenant farmers; they cheated
their patrons on rents and fees (such as the skeletal levy), evicted tenants
without the landlords' knowledge, sold land that the owners had lost track
of, misled tax collectors on land boundaries, colluded with militia groups
to forcibly secure harvests, and made their own vexatious demands on the
cultivators. In short, the contractors of Huicheng's corporate estates were
no mere farmers. Their interaction with estate managers involved patronage and power plays conducted within lineages, trade guilds, academies,
and public bureaus, where official connections were often brought to bear
in their favor.

The tenant farmers at the bottom of the hierarchy were in a rather different situation. Generally, those working the more remote sands were seasonal workers. Known locally as the *shamin*, they lived in straw huts temporarily erected on the dikes during planting and harvesting times. During slack seasons, they moved on to carry out other jobs in their boats. It was not uncommon for them to cut the crops prematurely and to flee the area in their boats. This practice of taking one's contractor by surprise was locally known as "harvesting green shoots" (*geqinghe*). Tenants working in the more mature polders formed stable communities with relatively secure tenure. Of course it depended on who their local contractors were. The elderly farmers in Tianma and Tianlu whom I interviewed recalled that during the early decades of the twentieth century, when village leadership as well as contract tenancy fell into the hands of local military strongmen, tenure became short and uncertain, and many levies were imposed. Payments had to be made before farmers were allowed by the hired guards to harvest their crops. It was difficult to run away, the old folks claimed, because they lived in communities with established populations and transportation routes, unlike "those out there in the sands." These were people who had failed at farming and become marauding bandits until they made enough to turn respectable once again. Tianma had long been regarded as "a den for bandits" by its neighbors, though the upwardly mobile members of the Chen lineage insisted that the troublemakers were the non-Chen households in a marginal section of the township encompassing two small villages in the recent sands.

The extensive reclamation projects conducted by the corporate estates and their functionaries meant that farmers who could afford the rental could farm a large area. In Tianlu and Tianma it was deemed necessary for a family to rent up to 30 mu. In view of the scarcity of nonagricultural employment, families rented as much as their household labor could manage. It followed that only the very poor or the migrant workers hired themselves out as year-round farmhands.

Land tenure in the periurban villages followed a slightly different pattern. Less land was available for the corporate estates to reclaim or to acquire. An active land market resulted in a rather fragmented pattern of land ownership and land use. A polder could be owned by numerous absentee landlords and rented by a variety of farmers at different stages of either losing or acquiring land. Uncle Luan, a sixty-five-year-old villager from the periurban Chengnan Xiang with whom I made friends in 1978, recalled that he and his brother farmed 10 mu of land located in two different villages. Traveling from one place to another took over an hour by boat. The problem of being spread thin was acute during planting and harvesting, or when summer storms hit.[12] At the same time the smallness of the rented plots made it natural for households to seek seasonal nonfarm employment, thus historically creating a more diversified employment structure and a more mobile labor force than those in Tianma and Tianlu Xiang. As the following section will show, the thriving commercial enterprises in town provided the much needed nonfarm employment.

In sum, though the landholdings of the corporate estates were vast, the processes by which they obtained revenue from the sands were quite indirect. Differential access to the revenue of the sands thus rested on a delicate balance of power among the managers of the town-based estates and their multitiered functionaries, which allowed the latter to rise up the social ladder and in time become respectable by moving from country to town. In the process of social mobility and political maneuvering, power and its associated symbols, embodied in the landowning institutions, reached far into the rural fringes.

Commercial Interests

Most of the corporate estates in Huicheng that made long-term tenure arrangements with large contractors extracted cash rent.[13] Cash income was then invested in commercial enterprises. Lineage documents that I have come across explicitly ruled that income after ritual expenses should be deposited with local banks and business enterprises to draw interest. Though the ultimate goal of the ancestral trusts was to accumulate income to purchase more land,[14] the ways in which the cash income was reinvested showed that the concerns of kin rarely obstructed the shrewd strategies of capital accumulation pursued by the commercial enterprises. The grain mills and brokers, for example, advanced credit to large growers in order to secure a steady supply of grain, just as fan palm merchants would give credit to growers for as long as four years in advance in order to ensure future supplies at agreed-upon prices. To the merchants, agricultural commodities were ready forms of capital. By controlling the supply of grain, fan palm, citrus fruits, and orange peel through financial arrangements with their growers, and by shaping market prices by virtue of their economic clout, commercial enterprises indirectly dominated the processes by which wealth was extracted from the rural hinterland. The operations of the county's most influential merchant institution, the Fan Palm Guild (Kuishan Huiguan), illustrate these shrewd strategies.

The palm merchants in Huicheng had devised a proper etiquette for conducting their affairs, and they regulated competition among themselves in the production and trading of the county's most prized commodity. For those who handled a large volume of trade, securing supplies at competitive prices was vital. It became customary for the larger merchants to advance credit to growers a few years ahead of harvests in return for a promise of fan palm at negotiated prices. Conflicts arose when growers, some of them managers of powerful corporate estates themselves, broke the contracts by selling their products to the highest bidder. The need for arbitration led to the formation of a guild in the early part of the nineteenth century. In the early twentieth century, the merchants from the different trades were linked by a chamber of commerce, which was also heavily armed. The *shangtuan*, a militia financed by the merchants for defense against bandits from the rural areas, was also used to discipline delinquent contractors and to extract various surcharges.[15] Its headquarters were built in 1842 (He 1965b, 143). The management body of the guild, Yuqing Tang, oversaw the four major divisions in the palm business: residue palm products, palm-drying, fan-processing, and interregional trade. Later, the management structure was reorganized around neighborhoods in Huicheng where palm enterprises were concentrated. Twelve wards (*jia*) were formed with two representatives each. The head of a ward (*jiashou*) served for a term of three years, but, more often than not, his reelection made the position almost hereditary. Two prominent members of the gentry were appointed by the guild as chief executives (*shoushi hangzong*). They did not have to engage in the palm trade, but were rewarded generously by the guild for dealing with imperial officials. I suspect that they were tax farmers during the period in the nineteenth century when the Qing government tried to collect commercial taxes. Nevertheless, their vital role in representing local economic interests was demonstrated by an interesting historical fact. The official letters of a magistrate in Xinhui, Nie Erkang, revealed that, after the Taiping rebellion, the Qing government tried unsuccessfully to collect the *lijin* (*likin*) tax through the Fan Palm Guild.[16] The fall of the Qing brought changes in the guild. The administration of the guild passed into the hands of a manager and his deputy. Under them were six subguilds based on specialized areas of the business: residue palm products (Lianxing Gongzhan), palm-drying (Lianhe Tang and Lianyi Tang), fan-processing (Lianhu Tang), palm accessories (Tongren Hao), and the interregional palm trade (Guangshun Tang). Each subguild elected its own manager and deputy.

The guild behaved like a monopoly. Newcomers in the trade had to pay a deposit (*hangdi*) as a guarantee. Extra fees were charged for enterprises that crossed the boundaries of specialization. Membership in the group for interregional trade was the most exclusive. Managers of the guild had at their disposal income from licensing fees and from its estate. Members feasted with gentry and officials every month, patronized communal festivals, and organized their own operas during the birthdays of the guild's patron deities, such as Guandi and Beidi. Heqing Hui, an association within the guild, was formed with a membership of 120 who contributed 2 taels of silver each. The sum was deposited in local banks for interest. Each year, for the celebration of the birthday of Beidi, the association and the Fan Palm Guild each took out 50 taels of silver as an advance for theatrical troupes hired for the occasion. The sum was redeemed after the revenue from the festival grounds was auctioned to the highest bidder.[17]

Members of the guild were also closely tied to local banks in Jiangmen and Huicheng. At the turn of the century, a great amount in overseas remittances was deposited in local banks at a monthly interest rate of 4 to 5 percent. The banks then offered credit to wholesale palm merchants at a monthly interest rate of up to 10 percent. In the first decade of the twentieth century there were five local banks in Huicheng. The thriving palm business in the following two decades brought the number to seventeen (Guan 1983, 2).

The interlocking economic and political power of the guild and its managers is illuminated by the career of Lu Zuonan. According to Guan (1983, 26–27), Lu was known as the "tiger with a smiling face." He started as a charcoal merchant, but his business brought him into contact with the fan-making workshops. Around 1918, he opened his own palm-drying and fan-making workshops in Huicheng. Within a few years he had joined the ranks of the long-distance traders and maintained a network of prominent brokers. He was first elected as head of a ward representing Sanyaying, the area south of the town where a majority of the workshops were situated. Backed by the Fan Palm Guild, he was elected to the board of directors of Huicheng's chamber of commerce in 1922. When the guild reorganized its management body, he assumed directorship. Two years later, he became chairman of the county's chamber of commerce, and transferred its militia forces to the guild. These he used to support the guild's effort to stop uncontracted sales of palm leaves. The militia also had the power to collect levies for regional military commanders, and so constituted a formidable political force.

However, individual enterprises as well as the trade as a whole encountered boom-and-bust cycles. The power of the guild declined when regional cores and interregional trade were seriously disturbed by the civil war and the Japanese occupation in the 1930s and 1940s. Growers in the rural areas such as Meijiang, Nantang, Qibao, and Lile Xiang broke the guild's monopoly by setting up their own workshops, hiring unemployed palm

workers from Huicheng, obtaining smuggled supplies, and altogether ignoring the trading rules set by the guild (Yu 1985, 36). In fact, the fate of
the Lianhe Tang, a subguild in the Fan Palm Guild, illustrates this usurpation of power. Lianhe Tang maintained some palm polders southwest of
Huicheng. During the Japanese occupation of Huicheng, the managers of
the guild scattered. When a few managers tried to collect rent from tenants,
their contracts were forcibly seized by local strongmen. Some palm polders
were then converted to rice fields. After the war, the subguilds and associations set up estate management committees in an effort to retrieve the
rights. In the case of Lianhe Tang, the efforts were rather futile because the
local strongmen had solidly carved out their sphere of control (Yu 1985,
35–36).

The shrewd handling of agricultural commodities was not the exclusive
domain of commercial enterprises. Institutions of charity and famine relief
played a part here too. In the late Qing, the functions of state granaries
(*changpingcang*) in Guangdong were largely taken over by the gentry-
organized communal granaries (*yicang*) in the townships. According to a
detailed study of the county granary systems by Chen Chunsheng (1987),
grain storage decreased despite a rise in the number of communal granaries. Chen claims that the decrease occurred because managers converted
grain supplies into cash, used them for usury, and converted the sums back
into grain only when the need for famine relief arose. A document on the
operations of Tongshan Tang and Renji Yihui (charity associations) in
Huicheng (Xinhui Cheng Tongshan Shantang 1936, abbrev.) supports
Chen's general observations. For twenty years after 1912, the managers of
the associations were leading merchants in Huicheng, usually those involved in trading fan palm, orange peel, and grain as well as owners of
pawnshops and local banks. Sums collected from various quarters were
converted into grain tickets, which were distributed to the needy from time
to time. The tickets could be redeemed at specified grain mills where the
association held constant cash deposits equivalent to over 100 shi of grain
(approximately 15,000 catties).

However, prominent merchant institutions did not always dominate the
market in Huicheng. Some restraints came from their own contractors.
Long-term arrangements for cash rent made these estates vulnerable, particularly in the first half of the twentieth century when monetary values
fluctuated during the warlord and Republican regimes. Runaway inflation
hurt the estates when they were paid cash rents that had become totally
devalued. Tenants were also hurt when worthless rent deposits were returned to them. Nevertheless, large contractors who received rent in kind

could manipulate market prices to their best advantage. An uncle of Cheng Mingfa in Meijiang Xiang recalled that his local landlord contracted with the managers of an estate in Huicheng for a portion of a polder. The tenant farmer had to pay the local landlord, who was a powerful contractor, in kind, based on a conversion from a cash rent. The conversion was based on grain prices at harvest time, which, unfortunately for the cultivator, were then at their lowest for the year. The rent collector was thus ensured a large supply of cheap grain from his tenants, which he subsequently deposited with brokers in town, selling only when prices were favorable. The villager was caught in a double bind: In a good year, grain was cheap, and he had to sell a great deal to make up the equivalent of the cash rent; during a bad year, grain prices were high but he had little to sell. Small-scale growers of cash crops had a similar problem with their contractors. Villagers in Chengnan and Meijiang Xiang often depended on large growers or town merchants for advance credit given against the promise to sell their crops at a price set by the creditor. At harvest times their resistance to selling at the usually low price brought in the large growers or the Fan Palm Guild itself, which often acted on behalf of the merchants to force the villagers to harvest the crops.

However, tough negotiations were necessary when the large growers resisted the contracted sales that the guild was attempting to enforce. In fact, a guild document of 1948 indicates that, during the war years and immediately after, there were many delinquent growers who owed substantial numbers of fan palm to the members of the guild—a sign of the tensions that existed among equally powerful entrepreneurs. The document listed the growers, the location of their fields, the wholesale merchants in Huicheng they contracted with, the type of fan palm to be sold, and the number outstanding (Xinhui Xian Kuishan Shangye Tongye Gonghui 1948). One of the local bosses of Meijiang Xiang, Chen Wendian, was a large grower. The document shows that he was in charge of a large polder in Meijiang that supplied eight wholesale merchants a total of 948,000 stalks of fan palm annually. These amounts were listed under his name, as well as under the names of Lianhe Gongsi and Sili Tang, two corporations under his control.

That the ancestral trusts with landed estates lost influence to their contractors during the turbulent decades of the 1930s and 1940s is confirmed by the fact that in several major townships local strongmen in the Huancheng area "bought" from them large tracts of land that were not supposed to be sold.[18] Until then, merchant institutions, together with the corporate estates, had dominated the rural landscape.

The Language of Class, Status, and Political Networking

The concentration of wealth and power with which the gentry and merchant elites in Huicheng were able to impress the rural population was not based solely on the control of land, commodity markets, or even charity. Class and status surfaced in practical politicking, which took institutional form in the county academies. Started as gentry-led institutions to promote local education, these academies became centers for political networking among the subcounty elites and between them and imperial officials. Their organization closely resembled that of a lineage, and their activities confirmed the ideals of lineage, territory, and literati culture. Together, they made explicit a system of authority diffused in the everyday social life of both elites and peasants in the region.

Three academies divided political arbitration in the county on a territorial basis. According to the Xinhui County gazetteer (1840, 86–87), Gangzhou Academy was established in 1752 by the county magistrate who assigned to it 1,100 mu of the sands. Local elites in Huicheng and its nearby townships took over its management in 1806. Jingxian Academy in Jiangmen was established in 1760 when the magistrate formed an estate for the academy by allocating it some disputed marshland southwest of Jiangmen and diverting 125 taels of silver from Gangzhou Academy.[19] Unlike its counterparts, Xi'nan Academy was established in 1845 by eight degree-holders of different surnames. Its estate was acquired through contributions from educated patrons from two subcounty administrative divisions in the southwestern part of the county, the Niudu Si and Shacun Si.[20] One of its initial goals was to aid aspiring scholars from the villages within the territory to sit for the civil service examinations.[21] By the turn of the century it had become a powerful political institution by securing an alliance of elites in Huicheng and in the southwestern part of the county. Its later charter made explicit its goals: to honor the learned and uphold the literati ideal, to arbitrate community affairs and settle lineage disputes, and, most interesting of all, to act as representatives of rural society against bureaucratic abuses, which were listed as vexatious demands from tax collectors, and accusations of banditry by state functionaries.[22] A house belonging to a He lineage in the Neighborhood of the Minister was bought to accommodate the soul tablets of the ancestors of the patrons and to serve as the center of social and ritual activities. The initial 1,694 tablets of various surname groups came from eight subdivisions (*jia*) of Niudu Si and Shacun Si. For the first seven years of its operation, the academy accounts showed an income of 27,948 taels of silver, made up of contributions from patrons who deposited the ancestral tablets and from landholdings acquired during the initial years of the academy. A portion of its income came from rent and interest payments from commercial enterprises in Huicheng (Xi'nan shuyuan quantu 1921, 51).

The academy's membership was determined by filiation, being limited to the descendants of the original contributors, and by territory, requiring residence in Niudu Si or Shacun Si. The management reflected the distribution of different surname groups within the membership. Each year after the spring rites, the management rotated. To form the management body, the eight subdivisions rotated their elected representatives according to the number of ancestral tablets from each surname group. Ritual pork was distributed after the rites and awards for scholarship were given on the basis of academic rank. An incomplete list of members in the academy indicates the vast social network it maintained in the rural communities. Several of the townships in the Huancheng area were included in the directory, and I am able to identify at least twenty-two members of the Chen surname from Tianma Xiang, three of the Liang from Chakeng, and one of the Huang from Tianlu. The Zhao of Sanjiang farther southeast and the Li of Qibao, both from areas with long histories of settlement, dominated the membership list. Many members had acquired academic honors, including a *Hanlin* (member of the imperial academy), 4 *jinshi* (metropolitan graduate), 11 *zuren* (provincial graduate), 94 *gongsheng* of various kinds (degrees obtained through contributions), 5 *wujinshi* (military metropolitan graduates), 6 *wuzuren* (military provincial graduates), and 40 *wuxiucai* (aspiring military scholars). Among them were also holders of academic degrees from the new-style schools, including 7 college graduates, 54 graduates of technical schools, 118 graduates of middle schools, 32 graduates of teachers' training schools, and 71 primary school graduates.[23] Many held administrative posts or conducted trade in other provinces.

The academies were arenas where politicking was conducted through the patronage and social networking of local elites. Participants employed different means of articulating their interests in response to changing times. An example of adjustment to new political environments was demonstrated by the leaders of Xi'nan Academy in the first decade of the twentieth century. In 1905, a few provincial graduates in the academy responded to the abolition of the civil service examinations by promoting the establishment of a junior and senior primary school. There was a hidden political agenda: The old property of Gangzhou Academy, which had been occupied by the Public Bureau for Reconstruction after the Red Turban disturbances and was then used by the Southwestern Bureau for the Security of the Sands (Xi'nan Shatian Baojia Ju), was targeted for the academy's expansion. Riding with public sentiments favoring new-style schools, the leaders of the Xi'nan Academy were able to take over the building from the bureau. Ten years later a leading member of Xi'nan Academy collected 10,000 Hong Kong dollars from overseas compatriots to establish a secondary school. It was, however, to be renamed Gang-zhou Secondary School to signify its broader perspective.[24] Though the proposed removal of the sign of the Southwestern School (Xi'nan Xuetang) from the building created a storm in a teacup and led to the headmaster's resignation, the schools gradually changed their narrow ter-ritorial focus. Teachers and administrators whose experiences stretched beyond the confines of Xinhui County were then recruited. Their gradu-ates rose high in the administrative hierarchies of the warlord and Re-publican governments.

The operations of the Xinhui Academy took after those of Xi'nan Acade-my, except that the social and political networks of its members repre-sented significantly new alignments among local elites. While the academy was being proposed and built, the Qing dynasty was already falling. The old-style gentry and merchants in Huicheng and Jiangmen were adjusting to the rather turbulent political climate and the changing definitions of authority among the successive governments of warlords in Guangdong. The establishment of the academy involved a wider circle of regional elites from the very start, because of a dispute over the disposal of the old county magistrate's office.[25] In 1915, provincial warlords were urging the sales of vacant government properties in response to an appeal by Yuan Shikai, the warlord in Beijing, for military contributions. The county head in Huicheng, backed by the province's director of navigation, made a deal to sell the property to a Yu lineage in Taishan, whose higher-order lineage hall was in Huicheng and bordered the old government office. A sum of 70,000 yuan of silver was secretly agreed upon. The Xinhui county head surprised the local elites by putting up a public auction within a week, hoping that they could not muster a competitive bid. The deputy head of the county's chamber of commerce, a local banker, became suspicious and contacted Liang Hongye, a leading member of the Xi'nan Academy.[26] It happened that elaborate rituals were scheduled in the academies the fol-lowing day to commemorate the birthday of Confucius. The suspicious members used the occasion to gather momentum for a competitive bid for the property. The auction turned into a fight between Xinhui and Taishan notables, with officials of the warlord government caught in between. On behalf of the public bureaus and the academies, two representatives went to Guangzhou to negotiate with provincial officials, pressing them to grant the property to the Xinhui coalition for a base price of 28,300 yuan. The Yu lineage reacted by sending a telegram to the finance ministry of Yuan Shikai in Beijing, suggesting that the Guangdong Provincial Government Properties Office conduct a public auction. The Xinhui elites finally turned to a native of Huicheng who was serving as adviser to the Guangdong warlord, Long Jiguang, at the time. Two days before the auction, Long Jiguang obtained Yuan Shikai's consent to give the property to the Xinhui coalition for a sum of 56,000 yuan. It is interesting to see how deeply involved the merchants in Huicheng were in the venture. The bulk of the expenses were borne by He Jintang, the chairman of the county's chamber of commerce and a local banker. The rest came from ancestral trusts of Huicheng's major surnames, the Li, Liu, He, Mo, and Huang.

It took eleven years, from 1916 to 27, to plan and build the Xinhui Academy, which towered over the northern end of Huicheng on the site of the old magistrate's office. Its stated goal was to supplement the power of the existing academies by creating a countywide alliance involving wealthy merchants, as well as securing connections with new warlords in the province. The checks and balances of power among the old gentry elites and the new bureaucratic officials were revealed in its management structure. The two provincial officials involved in the deal were appointed as honorary directors of the board. The managers were leading members of the Dongbei Public Bureau, the Xi'nan Academy, the Xinhui Chamber of Commerce, and a few prominent overseas merchants. They were joined by a hundred or so short-term trustees, who were also notables in the academies and the bureaus, and managers of trade guilds and ancestral estates. As with the Xi'nan Academy, ancestral tablets were solicited from contributing patrons, and the academy collected 634,000 yuan of silver within a year. As with other corporate estates in Huicheng, Xinhui Academy owned a variety of lands in the southeastern part of the county and received income from real estate in the town and from commercial activities.

An institution such as the Xinhui Academy shows how local elites who had formerly been affiliated with imperial authority adjusted to changing times. Endowed with a vast amount of capital and a dazzling array of leaders, the academy appeared to command an impressive political presence. However, it was no match for the entrepreneurial functionaries of the new Republican government. An incident in 1923 revealed its ultimate vulnerability. A military strongman stationed in Jiangmen demanded a "loan" of 100,000 yuan to support his troops. The managers of the academy initially refused. But when they were taken hostage by the troops,

40,000 yuan were exacted that very night and the balance was handed over a few days later.[27]

At about the same time, there were other examples of how elites in the cities joined with their rural counterparts to successfully promote their interests. One such venture was the Ningyang Railroad. The project was approved by the imperial government in 1907 and financed by Chen Yixi, a native of Xinning (Taishan County) who had migrated to the United States. The railroad was to link Taishan with Jiangmen, passing the northern edge of Huicheng. At two places in Xinhui, engineers met with violent opposition. For reasons of geomancy, they were forced to divert the route from Hecun, the place from which the He lineages in Huicheng claimed they had migrated. When the railroad reached Huicheng in 1909, similar concerns were voiced by the leaders of the bureaus and academies. They claimed a route through the hills behind Huicheng would break the "dragon vein" (*longmai*) that had generated numerous academic honors for the county. The leaders therefore gathered at the Mingluntang and drew up a petition to present to the county magistrate. However, county officials argued that since previous imperial officials had already approved the project, they should find a compromise. The railroad company promised to hire local people to staff its stations in Xinhui and to pay handsome compensations for the farmland the railroad appropriated. When the construction reached the outskirts of Jiangmen, another issue was raised. The leading members of the Dongbei Public Bureau claimed that a railroad bridge planned for the eastern end of the city would obstruct the normal flow of the river. They demanded that a canal be built to avoid potential flooding. When the engineers ignored their suggestions, the bureau members organized the militia from a dozen or so villages and descended upon the site, taking the engineers captive. They also petitioned the provincial government through colleagues in Guangzhou. The county government stopped the construction and called in troops to maintain order at the site. Finally a bridge without a concrete base was constructed. The technical compromise was ingenious, but not without tremendous costs and a delay of over a year.[28]

A later incident involved confrontations between Huicheng merchants and the new Republican government. In 1923 the Siyi Government Properties Office levied new taxes on what it claimed were "government properties", including the county's temples as well as a large stretch of Huicheng's south bank where commercial enterprises clustered. When militaristic functionaries of the office started to board up the shops that had refused to pay the taxes, a general strike was called by the city's merchants.

The county head finally arranged a settlement, but it was revoked by officials in the Provincial Bureau of the Sands. It took another round of petitioning to the provincial government by forty-two representatives from the merchant community before the original settlement was reinstated. The show of force successfully tested the organizing power of the Xinhui Chamber of Commerce, an institution established in 1907, which was assuming an increasingly significant role in county politics (Xinhui Cheng Yanhe Shanghu Weichituan 1924).

A new-style merchant activism had arisen to replace the waning influence of the ancestral trusts and the trade guilds during the transition from the Qing dynasty to the Republican regime. The entrepreneurs relied on new networks to promote their economic interests. At just about the time the Qing dynasty fell, a coalition of merchants proposed the opening of a port on the south bank of Huicheng. Known as the port of Gangzhou, it was promoted by merchants from Huicheng, Xiangshan, Taishan, as well as overseas merchants in Hong Kong. The project was started in 1910, and according to the minutes taken at the meetings of the board of directors, it continued into the Republican era. It accepted 120 patrons, who were each to invest 2,000 taels of silver. The person behind the project was a native of Gujing in Xinhui County who had gone overseas. The headquarters of the corporation were set up in Hong Kong, with a branch office in Huicheng. However, the plans to construct the port, an embankment, and an area for shops were thwarted by bureaucratic delays, opposition from communities whose land was affected, and a lack of funds stemming from merchant patrons' uncertainty over the political situation. After a few years the venture collapsed.[29]

Some entrepreneurs attempted to overhaul the management of ancestral estates and restructured the property relationships in rural communities. The Tangang Xingzuhui, for example, was an association formed with local and overseas funds to reconstruct the single-surname village of Tangang, which had been destroyed by community feuds in 1916.[30] Managers of the association raised revenue from overseas patrons, who secured priority shares in the association. Village land was rented by the association to those who returned to rebuild the community. The managers maintained a militia to keep public order and organize defense. They also arranged community festivals and published a periodical that lasted for more than twenty years.[31]

However, merchant activism on this scale required regional networks and thus generated its own problems. With increasing frequency it faced an array of political entrepreneurs in the Republican regimes who attempted to bypass traditional rules. At times, the merchants linked up with gentry elites to resist encroachment, as is shown by the politicking behind the establishment of Xinhui Academy. At other times, they directly confronted the new bureaucratic powers and negotiated settlements, as illustrated by their tax-resistance activities in the 1920s. Some even joined the ranks of political adventurers by making use of the local self-government structures to further their interests, as shown by the maneuvers of a group of village leaders in collaboration with merchants in Jiangmen to secure land for reclamation.[32] It seems that the early twentieth century saw the economic bases of the corporate estates and the merchants rapidly change with the volatile regional and overseas markets to which the highly commercialized economy was linked, and with the new demands of the warlord regimes.[33] The gentry-merchant coalitions in Huicheng transformed themselves from within to cope with this political environment.

Tax Farming

The tax resistance incident in Huicheng was a sign of larger political changes that local elites in Huicheng had to come to terms with.[34] Land tax during the Qing was relatively light. In the sands, people were exempted from taxation for the first few years, and taxes could be easily evaded long after the polders matured. Though a surcharge on the sands, known as the *shajuan*, had been levied since mid-nineteenth century, its collection was not very successful, as revealed by the complaints of Governor-General Zhang Zhidong (Nishikawa 1985). The responsibility for tax collection had been borne by corporate estates, town-based and otherwise. Focal ancestral halls were relied upon not only to pay the taxes on the land and on corvée labor registered under their tax accounts (*hu*), but also to collect sums due from their lineage segments. This was not disadvantageous to the taxpayers. At times lineage communities actively pursued such a strategy as a defense against subcounty functionaries who used tax collection as a pretext for making vexatious demands, because powerful estate managers could secure reasonable compromises. A reading of lineage genealogies shows that tax payments were one major preoccupation of estate managers, who repeatedly urged prompt payment of taxes by their lineage segments. The common practice for managers of wealthy ancestral estates was to pay the sums out of lineage funds first, with the stipulation that the segments pay back their share of the taxes.[35] For residents of communities such as Tianlu and Tianma, whose land was largely owned and whose land tax was paid by town-based estates, pressure from tax officials was not very strong. The old folks in Tianma were perplexed when I asked about taxes. Their response was, "What land tax? Our fathers paid rent to Wubentang (the focal ancestral hall), which took care of everything."

However, tax collection by ancestral trusts had its well-known problems. Though the managers sheltered lineage members from grasping tax officials, they could also turn against weaker ones, a practice specifically addressed as needing arbitration in the charter of Xi'nan Academy. Managers were known to extract tax payments from lineage segments by threatening to withhold ceremonial pork (a form of expulsion from the lineage) or to charge interest on delinquent kinsmen. Sums in arrears were disputed as estate management changed in time, rendering former agreements doubtful.

Furthermore, in a highly commercialized region, the introduction of the *lijin* (*likin*) tax on commodities in the mid-nineteenth century affected merchant institutions in a fundamental way. For example, the operations of the Fan Palm Guild showed the intricate methods used by managers to deal with taxes that were imposed. The two gentry members, supposedly representing the guild to the government officials, were generously rewarded with a yearly income of 2,000 taels of silver. The sum, I suspect, could be considered the guild's payoff to tax officials, that is, assuming that the two heads of the guild who were not in the trade were actually tax farmers.[36] Despite the complaints of a magistrate of Xinhui in the late nineteenth century, which revealed the difficulties of tax officials confronted by a powerful alliance of local merchants (Nie 1867), taxes were periodically imposed and collected through, for example, the Fan Palm Guild. As shown by a document of the Jiujingtang of the Fan Palm Guild (1856), the guild was once unexpectedly obliged to contribute 1,000 taels of silver to cover military expenses. Most of the long-distance traders were away in other provinces at the time. Consequently, the 238 enterprises in the fan-making trade each loaned out 4 taels of silver to tide the association over the crisis. In time, the commodity tax was collected to cover the amount. Instead of repaying those who had loaned the money, it was agreed that the 948 taels raised from the 238 enterprises would be invested in an estate for an association named Jiujingtang. After acquiring two properties for 800 taels, the merchants deposited the rest of the money to collect interest. Allowances were set aside to fund rituals on the birthday of the guild's patron deity.

With the advent of the Republican era, such institutional channels of tax collection tended to be bypassed. As the economic structures of the Qing dynasty faded with decades of warlord politics, successive Republican regimes stepped up their efforts to tap society's resources through new channels of taxation. As the 1923 incident of tax resistance in Huicheng shows, bureaucratic functionaries of warlord regimes invented unregulated levies and surcharges. Such acts became a plague not only to the estates and merchants in town, but also to the peasants at large.[37] The problem was due as much to the amount of the tax imposed by the government as to the method by which the tax collection was enforced. Local strongmen whose social mobility had been curtailed by the demise of the imperial order became the functionaries of the Republican government. Since they were not linked to the former political networks of the estates, trade guilds, academies, and public bureaus, they were able to manipulate tax farming with few institutional restraints. In the delta, the land tax had been the responsibility of the landowning estates, but the surcharges were split between the owners and the multitiered tenants. Miscellaneous exactions, such as passage fees and ritual expenses for local temples, fell entirely on the shoulders of the cultivators.[38] By 1930, the Republican government was attempting to bypass the institutional landlords and making contractors pay the taxes instead. These contractors were expected to obtain a receipt from tax collectors and then subtract the amount from their rent payments. The burden was ultimately passed on to the tenant farmers at the bottom of the tenancy structure. Not until the amounts owed were cleared were the farmers allowed to harvest the crops. Local functionaries who enforced such tax collection seized the opportunity to impose their own fees and terrorized peasants with threats of violence.

By the early 1940s, the wartime provincial government had gone further in dividing the sands in the delta into sections to install a tax-farming system. In Xinhui County, there were three tax-farming sections (Wu 1962). Rights to collect were publicly auctioned to the highest bidder. Militaristic local strongmen who won the bidding or their functionaries were free to levy numerous surcharges (Qiu 1941). Local officers of the new government who assumed headships in villages and townships or became captains of defense corps directly intruded upon communities to exact payments. The estates and the gentry-led parapolitical institutions in the county capital lost their mediating roles. The estates themselves fell victim to the competing interests of their large contractors, who made use of the monetary crises and direct tax responsibilities to take over the land they supposedly contracted out.[39]

Uncle Ye and Old Liang of Tianlu Xiang, together with the old farmers in Tianma and Meijiang, confirmed these observations in relating that during the 1930s and 1940s local strongmen in their communities were able to wrest land from corporate estates in town that were locked into long-term cash rents and ruinous tax payments. Such conflicts were illustrated by an interesting incident between a politician of the Mo surname in Huicheng and local functionaries who were the contractors of the Mo estates in Tianma. The Mo lineage had migrated from Enping in the mid-Ming to settle around the southern gate of Huicheng.[40] They held vast estates in Tianma and Tianlu Xiang. By the early decades of the twentieth century, local strongmen who supposedly collected rent for the estates were ignoring them. Mo Chaoxiong, a member of the county assembly, lawyer, and former secretary of the Nationalist Party in Xinhui, ran a newspaper called Minhui bao in Huicheng. His political ambition had brought him into conflict with the county head and the local bosses in Tianma. In August 1948, he ran an article written by his father on Tianma's history, using derogatory words about the Chen, who were enraged. When mediation by a Chen native who was also a member of the county assembly failed, the Chen mobilized a group of one hundred, marched into the printing office of the newspaper, and destroyed everything in sight. Mo managed to escape. The city police, whose heads were natives of Tianma, cooperated by staying away. Though a few stragglers were arrested afterward, they were released for lack of incriminating evidence. The incident illustrates hidden conflicts of interests between the urban elites, whose economic power was waning, and the "upstarts" from the rural fringes, who had established their networks with the warlord regimes.[41]

In sum, by the 1930s, the urban-rural structure of power based on a multitiered tenancy, with its complex checks and balances among the social strata, had become strained. With the gentry and merchants broadening their horizons to higher-level politics as their economic bases were being eroded, and with the Republican regimes attempting to tap directly society's resources, the dynamics of the subcounty political economy were increasingly determined by the tactical moves of local strongmen, who preyed upon the average peasants, usurped the patronage of the gentry-merchants, and paid only lip service to their new bureaucratic patrons. However, to complete the description of interlocking hierarchies of power embodied in the social, economic, and political institutions of the area before the accelerated disintegration of the traditional order, I now turn to their ritual linkages.

Ritual, Power, and Cultural Invention

In anthropological literature, ritual complexes are often interpreted as metaphors of worldview, as cultural texts that make explicit social roles and economic statuses otherwise submerged in everyday life, and as political dialogue.[42] It is important to appreciate how the state systematically attempted to impose its cultural priorities on society through ritual activities.[43] It is equally important to see how local elites and villagers both sought their respective places in and resisted against such a structure of ideological dominance, which changed over time as a result of these interactions. Joining the community of scholars who assume that power and commitment are juxtaposed in rituals, I want to examine certain popular rituals and temple festivities in the Huancheng area in the early decades of the twentieth century to show how peasants and the elites used cultural symbols to reinforce the structure of power to which they subscribed.

Rituals were organized according to several hierarchies. Kinship rituals in the Huancheng area ranged from offerings at domestic altars during the birthday and death anniversaries of close kin, to the elaborate and highly differentiating spring and autumn rites in the higher-order ancestral halls in the cities. Uncle Ye and Old Liang of Tianlu insisted that the ancestral graves of their lineages were situated in the hills at the back of Huicheng, and that their fathers had regularly attended the rites in the ancestral halls. Among the villagers, the upwardly mobile had contributed sums to the city's academies so that their ancestral tablets could be placed there for regular worship by a community of scholars. Closely linked with literati interests, the differentiated rights and obligations of the Chinese lineage were thus engraved on rural society.

As described in the townships of Chakeng, Tianlu, and Tianma, rituals of kinship were also intertwined with those of the territorial community. The latter included individual acts of devotion to a patron god, celebrations around an earth shrine, community exorcism ceremonies (*jiao*), and large-scale temple festivals that drew participants from outside the communities. Households constituting a small village made offerings to an earth shrine. The earth gods acted as guardians against strangers and evil spirits, and resources such as night soil or fruit trees on communal land were shared by households under their spiritual jurisdiction. Women performed their acts of devotion on occasions involving private concerns of births, weddings, sickness, and death. However, during the birthday of the earth god, the entire village, especially male heads of households, participated in the festivities. Ceremonial pork was distributed to those who contributed to the occasion. Beside the shrine there was often a shed for the village watchmen, where people congregated informally to discuss local affairs. Rights to settle in the village were often traced to genealogical ties with original residents.

As in rituals of kinship, the narrow territorial concerns of shrine-based rituals were not in direct conflict with state prerogatives. Subcounty administrators for taxes and public security since the Ming had built upon the *she*, a small village centering around an earth shrine. In the rural communities in the Huancheng area, the villages and *she* were referred to almost interchangeably. In Tianma, there was a shrine for every village; the name of the village was often that of the shrine.[44] Households in the *she* were also part of the ritual organization of community temples. During temple fairs, each *she* in a township became a unit for organizing contributions and activities. *She* heads occupied positions in the temple committees. In fact, just as lineage segments formed a level in the hierarchy of kinship organization, *she* and community temples with various followings formed part of a territorial-spiritual hierarchy.

Territorial boundaries were made most explicit during the *jiao* ceremonies, which centered around community temples. In Tianma and Tianlu, these ceremonies were performed once every two to three years in the townships' major temples. Who participated and what activities were organized were matters that went well beyond the confines of the local community. Opera troupes, for example, were invited from regional cities such as Foshan and Guangzhou. When Tianma staged its *jiao* during the turbulent decade of the 1920s, protection from without was sought, symbolically and practically. Members of the Village Defense League (involving Tianlu and Shenhuan Xiang), whose leaders were troublemakers in the eyes of the average villager, were obliged to keep a vigilant watch against possible attacks from bandits.[45] It was ironic that connections beyond the local communities were central to a celebration of community exorcism, an act of expelling strangers and evil spirits from within.

Apart from the rituals of kin and community, there were pilgrimage centers that attracted the faithful from afar. The Longmu Temple of Yuecheng up the Xi River and the Hongsheng Temple of Chaolian Xiang off the coast of Jiangmen were popular centers attended by the people in the Huancheng area.[46] Whether the temples drew attendance from local communities or not, the interplay between the literate and popular cultures, and between the power of the imperial bureaucracy and local society, was vividly represented by their pantheon of deities. While it is evident that belief in the hierarchy of gods, with the prescribed etiquette, fear, and faith in their functions and powers, replicated the practitioners' perceptions of the imperial order (Wolf 1974), it is important to see how cultural representations evolved from the beliefs and ritual actions of both individuals and groups. Through the ages, when a local deity had gathered a substantial following, it was not unusual for state authorities to bestow on it an imperial title and functions, thus incorporating it into the official culture. The popular deities in the Huancheng area and Huicheng were Beidi, Guanyin, Tianhou, Hongsheng, and Guandi, all given respectable places in the imperial orthodoxy. Local society, on the other hand, had exercised its selective preference in its judgment of which deities were efficacious and which were not. The hierarchy of deities, which ranged from the stove god to the Jade Emperor, and to which were added legendary folk heroes, community patrons, and Daoist spiritual masters, was the product of such an exchange among imperial bureaucrats, local elites, and the general populace.[47]

Two temple cults deserve some attention here, as they show how the ritual activities of kin, community, and political groups in the Huancheng area linked individuals to larger social units, differentiating social space and genealogical time, and articulating political interests. Elderly villagers in the Huancheng district had participated in the festivities of the Hongsheng Temple in Chaolian Xiang, which served as a political center for local lineages and communities whose elites had entrenched interests in Huicheng and Jiangmen. The temple cult had established its influence throughout the countryside and also attracted merchant and bureaucratic patronage from town. The Dilintang Temple was established just outside the southern gate of Huicheng around the same period. It became very prosperous during the early decades of the twentieth century due to the patronage of merchants, but it also drew groups of participants from the rural hinterland.

The Hongsheng Temple Cult

Hongsheng, known also as the god of the south seas (Nanhai Shen), was a popular deity in south China. Its earliest official recognition is said to have been granted in the Tang dynasty. Since then it had been given numerous titles. The populations on the southeast coast prayed to it for protection in long-distance trade and traveling. The full title of Nanhai Hongsheng Guangli Chaoming Longwang was given to the god in 1723.

The Hongsheng Temple in Chaolian Xiang dated from the Wanli reign of the Ming dynasty (1573–1620). According to local legends,[48] a degree-holder of the Lu lineage in Chaolian Xiang, who was a magistrate in Mencheng County of Anhui Province, prayed to a Hongsheng deity in the city when his mother fell ill. After she recovered, she asked to have the god's statuette taken back to Chaolian. As a dutiful son, he secured the consent of the locality to put up a new image of the deity in the temple and brought the old one back to Chaolian when he left his post. Initially, the statuette was stored with the Lu lineage of Beishang Village. On one occasion when the deity was being paraded, the procession stopped to rest at the waterfront near the Ou lineage settlement. The legend has it that the image became too heavy to be moved; after consulting the divine powers, the parties involved (the Lu and Ou lineages) set it up in the Tianhou Temple (the Empress of Heaven) nearby. The old temple was renovated to accommodate the Hongsheng, with a side hall for Tianhou. The Lu lineage continued to claim a connection with the deity by maintaining the right of its members to don a new robe for the deity every ten years. Moreover, the annual parade of the god began at the Lu settlement of Beishang.

When the cult of the Hongsheng Temple became identified with the entire township is not clear. However, residents placed their faith in two supposedly efficacious acts of the deity that held tremendous symbolic significance for Chaolian as a community. The first involved the edict in the third year of Kanxi's reign (1664) ordering the forcible removal inland of the coastal populations of counties such as Xinhui, Panyu, Shunde, Dongguan, and Xiangshan. The act was officially justified as a measure against coastal pirates, but it was in fact a strategic maneuver to prevent sympathizers of the previous Ming dynasty from responding to military ventures against the Qing in Taiwan. Divination in the Hongsheng Temple predicted that the dislocation would last for eighteen hundred days. The population of Chaolian was scattered inland into the mountainous areas of Heshan County. According to the legend, not until the deputy governor of Guangdong, Wang Lairen, pleaded with the emperor in a posthumously delivered memorial was the edict rescinded. It took four years and ten months, close to the time the deity had predicted. On returning, Chaolian residents put up a statuette of the deceased deputy governor in a side hall of the temple as an act of gratitude.

The second efficacious act of the deity occurred during the reign of Jiaqing (1796–1820). Six gangs of pirates ravaged the coastal communities in the delta. The gang, led by Zhang Bao, the son of a Dan fisherman in Jiangmen, made an alliance with another pirate, Guo Podai, and defeated the Qing troops many times. In 1809, Zhang Bao descended upon Xinhui County with his fleet. Seeing that the magistrate had set up defenses at Jiangmen, he turned on the nearby island of Chaolian. The community mustered all the village men to guard the major routes, and the two sides came to a stalemate. In fear and desperation, villagers are said to have appealed to the deity. They took an old model of a warship from the temple and placed it on the waterfront one misty morning, clamoring around it and brandishing flags and weapons. One legend holds that all the anchors of Zhang Bao's fleet broke at once. Subsequently, the pirates retreated to Guzhen in Xiangshan County and waited for a chance to attack Waihai Xiang outside Jiangmen. By that time, intertownship alliances had been forged with Chaolian. Led by a native of the powerful Chen lineage of Waihai who had a military title, the intertownship alliance sank one of Zhang Bao's junks and forced him to retreat from the area.

Though the cult of Hongsheng assumed symbolic significance for Chaolian as a community, it is clear that people occupying different positions in the bureaucracy were involved in its organization, establishing links beyond community boundaries. It was known that the deity had been bestowed imperial titles long before it became a deity of Chaolian. It had been brought to the local community by a native who was an imperial official in Anhui Province. Rituals at the temple closely involved two major lineages in Chaolian, the Lu and the Ou, who along with others who joined at a later stage, showed off their academic titles and officials among their members. From the time of its establishment in the Wanli reign of the Ming dynasty, the temple was renovated several times—in the forty-ninth year of Qianlong's reign, in the twenty-first and twenty-third year of Jiaqing's reign, in the thirteenth year of Tongzhi's reign, and in the thirtieth year of Guangxu's reign. The stone tablets engraved with the names of its patrons during the temple's periodic renovations revealed the social and political territory covered by the cult. Heading the list of patrons were imperial officials of various ranks posted to Xinhui at the time. Ancestral estates of the Lu, Ou, Li, and Chen, major surnames in Chaolian, followed. Contributions also came from neighboring townships such as Hetang, and from patrons as far away as Panyu and Gaoyao counties in the province. Juxtaposed with those of estate patrons and individual donors were contributions from managers of markets and river crossings and wholesale merchants in Huicheng and Jiangmen.[49]

Patronage was not limited to the sums contributed for the temple's renovations. The annual birthday celebration of the deity on the thirteenth day of the second lunar month also drew sponsors and participants from various quarters. Their activities followed prescribed rules and schedules and were pursued with appropriate etiquette. For example, before the four-day parade of the deity, the temple's managers fixed the route for the ceremony so that the deity would be received among the lineage settlements of Chaolian Xiang. The parade started at the Lu of Beishang in recognition of the fact that its native son had first brought the deity to the community. It was then taken to the Fifth District (Wutu), the economic and political center of the township, where a large market stood and where the Lu lineage dominated. Only after that did activities move to the settlements of other populous surname groups such as the Ou, the Chen, and the Li.[50] This sequence was said to have been fixed by the dominant surnames when the procession first began in the community. In this century, competition in other rituals was allowed a greater scope. Lu, the compiler of *Chaolian xiangzhi* (1946), recorded that lineages competed for the best opera troupes they could bring from Foshan and Guangzhou for the occasion. It was not unknown for the larger settlements to stage six or seven operas at once. Ceremonies were accompanied by lavish displays of lineage treasures at the ancestral halls. Offerings of cattle and lamb, luxuries reserved only for royalty, were made by the major lineages. The deity was paraded by village men dressed in official civil and military costumes, and the etiquette of the imperial bureaucracy was closely imitated.

Competition was not limited to lineages and villages in the township but involved merchants in Huicheng and Jiangmen as well. The processions were punctuated with bands of gongs and drums donated by merchant associations known as *ting* (pavilion). There were five major pavilions, sponsored by Xinhui natives in Foshan, Jiangmen, Xiangshan, Guangzhou, and overseas. Local merchants joined in by promoting parades of children dressed in costumes of legendary figures and standing on platforms known as *shiban*. The festivities culminated in a fireworks display and a competition known locally as *qiang huapao*, literally, grappling the rocket.[51] The winner was obliged to finance the expensive fireworks display the following year. Because of the cost involved, elaborate alliances were formed among social groups and associations to secure this ritual honor.

From its very establishment and from the subsequent changes in symbolic meaning it acquired, the cult of the Hongsheng in Chaolian reflected a historical process of social and economic change involving community-building as well as the creation of wider linkages through the township's upwardly mobile elements in commerce and in the bureaucracy. For example, there was an obvious change in the social rank of patrons between the first and second renovations of the temple. Patrons of the first renovation in 1784 consisted of individuals and ancestral estates. Subsequent contributors included shops, river crossings, and wholesale merchants. Step by step, the extra-community deity was drawn in to become Chaolian's patron deity, but the invention of local tradition did not pit community interests against the broader interests that the deity had stood for and that were legitimized by inclusion in the imperial order. By believing that the one who had brought the deity to the community was a native son, a member of a lineage as well as of officialdom, the legend reinforced the moral paradigm in which the legitimacy of lineage, community, literati, and imperial bureaucracy were thoroughly interwoven. What Chaolian residents had chosen to believe in—for example, the role of the Hongsheng in predicting their return from exile and in defending the region against pirates—assumed an enduring symbolic significance for the believers. One possible interpretation of the legends is that the first was an assertion of the rights of community against the coercive power of the state, while the second linked community defense with wider territorial alliances as well as with the protection of the imperial order against intruders. The legitimacy of the imperial order and its elements in local society were represented symbolically. The legends were texts composed of dialogues conducted with just such a cultural understanding as their background.

However, rituals surrounding the celebration of the deity's birthday demonstrated that ample room for maneuvering existed within the overall scheme of things. The lavish displays of lineage wealth, the competition for staging operas among lineage settlements, the participation of merchant associations, and the coalitions to sponsor the fireworks, all involved a constant reckoning of set boundaries as well as of new horizons opened up by social groups in and outside the township. In a sense, the ritual complex surrounding the cult of the Hongsheng in Chaolian was an arena for the constant invention of tradition. It illuminated a historical process in which cultural integration and differentiation took place at one and the same time.[52]

Other Temple Festivals

While the historical transformation of the cult of the Hongsheng in Chaolian continued to confirm the imperial tradition, other temple festivals staged in the early twentieth century revealed changes the area was undergoing. The *jiao* ceremony of Tianma was one such case. The Beidi Temple in Tianma customarily staged operas with its triennial *jiao* ceremonies. To avoid paying opera surcharges, community leaders discussed replacing the operas with puppet shows. However, after much debate they went ahead and invited troupes from Guangzhou, erected the stages, and hurried to pay the surcharges imposed by the county government.[53] The episode seemed to indicate a changing political environment. From the fall of the Qing, Guangdong was ruled by successive cliques of military strongmen. Communities found that the usual political networks with whom they had negotiated and who had defended them against demands from state functionaries, had changed. Local strongmen had bought up land from the disintegrating corporate estates in town and set up their own estates in the local community. They had also assumed important positions in the self-government structures that were created at the end of the Qing and were more vigorously promoted by the Republican regimes. As heads of the *xiang-bao,* or village and township self-government committees, they had become tax farmers for the warlords. In the 1920s and 1930s, these men increased their power as territorially based community leaders by taking over the management of the new ancestral estates. As tax farmers, they manipulated community rituals to their best advantage. I suspect that Tianma's decision to go ahead with staging the operas was made under pressure from these new leaders, who eventually would have pocketed a substantial amount of the opera surcharge they helped collect for the county government. They also rallied support from their counterparts in neighboring communities, such as militia from the Intervillage Defense stationed in Shenhuan and Tianlu Xiang to maintain public order during the festivities. A show of power was not lost on the Tianma community.

The changing power configurations underlying the staging of popular rituals was brought out in the temple fair of Dilintang Temple across from the south bank of Huicheng. Built sometime in the Ming, the temple was renovated as early as 1616.[54] The deities in the temple, the Beidi and the Guanyin among others, had always attracted a large following. The fair, held once every ten years, was a significant feature in local tradition. The one that was supposed to be held in 1930 was prohibited by the county authorities in view of the political uncertainties under the warlords and the rampant banditry. Nevertheless, local merchants used the excuse of the completion of a major road in Huicheng to stage the festivities in 1931. There was the usual display of religious items and crafts by shops in the vicinity of the temple. Elaborate stages were erected for the *jiao* ceremonies and the performances of operas. Rituals for community exorcism were performed for seven days by Buddhist monks and Daoist priests. The deities were paraded within the ward, but the route extended all the way to Dongjia Xiang at the eastern end of the periurban area. After three days of parades, the deity was returned to the temple. Musical bands from as far as neighboring counties joined in the festivities in front of the temple. The entire fair lasted for fifteen days.

An interesting point about the fair of Dilintang Temple was the major role town merchants and craftsmen played, compared with that of lineage organizations in the Hongsheng temple fair of Chaolian. The Dilintang's managing elite consisted of the directors of the city's chamber of commerce, who had independent militia forces (*shangtuan*) and ward fire brigades under their command. Public order was maintained through their cooperation with the county police forces. Entrepreneurial managers who negotiated with the county government for staging the fair had their own interests in mind. Temple grounds were auctioned to the highest bidder for food stands and for opium-smoking and gambling quarters. A substantial revenue accrued to these merchant strongmen, who by the 1930s had eclipsed the town's gentry leadership as the new political brokers. Though town-based, the temple continued to provide a means for forging alliances with social groups in the rural hinterland, who acquired fictive kinship ties with the temple managers and donated sums of money in order for the processions to be extended to them.

A Regional Nexus of Power

Around the time the Qing dynasty fell, the authority of the imperial government seemed far away indeed for the peasants in the Huancheng area. Local elites had taken over practically every state function: securing settlement rights and land tenure; organizing the construction of an agricultural infrastructure, such as that needed in land reclamation; controlling markets and commodity prices; paying taxes; overseeing public security, local defense, education, and charity; patronizing religious rituals; and, above all, sheltering the peasants from the arbitrary demands of state functionaries. Yet peasants continued to perceive with awe and respect the retainers of the emperor such as He the Minister and Mo the Eunuch. The grammar and vocabulary, if not the language, of the imperial mandate appeared to exert a hegemonic influence. Summarizing the historical material of the Huancheng area, I have attempted to explore the intriguing question of how the imperial state maintained its mandate to rule in the minds of the rural populace despite its negligible physical presence, and to understand the crucial role of the local upwardly mobile individuals in this enterprise.

It is well known among historians that subcounty elites were heavily relied upon by the county magistrates to administer the basic functions of the state.[55] To assume the role of political brokers, local elites had conjured up legitimizing mechanisms to make themselves acceptable to officials and respectable to the local community. The maturing regional economy provided them with ample though unequal access to the agricultural surplus. They made shrewd use of social and economic institutions that arose in the process of opening up the "frontier." Active political brokerage could be observed in the roles of the village guarantor (the *dibao*), of the village council head and the self-defense corps leader, of the members of trade guilds or offices often associated with the major temples of the market towns, of the literati representatives in the public bureaus and academies in the county capital, of the managerial elites in the corporate estates, and of tax farmers and large contractors. This constituted the range of "the rich and powerful," subject to varying degrees of social mobility within the framework of the multitiered political economy. State officials chose to interact with these elites not only because they were able to obtain a share of local resources through them, but also because the elites aspired to belong to the same social universe as the officials. They had common grounds for dialogue about authority as well as discipline.

Though organizationally rather weak, the imperial state had managed to diffuse a legitimate presence in society by maintaining just such interaction with the social elites. At times it suppressed challenging voices; at others, it incorporated them. Community solidarities were considered useful tools in the imposition of collective taxes and the maintenance of public security, that is, until their resistance and independence threatened the existing equilibrium. In powerful lineage communities literati members were subjected to the moral persuasion of the imperial bureaucracy. Nevertheless, some defiant literati implicated their kinsmen and brought about occasional purges. Claims for rights in the vast area of sands were granted with the understanding that state coffers were to benefit as well. Community temples were patronized by local officials, and parochial deities were granted imperial titles when they had gathered a following that might threaten its power. In a sense, the state and local elites mutually confirmed each other's legitimacy in their interactions. In the end it was not entirely the prerogative of officials to impose state power and sanctions; instead, local society actively sought its place in an encompassing imperial paradigm to which it subscribed and which it helped to sustain.

Just as the state diffused its presence in the informal arenas of politics with local elites, the latter were able to diffuse their authoritative presence in the interlocking institutions of kin, community, class, market, and popular religion. In the process of interacting with the populace, a homogenizing state culture sank its roots deep in local society. Historical materials on the Huancheng area show that local elites maintained a set of multiple roles by virtue of occupying the apical positions in a range of social and religious institutions. Fragments of the state culture they represented served as compelling models for local society. At times, these roles coalesced to provide an umbrella of control over rural society; at times they were vulnerable to challenge. In the Huancheng area, powerful managers of ancestral estates both dominated weaker members and protected them against state exactions. Local strongmen, on the other hand, sheltered the territories under their control from other predators so that they could prey upon them in their own way. The average peasants were therefore tied to their social patrons in relationships of power and dependence, exploitation and shelter, compliance and commitment.

The interlocking nature of social affiliations meant that the articulation of political interests took place in overlapping arenas. There was room for maneuver and selective involvement, which shielded the participants from direct, monopolistic coercion. No one party maintained a dominant power base, but in the process of their interaction they contributed to the maintenance of a social order and an underlying nexus of power. By interfering minimally in society almost by default and by recruiting into its ranks aspiring challengers with independent bases of power, the imperial state retained its authority while at the same time being culturally enriched by local customs.

By the early twentieth century, local power relations had undergone drastic changes. The managerial elites in town were losing their leverage over their own contractors. The commercial vitality that had once made them powerful was suffering in face of endemic political disorder. This development coincided with the efforts of successive Republican regimes to bypass the elites in order to control society through their functionaries. Local strongmen whose mobility up the commercial or literati ladders had been restricted by the end of the dynasty rose to the occasion. The institutional links between town and country, corporate estates and tenants, merchants and growers, government functionaries and village community, were shaken by this process in which the underlying assumptions of authority and power came under great pressure. As we have seen, such changes manifested themselves in rituals as well as in practical politics. Unraveling the traditional nexus of power were new actors: rising merchant activists in Huicheng and Jiangmen attuned to the political goals of the Republican regimes and of overseas connections, as well as local military strongmen engaged in carving their territorial enclaves out of the countryside. The fate of the gentry elites became even bleaker in the late 1930s and 1940s, when the Japanese occupation and the ensuing civil war made economic and social life in towns and cities virtually impossible. Was the stage set for new channels of communication between state and local society and for a restructuring of authority?

CHAPTER 5

The Reign of
Local Bosses

If one plays a Chinese domino game, one can appreciate what the peasants in the Huanchang area meant when they referred to their communities' *da tian er*, territorially based local bosses, who dominated the rural landscape in the 1930s and 1940s.[1] Allegedly uneducated, corrupt, militaristic, and arbitrary in the exercise of their power, they were associated with acts of extortion, smuggling, encroaching upon markets and land, vexatious demands for taxes, and, to top it all, the indiscriminate use of violence. In the eyes of their victims, they lacked even the redeeming ethic of social banditry exemplified by the characters in the classic novel *The Water Margin* (Shui hu zhuan).[2] The local bosses were also considered to have official sanction; according to Uncle Ye and Old Liang of Tianlu Xiang, a popular local saying of the time held that "if you have a badge, a uniform, and a gun, you rule the countryside." Such a saying would not have applied to the local strongmen of only a few decades before.

In the imperial past, banditry was a rather fluid cultural concept. The notion that "chengzhe weiwang, baizhe weikou" (those who succeeded became king and those defeated, bandits) was assumed. In this regard, the legitimacy of the imperial system was seldom questioned either by the literati or in the popular culture. Popular culture treated favorably the legendary figures who robbed the rich, aided the poor, fought corrupt officials, and rebelled against unjust imperial power. The culture of resistance also allowed bandits to turn legitimate. Occasionally they responded to the government's beckoning (*zhao an*) to surrender and join the ranks of the bureaucracy.

The Huancheng area did not lack these characters. As described in the previous chapters, peasants in the sands sought protection from them just as estates in Huicheng and Jiangmen depended on them for the management of land reclamation and tenure. Local strongmen assumed the multiple roles of clients to town-based enterprises, patrons to peasants, and predators. It was true that at the rural fringes marauding self-defense corps and their captains were no more than bandits in uniform. In the areas around the market towns, they were probably leading members in secret societies. Nonetheless, the political economy of the sands also sustained powerful mechanisms of social mobility through which they were recruited into the commercial and literati networks in Huicheng and Jiangmen. In the popular mind, their power had limits, and they also turned legitimate in time.

In this chapter I ask who, with the fall of the Qing dynasty's overarching system of political legitimacy, became the dominant forces behind the structuring of state-society relationships and the redefinition of authority? The successive warlord regimes in Guangdong altered the local configurations of power, a major component of which was the emergence of a new breed of local bosses and their territorial bases. Peasant victims were obviously fearful of them. Did their behavior significantly change popular perceptions of power and authority? If it did, how should we interpret peasant motivation and behavior in the land reform campaigns against these bosses? If they did not, how were the values of the traditional order sustained in an era of apparent crisis in the economic and social spheres?

The question touches on the related issue of the extent to which solidarities of kin and community, features for which this area was known, were preserved in an age of endemic political disorder. Historians of the Republican era have readily pointed out the volatile political dynamics created by a lack of centralized authority, which resulted in the predatory activities of bureaucratic and military adventurers.[3] Skinner (1971) suggests that rural communities faced with dynastic crisis in the late imperial period turned inward in self-defense. Huang (1985) elaborates the idea of community closure in the Republican period by arguing that different degrees of commercial activities in north China villages led to two major patterns of social differentiation in rural communities, which in turn shaped their ability to accommodate or resist the pressures of the new bureaucratic elites. Social disintegration in the more commercialized villages made these vulnerable to the demands of bureaucratic adventurers, whereas community solidarity in the less commercialized villages enabled these to maintain autonomy against predators. My observations in Huancheng suggest that while the periurban communities were hurt by the chaotic politics of the warlord era, those in the rural fringes were not as enclosed and sheltered as might have been expected. Was this largely because of the maneuvers of the local bosses?

Underlying these historical questions are conceptual ones: How do we analyze the nature of communal solidarities when the political leaders on whom villagers depended and to whom they responded were rapidly changing their character during the Republican era? When we analyze the attachments of peasants to their village community after the Communist

revolution, how shall we incorporate the history of these decades of unprecedented upheaval? Moreover, what analytical connections can we
make between cultural values and political economy in order to meaningfully conceptualize social change as experienced by those drawn into it?

Competing Paths to Wealth and Power

Most historians would agree that general lawlessness in the Chinese countryside during the late Qing and early Republican periods was the rule
rather than the exception. In their efforts to apply moral sanctions and
administrative control, metropolitan elites had devised schemes to incorporate local power-holders into the formal bureaucratic organization. Local self-government (*difang zizhi*) was promoted by both the Qing and the
Republican regimes in the first two decades of the twentieth century, but it
was a rather futile effort (Kuhn 1975). Those who had to be relied upon for
this purpose could hardly hold their own ground. In Huicheng the gentry-
merchant coalitions in the ancestral trusts, academies, and trade guilds
were facing challenges from all sides. Efforts to bureaucratize local leadership created opportunities for militaristic functionaries, who only accelerated the elites' decline.

The pains of transition in Huicheng could not be separated from the
political upheavals of the province as a whole. Central political authority
had disintegrated. Guangdong was ruled by a succession of warlords and
coalitions of their military commanders from 1913 until the eve of the
Japanese occupation. The situation was aggravated by more than seven
years of war with the Japanese, followed by the civil war between the
Nationalists and the Communists in the late 1940s.[4] Political turmoil at the
provincial level trickled down to the local economies, because in order to
support their armies the militarists devised ruthless means to increase
revenue. Provincial finances from 1912 to 1941 were supported by taxes,
government bonds, and loans, with taxes constituting 60 percent of the
total revenue. However, military expenses often exceeded tax revenue.
Monetary crises were brought about by the overprinting of paper money
and by the forcible takeover of bank reserves. The crises deeply hurt the
commercial economy of the delta. The regimes also established numerous
offices for the collection of taxes on new items: the stamp duty bureau, the
commercial registration tax bureau, the prohibition bureaus for opium and
gambling, the government properties bureau, the sands bureau, and so on.
Revenue collection was complicated by its reliance on tax farming. Collection rights were auctioned to entrepreneurial tax farmers who were well

connected with bureaucratic officers of the regimes.[5] In Huicheng, the incident over Xinhui Academy was just one of the efforts made by regional warlords to increase revenue by auctioning off government properties. The project to convert waterways into roads on the south side of Huicheng was another example. In the autumn of 1932, the new heads of the county and the construction office took over its management. In collaboration with some local notables, the Xinhui County Office of Road Administration was set up to levy 60,000 yuan in construction fees. The revenue was fought over by opposing factions, and contractors stalled the work. The project had not been completed even by the time of the Communist takeover.[6] Table 5.1 lists the numerous taxes and surcharges in the Jiangmen-Huicheng area and the remarkable variety of tax farmers and collection agents during the Republican period. These were largely local merchants who secured ties with the military regimes. Their tax-farming maneuvers had a serious impact on social life in Huicheng as well as in the surrounding rural communities. In sum, the former institutions of tax collection and political mediation were bypassed as the warlords sought a new stratum of functionaries through whom to exploit local society for the purpose of raising revenue.

The great area covered by the sands made their revenues a source of fierce competition. Xinhui was one of the counties with vast alluvial fields where provincial warlords had set up an independent bureau of the sands. The bureau was bolstered by crop-watching and anti-smuggling forces, largely to ensure the collection of revenue.[7] However, in an environment where the sources of legitimacy were problematic, the right of collection became arbitrary, resting as it did on the use of force. In the sands, captains of the self-defense corps stationed themselves at strategic points to demand payments. The old folks with whom I made friends in Tianma recalled that during the harvest the local military would set up straw huts at the crossroads on land and water. They extorted tax payments for landlords and for government agencies before giving out receipts, a practice known locally as securing grain tickets (*da hepiao*). Peasants were not allowed to harvest until they could show such tickets. The local bosses and their followers inspected boats transporting grain and confiscated entire boatloads on the slightest pretext. On top of the taxes, they added their own demands, such as passage fees, protection fees, landing surcharges, and the like. Their networks were not confined to the villages and waterways far away from town. One of the local bosses of Tianma, Chen Shipei, had acquired land from the Mo and the He estates up to the southern edge of Huicheng. Uncle Luan of Chengnan Xiang remembered that his functionaries came around to extract payment at least twice a year, during

Table 5.1.   Selected Taxes and Surcharges in Xinhui County, 1920s–1940s

Taxes and Fees	Year Created	Collector	Specifications
Garbage fees	1925	Garbage-disposal company	Collection was later taken over by the County Bureau for Garbage Disposal.
Fees on garbage cans	1925	Neighborhood directors	Collection was supervised by the police station of the First District of Huicheng.
Fees on fishing boats	1925	Finance Office of the Five Counties	The office was created by military regimes in the Republican period and covered five counties west of the Pearl River delta.
Fees on prostitution houses	1925	Private company	The Jiangmen and Huicheng police stations later doubled the fees and collected their share.
Fees on firearms licenses	1926	County chamber of commerce	A military commander asked for a sum of 10,000 yuan for his troops. The chamber of commerce therefore collected 5 yuan each from its members to make up the sum.
Surcharge on sugar	1926	Private companies	The companies contracted with a branch of the Provincial Sugar Corporation in Xinhui.
Fees on village operas and puppet shows	1926	Village offices	There were three grades of fees depending on the scale of the theatrical troupes.
Surcharge on fan palm	1926	County government	The surcharge was used to finance the County Middle School.

(*continued*)

Table 5.1. (*Continued*)

Taxes and Fees	Year Created	Collector	Specifications
Stamp duty on opium	1927		The tax was enforced by the Wuyi Opium Prohibition Office.
Fees for licences of opium dens	1927	An opium racket in Huicheng linked to an opium trading company	The company collected a percentage of the daily sales from seventy or so dens.
Land surcharge	1927	The captain of the self-defense corps in the Southwest District	Troops were sent to the townships to collect.
Fees on boats	1927	Police stations	The head of Jiangmen's police department imposed the fees on boats moored along the embankments. The police station in Huicheng followed.
Fees on gambling houses		Private companies	The Provincial Finance Department auctioned the rights to collect a percentage of profits to private companies.
Fees on pig slaughter	1930	Slaughterhouse in Huicheng	
Fees on religious items		County government	The county government also auctioned monopoly rights for selling religious items in temples to temple managers, who delivered the fees to the county office.
Beggars' fees		Secret societies	Certain secret societies in Huicheng set up a "beggars' association" to collect fees from shops and to guarantee that the payers were not harassed by hoodlums.

Source: Zhao Gongqing 1986, in *Xinhui wenshi ziliao xuanji* 22:58–63.

spring ploughing and at autumn harvesting. What if the peasants did not pay? "These bullies threatened to beat us up or tear down our houses," Luan and his friend Old Yong replied. Could local bosses in their own village give them some protection? "They were all in it together. Mo Bao and Li Yao, both bosses at Chengnan, cooperated with Chen Shipei. They were in the palm-drying business and were dependent on palm leaves harvested from his estates. Those of us who rented land from large growers like Chen Shipei also hired ourselves out to cut palm leaves for them. Local hoodlums who worked for Mo and Li watched us closely."

From the perspective of the regional warlords, those who could most effectively collect and share revenue from the territory under their control were their chosen administrators. As new taxes and surcharges were invented, new offices and administrative titles proliferated. The earlier institutional linkages to rural society were increasingly undermined.

Military Adventurers

Local strongmen were relied upon not only for revenue collection but also for political maneuvers. The use of their organized power was not limited to the warlord regimes. The first decade of the twentieth century saw members of the Tongmeng Hui[8] in south China recruiting support through channels provided by the secret societies, notably the Triads.[9] During the uprisings to overthrow the Qing in September 1911, various groups joined the Republican army (*min jun*) (Li and Lu 1962, 40–41). They were quickly drawn into the military politics of the region. Warlords who doubted the loyalty of these groups tried to get rid of them for fear that they would go over to competitors. In the subsequent pacification campaigns, individuals as well as entire communities suffered heavy losses, depending on whom they were accused of having sided with. Zhang Zhengshi, a provincial graduate and a member of Nanzhou Academy in Guangzhou, was assigned to Xinhui by the warlord Chen Jiongming soon after the Qing dynasty had fallen. He collaborated with members of the Dongbei Public Bureau of Jiangmen and Xi'nan Public Bureau of Huicheng to root out members of the Triad in the Republican armies, and directly participated in the campaigns in the townships of Qibao, Chengnan, Shanghengsha, and Chaolian.[10] Cai Guoying, a degree-holder from Jiangxi and the deputy of the warlord Long Jiguang, was given the power to execute immediately after arrests were made. It was alleged that executions were conducted every day outside the northern gate of Huicheng. His actions triggered resistance from villages and prompted Long to replace him with Yan Dezhang, a military officer from Guangxi. It seems that Yan was no better. He gained notoriety by interfering in the community feuds of 1916 between the Chen and the Lin in Shuangshui, southwest of Huicheng. Siding with the Lin of Luokeng, Yan and his troops stormed Chenchong with the excuse that they were rooting out rebel Republican troops. Soon afterward, another commander from Guangxi, Wang Chuxian, inflicted heavy casualties in Longquan Xiang, southeast of Huicheng, in another power struggle between Guangdong and Guangxi commanders. Yuan Dai, a local boss who sided with the Guangdong warlords, stationed himself at Longquan. In an attempt to drive Yuan out, Wang stormed Longquan from his base in Huicheng. When the township's militia resisted, he returned with a larger force, killed some villagers, and burnt down a number of houses.[11]

Bands in the delta that had been dispersed by the warlord armies regrouped under the leadership of a certain Lu Man, a local boss with close ties to the delta's underworld. They formed an alliance named "Liang Yue Guang Yi Tang" (the Association of All-Encompassing Justice of the Delta). The association boasted a membership of over two thousand who swore to abide by strict principles of behavior, urged people to defy the warlords, demanded a fair distribution of the spoils, and showed sensitivity to the poor peasants, as well as encouraging mutual help. Other leaders followed suit, and the rural counties in the delta saw the formation of numerous brotherhood associations, ranging in size from a few hundred to a thousand or so members.[12] However, as the political instability continued under competing armies, the large bands were used as leverage in military maneuvers. Wooed by one military commander and persecuted by another, they constantly adjusted their allegiances to the fluctuating political fortunes of their military patrons.

By the time the delta was occupied by the Japanese army in the late 1930s, the wartime Nationalist government had recruited many local bosses as the captains of resistance forces. Lu Man, for example, was appointed as the commander of Guangdong's First Guerrilla Corps in 1939. Based at Shiqi in Zhongshan County, he led over ten thousand men whose local leaders had given him their allegience. The troops were partly financed by the Nationalists. His subordinates were allowed to smuggle, operate gambling and opium houses, become tax farmers, and seize land and property from those fleeing the war zones. Most maintained their independent bases and shifted their allegiances with Machiavellian shrewdness.[13] For example, when Lu Man detached himself from the Nationalists when they discontinued military aid, several of his deputies defected to the collaborator government at Guangzhou.

Among the bosses who controlled the sands, a few are worth mentioning because their adventures interconnected in various ways. In the late

1920s, Liu Faru of Dongguan County was one of the heads of the Guangdong Tang brotherhood who joined the Nationalist guerrilla forces at the beginning of the war. He later defected to the collaborator government and became head of the self-defense bureau of Dongguan's Minglun-tang, the county academy, controlling the collection of grain and fees for over 60,000 mu of sands (Qi 1964, 66–86). Yuan Dai established his base in the sands at the border of Zhongshan, Shunde, and Xinhui counties. He was appointed the commander of a detachment, maintaining allegiance to the Nationalist wartime government. Under him were eleven deputies, each with his own armed followers. They formed a corporation, named the Minli Gongsi, to manage contract tenancies in the sands and conduct tax-farming operations. During the harvest, armed guards of the corporation posted the red and the black grain tickets (*hepiao*) for the collection of fees. The sums posted on red tickets were collected in the name of the army unit for resistance against the Japanese, and those on the black tickets were protection fees collected by the secret societies.

Based in Macao, Zhao Qixiu of Sanjiang rose to prominence during the Japanese occupation period. He participated in the formation of the peasant association in 1926. After the Nationalist government turned against the movement, he fled to Indonesia and worked in a mine for a time. He later returned to Macao to head a smuggling operation, for which he was jailed, but he escaped in the chaos of the Japanese advance. He was not formally involved with the military until the early 1940s. At the time, Hong Kong was occupied and Macao had become an uneasy haven for refugees. Zhao specialized in transporting goods from Macao up the Xi River to the Nationalist-controlled areas in northwestern Guangdong. Together with his brother, who was living in Sanjiang, he also helped resistance forces escape from the occupied areas. To escort his convoy, he maintained his own forces, later given the title of Xinhui Yiyong Youji Dadui (the Xinhui Guerrilla Corps of Righteousness and Bravery). At the time Nationalist generals made every effort to incorporate local strongmen like Zhao into their military networks, giving them the title of adviser. As expected, Zhang Fagui, the commander of the fourth war zone (covering Guangzhou and its vicinity) gave him the title of adviser with the rank of a major-general and used his radio station to collect information from the occupied territories. Since Zhao's troops also operated in the Siyi area, Yu Hanmou, commander of the seventh war zone, gave him a similar title. After the war, however, he was dismissed by the provincial chairman, Song Ziwen, and later implicated in a feud between Sanjiang and Longquan Xiang. He fled after an arrest warrant was issued against him. The reputation of his networks is confirmed by the fact that during the initial months of liberation a pro-Communist shipping company that operated the route between Macao and Kaiping relied on Zhao's forces for escort. Zhao eventually settled in Hong Kong. In 1953 he was even given a title by the British crown for having helped war refugees. Zhao's career captures the ethos of a turbulent era.[14]

After the Japanese surrender, the Nationalist regime continued to use these local strongmen in the pacification campaigns against Communist sympathizers. They were given petty bureaucratic titles allowing them to engage in tax farming, recruit soldiers for the civil war, break trade unions, and arrest political suspects. To appreciate how social life was shaped by the maneuvers of these local bosses in the 1930s and 1940s, I now turn to the situation in the Huancheng area in more detail.

The Fall of Huicheng

Once the Japanese army captured Guangzhou in October 1938, provincial politics started to revolve around the maneuvers of three major contenders for power: the Japanese army, which occupied big cities and major transportation routes; the Nationalist wartime government in the northern and western parts of Guangdong; and a growing Communist movement in guerrilla bases in the rural fringes. On the eve of the Japanese occupation, Huancheng was the stronghold of the Nationalists. According to a Communist party document that recorded areas under Communist influence, peasants in Xinhui had relatively little exposure to the party's activities. Guerrilla bases grew during and after the war at Heshan in the northeast, at Gudou Mountain bordering Xinhui and Taishan counties in the southwest, and at Wugui Mountain in Zhongshan County to the southeast.[15] When Huicheng fell in early 1939, the county government moved to the market town of Shuangshui southwest of the city and separated from it by the Tan River. Sandwiched between the Japanese-occupied cities and the Nationalist base at Shuangshui, the Huancheng area became a no-man's-land. The Nationalist troops in the southwest organized token resistance by ambushing Japanese soldiers near the city. In retaliation, the Japanese searched the periurban villages for suspects and destroyed property. When Communist-organized resistance grew, they made occasional surprise attacks from their bases in the hilly areas north of Huicheng.

The periurban villages bordering Huicheng and Jiangmen suffered the most destruction, as illustrated by the experience of Dalong Li on the southwestern edge of Huicheng. A few weeks after the Japanese took Huicheng, their troops marched into the village, ordered a dozen or so adult males out of the watchmen's shed, and shot them.[16] The reason for this slaughter was that Nationalist troops had had a skirmish with the Japanese military a few days before and had retreated through the village outside the western gate of Huicheng. Another account alleges that more residents were killed and that their bodies filled up the village pond. After the massacre, the soldiers burnt down the periurban villages bordering the city in order to create a safety zone between themselves and the rural areas. Such zones became known as "the three bare zones" (*san guang didai*). On several other occasions Japanese soldiers marched into communities along the road linking Huicheng to Jiangmen and killed at random. Survivors remember that the waterway at Duhui and Qibang Xiang ran red with the blood of victims who were thrown there by the soldiers.

The Japanese established their headquarters next to the county library at the center of Huicheng, set up checkpoints at the eastern, western, and southern gates, and drafted laborers to build forts in the hills north of the city and to cut down palm and orange groves. This was done to provide the forts with an unobstructed view of the unoccupied areas farther west. Occasionally the Japanese fired artillery at the surrounding villages as far as Tianma and Sanjiang. One observer recorded that the shells once hit a ferry crossing the Tan River from Tianma to Shuangshui, killing many passengers.

With the help of local collaborators, the Japanese began their military rule in Huicheng.[17] Liang Borong, nicknamed Rong the Wastepaper Collector, was a seventy-year-old Daoist priest who went about Huicheng's streets gathering wastepaper for ritual purposes. He was among the first to be chosen by the Japanese for his knowledge of the city. Out of fear, he introduced the officers to a Lei Hong, a patron of the Aiqun Charity Association, which buried the city's poor and homeless and to which Liang's temple was linked. Assisted by an unemployed teacher and local detectives, an informal group of collaborators was formed.

Some of the city's population had already fled to the nearby rural areas. Many businesses closed down, and handicraft workers were left jobless. Residents in rural communities were also nervous. Chen Mingfa remembered that as a child he fled with "his entire village" when two Japanese soldiers strayed into Meijiang Xiang. In fact, there was a great deal of movement between town and country. While hordes of town residents fled to Meijiang and to the villages farther southwest in order to avoid getting in the way of the Japanese soldiers, many unemployed handicraft workers in the periurban townships, such as Chengnan, Siya, and Dongjia, migrated either to nearby market towns such as Lile, which was controlled by two local bosses named Zeng Huan and Chen Peng, or to Xiaolan in neighboring Zhongshan County, or up the Xi River to the city of Zhaoqing and to Guangxi Province, to which the Nationalists had retreated.

After the Japanese military had defined the boundaries of the occupied territory, the area quickly recovered from its initial shock. Traffic between Huicheng and the rural areas was partially resumed. Peddlers who traded between Huicheng and the neighboring market towns had to carry documents issued by the Japanese authorities for safe passage. Nevertheless, itinerant traders conducted a profitable but risky business. In Chengnan and Dongjia Xiang, one or two members of most peasant households engaged in the trading of orange peel, vegetables, fruits, fish, river shrimp, and sundry items such as cloth, yarn, oil, and small tools. Elderly villagers give accounts of peddlers carrying these Japanese documents being harassed by soldiers who supposedly belonged to the resistance forces. An employee of a harness shop in Huicheng who transported goods to and from the unoccupied market town of Daze recalled that business associates in Daze warned him of the dangers. He was told that peddlers with a Huicheng accent were automatically suspected of being Japanese spies. One such peddler was shot merely because Nationalist troops found a safe conduct document in his pocket (Yu Ziliang 1982, 25). Most of the peasants in the Huancheng area who customarily attended the markets of Huicheng and Jiangmen[18] diverted their activities to neighboring market towns, which included Daze to the west of the Huancheng area, Xiaogang and Shuangshui to the southwest, Sanjiang to the southeast, Lile to the east, and Dongjia and Tianma within the Huancheng area itself. Each of these towns was dominated by local bosses who maintained a tense equilibrium with both the Nationalist and the Japanese armies. Peasants who continued to sell their produce to town residents clustered at the bridges at the south bank of Huicheng and clung stubbornly to the Chinese currency in preference to that issued by the Japanese military.[19] Money changers sprang up in the periurban area in order to facilitate such marketing activities. Food growing was profitable. Cheng Mingfa recalled that villagers in Meijiang converted palm polders to grain and sweet potatoes, which were then sold to town residents at very high prices. In a few years those who rented land were able to buy it from the landowners in town. While peasants farther away from Huicheng enjoyed relative security during the war, those in the periurban townships and Huicheng were the hardest hit. Not engaged in farming, they depended on the supply of food, which was vulnerable to blockades by both sides. In our discussions in 1978, Old Yong of Chengnan Xiang recalled that the daily wage he earned as a laborer gave him between 4 to 10 ounces of grain. In the early 1940s, he gave away one of his younger sisters to a trader who was recruiting "brides" to be taken to the areas up the Xi River where more food was available. He gave away another sister as concubine to a policeman in Huicheng and worked on his "brother-in-law's" palm fields. His family could not survive on the meager supply of food he purchased with his wages. After his mother died of famine-related disease, he peddled orange peel by collecting it in Dongjia Xiang and selling it in Jiangmen. He even collected night soil in Huicheng and transported it to peasants in the neighboring townships. However, he was scared off from this activity after hearing rumors that peddlers had been lured into houses and killed and their flesh sold in the market in Huicheng.[20] He finally made his way to Tianma and hired himself out as a year-round laborer. But his plight did not end there. As an outsider, he was threatened with being drafted either as a laborer for the Japanese military or as a village militiaman under a local boss.[21]

The Local Bosses of Huancheng

The Japanese occupation complicated the already unsettled political situation in the entire Huancheng area. When Huicheng and Jiangmen fell, the city militia that belonged to the Fan Palm Guild and the chamber of commerce fled to the townships of Nantan, Meijiang, Tianlu, and Tianma.[22] Local strongmen in the townships led villagers in the defense of their territories against the marauding militia. The managers of Wubentang, the focal ancestral hall of Tianma Xiang, for example, negotiated and bought many arms from the fleeing militia and from the retreating Nationalist troops. The sudden accumulation of weapons made the local strongmen in Tianma and Tianlu Xiang political forces to be reckoned with.

Among notable local bosses were Ye Yi and Ye Ziqun of Tianlu; Chen Qin, Chen Shipei, and Chen Shifeng of Tianma; and Chen Ermou and Chen Wendian of Meijiang.[23] The backgrounds of these men were diverse. Known as Yi the Fat, Ye Yi of Tianlu was a poor member of the Ye lineage who rose to power by gathering village toughs around him to exact payments from peasants and travelers. Ye Ziqun, on the other hand, was from an educated family and had made some money from charity operations entrusted to him by overseas members of the township. Chen Shifeng of Tianma also had an educated background. His father and grandfather had obtained minor degrees in the civil examination system and had been managers of ancestral estates in the township. Chen Wendian of Meijiang was a bureaucratic functionary, whereas Chen Ermou gained a fortune from his agricultural enterprises and bought up land from the declining corporate estates in Huicheng. These men created powerful enclaves between the areas occupied by the Japanese and Nationalist troops. On the one hand, they allied themselves with regional militarists, notably Zhou Hanling and his chief rival, Zhao Qixiu, who were in control of troops claiming allegiance to the Nationalists. On the other hand, they became political brokers for the Japanese forces.

The need for political brokers arose in early 1941, when the Japanese military established "associations for public order" (*weichihui*) in Huicheng and in the villages bordering the city. Led by local collaborators, the associations maintained their own police forces and supplied the Japanese troops with food, tax revenue, and laborers. The associations also issued passes for a fee, which became a lucrative operation. Subsequently local bosses in the periurban townships appointed themselves as village and association heads.[24] Heads of townships farther away from Huicheng, such as Tianma, Tianlu, Chakeng, and Dadong, were linked to the Japanese military power through personal ties with the managers of the public order associations. At about the same time, the collaborator government organized its own security forces. Though stationed in Huicheng, they were connected with military groups in the surrounding rural communities. In the popular mind, two types of village representatives emerged. "There were those who could write a little but were powerless figureheads; they gained no advantage, and risked losing their heads. There were also those who were illiterate, but powerful and rich nevertheless."

A complicated political network existed. In Tianma, for example, local strongmen allied themselves with different extra-community power groups. Chen Qin joined the collaborator government in Huicheng. Chen Shipei was a captain of the guerrilla forces for the Nationalist army, and Chen Shifeng claimed the position of captain of the township's self-defense corps. There were also plainclothes policemen working directly for the Japanese military in town. The local bosses maintained a tense balance of power, as the following episode reveals. In 1943 Chen Shifeng invited representatives of various power groups to a banquet to celebrate the completion of his new house. Here one found the captain of the Japanese troops in Huicheng exchanging toasts with military personnel from Nationalist headquarters. However, each guest brought an entourage of armed guards, who took up positions outside the banquet hall (Yu Ziliang 1982, 24).

Conflicts of interests among the local bosses did lead to intrigue and murder. There was the well-known case of Chen Ermou in Meijiang Xiang. Chen was a rich peasant who had acquired over 300 mu of palm and rice fields from corporate estates in Huicheng. His eldest son had assumed the post of village head in Meijiang and had offended some rivals. One of them was Chen Wendian, whom the Japanese had picked to recruit laborers for construction projects. Potential victims in Meijiang paid Chen Wendian fees to avoid being drafted, but when he forcibly drafted two of Chen Ermou's farmhands, Ermou's sons threatened to tear down his house. Chen Wendian mobilized his own followers in the self-defense corps for a confrontation, but elders in the village stepped in to mediate. Chen Wendian thereupon allied himself with a disgruntled plainclothes policeman from Tianma who had once been shot at by Ermou's son when he tried to cross one of his fields. One evening Chen Wendian assembled a group of policemen from Huicheng and Tianma and marched into Chen Ermou's house. Without any excuse, the attackers rounded up the surprised men and shot them. Hoodlums from Tianma who came with the attackers ransacked the house and robbed others in the vicinity. Chen Wendian took over the properties and established himself as a large grower of fan palm. He continued to dominate Meijiang after the war, and was a powerful figure in the eyes of wholesale palm merchants. A record of the Fan Palm Guild in 1948, for example, showed that he sold huge quantities of fan palm to its members. In 1952 he was arrested and shot by the Communists. Chen Mingfa's uncle said that villagers in Meijiang Xiang did not miss him. Though Chen Ermou was a shrewd and rather unpopular landlord in the community, villagers thought it unforgivable of Chen Wendian to seek help from outsiders in order to plunder his own community and kin.

The second and more serious episode broke out between local bosses in Tianma and Tianlu Xiang. The two communities bordered each other, and conflicts over trespassing often arose. In the 1930s, local bosses had taken up strategic positions at the confluence of the Tan and Xi rivers in order to extort passage fees from travelers. Chen Shipei and Chen Qin of Tianma and Ye Yi and Ye Ziqun of Tianlu competed fiercely for control of the waterways in order to smuggle commodities through Japanese-occupied territories. Under their rule, the daily markets in Tianma and Tianlu thrived. Gambling houses and opium dens, stimulated by the active markets, which would otherwise have been diverted to the cities, did brisk business. Peasants in the periurban townships who used to attend markets in Huicheng now came to Tianma and Tianlu instead. In fact, like Lile under the local boss Zeng Huan, Tianma's unusual fortunes earned it the reputation of "Little Macao."

As in Meijiang, local bosses in these communities rapidly bought up land from the disintegrating corporate estates in town, at times forcibly, in order to set up their own estates. The old folks in Tianma recalled that Chen Shifeng and Chen Shipei extended their landholdings "all the way into Huicheng," and claimed that the bulk of the township's thirty-eight an-

cestral estates were set up during the 1930s and 1940s. As described earlier, they showed me a three-story, Western-style bedchamber type of
ancestral hall built by one of the local bosses, with a primary school attached at the side. It seems that even when local bosses became nouveaux
riches through unorthodox means, they actively pursued traditional cultural symbols to earn respectability in the community.

What triggered the feud between Tianlu and Tianma was a dispute.
Chen Chulin of Tianma had quarreled with the Ye brothers over the operations of an extortion racket. Because the most powerful bosses of Tianma
were on good terms with the collaborator government in Huicheng, and
those of Tianlu leaned toward the Nationalists, Chen Chulin accused
Tianlu Xiang of harboring Chinese troops. As a result, the Japanese military instructed the collaborator government to station soldiers in Tianlu.
This act outraged the local bosses there. To make matters worse, the troops
looted households and raped some women. Mobilizing the outraged villagers, Ye Yi and Ye Ziqun rounded up the soldiers in a surprise attack.
Except for a few who escaped to Tianma, the soldiers were all drowned.
The Japanese military bombed Tianlu in retaliation. As the villagers dispersed under the bombing, Japanese troops marched into the township
and razed the houses to the ground. In the wake of the Japanese attack,
local bosses from Tianma led their men into Tianlu and looted the township, even carting off bricks and bridges. Most of Tianlu's four thousand
residents fled to the surrounding communities of Shuangshui and Nantan,
and only half of them eventually returned. Ye Yi himself was later killed by
a disgruntled follower. For years after the incident, residents of the two
townships did not intermarry or attend each others' market. The two
episodes I have described are examples of conflicts occurring within and
between rural communities that were aggravated by the maneuvers of
local bosses who brought the power of outside patrons to bear on the
situation.

After the Japanese surrender in the summer of 1945, the Nationalists
returned to set up the postwar county government at Huicheng. Some
Japanese collaborators in town were arrested and shot, but local bosses in
the rural communities remained unscathed. The Nationalist government
continued to award the title of captain as well as village and township
headships to local bosses who had maintained ties with it during the eight
years of war. As for those who were obvious collaborators but were still
heavily armed, the Nationalist government left them alone, as there was
little it could do to contain their power. Chen Shipei of Tianma, for example, who maintained a large arsenal, made a fortune in 1948 by renting his
weapons and men to local bosses in Longquan, who were feuding with

Sanjiang Xiang over reclaimed land. In fact, the provincial director, Song Ziwen, sent a gunboat to the area, planning to confiscate the arsenal. The gunboat was sunk by the village militia before it could reach the area of conflict.

After the Japanese military were out of the picture, conflict between the Nationalists and the Communists intensified. Nationalist commanders in Guangdong stepped up their efforts to recruit armed local bosses in order to suppress a growing body of Communist sympathizers. Local bosses in the Huancheng area sided with Nationalist commanders who controlled the town. In Tianma, they were active in the reconstituted township council. Subtownship divisions for public security (*bao*) were reduced from seventeen to twelve,[25] each with elected heads. In addition to taking care of matters related to the formation of a peasant association, a credit cooperative, and an arbitration body, the self-appointed leaders of the township council were members of a committee that managed a community fund made up of 20 percent of the annual income of all the ancestral estates. A primary school was built in the spring of 1945 largely with these funds. Most important of all, the council was given the task of organizing a police force; they built five small watchtowers at strategic sites in the sands belonging to Tianma, participated in a self-defense league (*lianfang*), and provided recruits for the county government.[26]

The Deepening Political Crisis

In their efforts to step up the suppression of Communist activities, the Nationalist government mobilized forty thousand troops in Guangdong.[27] However, the intensifying civil war between the Nationalists and the Communists in other parts of the country necessitated the transfer of the regular army (the Forty-sixth Army) to the north in early 1947. The regional security forces and the self-defense corps in Guangdong therefore assumed all responsibilities in the pacification campaigns. Taking advantage of the fact that they had men and arms on which the government depended for tax collection and for the campaigns, local bosses scrambled for petty bureaucratic positions in the county and village governments as well as in the security forces. The bosses in the Tianma and Tianlu Xiang, for example, extended their political networks by moving to Huicheng. Ye Ziqun, head of the self-defense corps of Tianlu Xiang, assumed the post of the head of the township and bought himself a seat in the county assembly. The pro-Nationalist Chen Shifeng of Tianma became the head of security in the county. Chen Qin of

Tianma, whose ruthless methods of drafting laborers for the Japanese military had earned him the nickname of "The Hound," became a plainclothes policeman in the public security office. Another native of Tianma, Chen Zhenhua, became a member of the county assembly. The Chen of Tianma became so influential that when the township's primary school celebrated its third anniversary in 1948, the occasion warranted a visit from the then county head, Tang Canhua.[28]

As will be shown in this section, the pacification campaigns not only sapped the resources of the Guomindang (Kuomintang, KMT) government in Guangdong, but also strained to a breaking point the already tenuous relationships among the provincial government, the local military, and the general public. Progressive intellectuals grew uneasy over the blatantly predatory acts of bureaucratic officials. Most administrative positions were for sale to the highest bidder. The most lucrative positions were the county head, the county tax collector, the administrator of granaries and government warehouses, and the heads of townships, villages, and local security forces.[29] Because these assignments could be easily revoked and given to a higher bidder, politicians who pooled their resources to bid for an important official post often skimmed the cream of the territories under their administration as quickly as possible. The town merchants, the urban poor, and the peasants were further burdened by incessant demands for grain and labor corvée. There were also numerous indiscriminate acts of terror by the security forces.[30]

The county government that the local bosses linked up with was plagued with one scandal after another. A notable case in 1947 implicated the county head himself. A lawsuit was brought against this individual by political enemies in Dasha Xiang, who accused him of embezzling tax revenues from fifty sources and more than 200,000 catties of grain in 1946. He was also charged with corruption in labor conscription and police work. Village officers and prominent households in the township provided incriminating evidence to the provincial chairman who was obliged to look into the case. However, when the case was brought to the Xinhui county court, the accused did not even bother to appear before the judges. Moreover, the judge in the case was soon transferred to Dongguan County, and the trial was postponed indefinitely. It was only too obvious to the public that a powerful patron had stopped the investigations.[31]

An incident that severely discredited both the county and the provincial governments in the eyes of the public was the feud between Sanjiang Xiang and Longquan Xiang in the summer of 1948. The Zhao of Sanjiang Xiang had been pioneers in the area and had long controlled the marshes to the south and east. These marshes were worked by migrant farmers from surrounding communities. By the turn of the twentieth century, the mature polders supported prosperous communities, one of them being Longquan Xiang. According to a report in a local paper,[32] strongmen in Longquan resented the fact that ancestral trusts in Sanjiang Xiang continued to collect skeletal fees from the cultivators of the land in Longquan. The relationship between the two rival groups was further strained by conflicts over the control of the smuggling routes between Jiangmen and Macao during the decade before and after the Japanese occupation. Since June 1947, Sanjiang Xiang had built a line of fortresses in response to the government's call to step up pacification activities. The strongmen in Longquan interpreted this act as a show of force by the Sanjiang bosses in an attempt to take over the smuggling routes. They retaliated by attacking the fortresses and killing some village militiamen. They also ambushed and looted a convoy from Sanjiang. These incidents triggered a massive buildup of weapons and men by both townships; by June 1948, a head-on clash was imminent. Sanjiang was armed with two hundred machine guns, ten small cannons, over fifteen hundred small arms, and twenty motorboats; it also mobilized some seven hundred village militiamen. Longquan Xiang had fewer arms but was able to mobilize about a thousand village militiamen. In fact, it had hired arms and men from Chen Shipei of Tianma. The leading organizer for Sanjiang Xiang was a member of the county assembly; his counterpart in Longquan Xiang was the secretary of the Nationalist party in Xinhui County. Both allegedly had acquired vast estates in the sands. The county government appealed to the provincial chairman, Song Ziwen, for help. Song sent two gunboats to the area supposedly to stop the feuds. However, the militiamen from Sanjiang stopped the gunboats before they reached the scene of the fighting, inflicting heavy casualties. The public was not sympathetic to the provincial chairman. A local newspaper wasted no time in quoting the proverb, "He not only failed to steal the chicken, but also lost his handful of rice." After a week of fighting and heavy losses on both sides, a cease-fire was finally negotiated. The government, however, insisted that both townships should pay compensation for the loss inflicted on the gunboats and for the expenses of mediation. Furthermore, they were to contribute part of their weapons and men for the pacification campaigns.[33]

The security forces and local police contributed their share to the county's disorder. With the authority of their uniforms and the power of their guns, they plundered the city neighborhoods and the surrounding townships. Policemen forcibly entered homes and made arbitrary arrests, extorting money from those whom they accused of being Communists. Others took the liberty of stopping and searching passersby on the street and then robbing them.[34] A touchy issue concerned the draft of soldiers and laborers. Every county had to provide its quota of recruits, based on the male population.[35] Many administrative positions in the county, such as the headship of districts and villages, had quotas of recruits attached. It came down to a matter of who could forcibly round them up. A peasant in Duhui Xiang, a community within the Huancheng area, had a bitter story to tell. His family was looked down upon by fellow villagers because his father was an outsider whom his widowed mother had married. He had once quarreled with the son of the head of the village self-defense corps. The latter came to the home of the young peasant with his men and took him off to the conscription station. Fortunately he managed to escape after three months.[36]

While unfortunate individuals found it difficult to avoid trouble, whole communities took up arms against what they considered the predatory advances of the authorities. In 1947, communities on the Xinhui-Zhongshan county border organized a self-defense corps to fight "unidentified troops" who were harassing the villagers.[37] In others, village militiamen ambushed county tax collectors and their guards who were pressing for taxes and food.[38] In the meantime, boat services between Macao and Jiangmen were forced out of business by piracy and customs extortion.[39] Master Zhang, a carpenter who lived in Xiaogang Xiang, southwest of the Huancheng area, fell victim to such endemic disorder. In a conversation with him in 1978, he told me that he and his brother sold their family plot at the end of 1947 in order to start a business making wooden buckets in Jiangmen. With 100 Hong Kong dollars in his hands, he went to Macao to buy lumber and iron sheets. On the return trip, the boat was stopped by pirates at Gujing. Robbed of his capital, he tried to start the business by borrowing lumber from a wholesale merchant. Realizing after a year that he would never be able to repay the debt, he quickly folded up his business and fled back to Xiaogang Xiang. He and his brother tried to support their families by renting 11 mu of land but could not make ends meet. In 1949, he came to Huicheng to work in a wooden bucket shop, but business was too uncertain at the time. He finally returned to Xiaogang to become the village carpenter.

City police and local bosses also fought over the distribution of spoils. In Gujing, a market town south of the Huancheng area, a gun battle broke out between policemen from Huicheng who intended to raid a prosperous gambling house and local bosses who were fearlessly defending their lucrative businesses.[40] In the eyes of the public in Huicheng and its vicinity, the Nationalist government was not only unable to provide basic security, its agents were also the major sources of violence. Four years after the Japanese surrender, even the most unconcerned among the public seemed skeptical about what remained of a state structure.

Changing Minds: Intellectual Doubts

Intellectuals in Huicheng and Jiangmen were rapidly changing their minds about the Republican order. Many had been students in the modern schools or had returned from Guangzhou. Before the Japanese occupation, they had participated in a variety of anti-Japanese activities organized by the county Nationalist party and by organizations that were fronts for the underground Communist party.[41] There was the Spring Reading Group, with twenty or so members, organized by teachers at the Jingxian Commercial Academy in Jiangmen in 1937 and led by two underground members of the Chinese Communist Party. The membership included students from Xinhui Teachers College and Xinhui Number One Secondary School, several of whom were later recruited into the party. Through the reading group, leftist magazines such as *Dazhong zhexue* (People's Philosophy), *Zhengzhi jingji xue* (Political Economy), *Qunzhong* (The Masses), *Jiefang* (Liberation), and *Jiuwang ribao* (Resistance Daily) were introduced to the members. There was also a mobile theatrical troupe with a hundred or so members largely from Xinhui Teachers College and Xinhui Number One Middle School. The leader again was an underground member of the Communist party, who taught at the Jiangmen Workers' Children School. The troupe devoted its energies to public performances protesting the Japanese military presence. A similar organization was the Qingqing Resistance Work Team, established in the summer of 1937 by a group of students who had returned from Guangzhou and comprising forty to fifty members in all, with its headquarters at the Guanghua Primary School in Huicheng. Another organization consisted of twenty or so school teachers who published a semimonthly magazine for young children from their base at a primary school in Huicheng. Pro-Communists participated in the activities organized by the Nationalist party. Two of them joined the Women's Association of the Nationalist party, which was made up mostly of students from the Xinhui Teachers College. A combined force from leading schools in Huicheng, such as Gangzhou Middle School, Xinhui Number One and Number Two Middle schools, Pingshan Primary School, Mingyuan Middle School, and Xinhui Teachers College, organized the Xinhui Wartime Rural Work Training Camps in the summer of 1937 and 1938.[42] The camps were designed to train cadres to promote rural cooperatives, education, and defense. From the directory of trainees, I saw that several of the townships in the Huancheng area were involved, including Shenhuan, Tianma, Tianlu, and Dongjia. Most of the trainees had been active in the village schools, the credit cooperatives, and the youth resistance corps (Xinhui Xiangcun Gongzuo Xiehui 1938). However, it seemed that villagers were a little ambivalent about these new-style edu-cated members of their communities. A trainee from Tianlu reported that his attempt to expand primary education in the village by adding short-term courses went rather smoothly. He also noted the formation of a two-hundred-member credit cooperative. However, other activists were deal-ing with village schools run by ancestral estates and had great difficulties with peasants who were suspicious of them and their nationalist appeals. Worse still, entrenched local bosses accused them of being traitors.

After the war, with the help of the underground in the Chinese Com-munist Party, some intellectuals infiltrated the county government and the educational institutions in Huicheng. The underground used a ship-ping company in Jiangmen as a front to make contacts and to transmit party directives. Occasionally a merchant by the name of Chen Ning would transport a load of wood and charcoal from Guangzhou to Jiang-men and stay with his business contacts at the shipping company's quar-ters. He was none other than the chief coordinator of the underground sent by the South China Bureau of the party to direct activities in the Siyi area (Li and Hong 1952, 2–13). According to the account of Wen Zhiyu, a former underground organizer in Jiangmen, the Democratic Alliance (Minmeng) was active in 1948 and 1949 (Wen 1983, 83–93). The out-lawed organization maintained its headquarters in Hong Kong and worked closely with the party to recruit left-leaning elements. Core mem-bers were trained as cadres in preparation for the area's eventual political takeover. Activists also gathered information on the Nationalist govern-ment. Information was compiled monthly as "News from Jiangmen and Xinhui" (Jiangmen Xinhui dongtai) and sent to the headquarters in Hong Kong (Wen 1983, 84).

Gradually Communist sympathizers assumed positions as heads of bu-reaus and departments in the county's educational administration. Some became the headmasters of schools in the large townships. A social club was formed in Jiangmen to recruit young politicians and to organize their election to the county assembly (Li and Hong 1952, 4). These representa-tives used every means to discredit the Nationalist party. They revealed the corruption and the incompetence of the county government and com-plained about tax burdens. Their political activities were supported by those who had gained control of several prominent county newspapers. Some lawyers and doctors were also active. A woman doctor used her office in Huicheng to supply medicine to the guerrilla bases and occasion-ally provided treatment for party cadres wounded in the fighting. In the meantime, a steady stream of intellectuals left the two cities to join the Communist guerrillas at their bases. By the spring of 1949 when the collapse of the Nationalist government was imminent, entire schools had moved to the base areas.[43]

Members of the Democratic Alliance finally linked up with the party underground in the Jiangmen-Huicheng area in March 1949 and set up the Jiangmen City Work Group (Jiangmen Chenggong Xiaozu) to accelerate the work of infiltration. On the eve of the takeover of the two cities, these activists completed two important tasks. First, they managed to "convince" leading merchants in town to keep their militia independent of the Nationalist county government.[44] Second, through the chamber of commerce, they obtained the plans for the government's retreat and acted quickly to protect factories, warehouses, and other material resources. Unlike the peasants in the area who were as frightened of the Nationalists as they were suspicious of the Communists, these leftist intellectuals were actively preparing for the new regime. It is important to note that in the affluent regional core areas of Guangdong, the Nationalist forces remained in control until the very end of the civil war. Except in the case of a few guerrilla bases, the peasants were generally not exposed to the program of the Communists. Those who joined the underground were largely city intellectuals motivated more by political idealism than by material interests.[45]

Changing Sides: Military Defections

A succession of regional military commanders had tried without success to root out the Communists' guerrilla bases in the border regions of Taishan, Xinhui, and Heshan counties. In December 1947, the former commander of the anti-Japanese forces in the area, "the lord of the Six Counties," Zhou Hanling, took over the operations.[46] Zhou was already influential when he organized anti-Japanese guerrilla forces in the Nationalist-controlled Shuangshui area southwest of Huicheng. Politicians in Guangzhou were wary of his ambitions. He was considered to be the "local snake" (di-toushe), who would take credit but reject orders (Lu 1965, 48). They gave him the titles of the province's deputy commander of pacification campaigns for the first district and director of pacification for the five counties on the delta's western front, but they assigned officers from the regular army units to work with his security forces. The real intention was to neutralize him. Out of frustration, Zhou and his deputy, Peng Qiuping, regrouped former anti-Japanese guerrilla forces and trained them independently. Known as the Zhou family troops (Zhoujia bing), they were a force to be reckoned with. However, by October 1948, the ineffectiveness of the pacification campaigns gave the provincial government the opportunity to strip Zhou of his official positions. He was replaced by Li Jiang, a rival commander in the security forces in Guangzhou. The political tug-of-war made some of Zhou's officers feel uneasy, for they found themselves caught in the power struggle between a disintegrating government and a growing political movement. One leading officer who decided to defect to the Communists to save himself was none other than Zhou's deputy, Peng Qiuping. He called a secret meeting of his officers in October 1948, secured their support, and contacted the underground in March 1949. From then on, Peng stepped up his efforts to persuade Zhou to defect and quietly waited with his officers for the moment to act.

On October 5, 1949, the People's Liberation Army (PLA) entered Guangdong from Jiangxi along a major highway linking the two provinces. Without any resistance from the enemy, it swept through Wengyuan and Xinfeng counties. On October 13, it crushed the last line of defense put up by the Nationalists in Conghua, and by the early evening of October 14 marched into Guangzhou. Within days, as quickly as the soldiers could march, the Communists took Shenzheng, Foshan, and Sanshui, strategic towns in the Pearl River delta, and headed toward Jiangmen. The Communist advance was "as swift and crisp as splitting a bamboo." Residents of Jiangmen watched the retreat of the Nationalist forces toward the southwest. It was a familiar scene. The weariness of the soldiers, the defeated spirit of the officers, the desperate maneuvers of the commanders to save their spoils, and rumors that bandits in the area were growing restless—all pointed to the end of an era.

In the wake of the Nationalist retreat, rumors of bandit attacks from Lile to the west of Huicheng and from Tianma in the south heightened anxiety in the cities. Marauding soldiers who looted along their way added to the fear. In Jiangmen, the self-defense corps rose to the occasion by threatening to disband unless the merchants compensated them generously. The chamber of commerce in Jiangmen hurriedly supplied them with guns and wages, but the merchants in Huicheng were so devastated by the unstable political situation that they collected only half the demanded sum.[47] Consequently, the matter of protection was left to resolve itself. Local strongmen in the surrounding townships collected arms from deserting soldiers and fortified their bases.

After taking Guangzhou, the PLA and the regrouped guerrilla forces in the delta joined up at the Heshan base area within a few days and headed toward the lower reaches of the Xi River. The county head of Xinhui fled south. Li Jiang, the commander of the security forces, retreated to the mountainous areas at the border of Xinhui and Taishan counties. Zhou wavered. On the one hand, he agreed with Peng that they should side with the approaching Communist forces, and even made an attempt to arrest the county head of Xinhui; on the other hand, he took his troops back to his old base west of Huicheng with the intention of waiting for the next turn of political events. Before he reached his destination, the officers under Peng's control defected to the approaching Communists. With hardly a shot fired, the western front of the delta came under the control of the Communists (Peng 1980, 229–42). Almost simultaneously, a company of the provincial security forces that had retreated from Guangzhou broke off from the march and stayed temporarily in Jiangmen. The suspense created by the power vacuum finally ended with the defection of these troops. The acting commander of the company, Yun Han, had had previous contacts with the Democratic Alliance. According to Wen Zhiyu (1983, 90–93), the underground sought out Yun Han and arranged for the defection of his troops, who numbered about eighteen hundred. A liberation ceremony was staged on October 23, 1949. On the same day, Huicheng was taken by the Communists without resistance. By that time the underground had surfaced to assume administrative control. General order was maintained by the troops until the arrival of the army units from the guerrilla base at Heshan the following day. By October 25, 1949, the Jiangmen-Huicheng area was under the control of the Jiangmen Military Committee.

The End of an Era?

The Administrative Offices for Central Guangdong (Yuezhong) were established in Jiangmen. Of the five leading cadres, one was a native of Kaiping, one was from Zhongshan, two were from Xinhui, and one came from Enping County.[48] The Jiangmen Military Committee set up headquarters in Huicheng, with the political commissar of the Heshan guerrilla base, Zhou Tianhang of Kaiping County, as its director. The Xinhui County People's Government also established its offices in Huicheng. Under it were the offices of public security, the county peasant association, the women's league, the business league, and the offices for tax collection and grain control and storage, among others. A host of mass associations were also formed, including the Progressive Teachers Association and the Progressive Youth Association. Most of the officers were local residents.

The immediate task of the military committee was to disarm the region's dispersed security forces as well as the heavily armed rural communities. The self-defense corps of Jiangmen under Chen Chi and that of Huicheng were among the first to be disarmed. By mid-November 1949, the most heavily fortified townships—among them Sanjiang, Longquan, and Tian-ma—were simultaneously disarmed. Led by local informants, seventy to eighty soldiers marched into each of the townships, rounded up the local bosses and village elders, and confiscated their arms.[49]

The reaction of the residents in the area to the political takeover was not totally negative and might best be described as ambivalent. Even an anti-Communist publication in Hong Kong later made the following admission:

> So Jiangmen and Huicheng were liberated. At the time, there were those who naturally maintained an anti-Communist position. There were others who wanted to wait and see. But generally, people were willing to accept the new Communist government. A majority of them not only were willing to accept the Communists, they welcomed and supported the change. This applied particularly to students and workers. More people welcomed the Communists than mourned the passing of the Nationalists. Assuming that every emperor demanded taxes, they at least hoped that the policy of the Communists would better suit their interests (Li and Hong 1952, 14).

Uncle Ye and Old Liang, among other elderly villagers, recalled that the commotion accompanying the change of regimes in the county capital and Guangzhou seemed vague and distant to those in the villages. Some reper-cussions from the political uncertainties of Huicheng and Jiangmen were felt in the uneasy preparations being made by the local bosses. The villagers were worried about the Communists because they had been told horror stories of properties being confiscated and women forcibly "commu-nized." Neither the leftist intellectuals nor the ordinary peasants could foresee what the new regime would entail. At this historical juncture, some centralized structure of authority seemed desirable to both. For the intel-lectuals, the key concerns may have been national pride and political idealism. For the peasants, what mattered most was a secure livelihood; they hoped at least for political stability and social order, regardless of the slogans the new leaders proposed. There was also a prevalent fatalism, as Uncle Ye of Tianlu recalled during an interview in 1983:

> Dynasties had risen and fallen. Political glory was reserved only for heroes. Thousands perished to make possible the rise of generals. So what could we ordinary peasants expect from those with power? As long as the stomachs of our family members were filled, and our sons could see to our old age, we considered ourselves lucky and our lives full. We asked no more from the officials.

Local Leadership and Cultural Change

As described in earlier chapters, the prerevolutionary economic landscape of the Huancheng area had provided local elites with multiple bases of power. In times of relative peace, the corporate estates and merchants in Huicheng and Jiangmen had prospered as a result of their differential access to the wealth of the sands. A repeated process of social mobility sustained a rural-urban nexus of power. Aspiring elites actively sought a place in the imperial hierarchy while at the same time sheltering rural communities against direct state encroachment.

However, the disintegration of the central authorities in the warlord era saw the corresponding rise of militaristic strongmen in the rural fringes. Dominating particular territories with their guns, they and their outsider patrons created a new political stage and a volatile structure of power. Even if peasants continued to be bound by tradition, cultural assumptions among a new kind of city intellectual were changing, shaping and being shaped by this new pattern of economic interests and clash of ideologies. The question is, to what extent did the new political conditions affect rural life?

On the surface, one may argue that what one saw in the Huancheng area was a process similar to Skinner's community closure during times of endemic disorder. It would seem on the basis of Skinner's model that in the 1930s and 1940s, when traditional channels of mobility to the cities became blocked, communities in the rural fringes turned autarkic in self-defense. The parochial concerns of these communities in south China might lead one to agree with the observations of Philip Huang (1985) for north China, that a high degree of social solidarity in the less commercialized areas offered communities better defense against the demands of Republican officials.

However, a closer look at the local configurations of power in the Huancheng area raises intriguing analytical questions. Was the apparent cellularization of community boundaries under the local bosses a defensive move? How autarkic or enclosed were these communities? Granted that local bosses had their independent territories, could they have held their ground against competitors without the wider network of military and bureaucratic patrons? If they could, the shrewd shifting of allegiances seems quite unnecessary. In fact, the territorial structures they carved out involved an intense tug-of-war among higher-level competitors as well. The backing of their patrons reinforced the local standing of the lesser bosses because it could be brought to bear in disputes, as demonstrated in the feud between Tianma and Tianlu Xiang in 1939 and again in the feud between Sanjiang and Longquan Xiang in 1948. The reasons for conflict and the degree of damage that it brought about went far beyond those of community feuds. The vertical networks of patronage between extra-community power groups and local bosses blurred the boundaries of local solidarity. The intervention of military patrons from outside the community increased the violence and the destruction. The power of the warlord regimes was thus embodied in and at times magnified by the maneuvers of the local bosses. From the agonizing experiences of the villagers with whom I became friendly, it appears that residents in the periurban townships as well as those in the rural periphery were exposed to a rather different kind of power—direct, unmediated, personal, and arbitrary.

Of course, affiliations with extra-community patrons did not mean that local bosses were mere bureaucratic agents. The warlord regimes were probably more dependent on them than the bosses were on the warlords. By being able to keep much of the revenue they extracted, the local bosses diverted resources that in the empire's heyday would have been drawn into the cities and the periurban townships through the upward mobility of rural residents. Compared to the relative decline of the periurban townships, communities such as Tianma, Tianlu, and Sanjiang experienced an unusual boom period. Marketing networks became more elaborated and revenue accumulated as refugees fled the war-torn zones and redirected their energies and resources. The militaristic maneuvers of local bosses could be arbitrary and frightful, but they offered material benefits as well.

This brings us to an analytical question: What were the cultural implications of this rechanneling of wealth and power to the rural periphery? Not only did the villages enjoy a new "openness" in terms of expanded market networks and associated prosperity, but also the nouveaux riches were able to acquire land from the town-based trusts to establish their own estates, to build ancestral halls, to contribute to elaborate temple festivals, and to pursue cultural symbols of kinship and community solidarity.

Therefore, although the traditional symbols of power were disintegrating in the cities, their importance was intensified and their forms enriched in the rural periphery. Basking in their hard-earned prosperity, how did the peasant victims then view the militaristic power of the local bosses? Did the bosses' efforts to turn respectable make their political adventures appear more illegitimate? The question is pertinent; very soon after the Communist takeover, the local bosses in the area were literally exterminated in the "anti-bully" campaigns. Were their fellow villagers, who joined in the attacks with a vengeance, merely removing what they perceived as excesses of the traditional system?

CHAPTER 6

Understanding Revolution: The Language of Class

To consolidate their control over the vast and varied countryside, the new political leaders needed to convince the peasants of the value of what they had been promised. There were no doubt self-serving individuals among them, but unlike the earlier military adventurers, many genuinely believed in their vision of a better society. They had also secured the means—the Marxist ideology and the Leninist party organization—with which to achieve their goals.[1] By the time the entire country came under Communist control in 1950, the new leaders had accumulated more than two decades of experience in political work in the rural areas. They had confronted a variety of social groups but had also gathered support from them. The Communists' difficulties sometimes pointed to the resilience of primordial sentiments embedded in established social relationships. Nevertheless, the village communities that were swept into political campaigns in the next decades were certainly exposed to the Communists' intrusive attempts at state-making and party-building.[2] It would be naive to assume that a majority of the peasants welcomed the revolution with the enthusiasm that befitted their class interests as defined by the Communists. It is equally naive to suppose that the Communists established their power without mass complicity. In what way did their interests coincide? The way in which the party and the peasants interacted, though often ambivalent, provides an important perspective on how and to what extent the revolution touched rural society.

In this and following chapters I intend to analyze the reconstruction of the political economy and its associated cultural dynamics in the Huancheng area. The process involved a long series of forced encounters between traditional social affiliations and cultural values that had been built up through the centuries and had withstood profound challenges in the warlord era, and a highly organized party armed with an ideology to establish alternative claims to authority. However, the revolutionaries themselves, from village activists to national leaders like Mao Zedong, were in varying degrees steeped in the traditional culture. To what extent did their uneven attempts to break with the past color the process of political transformation?

It is intriguing to compare the power of the party-state with that of the imperial state and the warlord regimes. At the turn of the century the imperial state hardly had the power to reach rural society but nonetheless remained largely legitimate in the popular mind. The warlords attempted to extract revenue directly from the countryside but in the process undermined their power to govern. In the 1980s, the Chinese Communist Party has secured unprecedented compliance from rural society in the name of socialism, but has it acquired the legitimacy it expected?[3] Rural revolution fostered an evolution in the lives of the peasants in response to a political organization determined to reach them. It embodied changes not only in the nature of social and political affiliations and in the production and distribution of material resources, but also in the structuring of a dialogue between peasants and politicians that determined who were the heroes and the villains, who should be in positions of power, what were the bases of authority, how leaders should act, and what the conventions of social living should be.[4] Peasants in the Huancheng area opened such a dialogue in 1950, thus initiating a compelling web of relationships between the state and the community, the party and its rural cadres, and the cadres and their constituents. The motives of those involved were mixed, and very often the outcomes were unexpected and the consequences unintended. But revolution was enacted and understood by the participants through the evolution of these relationships.

The Language of Class

Since the formation of the Chinese Communist Party in 1921, Marxist intellectuals had debated the role of the peasantry in the revolutionary movement. They had wavered between imputing a progressive potential to peasants and doubting their tradition-bound mentality. Chen Duxiu, who believed that a bourgeois-led national revolution would occur before a proletarian one, was particularly skeptical: "The peasants are scattered and their forces are not easy to concentrate, their culture is low, their desires in life are simple, and they easily tend toward conservatism. . . . These environmental factors make it difficult for the peasants to participate in the revolutionary movement" (Meisner 1967, 242). Li Dazhao, on the other hand, recognized the peasants' dubious value, but in his article "Land and the Peasants," published in 1925–26, he advocated organizing them as militants.[5] Influenced by Lenin's ideas on imperialism, Li believed that China was a "proletarian nation." It followed logically that the peasants constituted a majority in this exploited entity. Believing in their ardent "national tradition," Li felt that they should be given due encouragement in the class struggle to realize their political potential. His voluntaristic interpretations of Marxism and peasant nationalism heavily influenced Mao Zedong, who continued this line of thinking in his own mobilization of the peasants.[6]

For Mao, the party's role in promoting the class struggle was taken for granted. His political approach was based on an understanding of crucial class relationships in rural society.[7] In evaluating how various classes would act to maintain or change the status quo, party cadres were to distinguish friends from foes. Nonetheless, there was a flexibility in Mao's class analysis. In the article "On Contradictions," Mao outlined his philosophical views, pointing out that both the target and the intensity of the class struggle were contingent upon historical circumstances. Policies about the alignment of class antagonisms and loyalties changed according to the principal political tasks to be pursued.[8] Despite lively and at times violent disagreements over the class issue, the Communist movement that had been dominated by Mao since the 1930s assumed that the class struggle would be used to transform society.[9] At the same time, class policies also applied to the recruitment of party cadres. The party had enrolled the very poorest in the villages under the assumption that they were politically reliable. On the other hand, these activists were balanced by a large number of technical and intellectual cadres drawn from different class backgrounds. In the 1930s and 1940s, many city intellectuals from well-to-do family backgrounds had joined the Communists in the base areas. Some subsequently became leading party members. However, as liberation approached, strict working class criteria again came to the fore.

Class and Leadership

The earlier political economy of Huicheng and its rural vicinity posed special problems for the class policies of the party. An important one involved party leadership itself. The Huicheng area was one of the last to be taken over by the People's Liberation Army (PLA). The Japanese military had controlled it from 1939 to 1945, and military adventurers had held on to it until late 1949. The change of power was the result of military defections coordinated by a small group of underground cadres and city intellectuals. The vast majority of the peasants were little exposed to or involved with the political movement. The Communist base area closest to Huicheng was in the hills of Heshan County to the north. When the Nationalists fled from Huicheng in October 1949, the guerrilla forces from Heshan were the first to arrive. The provisional military committee set up at Huicheng consisted of cadres from that base. Zhou Tianhang, the political commissar, who was a native of Kaiping County, became the head of the Jiangmen Military Committee that administered Xinhui County. His deputies were leading members of the underground from Huicheng and Jiangmen (Li and Hong 1952).

From the start, the local activists were a source of difficulties for their political superiors from the South Central Party Bureau at Wuhan, and later for the Party Central Committee in Beijing after the South China Branch of the bureau became independent from Wuhan. Not only were a substantial number of them intellectuals from well-to-do families, they were also used to making independent decisions in the isolated circumstances of the underground. Moreover, they were native Cantonese and had serious differences with the party leaders who had marched south with the PLA. According to them, the *lao dage* (big brothers) were rigid in their class policies and not at all sensitive to local sentiments. The Wuhan cadres, on the other hand, were treating their class backgrounds as politically unreliable. Guangdong's lineage communities with their corporate estates were organizationally powerful and culturally exclusive, features considered by the national party leadership as major obstacles to rural revolution. The new leaders did not wish to see them protected by the dubious class interests of the local cadres.

Judged by class criteria, the backgrounds of many of the Cantonese cadres were highly suspect. Statistics compiled by the Guangdong provincial government in 1950 show that those serving at or above the county level were relatively well educated and probably from families who could afford to pay for such education. Most of these cadres were students recruited through resistance activities during the Japanese occupation. Major political officers had worked for a long time in the guerrilla bases in the Kejia (Hakka) regions of Guangdong. After the Japanese surrender, many activists went underground to escape persecution by the pro-Nationalist military. Their undercover work had at times required contacts with administrators of the Nationalist regime. Such activities turned out to incriminate them when the uncompromising class politics of the party were deployed against them.

According to the statistics compiled by the Policy Institute of the Party Central Committee's South China Branch, local activists occupied prominent positions in the provincial government. The provincial chairman, Ye

Jianying, and his two deputies, Fang Fang and Gu Dacun, were typical examples. As shown in tables 6.1, 6.2, and 6.3, the provincial government, the prefectural and county governments, and the First Provincial People's Congress included a large number of members with commercial and intellectual backgrounds. The tables also show the number of military cadres from outside Guangdong whom local leaders could not ignore.[10]

In fact, class tensions marred the first major political campaign, aimed at land reform, from the start. Activists in the villages continued to receive mixed signals. On the one hand, the deputy provincial chairman, Fang Fang, who was Cantonese, urged gradualism. In the land reform schedule outlined in 1950, he planned campaigns in three out of ninety-nine counties, and if conditions allowed, they were to include seven periurban districts of Guangzhou. Altogether, the initial program would have involved forty-three districts with about two million people out of an estimated total population of 27,460,000 in the province. Cadres were urged to be sensitive to rich peasants and to emigrant families, and to distinguish carefully between commercial interests and "feudal exploitation."[11] He asserted that rural trade, handicraft, and subsidiary activities were to be considered conducive to the development of productive forces and therefore should not be categorically attacked. In sum, he pleaded for caution in dealing with the complicated and delicate class relations that characterized a highly commercialized and urban-oriented economy supported by overseas ties.[12]

Despite Fang Fang's cautions, the campaigns were intensified in November 1950. The provincial government extended the campaign area to eleven counties and expected land reform to be completed before spring planting the following year. In the New Year's Day editorial of the *Nanfang ribao* (Southern Daily), the language of class struggle was uncompromis-

Table 6.1. Committee Members of the Guangdong Provincial People's Government

Place of Origin	Number
Guangdong (outside the Pearl River delta)	22
Guangdong (within the Pearl River delta)	6
Other provinces	9
Unknown	4
Total	41

Source: Guangdong qingkuang huibian, by Zhonggong Zhong-yang Huanan Fenju Zhengce Yanjiushi, 1950, 45–51.

ing.[13] Another speech made by Deng Zihui, the deputy chairman of the South Central Military Committee, explicitly targeted local cadres: "Recently some local cadres have been restrained by technical terms and are overcautious. Landlords have therefore manipulated them in order to sabotage the land reform."[14] An earlier editorial representing the views of the South Central Bureau had raised criticism to an ideological level. The class attitudes of the Cantonese cadres were openly doubted. The editorial insisted that the peaceful division of land (*heping fentian*), a political act it accused local cadres of committing, "borders on reformism and is not compatible with the revolutionary means of Marxist social transformation. . . . Land reform should be a 'systematic and violent' struggle" (Dong 1953, 5). These views were echoed by Tao Zhu, later head of the South China Branch Bureau of the Party Central Committee. The change of tone could be attributed in part to the anxiety of the leaders over the Korean War and to the associated fear that the delta was vulnerable to infiltration and attack. It also reflected the deepening schism between the local cadres, represented by Fang Fang and Gu Dacun, and those influential in the South Central Bureau, represented by Tao Zhu and Deng Zihui.

In one campaign after another in the early 1950s, local cadres were hounded out of the party for having "feudal" class backgrounds and for having served as administrators in former regimes, offenses for which they were labelled "counterrevolutionary." As described in the previous chapter, Communist sympathizers in the Jiangmen-Huicheng area who surfaced to assume administrative posts after the Communist takeover were largely city intellectuals. They were the first victims of class rhetoric among the ranks of the cadres. A major event in the witch hunt was the Jiangmen Incident. In late 1951, Wen Zhiyu, an underground member of the Jiangmen City Work Small Group and chairman of the Jiangmen Business League, was accused of espionage. When evidence for these accusations was not forthcoming, the campaign was toned down. Nonetheless, the incident implicated many former underground members who had risen high in the city's administration. Special investigators were sent from the South Central Bureau of the party. In the ensuing shake-up of the Jiangmen administration, the mayor was dismissed on charges of corruption and several others were jailed. Wen Zhiyu was tried at a mass meeting and sentenced to a labor camp.[15]

One can detect a similarly uncompromising tone in the local newspapers reporting on the land reform campaigns in the county.[16] The struggles among the party leadership colored the campaigns at the rank-and-file level. When local cadres with intellectual backgrounds were rooted out

Table 6.2.   Delegates of the First Provincial People's Congress, 1950

Delegates	Total	Class Status				Education					
		Workers	Peasants	Others	Unknown[a]	Illiterate	Primary	Junior Middle	Senior Middle	College and above	Unknown[a]
Political party members	40	3	—	32	5	—	—	—	9	24	7
Government personnel	14	—	2	10	2	—	2	2	5	3	2
Military personnel	30	5	9	15	1	3	15	5	4	—	3
Mass organization members	32	7	—	24	1	—	5	4	5	17	1
Special-interest groups[b]	49	—	—	39	10	—	1	4	6	28	10
Regional delegates	637	111	166	336	24	46	236	103	112	104	36
Ex-officio[c] representatives	43	2	1	34	6	—	2	4	14	16	7
TOTAL	845	128	178	490	49	49	261	122	155	192	66
PERCENT	100	15.1	21.1	58.0	5.8	5.8	30.9	14.4	18.3	22.7	7.8

Source: Guangdong qingkuang huibian 1950, 25.

[a]A number of delegates were classified as unknown because they had not yet arrived when the
[b]Special-interest groups include technical specialists, educators, overseas Chinese, industrialists,
[c]Compared to table 6.1, the ex-officio group includes three more cadres of Guangdong origin and

from the county leadership and even higher up, activists in the villages were recruited from among the very poorest for their assumed political loyalty rather than for any technical administrative skills. In the hands of these activists, class politics turned increasingly doctrinaire.

However, recruiting the very poorest posed its own problems. Compared to many provinces in the south central area of China, the Pearl River delta of Guangdong had a large number of mobile laborers, petty traders, and handicraftsmen who joined the Communists with very mixed motives. As shown in table 6.4, their participation is reflected in the composition of the leadership of the township administrations. A similar differentiation among peasant households can also be seen within the

Sex			Age						Place of Origin		
Male	Female	Unknown[a]	Under 26	26–45	46–65	66–70	70 and over	Unknown[a]	Guangdong	Other Provinces	Unknown[a]
39	1	—	1	22	9	—	2	6	29	6	5
14	—	—	—	9	3	1	—	1	6	7	1
29	1	—	5	23	—	—	—	2	8	20	2
23	9	—	1	27	3	—	—	1	24	6	2
38	1	10	—	22	16	—	1	10	31	8	10
541	89	7	71	431	110	6	10	9	598	27	12
41	2	—	—	18	18	—	—	7	31	8	4
725	103	17	78	552	159	7	13	36	727	82	36
85.8	12.2	2.01	2.0	9.2	65.3	18.8	1.5	4.3	86.0	9.7	4.2

Congress was convened.
progressive members of church organizations, and ex-KMT officers.
one fewer from outside the province.

Huancheng area. As shown in table 6.5, the periurban township of Dongjia consisted of peasant households that were more polarized than those in Tianlu Xiang, a township 6 kilometers from Huicheng.[17] Old cadres in Huancheng admitted in retrospect that in uncertain political waters they found it safer to be leftist rather than rightist. Chen Sheyuan, a tenant farmer who had acquired some accounting skills from a village school in Meijiang, recalled that he was not allowed to join the township's Poor Peasant League because he was not poor enough. The following sections will show that peasant activists were recruited from among the very poorest in the periurban townships, whereas the activists in Tianlu Xiang were largely poor and middle peasants.

Table 6.3. Backgrounds of Leading Cadres in the Prefectural, Municipal, and County Governments, Guangdong Province, 1950

Administrative Level	Total	Education						Age					Sex		Date of Recruitment				
		Primary	Junior Middle	Senior Middle	Technical College	University	Other	Under 26	26–35	36–45	46–55	56 and over	Male	Female	mid-1920s	1928–37	1938–45	Others	Jan. 1949
Province	1	—	—	—	—	1	—	—	—	—	1	—	1	—	1	—	—	—	—
Prefecture	24	2	10	7	1	4	—	—	8	13	3	—	24	—	3	9	9	—	3
County	129	3	44	44	1	34	3	2	76	47	—	4	129	—	1	13	111	4	—
TOTAL	154	5	54	51	2	39	3	2	84	60	4	4	154	—	5	22	120	4	3
PERCENT	100	3.2	35	33.1	1.3	25.3	1.9	1.3	54.6	39	2.6	2.6	100	—	3.25	14.29	77.92	2.6	1.94

Family Background[a]

Administrative Level	Total	Workers	Handicraft Workers	Poor Peasant	Middle Peasant	Rich Peasant	Landlord	Petty Capitalist	Capitalist	Urban Poor	Independent Professions	Other
Province		—	—	—	—	—	—	—	—	—	—	1
Prefecture		1	1	3	8	3	4	2	—	1	—	1
County		2	3	19	46	12	25	9	—	5	5	3
TOTAL		3	4	22	54	15	29	11	—	6	5	5
PERCENT		1.94	2.54	14.2	35	9.74	18.8	7.1	—	3.8	3.24	3.74

Source: Guangdong qingkuang huibian 1950, 9–19.

[a]In terms of their own class status, 44.1% were students and 32.4% were from the independent professions category.

Table 6.4. Background of Township and Village Cadres in Guangdong
and Hunan Provinces, 1952

	Peasants (%)	Others (%)	Impure Elements (%)
Guangdong (a sample of 15 town- ships)			
Key cadres	76.00	22.5	1.33
Other cadres	78.10	20.07	1.20
Hunan (a sample of 13 townships)			
Key cadres	86.11	12.50	1.84
Other cadres	86.30	12.58	1.12

Source: The figures are taken from *Zhongnanqu yibaige xiang diaocha tongji biao*, compiled by Zhongnan Junzheng Weiyuanhui Tudigaige Weiyuanhui Diaocha Yanjiuchu, 1953, p. 110.

Note: Impure elements refer to landlords and former officials of the KMT.

Cultural Dynamics in the Class Struggle

The highly charged class politics increased the practical difficulties of the land reform campaigns in the villages. Major problems had arisen from applying such policies to the land tenure system and its culturally accepted system of rights and duties. The first set of problems involved the definition of landlordism. Huicheng's numerous corporate estates produced an array of "landlords" and an equally wide range of "tenants." However, those who wielded the greatest economic power in the sands were not always technically landowners. Traditionally, the managers of corporate estates in Huicheng had pocketed the cash rents and rent deposits from their contractors, themselves local strongmen who could hardly be categorized as poor and exploited. With the demise of the ancestral trusts and other corporate estates in Huicheng during the 1930s and 1940s, a new stratum of landlords had been created in the rural areas. These were local bosses, such as Chen Shipei and Chen Shifeng of Tianma, who took over the control of the estates of the He and Mo lineages on a large scale.

Others also seized the opportunity to acquire land. Villagers from Tianlu and Meijiang Xiang recalled that, after a year or two, tenant farmers who had profited from the production of food during the war were able to buy the land they had rented and accumulate more to be rented out or to be farmed by hired laborers. While villagers loathed the way in which the local bosses had acquired their wealth, they showed sympathy for those

Table 6.5.   Class Compositions, Dongjia and Tianlu Xiang

A. Class Composition of Dongjia Xiang, 1955[a]

Class Status	No. of Households	Percentage
Poor peasant	342	46.9
Lower middle peasant	78	10.6
Upper middle peasant[b]	83	11.3
Rich peasant	29	3.9
Landlord[c]	30	4.1
Others (farm laborers, small rentiers, petty traders, handicraft, etc.)	167	22.9
TOTAL	729	99.7

B. Class Composition of Xian Village, Tianlu Xiang, 1952[d]

Class Status	No. of Households	Percentage
Poor peasant (hired hands, others)	92	53.8
Lower middle peasant	51	30.0
Old middle peasant[b]	20	11.6
Landlords and rich peasants	8	4.6
TOTAL	171	100.0

[a]The figures in table 6.5A are taken from records in Dongjia Brigade.
[b]The term "upper middle peasant" was used only after the land reform and during collectivization to distinguish this group from old middle peasants, who were treated more harshly during the land reform. Upper middle peasants could be poor middle peasants who had achieved a comfortable level of income after liberation.
[c]Landlords include managers of ancestral estates and those who owned land but who also engaged in trade and industry.
[d]The figures in table 6.5B are based on interviews with cadres who conducted the land reform in Xian Village. At the time, the village population was around 600.

landlords and rich peasants who had followed what peasants considered the legitimate channels of social mobility. Chen Mingfa, who later became the party secretary of Meijiang Xiang, told me in an interview in 1980: "One could blame these tenant households for profiting in wartime at the expense of others," he said, "but they had worked hard for generations to acquire a piece of land and did not have the chance to lord it over others before the revolution came. Unfortunately, they were all classified as landlords during the land reform. In Meijiang, out of the 500 or so households, 80 were labelled landlords. This was immoral."[18]

Other popular assumptions about the rights and obligations associated with landowning posed similar problems. For those who secured settlement rights in a village by tracing ties to a focal ancestor, or who were entitled to use the land of an ancestral estate whose management rotated among senior lineage members, private ownership of property was not the only means to a livelihood.[19] In the popular mind, people who owned property did not hold it forever. Properties broke up with family divisions. A poor lineage member could also expect charity and aid from the corporate properties of his kin groups. These properties held through various genealogical and territorial claims, involved changing benefits and obligations, supported and protected by the locally powerful. Landlordism thus represented a legitimate channel for social mobility in the process of community- and lineage-building, in conjunction with a system of authority buttressed by literati culture and official connections. It seemed that peasants felt more animosity toward the usurpers in such an order than toward those who rose within it. Chen Mingfa recalled asking himself many times during the land reform, "Should peasant households who acquired a few mu of land for themselves during the war, or who happened to be the lineage elders appointed to manage an estate for a term, be held responsible for a crime they hardly committed?"

Such questions also applied to the treatment of emigrant families and small rentiers.[20] Former activists recalled during an interview with me that they were uncomfortable about the struggles against these households. They held the opinion that "these properties were products of the hard labor of their kin overseas. Moreover, emigrant households consisted largely of women and children. What could you expect them to do if you take away the rental properties? Some wealthy emigrants had contributed to community education and charity. It seemed heartless to go after their families." A document summarizing the results of the land reform activities between October 1951 and February 1952 listed 57 households in Huicheng labeled as emigrant landlords and 1,092 households as "small rentiers," many of which consisted of the dependents of emigrants.[21] Despite the ambivalence expressed by former activists, the properties of these small rentiers were seized in the more uncompromising phases of the land reform.

Other cultural factors also entered into the political decisions. One case involved a small rentier in Huicheng who held land in Chakeng Village. Pressured by activists from Chakeng, he paid back 500 catties of grain, and another 500 catties were secured after he was tortured. Note, however, that he was not a member of the Liang lineage in Chakeng. Moreover, the peasant representatives who pressured him were of the Yuan surname, probably from the Yuan lineage historically subservient to the Liang. It appeared in this case that, despite the mobilization of the "underdogs" of the village, the easiest targets in the struggle remained the outsiders who could not muster community support.

If it was difficult for political activists to decide who were the "land-lords" and what constituted "feudal exploitation" (*fengjian boxue*), the selection of class allies was no easier. The party relied on poor peasants and hired hands to support its programs because they were considered to be the most downtrodden in the traditional society. However, the expected class sentiments did not come readily. As mentioned earlier, tenancy in commu-nities such as Tianma, Chakeng, and Tianlu was tied to lineage and com-munity membership. The social distinction between villager and outsider was just as important economically as that between landlord and tenant. The livelihood of landless peasants was no doubt precarious, but those institutions that were culturally obligated to support them in various ways provided a measure of security. In sum, popular ambivalence toward the language of class shows how relationships permitting the extraction of agricultural surplus were embedded in rural social institutions, the rights and duties associated with which had historically been held legitimate in the popular mind. Even if the support that their elites were morally obliged to give was not always forthcoming in material terms, it would have been difficult to claim that the peasants had lost faith in the traditional order.

Class, Corporate Estates, and Commerce

Documents of the land reform list 97 ancestral trusts, which were identified as the area's largest landlords based in Huicheng.[22] From a sample of 85 of them, they owned a total of 15,144 mu of land spread out over three counties, with 5,412 male beneficiaries, that is, 20 percent of Huicheng's population at the time. The largest estate, that of He Wenyi, owned 6,449 mu of land, of which 5,930 mu were located in Jiuzisha to the southeast of the Huancheng area, and had 1,792 male beneficiaries. To avoid implicat-ing and alienating a vast number of people, the cadres were instructed to single out the estate managers, who were often the most influential figures on the local scene. Branded as "ancestral hall termites" (*citang baiyi*), they were accused of embezzling lineage funds and of using them for usurious purposes. The interests of the average kinsman who was entitled to a share of benefits were pitted against those of the estate managers, who were said to have abused the rules for selfish reasons. The accusations against the managers as usurpers of collective property did not undermine the right of the kinsman to that property. One may even suggest that such attacks on corporate estate managers unexpectedly restored lineage members to a more equal place in the structure of benefits. In fact, concerns based on the genealogical aspect of kinship continued to surface after the revolution, even though their material foundation had long since disappeared.

On the basis of class interests, tenants, whether they were kinsmen or not, were encouraged to claim a share of the estate land and its income. However, the highly commercialized nature of the estates made it difficult to disentangle income made up of rent and usury from that derived from commerce, the latter being a protected category along with the rich-peasant economy.[23] The He Wenyi estate with its vast landholdings and large number of beneficiaries posed a serious problem. Although the traditional distribution of the landed wealth was not even, many lineage members had reaped substantial benefits. The estate owned 50 percent of the sands in Jiuzisha, but its beneficiaries were town residents engaged in non-agricultural activities. Who should be classified as landlords and what could be confiscated as the product of "feudal exploitation" were complicated issues that the new regime was unable to resolve completely.

The verdict on Liu Yiji, Huicheng's largest fan palm enterprise, was a case in point. Though it controlled palm production and marketing in the area, it could be held responsible for only 86 mu of land. At the beginning of the land reform, tenants in Tianlu Xiang put forward their claims and were compensated accordingly. However, as the campaigns gathered momentum, those members whose livelihood was more loosely connected with Liu Yiji began demanding astronomical sums. The managers, who had fled to Guangzhou, refused to cooperate. Exasperated cadres held the managers responsible for the death of two peasants and demanded 600,000 catties of grain to be paid out in installments. Though the case was publicized in the local newspaper as a reasonable settlement between peasant and commercial interests, it had a negative effect on merchants, who were already cynical about the government's professed moderation toward them. Moreover, the demise of the commercial enterprises brought unexpected hardship on those peasants in the rural areas whose household incomes were supplemented by handicrafts and the trading and processing of local cash crops such as palm and orange peel, and whose household economy had often depended on credit extended by rich peasants and merchants.

A special committee was set up in Huicheng to process peasant claims against landlords who resided in town. Its work was to distinguish the "feudal exploitation" against which claims could be made, from the commercial interests that should be protected. Within four months the committee received 2,273 claims from the surrounding townships, out of which 1,781 cases were settled; 133 fugitive landlords were forced to return to the villages in order to face "political struggle," and a total of 4,945,501 catties of grain were returned to tenants. However, as the land reform campaign intensified, cadres admitted that "leftist excesses" were committed during the confusion. On November 5, 1951, three thousand peasants marched into Huicheng demanding compensation from the estate managers. Their action created a general panic, not only among the residents in town, but also among party cadres conducting the struggle sessions.

In sum, the attack on the town-based ancestral trusts and the commercial enterprises caused confusion among those involved. The economic structure upon which these institutions had based their ability to extract the agricultural surplus had started to weaken during the early decades of the twentieth century. It met its final end in the land reform in 1951. However, the questions of who benefited from the changes and what popular expectations were associated with them remained unresolved.

The Language of Vengeance and of Opportunism

The day three thousand peasants flocked into Huicheng was the high point of the campaign to "retrieve rent and rent deposits, and to struggle against bandits and bullies" (*tuizu tuiya, qingfei fanba*), which preceded the attempt to determine the class status of peasant households and the subsequent redistribution of land. It aimed at mobilizing peasants to identify those they most hated and feared. The party hoped that through public denunciations of the local bosses the peasants would build up confidence in their class interests and power.

However, a closer look at these activities reveals a different situation. In the Huancheng area peasant participation fluctuated between two extremes. In the townships farther away from Huicheng, where local bosses had dominated for more than a decade, peasants were fearful and reluctant to identify the bosses. In Tianma, Chen Shifeng and Chen Shipei had already fled to Hong Kong. A few bosses who remained in the villages or had fled into town were arrested, including Chen Yin (The Hound) of Tianma; Ye Ziqun of Tianlu; Chen Wendian of Meijiang, who had murdered his rival Chen Ermou; Liang Richao, who had killed a rival to assume the headship of Yuanqing Xiang in the 1940s; and Liang Letian of Chakeng. However, the aura of their power remained. Villagers were afraid that once the land reform work teams had gone, the followers of the local bosses would take their revenge.

Such fears were not unfounded. Dispatches from work teams in a township south of Jiangmen vividly described the problems.[24] Xinsha Xiang was situated in the sands south of Jiangmen and immediately to the east of the Huancheng area, with 783 households and a population of 3,416. For two decades it had been dominated by several captains of self-defense forces linked to a secret society named Jiulongtang. When the campaign began, 30 households were identified as landlords and 103 as former functionaries of the Republican regimes. According to the dispatches, several individuals of dubious status had found their way into the peasant association, the market and supply cooperative, the irrigation association, and the village police. Wu Qun was one such figure. As the head of the peasant association, he formed an executive committee consisting of "a petty trader, a small owner-cultivator, two former militiamen, two old women who had no influence, and a landless peasant who never dared to show up in the association meetings" (Xinhui Xian Siqu Tugaidui 1952, 1–2). It was claimed that Wu had polarized the activists. He accused the head of the newly established Poor Peasants League of hoarding the grain taxes. He warned owner-cultivators that they would not be spared in the subsequent campaigns. Those identified as struggle targets fanned the uncertainties of the situation by saying, "You dare to struggle against me before the assignment of class statuses! Don't you know that some tax collectors in Zhongshan County have recently been killed? . . ." (ibid.).

In cases where peasants' fears were overcome, their activism revealed a mixture of greed and vengeance. As in the case of Chakeng Village, physical torture was used to obtain confessions of "hidden treasures." According to a land reform report on the village, activists who wanted to acquire the "fruits of struggle" (*douzheng guoshi*) urged the peasants to "tie up Liang Letian's [a village notable] entire family and see if he dares not to confess." Others cautioned, "Torturing him to death would not yield the fruits; we may even drive away other landlords. When Sanjiang Xiang started 'dragging' (torture), three landlords in Chakeng fled" (Yuexiqu Dangwei Zhengce Yanjiushi 1952, 4–5). When party work teams tried to steer the peasants away from purely economic motives toward political ones, they found that the desire for vengeance surfaced instead, as described in the same report (ibid. 7):

When an exploited household head, Liang Zou, struggled against Liang Letian, he focused only on economic exploitation. He asked, "Letian, you bastard, you owed Zuoqi [his deceased brother] three years of wages, amounting to twelve baskets of grain a year. So he was cheated of thirty-six baskets. Are you not going to pay back the debt?" He was then asked, "How did your brother Zuo die?" "He died of sickness." "How did he die of sickness?"

"Liang Letian refused him wages and he could not afford the medicine, so he died . . . ." "Does the repayment of money suffice?" Then the issue emerged. When he questioned Liang Letian a second time, he changed his accusations: "Letian, you bastard, my brother Zuo worked as a year-round farmhand for you in 1941. . . . In 1947, he fell and hurt his chest while loading grain, and you refused him money for medicine. When he died, we could not even afford a coffin. He was just wrapped up in a mat. I want you to repay the blood debt with your life . . . ."[25]

In the periurban townships an atmosphere of opportunism prevailed. Activists rushed into town to claim the "fruits of struggle" indiscriminately, a phenomenon the rural-urban committee branded "looting during a fire" (*chenhuo dajie*). The language of vengeance and opportunism was heard most clearly among the "brave elements" (*yonggan fenzi*). These were the mobile, street-wise laborers who congregated in the periurban townships and who readily joined the party work teams as local activists.[26] They seldom belonged to the dominant lineages in their communities. Not entitled to build houses or too poor to rent land, they hired themselves out to do odd jobs and were drafted as laborers and soldiers during the war. They had nothing to lose in rallying behind the banner of class, which offered a means to acquire recognition, economic benefits, and power they could never have imagined. Party cadres trusted that they harbored the greatest number of grudges against the old society and therefore viewed them as good allies. But in fact, the vengeful behavior of this group was not in the interest of the party, because it created fear and suspicion among fellow villagers. In Chengnan Xiang, for example, an activist brought a case against an owner-cultivator, accusing him of forcibly buying some palm fields and terminating a tenancy. Not daring to argue with the aggressive and vocal "officials," the farmer sold his property in order to pay his accuser. Fortunately, the case was reviewed by the rural-urban liaison committee, which reversed the verdict. The committee ruled that the farmer had been victimized by the "arbitrary, opportunistic accusations of bad elements" (*Fan fengjian*, April 1952: 11).

A detailed though incomplete account of the land reform campaigns in the county lists the range of people being "struggled" against.[27] They were the township and village heads, the captains of self-defense corps, emigrant landlords or their close kin, and the functionaries of the Republican regimes. Many people in the Huancheng area were included. The notorious Chen Wendian of Meijiang Xiang, for example, was publicly tried and shot, along with five of his followers. The elderly wife and the daughter-in-law of his rival, Chen Ermou, whom he had murdered, were also tried.

Liang Richao of Yuanqing Xiang was tortured and then shot, along with three others. Six others were beaten and imprisoned. In Chengnan Xiang, twenty-two local bosses were arrested and publicly tried. Eight were shot, five killed themselves, and the rest were imprisoned. In Jiaotou Xiang, twenty-two people were arrested, six were killed, and five committed suicide. The local rich who had not accumulated blood debts (*xuezhai*) had their properties and houses confiscated, a punishment locally known as *saodi chumen* (to be swept out of one's house).

The Traditional Order Unraveled

In tearing down the former bastions of power, the land reform work teams targeted activists to build new political institutions. As soon as they arrived at the villages, they sought out potential members for the new peasant associations.[28] Village leaders during the interregnum were forced to step aside. The new peasant associations consisted of poor peasants and landless laborers, who were groomed as future village cadres. Supervised by the work teams, the activists helped select peasant representatives, conducted village congresses, and assumed administrative functions. They also shouldered the propaganda work in the land reform campaigns. Up to that point, fellow villagers were mere observers. Only the local bosses, who had been singled out to be struggled against, and the activists were seriously involved. However, when the work teams proceeded to the next stage of the land reform, in which the class status of every peasant household had to be determined and then acted upon in order to redistribute land and properties, everyone found himself drawn into the political whirlpool.

Party guidelines divided the rural population into five broad categories: landlords, rich peasants, middle peasants, poor peasants, and landless laborers. Landlords were those who lived entirely off the labor of others. Rich peasants, on the other hand, engaged in labor, but obtained a significant portion of their income from rent and from hired help. Middle peasants both owned and rented land. They even hired laborers on a short-term basis during the planting and harvesting seasons. To be given middle-peasant status, less than 25 percent of one's total income had to come from the labor of others. Poor peasants were tenant farmers who hired themselves out for short periods. Landless laborers were those who could not afford to rent land at all.[29] However, in a commercialized economy such as Huancheng's where members of households engaged in various forms of agricultural and nonagricultural work, it was as difficult to decide what constituted principal labor (*zhuyao laodong*) as it was to determine the amount of "exploitation income" (*boxue shouru*).[30] The lack of clear-cut boundaries allowed room for maneuver. Neighbors and kinsmen found themselves locked in anxious negotiations and mutual accusations. A common strategy nevertheless emerged from the chaos: everyone claimed to be as poor as he could get away with. Before the question of class status had been settled, those who possessed resources did not dare to rent out land, extend credit, or hire laborers for agricultural tasks, and this disruption of the economy further threatened the meager livelihood of those who depended on occasional work to supplement their incomes.

After agonizing negotiations between members of the work teams, local activists, and peasant households, class status was determined, posted by the peasant associations, and publicly confirmed. The Huancheng area saw two distinct patterns of class compositions. In a periurban township such as Dongjia, the community was polarized. Landlords and rich peasants who maintained ties with commercial enterprises in Huicheng were numerous. Tenant farmers, small rentiers, landless laborers, and petty traders also made up a large percentage of the population. There were relatively few middle peasants. In townships farther away from the cities such as Tianlu, the majority were classified as poor and middle peasants.

The two types of communities faced different problems when land was redistributed. In Tianlu Xiang, the existing production arrangements were disturbed only minimally. Most households stayed where they had been farming. Those who had rented from local landlords or large contractors were allowed to claim this land as theirs. Migrant farmhands were entitled to claim land from the communities where they farmed, but the exclusiveness of local surname groups caused many to return to their native villages. The Liang of Xining Village in Tianlu continued to occupy the township's best land and bitterly opposed the attempts of other surnames to take a share. The periurban township of Dongjia Xiang faced a different set of problems. Rich peasants with commercial interests in town refused to have their land and properties confiscated and claimed protection under the land reform laws. A large number of migrant farmers returned to Dongjia to claim their shares, heightening tensions in the already land-scarce community. Furthermore, the old land tenure system had created landholdings consisting of small parcels of land spread over several communities, and their reorganization required a great deal of land swapping among former cultivators. As a result, endless disputes arose over the terms of exchange.

After the commotion caused by the land reform campaigns, the work teams finally left the villages in 1952 and the peasants resumed their livelihoods. However, it would be naive to say that social life settled back to its old rhythms. Everyone had acquired a new label—a class status—which not only entitled him to the land he worked on, but also weighed considerably in his dealings with the new government. At this juncture, criteria such as village membership and kinship affiliations were still important, but new voices and motivations had emerged from the political struggles. Most important, the class labels had entered into the everyday language of both town and village.

The Emerging Rural Leadership

A major indicator of the importance of the language of class in the villages was the emergence of a new rural leadership whose legitimacy was created and reinforced by the party. From the campaigns against local bosses to the redistribution of land, the very poorest were recruited to the new peasant associations in every township. Middle peasants were allowed to join the associations but were seldom included as core political members. The party planned to create a new corps of local cadres made up of peasant activists whose members came from what they considered reliable class backgrounds and who could be expected to be loyal to the party. They were to become agents of change from within the villages.

Two types of activists emerged on the Huancheng social landscape. In the periurban townships such as Dongjia, Dajiao, and Chengnan, activists were tenant farmers and hired hands who had seen the world outside their villages. Such a recruitment policy reflected the historical tradition of a mobile population engaged in petty trade and handicrafts, an important component of the Huancheng area's socioeconomic life since the Qing dynasty. However, the channeling of resources to the regional periphery during the war and the direct impact of the military occupation of Huicheng brought about serious social dislocation in these communities. Livelihoods had become uncertain and social hierarchies volatile. What the Chinese Communist Party (CCP) termed the "brave elements" were largely the products of such social disintegration. In townships such as Tianlu and Tianma that lay farther away from Huicheng, activists consisted of poor and middle peasants who, in good years, had been given some education in the free schools operated by ancestral estates. They held grudges against the old society but were at the same time entrenched in relationships of kin and community. Most were farmers with a relatively stable livelihood. In fact, for them the destructive impact of the war had been somewhat buffered by the local strongmen in their villages. Under the bosses' territorial control, ironically enough, traditional ideals of thriving markets, landownership, kin solidarity in the forms of ancestral estates and halls, and community exclusiveness were upheld. On the other hand, although they were more entrenched in the socioeconomic networks of their communities than their periurban counterparts, they shared with them certain attitudes toward the patronage of the party. They felt indebted to the "great benefactor" (*da enren*). They urged peasants to appreciate the "kind favors" (*enqing*) that Mao Zedong had bestowed on everyone, and hence to support the revolution.[31] Their work style continued to be shaped by the traditional cultural orientation toward patronage and personal charisma that was familiar to their fellow villagers.

In order to bring out the nature of the new leadership, it is necessary to look at the profiles of a few activists who were recruited into the peasant associations during the land reform. These individuals became township officials after the land reform campaigns and were later recruited into the party. For the next three decades they were the vital links between the villages and the state. Their interests, perceptions, and work styles greatly influenced the processes of rural transformation. It would be wrong to assume that they functioned as traditional village leaders. Their very emergence onto the rural scene was intimately tied to the party's class policies and revolutionary program. As later events show, even if fellow villagers expected them to behave like traditional leaders, and in fact pressured them to do so, the party did not intend to share power and would flex its political muscle to maintain control. The political middlemen were soon to become men in the middle.

Xu Decheng was a native of Dajiao Xiang, a community of a thousand inhabitants located near the county road that links Huicheng to Jiangmen. Xu's father rented a few mu of land from a landlord in Huicheng. He himself helped his father in the fields, collected river shrimp, and sold wild vegetables. He recalled that life before the Japanese was tolerable for the family. As the only son, he was sent to the village school for three years. His father could afford to pay the school a few baskets of grain. However, when the Japanese military occupied Huicheng and Jiangmen, Dajiao Xiang was caught in the path of the fighting. His father died, and two of his sisters died of starvation-related diseases. He sent another sister to work as a maid to a family in town and left for Guangzhou to work on odd jobs. His mother and a younger sister stayed in the village and survived on petty trading.

After the war Xu returned to Huicheng and worked in a grain store. When he lost the job in 1948, he became an apprentice in a paper-dyeing workshop in Jiangmen. He remembered watching the retreating KMT armies in late 1949. He returned to Dajiao in 1950 and joined the land reform work team in 1951. By this time the campaigns "to support Korea against American aggression" had begun. He and another young activist,

Zhou Yi, took over the propaganda and militia work in the township. With a touch of nostalgia he recalled how impressed he had been with the enthusiasm of student volunteers from Guangzhou, but he also remembered that fellow villagers were reluctant to speak out against local bosses for fear of revenge.

Huang Tao was among ten or so activists recruited by the work team that came to Chengnan Xiang in 1951. Huang's father was a handicraft worker in Huicheng, but the family lived in Chengnan Xiang on the south bank of the county capital. Like Xu Decheng, he also attended an old-style school for three years and did odd jobs to supplement the family income. During the Japanese occupation his father returned to the village to farm. From then until liberation, Huang and his brother worked the 10 mu of land that the family rented in Chengnan and Tianlu Xiang. In his spare time, he caught river shrimp for the markets in town. Not belonging to either of the two major lineages in Chengnan—that is, the Nie and the Li—he was quickly recruited by the land reform work team when it first arrived. In an interview in 1981, Huang recalled that

> when the work team came, its members sought out the very poor. There were cadres, teachers and students from Huicheng and Jiangmen. We even had a few students from Guangzhou. The team members stayed with us poor peasants. We worked in the fields and ate together. Then they asked us to describe the circumstances of each of the households in the village. They taught us the nature of class relationships—who worked for whom, how the harvests were shared, who was enjoying the fruits of our labor. They seemed moved when we described the bitterness [*ku*] in our lives. Then they suggested that we must act to "grasp power in our own hands" against feudal exploitation. They reassured us that the Communist party was serious in its desire to bring about a better life for the poor peasants. The students were so young and hopeful about the revolution. But they knew so little about our fear of the local bosses. When the team left the village, who could protect us from the bosses' revenge? Still, I admired their willingness to take on hardships with us.
>
> I introduced the team members to some other poor folks, and after a few secret meetings (because we were afraid that the local bosses would sabotage the team's efforts), we set up the "small group of poor peasants" [*pinnong xiaozu*]. There were ten of us. Rich peasants were excluded. Some middle peasants were invited to the meetings, but they were not given any posts. Sometimes, our meetings went on from night until daybreak. We were fearful and at the same time very excited. Life had been so bad that it was worth the risk. We all had the attitude of martyrs. Between liberation and land reform, the government kept the old village militia in order to maintain a minimum of order. Other activities were organized by a village association that was run by

old bosses. However, in mid-1950 the militia was disarmed. A new association took over and a core group of leaders [*zhuxi tuan*], composed of poor peasants like me, was set up. We were never elected by poor peasant representatives in the *xiang*. The work team just asked us to join in. Some of us had a few years of school, but the chairman of the *zhuxi tuan* could neither read nor write. It was 1951. I was given charge of the village militia. The party believed that it was important to maintain armed power to prevent sabotage by the former bosses. They never yielded voluntarily. Under the direction of cadres from the work team, we mobilized fellow peasants to attack them. We had to arrest a few big ones and shot them right in front of the masses before the poor gathered enough courage to speak out. The economic landlords had a much easier time, but they cheated a great deal by hiding their properties or transferring them to relatives in town. After the anti-bully campaign, more households joined us. It was difficult to be neutral. You were either for the land reform and the revolution, or you were the enemy. On looking back, of course we committed mistakes. We allowed relatives who were class enemies to join, and often enough the rhetoric that party cadres insisted upon scared away friends. After we fixed class statuses, we took a great deal from the landlords who resided mostly in Huicheng. We marched there to attend the mass meetings against them. The district office also sent me to attend mass meetings in the neighboring townships of Meijiang and Chengxiang. We were called land reform volunteers. When I was out of my village, I was given an allowance by the district association, and the Poor Peasants League arranged for laborers to help my family. At that time land was still rented, though the rent was much reduced. We finished fixing class statuses and immediately went about distributing the land. Then our work was reviewed in 1953. Soon afterward the township government was formed. I was appointed head of the township and drew a salary from the district office. The land reform work team had left then. During the land reform campaigns, we did not have party members in the village. It took us a while to find out who the party members were in the work teams. It was all a bit secretive because we could not tell who the enemies were either. After the review of the land reform in 1953, a Party Youth League was set up in the village and cadres persuaded me to join. I remember that our party branch was set up the same year as our first agricultural producers' cooperative. It was March 1955. Five of us joined.

A third man, Lin Qing (known as Uncle Lin) of Tianlu Xiang belonged to a different breed of peasant activist. When I interviewed him in 1981, he was fifty-three years old. He looked back on his thirty-year career with mixed feelings.

I am a native of Xian, a village in Tianlu Xiang. Before the revolution, it was dominated by powerful surnames. They had established ancestral halls and estates, but the Lins did not. When the Ye fought with the Chen of Tianma, we joined in. The Chen and the Japanese burnt our entire village. The Liang in Xining were as fierce as the Ye. They had the best polders. No outsider could rent them, not even people from Tianlu.

My father rented some land from the Ye. When I was nine, I attended the village school for two years, though half of the time I was taken out of school to help with family chores. I can read but I can hardly write. Few of us ever traveled out of the village for any extended period of time. When the Communists came, I was sought out. Xian had about six hundred villagers. I shared the work with another activist. We coordinated with those in other villages to set up a new peasant association in Tianlu. There were few hired hands in the association. Most of us were poor and lower middle peasants [*pin xia zhong nong*]. With the support from the work team, we took over the administration from the old village association. Actually, the chairman of the association was a poor peasant and a decent man, but the work team did not trust him. At the time of the land reform, many of the big local bosses had fled. We were able to single out a few small landlords and then distributed the land without much fanfare. We sought advice from the lineage elders [*fulao*] because many wealthy households had fled. Though the bosses were powerful, peasants had habitually gone to the elders to settle disputes. These elders had mediated in the feuds that tended to flare up between Tianlu and Tianma, as well as among their segments. The local bosses who stirred up trouble and invited destruction on the villages had committed such great moral crimes [*shang tian hai li*].

The students who came from the cities were full of enthusiasm. They tolerated a great deal of physical hardship. When I worked in the fields, I mixed tea with fried rice powder for lunch. The students ate with us. Nowadays, young people in our village bring soda and cakes and call this progress! After the village land was redistributed, I farmed my family's share. For two years I was not involved with mobilization work anymore. I was happy with what I was given, and I wanted to provide my family with a good livelihood. I joined a mutual aid team and worked very hard on the family plots. The party tried to convince me to join and be a cadre full time. I refused. You were freer if you were on your own. I did not have to go to any meetings. But I finally joined in 1956 when the district office sent a work team to the village to set up cooperatives.

When the local bosses were rounded up, publicly denounced, imprisoned, and shot, peasants in the Huancheng area were finally convinced that the reign of the military adventurers was over. What they were not sure about was the bosses' replacements. Social hierarchies were rapidly being redefined. Activists rose to prominence through peasant associations that assumed increasingly important functions. The activists got the anti-bully campaigns off the ground and also conducted village congresses to ratify decisions passed down from party superiors at the district office. The associations wielded unprecedented power over village life when they helped the land reform work teams determine class statuses. Every household was anxious to receive a good classification. The poor were grateful to them when granted recognition and promised a future. Affluent households, on the other hand, pleaded and bribed. The reorganization of social hierarchies made community life intensely volatile during these campaigns. When the land reform work teams finally left, an obvious question remained in everyone's mind: Were the activists and the peasant associations there to stay?

It seemed they were. Township governments were set up immediately afterward. The core members of the peasant associations were recruited into branches of the Party Youth League and became salaried cadres in 1954 when they joined the party. The district office assigned each township five salaried cadres, addressed with awe and skepticism by the peasants as the "five great leaders" (*wu da lingxiu*) in their villages. Those who were busy with official duties had former landlords and other disenfranchised elements farm their land. From activists to party cadres, the underclass in the villages of the Huancheng area got its first taste of bureaucratic power.

The emergence of the two types of activists on the rural landscape was no historical accident.[32] The Communist party, in its first major attempt to build a new political economy based on its goals, saw in the rural underclass a potential ally. Those who joined the party as activists and later as cadres were motivated by various socioeconomic circumstances. They used the language of class and revolution shrewdly in order to maneuver their way through the entrenched interests and cultural complexities of their communities. In the process, they established positions of power and changed the nature of their relationships with fellow villagers and the party-state. These activists were later referred to as the land reform cadres (*tugai ganbu*), as distinguished from later generations of cadres recruited during successive political campaigns. As I will show in later chapters, each generation of cadres had its unique background and was recruited according to the political needs of each stage of party-building. Each maintained political resources, work styles, and attitudes that distinguished them from later generations. The land reform campaigns marked the beginning of a long-term relationship between party and cadre. In the new political stage that was being set, the stance that the several generations of cadres adopted in relation to bureaucratic power colored subsequent developments, even if they did not determine their direction.

How Was Revolution Understood?

Revolution meant different things to different people. Immersed in the language of class, party intellectuals may have interpreted peasant support of the land reform campaigns as an expression of proletarian class sentiment, but the evidence points to other motives and concerns as well. It seems that the peasants joined the revolutionaries partly to obtain "yi tian, er niu, san poniang" (first, land; second, cattle; third, a wife). Apart from material goals, there were moral ones. Peasants' attitudes toward local bosses had been ambivalent. They could be effective patrons and protectors, though their predatory behavior represented a severe abuse of traditional legitimacy. The strong note of vengeance in the anti-bully campaigns deserves attention. It seems that peasants wanted blood debts paid in order to restore equilibrium. The Communists promised them the means and effectively delivered. With injustice avenged and with the promise of material benefits, peasants looked forward to a period of peace, order, and prosperity largely within the traditional frame of reference.

Could the circumstances of the early 1950s be considered the beginning of another dynastic cycle, with local leadership being seen as a new form officialdom in the popular mind? One could probably argue such a case, especially when the resilience of imperial traditions in rural society was repeatedly demonstrated by self-proclaimed emperors who attracted large followings.[33] However, the party's class policy did not conform to the traditional order for the peasants who had supported the revolution. Among the three major social affiliations interwoven in the lineage-dominated political economy in the delta—class, kin, and community—the land reform removed whatever class power remained in the hands of the estate managers, although kin and community loyalties were left undisturbed at the time. The military adventurers and their local representatives in the villages had also disappeared from the political scene. Local leadership increasingly relied on a new bureaucracy, a party-state attempting to exert direct control and to hold an ideological monopoly over all potential challengers. The rural underclass had emerged with political capital that was clearly linked to the dominance of the party. The two were becoming inseparable. The political reality in which these activists were now playing central roles gradually altered perceptions of power and authority among the rural populace.

Were Chinese peasants in the twentieth century passive spectators watching history unfold, or were they creative actors improvising on a turbulent political stage? They were both. Nostalgia for the imperial past, the language of vengeance, the feeling of moral indebtedness to political patrons, the opportunism of the "brave elements," and communal ex-clusiveness—all these popular attitudes continually surfaced and sub-merged in the peasants' relationship with the party. The process of getting to know each other took place against a background of moral dilemmas that made such contacts fitful and painful but seldom hopeless. These experiences shaped the peasants' new cultural and historical con-sciousness. Together, peasants and party cadres began unraveling the tra-ditional order that prior generations had created in the light of their own ambivalent choices.

The headquarters of Dongjia Brigade in 1978.

A river crossing on the way from Guangzhou to Xinhui in 1980; there were few private transport or travelers then.

The site of the daily market at Tianlu in 1980; marketing activities had not yet been revived.

The paper-making factory, Huancheng Commune. (1979)

A local brick kiln, Jiangzui Brigade. (1979)

Women working in a glass
tube–cutting factory, Dongjia
Brigade. (1978)

Women working in the fan palm factory, Huancheng Commune. (1979)

Women and children waiting outside the headquarters of the Sancun Brigade of
Tianma; the men were discussing production problems. (1981)

A family of Dan fishermen transporting goods on their boat, Tianma. (1982)

Collective grain drying in Meijiang Brigade. (1980)

Individual grain drying in Meijiang Brigade after production responsibilities had
been given to individual households. (1982)

CHAPTER 7

Losing Ground:
Community Cellularized

In the 1950s if a Guangdong peasant was asked where he came from, he gave the name of his village or township (*xiang*). In the 1980s, he would give the name of his brigade. Although the *xiang* and the brigade were one and the same physical entity, they had very different meanings for those who lived in them. What peasants identified as the *xiang* embodied long-established relationships governing settlement and land tenure rights, marketing networks, temple alliances with other communities, kin solidarities linked to higher-order ancestral halls in Huicheng, and political affiliations with town notables in public bureaus and academies who had come from the villages. The brigade, on the other hand, embodied few of the above ties. Instead it was a unit to which peasants were confined by a system of household registration enforced by the state and backed by a rationing system. The resources of the brigade became the dominant if not the sole source of livelihood. Its management policy was shaped by procurement quotas and state prices and the priorities of rural cadres who had been drawn into the political whirlpool of a national party bureaucracy.

After the land reform, the managers of the town-based ancestral trusts dropped out of sight, as did the local bosses linked to the military regimes of the Republican decades. Village economies in the 1950s continued to be connected to institutions in Huicheng, but the latter no longer consisted of the wholesale enterprises and their credit networks, nor was arbitration conducted in the guilds and the academies. Instead, villagers came into contact with the department of commerce and its various corporations, the food grain bureau, the pricing bureau, the state banks, and the county planning committees. Former leaders among town merchants who chose to work with the new government became members of the Industry-Commerce League (Gongshang Lian), an organization formed in the early 1950s under the supervision of the party committee of the county. Community, a principle of social affiliation left undisturbed in the land reform, became the major target of transformation under the socialist program of the party from then on. The process of redefining the central social institutions and town-based relationships of the village lasted for the next three decades. It involved much more than the substitution of one set of labels for another.

Administrative Changes

To facilitate the various political campaigns aimed at transforming the rural economy, the new government made many administrative changes at the subcounty level. In 1951, the First District in the county consisted of sixteen townships, with district headquarters in Sanjiang. In the autumn of 1952, when the land reform was in progress, the First District was split into two. The southeastern part merged with other townships centering on Sanjiang and remained the First District, but the area covered by today's Huancheng merged with the Upper Xianxian Xiang of the Second District to become a new Tenth District, consisting of eleven small townships.

In 1953, many of the districts in the county were given the status of market-town (*zhen*) government. However, in an effort to centralize the administration of the collectivization campaigns, the county government, which was renamed the County People's Committee in 1955, abolished these market-town governments and turned them into district offices (*qu gongsuo*, an executive branch of the county committee). During that time, the then Huancheng District Office incorporated three more small townships in the periurban area of Huicheng as well as the Wuhuan Xiang, which was separated from Shenhuan Xiang in the southeast. Following the campaigns to collectivize the rural economy, administrative centralization continued. From 1956 to 1958, the small townships in the Huancheng District merged into five enlarged townships (*da xiang*) and then into two: the Huancheng and the Sanhe Da Xiang.[1]

Despite the administrative changes, the *xiang* remained active sociopolitical units. In the Huancheng area, there were fifteen such units in the mid-1950s, as shown in figure 7.1. This was where the party-state set up its lowest level of political organization. At the time of the land reform campaigns, a peasant association with a core of political activists was organized at every *xiang*.[2] After the review of the land reform in 1953, *xiang*-level governments were established. Under the direction of the district office, they became the key units for policy transmission in agricultural production, trading and credit, tax collection, household registration, and public security. Peasant activists were recruited into the Party Youth League and then into the party itself once a local branch was established. They monopolized the salaried posts of township head, deputy head, staff members for civil affairs, accountant, and militia captain. The

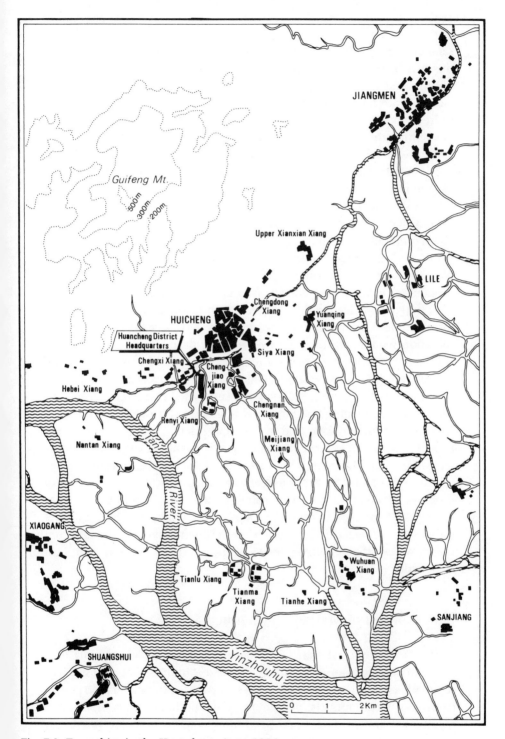

Fig. 7.1. Townships in the Huancheng Area, 1956

salaries were small, ranging from 5 to 25 yuan. According to Chen Mingfa, this was because their families had been allocated land during the land reform, and former landlords had been "assigned" to help the cadres' families with farm work while the cadres attended to political tasks. The cadres' work was overwhelming at the time, as the responsibility for implementing the next stage of party policies—the collectivization of agriculture—rested upon their shoulders.

The bureaucratization of the *xiang* took place in the context of the party's plan to transform the national economy into a socialist one. Steps were taken soon after the land reform to nationalize industries and handicrafts; to control commerce by the unified procurement of grain and other principal commodities; to implement a system of planned production targets, prices, and rationing; and to collectivize agriculture. The first three goals aimed at bringing the rural sector within a centrally planned national economy; the last was to change its internal organization.

Although party leaders differed over the form and pace of socialist transformation in the Chinese countryside,[3] they generally agreed that collectivization would help the state oversee agricultural production and that collective units led by party cadres would be more manageable than households each having its own economic strategies, social networks, and political priorities. A well-planned and supervised rural sector would allow the government to build up a stable urban industrial sector sheltered from fluctuations in food and agricultural prices. Logically, this would benefit the rural areas as well.[4] To evaluate the dynamics of socialist transformation in the Huancheng area, a brief description of its larger economic structure is necessary. Peasants perceived this structure as a source of economic benefits as well as constraints. It determined their strategies during the campaigns to establish cooperatives and later collectives. How the peasants interacted with the broader economic system through rural cadres reveals their changing views of the nature of the state and local leadership.

State Control of Marketing Channels

In March 1950, the national government established the Ministry of Commerce to oversee commodity prices and trade.[5] By 1951, the ministry had set up fifteen national corporations to supervise the trading of food grains, cloth, salt, local products, petroleum, coal, and industrial equipment. It maintained branch offices and purchasing stations from the provincial down to the subcounty levels, a complex that represented the state commercial sector, and it was supported by a network of supply and marketing cooperatives (*gongxiao she*) administered by a national bureau. The number of these cooperatives grew from 22,817 units in 1949 to 35,096 units by the end of 1952. In 1952, the cooperative network was responsible for 49.7 percent of the state's purchases of grain, 79.9 percent of its purchases of cotton, and large percentages of its purchase of jute, wool, tobacco, and silk cocoons (Shangyebu 1984, 8).

In using the cooperatives to facilitate a rural-urban exchange, the government was explicit in its political goals. An editorial in *Renmin ribao* stated:

> Cooperative business maintains an important position and function in our national economy. . . . Cooperatives operate more than 132,000 retail stores and over 35,000 mobile trading stations in the country. . . . The volume of production material they circulated has increased 30 times from 1950 to 1953. . . . They reinforce and expand the leadership of the socialist economy, dwarf the influence of private commerce in the rural areas, promote cooperative activities, and reinforce the peasant-worker alliance. . . . In other words, the work of the cooperatives is economic as well as political.[6]

The state played an important part in the operations of these supply and marketing cooperatives. A survey reported by *Renmin zhoubao* (Zhongyang Weiyuanhui Shejikaohe Weiyuanhui 1953, 52) showed that 23 percent of their capital was put up by members, 19 percent by the government, and the rest was borrowed from state banks. They bought agricultural products from the peasants on credit and repaid them with commodities produced in the increasing number of nationalized industries. By being able to secure favorable terms from state enterprises, they gained a distinct competitive edge over private entrepreneurs.[7]

Private traders tried to compete by offering grain producers prices up to 20 percent higher than the state's. The government countered their efforts with political maneuvers: charged with illegal price manipulations, the merchants were often arrested and fined, and their goods were confiscated.[8] Private interests were further suppressed in 1952 by the "Three Anti" and "Five Anti" campaigns, which attacked alleged corruption and associated misdeeds in the urban sector. Besieged in this way, private commerce rapidly diminished. In wholesale trade, the volume of business conducted by state enterprises increased from 23.2 percent in 1950 to 71.5 in 1957, whereas that of private enterprises dropped from 76.1 to 0.1 percent in the same period. For retail trade, the state sector increased from 6.9 percent in 1950 to 37.2 percent in 1957 and 90 percent in 1978. The private sector started with 88.3 percent of retail trade in 1950 and ended with 6 percent in 1957 and 2.1 percent in 1978 (Shangyebu 1984, 40, 484). The historically commercialized rural economy of Guangdong felt the pressures of state control very deeply because the leading provincial cadre, Tao Zhu, was adamant in collectivizing the private sector along the political lines laid down by the national government. In a speech made in 1953 to provincial delegates, he warned that the state sector in Guangdong constituted only 30 percent of the total wholesale trade and 40 percent of the industries. In his view, the proportions must be reversed (Tao 1953). In Huicheng and Jiangmen, the socialist transformation of private commerce and industries got underway after the "Three Anti" and "Five Anti" campaigns. The former County Chamber of Commerce was replaced by the Committee for the Industry-Commerce League after July 1950. Leading merchants were invited to join, though some declined. According to He Zhuojian,[9] the measures leading to the fusion of state and private interests were harsh. Tax officers who audited private enterprises demanded enormous back payments. The tax burdens and the competition from state enterprises caused many private operations to close down. He Zhuojian's own publishing shop was forced to sell a large amount of printing equipment at extremely low prices in order to pay the taxes imposed (He 1986, 45).

The county government stepped up the collectivization of private enterprises at the end of 1955. He Zhuojian and Li Hong, the secretary of the committee of the Industry-Commerce League in Huicheng who was also a party cadre, attended the provincial conference of Industry-Commerce Leagues. Upon their return, a county-level conference was convened in January 1956. Representatives, who consisted of 160 members of the work team for the socialist transformation of private enterprises, elected an executive committee for the league. The transformation process was officially inaugurated with parades and festivities in Huicheng, where every shop was given a large "double happiness" sign to be hung out front. Statistics compiled in December 1956 show that 688 private entrepreneurs with a total capital of 800,000 yuan, were socialized (He 1986, 49–51). Of this number, 505 members, with a total capital of 640,000 yuan, were located in Huicheng. Thirty-eight private industrial enterprises with 162 shareholders and a capital of 468,848 yuan were transformed into eight joint enterprises with the state.[10] This figure did not include a printing factory, a wine-making factory, and a tobacco factory with 27 shareholders and a capital of 27,595 yuan, for these had merged with state factories earlier in the year. In addition, 168 commercial enterprises with 343 shareholders and a total capital of 171,788 yuan were transformed into thirteen joint enterprises with the state.

Almost simultaneously, handicrafts in Huicheng and the surrounding rural areas were collectivized. My interviews with Master Zhang, the carpenter from Xiaogang Xiang, revealed part of the picture. In 1951, he returned to Huicheng to work for his old employer, Li Qi, earning a monthly wage of 28 yuan. At the time there were two types of unions. The workers were urged by the new government to join the handicraft workers' union. The other union was a league of employers who negotiated the terms of business with government cadres involved with the management of these enterprises. This was a time of transition, when the enterprises were jointly owned by the state and private interests. The cooperativization of handicrafts started in 1953 when Master Zhang joined four others to form a mutual aid team. In November of the same year, a friend who had become a cadre in Huicheng convinced the team he was with to join a wooden tools cooperative whose headquarters were on the street bordering the southern bank of Huicheng. Its twenty members distributed 75 percent of its net income based on the shares held by each member, and used the rest to acquire machines for collective use. The high tide of collectivization came in 1956. Master Zhang's cooperative, which specialized in manufacturing wooden buckets, joined a larger cooperative consisting of makers of furniture, small boats, and agricultural tools. The 110 members were grouped into four factories: the Sanhe Agricultural Tools Factory (in Tianma Xiang), the Chengdong Agricultural Tools Factory (near Huicheng), the Huicheng Furniture Factory, and the County Number Two Light Industry Agricultural Tools Factory.

The process of collectivization was not without its problems. Most of the members felt that their work schedules and autonomy were unnecessarily restricted. Profits were locked into the collective. Those who had run their own businesses resisted collectivization in various ways. Two of Master Zhang's distant relatives, owners of the Zhang Brothers Enterprises, had a particularly hard time. He sadly remembered a younger brother who killed himself, unable to face pressure from the cadres. His widow survived by remarrying, but had to give away her son. The older brother reluctantly joined and drew a monthly income of 60 yuan. The brother of Master Zhang's old employer joined the cooperative with a capital of 4,000 yuan. It was not until the late 1970s that his capital and the interest accrued were returned to him. The workers who joined were not always in agreement. Conflicts arose over the evaluation of wages. The older workers demanded higher wages because of their greater experience, while younger ones claimed more because of their greater speed and efficiency. It was not uncommon, according to Master Zhang, for people to come to blows in the meetings.

All in all, the shrinking of private enterprises in town had a serious impact on the village economies. It meant that peasants had to rely more and more on state agents. With few competitors, the state was able to impose its policies.

State Procurement of Grain

Nationally, the unified purchase of grain by state agents largely eliminated private trading by November 1953. Peasants were required to sell fixed quotas of grain at official prices. After meeting the procurement quotas, they were then allowed to sell at state-supervised grain markets. Private grain merchants and grain mills were to conduct business only with state agencies. Similar policies were extended to the trading of vegetable oil and raw cotton in 1954. From time to time, the compulsory grain purchases generated fear and confusion. As described in retrospect by a Chinese study (Shangyebu 1984, 56), the government was ill prepared to set up a realistic system for the unified procurement of grain based on estimates of individual production. It set guideline quotas subject to negotiations, but peasants were unsure how much grain the government intended to procure. Many feared that the more they produced, the more they would be compelled to sell. In 1954, when natural disasters caused crop failures, the government took 7 billion catties beyond what would have been realistic adjustments, thus drastically shrinking peasant reserves. The study acknowledges that anxiety over grain procurement stirred unrest in the rural areas.

To reduce peasant anxiety, the government in August 1955 implemented the "three fixed" (san ding) policy. Each grain production unit, whether an individual household or a cooperative, was assessed for how much grain it produced, how much it needed to consume, and how much it had to sell to the state. The fixed amounts of procurement were guaranteed for three years.[11]

Grain procurement was particularly worrisome in the Pearl River delta, which had historically relied on grain imports because of its highly valued production of cash crops. A large and inflexible procurement quota meant that there was even less grain reserved for an extremely dense population. If more land was used to grow grain, the cash crops that yielded higher returns for the peasants suffered. Despite these widespread concerns, the provincial government remained inflexible, as indicated by the speech of Tao Zhu in 1953. He insisted that Guangdong not only be self-sufficient in grain but that it also reserve a portion of its grain for national allocation. Production targets for the five-year plan aimed at a 35 percent increase over the 1952 record (Tao 1953, 14–15). Another document of the Guangdong Provincial Government in the same year carried a threatening tone: "If the failure to fulfill the government's increased production quotas is due to tardiness and a disregard for government planning, [households] will be obliged to sell the fixed amount of grain to the state all the same."[12] The uncompromising policies of grain procurement hurt particularly those counties that specialized in cash crops. In Xinhui the problem was serious enough to be put on the agenda for discussion at the first plenary session of the People's Political Consultative Conference organized by the Xinhui County Committee in November 1956 by a leading party official, Dang Xiangmin. He acknowledged that the county had overemphasized grain production, thus hurting both the crops and the subsidiary activities.[13] Table 7.1 does not show an increase in the acreage allocated to grain production, but because fertilizers and labor were concentrated on grain crops, cash crops that needed sustained care suffered. These factors, coupled with the growers' loss of incentive due to the restrictions in marketing, caused substantial drops in the county's citrus crop: 17.6 percent from 1954 to 1955 and another 34.4 percent in the following year. In 1957, only 146,621 picul were harvested, indicating another drop of 53.9 percent.[14]

Furthermore, state purchasing stations generated serious bureaucratic problems. A document from Xinhui County confirms this observation with some sobering facts:

> The county has 23 grain offices, 78 local stations, 151 storage houses of varying sizes with a storage capacity of 120,000,000 catties. There are also 23 state and collective workshops for processing grain, and 428 cadres . . . who are responsible for procuring grain from the county's 500 agricultural collectives and for supplying grain to the 80,000 residents. . . .
>
> Previously we were not clear on how to make grain procurement serve agriculture. We were bogged down by technical difficulties that were adverse to production. For example, peasants had to queue to sell their grain. For each picul, they went through seven barriers: registration, queuing up, grain inspection, filling out inspection forms, weighing, accounting, and payment. The process involved a seven-to-eight-hour wait. The impatient ones dropped off their load and went to the teahouses instead. Women and the elderly crowded at the door with crying children. Some peasant masses needed money from the grain sales for their children's medical fees. Yet after a whole day's wait, not only did they not get the money for the doctors, but also they had to endure sun and rain. The negative effect on labor and time was more serious.

Table 7.1. Grain and Citrus Production, Xinhui County, 1949–82

Year	Rice (Double-Cropping) Area (Mu)	Yield per Mu (Catties)	Citrus (Planted Area)	Citrus (Harvested Area)	Total Citrus Yield (Picul)
1949	—	—	28,839	16,338	253,309
1950	—	—	33,823	16,510	264,820
1951	—	—	39,308	22,792	265,376
1952	—	—	39,993	26,194	335,275
1953	—	—	40,764	31,939	411,415
1954	699,125	581	38,793	32,258	589,39C
1955	691,845	610	36,513	32,223	485,529
1956	682,433	658	41,460	34,227	318,430
1957	666,223	658	32,542	23,219	146,621
1958	614,809	811	35,067	13,543	53,755
1959	606,790	788	29,519	7,707	10,531
1960	605,835	735	30,814	10,500	20,913
1961	644,012	702	24,881	13,325	38,486
1962	654,351	754	17,627	9,631	12,835
1963	631,996	956	13,589	8,220	32,589
1964	627,974	795	23,065	6,391	9,957
1965	622,459	902	31,692	5,771	19,192
1966	624,666	976	33,619	11,324	32,009
1967	673,929	973	32,030	22,184	86,746
1968	629,242	958	30,376	22,732	135,615
1969	650,520	950	25,890	20,379	148,408
1970	657,132	912	22,065	16,728	142,197
1971	658,892	964	20,504	12,719	115,465
1972	643,497	895	20,007	7,306	54,376
1973	634,457	886	19,417	5,102	26,787
1974	645,148	1,032	17,191	5,102	16,993
1975	644,750	874	16,591	4,187	7,400
1976	642,652	884	15,535	4,303	8,483
1977	612,113	1,145	15,137	6,073	38,150
1978	611,266	931	16,327	5,709	36,056
1979	604,636	1,044	17,134	5,376	28,011
1980	596,230	1,186	17,559	—	51,995
1981	556,310	973	—	—	—
1982	544,860	1,170	—	—	—

Source: Xinhui xian nongye quhua baogaoji, compiled by Xinhui Xian Nongye Quhua Bangongshi, 1983, 292 and table 5.

If one estimates that to sell a picul of grain takes half an hour, then for the county to procure the yearly 240,000,000 picul, it would need 120,000,000 hours, equivalent to 1,200,000 labor days. . . . In sum, slow procedures for procurement and storage damage summer planting and winter ploughing. The masses complained, saying that the cadres at the grain offices were "granary mice." . . . The party committee was also critical. Our cadres are in fact working very hard day and night but are blamed unnecessarily. Cadres in the grain office therefore do not see a future in their work, saying that they were at the bottom of the hierarchy; that if they do their best, they end up in the hospital; if they make an error, they end up in the courts. . . ."[15]

Restrictions on Cash Crops

The pressure of grain quotas indirectly affected the production of cash crops. In 1954 tensions were compounded when marketing restrictions were directly imposed on a variety of such crops. The national government divided agricultural products into three categories. The first consisted of those under the state's program of unified purchases and sales. Products in the second category could not be sold in rural markets until state purchases had been made. Even then prices were regulated, and long-distance trade required official approval. The third category encompassed local specialties that could be traded freely in rural markets. Private trading restrictions and low prices set by the government caused some local products to virtually disappear from rural markets. There were shortages and overstocking. In the plenary session of the People's Political Consultative Conference of November 1956, another leading county cadre, Chen Jiangtian, admitted these problems. He stressed the point that in light of Xinhui's commercialized economy, state policies and their implementation had not been realistic. He claimed that peasants were unwilling to produce because prices were too low, causing shortages, but stated that bureaucratic bottlenecks in procurement also wasted perishable commodities. He noted that at one point watermelon and winter melon had both been in short supply in Huicheng, while the melon crops in the rural hinterland were rotting because of collection delays by the local agencies. As a result peasants suffered considerable losses and city supplies were very tight. Chen also admitted that the price of pigs had been set too low and that he had drawn criticism from pig farmers.[16]

Fifty percent of Huancheng's land was devoted to cash crops, the most important of these being citrus and fan palm. As described in chapter 2, fan palm production and marketing had been channeled through the Fan

Palm Guild, whereas with citrus these processes were far less centralized. Wholesale fruit merchants in Jiangmen and Huicheng had relied on peddlers from Chengnan and Dongjia Xiang to collect citrus from peasant households, each of whom produced a small amount. When supply and marketing cooperatives were set up in the villages in 1952, they took over most of the buying. At the time the farmers could still sell to private traders or to one another in rural markets. However, between 1954 and July 1956, citrus was placed in the second category of agricultural produce in the government scheme. Sales through private channels were discouraged until state quotas were met. Villagers in Dongjia Xiang recalled that in 1954 angry growers staged a demonstration in Jiangmen against the alleged corruption of state agents. The harvest had been good that year, and government agents were very selective. When agents came to the villages to buy from particular orchards, farmers who were left out and could not sell elsewhere protested strongly.

A survey of county and provincial papers reveals that official policies fluctuated sharply in the mid-1950s. On the one hand, the government did try to relax marketing restrictions for local cash crops because there were serious shortages in daily vegetables. An article in *Xinhui nongmin bao* (October 28, 1956) reported that trade revived after a relaxation of policy in July. Items such as barley, beans, peas, melons, ginger, garlic, sesame seeds, eggs, piglets, and young poultry reappeared in the rural markets. On the other hand, official pronouncements repeatedly stressed that relaxation applied only to local agricultural specialties and warned against private trading. In November of the same year, the county government published a directive, specifying in minute detail the various categories of agricultural products under state control.[17] It was followed by another directive from the provincial government, urging stronger regulation of free markets and stressing the lack of leadership in rural marketing.[18]

The fluctuations in policy did not occur simply in response to changes in the local situation; they reflected fierce debates among the nation's top economists and political leaders[19] and expressed the tensions involved in imposing central planning on a society of small producers and private traders. Policy fluctuations became a problem in themselves in the eyes of the peasants, who refrained from producing crops that required large capital investments and long-term commitments. The changing pattern of citrus production provides a good illustration of the problem. Except for 1953, which represented the peak of recovery, citrus production continued to fall despite some efforts in the mid-1960s to revive it. By 1980, only 17,559 mu of orchards were left. Citrus production in Xinhui demonstrated the difficulties confronting rural communities in relation to the state. In contrast to the situation in the following decades, agricultural production and marketing in the mid-1950s continued to mix private, collective, and state interests, allowing some room for maneuver. But by the mid-1970s, rural communities had little choice left. (I will return to the near extinction of citrus production in the Huancheng area in chapter 10.) It seems that when the pressure for more grain procurement increased in the 1970s, government agencies were also able to monopolize institutional channels to impose their priorities on the local economies. Both cadres and peasants complained bitterly about the loss of income and autonomy, but the question remains as to why they were not able to resist state impositions. To address this question, we must turn to the internal transformation of the villages themselves.

Collectivizing Agriculture

Just as macroeconomic structures were being changed by the decline of private commerce and by the imposition of quotas and prices by the state, the organization of agriculture at the village level underwent a rapid transformation that led to the rise of a new stratum of managers. As with the land reform programs, the collectivization of agriculture was not new to the regime; party leaders in the Yanan era had systematically experimented with it.[20] Depending on when the land reform campaigns ended, different forms of collectivization were introduced on a trial basis as early as 1951.[21] Party leaders were cautious, as is indicted by a document of the Central Committee of the CCP dated December 1953, which decreed that, from the winter of 1953 to the following autumn, the number of agricultural producers' cooperatives (APCS) was to increase from 14,000 to 35,000. The entire country was divided into regions practicing varying degrees of collectivization. By 1957, about 20 percent of peasant households belonged either to a mutual aid team or to a cooperative.[22]

In Guangdong, Tao Zhu proclaimed the completion of land reform in 1953 and directed the cadres to turn their attention to agricultural production. Their major task was to convince peasants to embrace collective agriculture. In the initial stages, mutual aid teams (MATS) and lower-level agricultural producers' cooperatives were to be promoted. The process would not be easy for either masses or cadres, he warned. Private entrepreneurship was strong among peasants and cadres, and there was little experience in managing cooperatives to draw from. Tao Zhu suggested that cadres should start with seasonal mutual aid teams on a large scale.

These would then be stabilized into year-long arrangements. Only if conditions allowed were cooperatives to be tried (Tao 1953, 10–13).

Collectivization in the Huancheng Area

Once the directives had reached the county level of administration, the party committee leaned heavily on rural activists and on the district and township cadres to launch the programs. As the land reform drew to a close in 1953, villagers in the Huancheng area were settling down to their family plots, but the newly recruited cadres had already been instructed to lead the movement of organizing mutual aid teams and agricultural producers' cooperatives by personal example.

The twenty-year-old Chen Mingfa formed the first MAT in Meijiang Xiang with a few relatives and friends. He was a member of the Party Youth League and the head of the community of two thousand, all surnamed Chen. He also helped activists from small villages within Meijiang to form their own MATS. Chen Mingfa was regarded as a sincere and competent man. He was articulate and was known among his peers as "the peasant theorist." He had a few years of village education and had also lived with his uncle in Hong Kong. His worldliness inspired a degree of respect from fellow activists. The Party Youth League relied on him to do propaganda work. Among his helpers were a farmer named Chen Mingzhi and a young farmer, Chen Sheyuan, who knew simple accounting and was the deputy leader of the Party Youth League in Meijiang. All of them had been active during the land reform campaigns.

Apart from organizing mutual aid teams, they experimented with a unit known to them as *mai chan zu*. These units were small, comprising ten or so households. Members pooled their rice fields and cultivated them together. The group leader kept an account of income and expenses. After the harvest, he paid the taxes, sold the crop to the state agents, subtracted other expenses, and distributed the rest to the member households. Thirty percent of the income was distributed based on labor contributions; the rest was allotted according to land contributions. The group's orchards and palm fields were not pooled; each household worked on its own and bore the expenses involved. Since they received seasonal help from other group members, individual households kept 70 percent of the harvest and pooled the rest into collective income. Conflicts did arise, especially when members of the group decided to concentrate on their own palm fields and orchards rather than on the rice fields. However, group members were often close relatives and differences were dealt with as "family squabbles."

When asked whether he thought concerns of kin had contaminated what the party upheld as socialist relationships of production, Mingfa justified the arrangement by saying that land reform had eliminated the exploitative aspects of kinship embodied in corporate estates and that kinsmen could therefore collaborate on more equal terms. Technically speaking, the Chens in Meijiang were all agnates, he recalled: how could they not form cooperatives in association with one another? After all, they were tied to the land they had acquired in the community and to the taxes and quotas that came with it.

The first two lower APCs in Chengnan Xiang were organized in March 1955, and, as in Meijiang, they consisted of agnates. The thirty-three households of the Number One Cooperative came from the Nie lineage, and the thirty-two households of the Number Two Cooperative came from the Li lineage. It was a proud occasion for the local activists, because party cadres from the district office came to attend the ceremonies. Huang Tao, the township's deputy head, was somewhat embarrassed by these events. Only months before, he and fellow activists had learned that the county wanted to organize cooperatives. They had immediately mobilized the poor peasants in their village. However, the district party cadres were just beginning to monitor the progress of trial cooperatives in the neighboring township of Dongjia and were surprised by the hasty actions of their subordinates. Huang was subsequently chastised by his superiors for having committed "adventurism." However, past mistakes were soon forgiven. The party branch in the township was formed at the same time as the cooperative, and despite their mistakes, Huang Tao and four other activists were sworn in as the first group of party members. There were middle peasants in the Party Youth League, but only poor peasants were allowed to be party members. Huang Tao was considered poor enough, and possessed the added advantage of belonging to neither of the two dominant surname groups. The same applied to another deputy head of the township, Wu Zong. The two cooperatives, however, were headed by their own kinsmen, and Huang had made sure that the leaders were of poor peasant backgrounds. Like Chen Mingfa, he held that kinship and cooperatives did not contradict each other. His party superiors wanted cooperatives that were successful. "If kin groups worked better, so be it, so long as the richer members did not exploit the labor of others."

Around the same time that Huang Tao organized Chengnan's cooperatives, Chen Mingzhi and Chen Sheyuan set up the first APC in Meijiang Xiang. It consisted of forty households subdivided into production teams of ten to twelve households. Members held shares whose value was based on their contributions in land, tools, and labor. Each household had very different resources, because during the land reform every person was allocated land according to a per capita estimate of what the township "owned." In Meijiang, an adult was entitled to a value equivalent to 1,300 catties of grain, which meant that he could select land whose annual yield was valued at this amount. Peasant household often chose a combination of rice fields, palm fields, and fruit orchards. Chengnan Xiang had fewer resources than Meijiang, so the per capita distribution was set at 1,100 catties. Nevertheless, a villager in Chengnan estimated that during the mid-1950s, a family of four or five could comfortably earn 500 yuan from the palm fields, 200 yuan from a few mu of rice, another 100 from citrus fruit, and some additional income from forty or so lychee trees on the dikes.

The larger cooperatives were subdivided into work teams. As the leaders in Meijiang Xiang, Chen Mingzhi and Chen Sheyuan consulted with team leaders to set production plans, saw to the payment of taxes, and negotiated the sale of their crops to state agents.

Enthusiasm for cooperatives varied. Ironically, reluctance was frequently greatest among households classified as poor peasants, who had been given the opportunity to choose the best land and tools. Those with strong laborers among them were particularly reluctant to join the cooperatives. They were protective of their newfound resources and eager to make it on their own. Those who were persuaded to join bickered over remuneration standards for the properties they pooled. Cadres found it difficult to balance conflicting interests among friends and relatives.[23] Chen Sheyuan recalled that his cooperative was given discounts to buy tools, seeds, and fertilizers by the supply and marketing cooperatives, and that the credit cooperative promised interest-free loans. However, these advantages were not attractive enough to households who had flexible alternatives. It was clear to villagers at the time that being on good terms with cadres was useful but not essential. Peasants who chose not to join the cooperatives could rely on friends and relatives for credit and were able to purchase the major production items they needed in the rural markets. So long as they paid their taxes and delivered quotas to state agents, they were generally left in peace. If they complained about government-imposed prices, so did members of cooperatives.

At times, it seemed better to stay away from the government bureaucracy. Cooperatives with cadre members were obliged to set a good political example, even if it was not in their best economic interest. Chen Sheyuan admitted that he and fellow activists were under pressure from superiors to follow the party line closely. Not only did work teams from the county visit them periodically, but they were also recruited into these teams to participate in campaigns in other communities. The party committee of the county organized training classes before every mobilization and followed them up with review sessions afterward.[24]

However much the cadres were involved with the political goals of the national and regional party organization, they had to deal with social relations and sentiments in their local circles. Reluctant relatives, for example, could be embarrassing. Chen Sheyuan's uncle was pressured to join his nephew's cooperative but withdrew three times. The stubborn old man was a poor peasant who had obtained 3 mu of palm fields, 6 mu of orchards, and 1 mu of rice. With a household of seven, he decided to make it on his own. At the urging of his nephew, he reluctantly joined the cooperative but immediately backed out, claiming that the cooperative had set the value of his land too low. He eventually rejoined but quit a second time over the members' estimate of the value of his labor. Having joined for the third time, he quit again after disagreeing with the cooperative over the value of a boat he had sold to them. "I was a laughingstock among skeptical villagers," complained Chen Sheyuan, "because I could not even convince my own uncle."

Peasant households in Tianlu Xiang were even less enthusiastic, as indicated by the fact that at the end of 1955 there were only three cooperatives (out of a total of 942 households in the township). However, during the course of 1956, when the rest of the county was being mobilized for the formation of the higher agricultural producers' cooperatives, local cadres hastily turned the seven villages into eight cooperatives.[25] Although they were vulnerable to political pressure from party superiors, the cadres retained a degree of freedom in implementing national policies. Very often personal grudges overrode political prudence. A middle peasant in Tianlu Xiang, for example, had refused to join a cooperative when invited. After a typhoon broke a dike and flooded out his fish pond, he decided to join. However, the cadres wanted "to teach him a lesson" and refused his request. Chen Mingzhi and Meijiang recalled that the way they would treat a recalcitrant villager was "to give him an unworkable piece of land stuck in a far corner, and to let him scramble back to the cooperative after a year of ordeal." Despite evidence of ambivalence and conflict among both peasants and cadres, joining the cooperatives remained largely voluntary in the Huancheng area. Personal ties among members were strong and were often used to exert pressure to join. Moreover, to be attached to the state sector was not without its advantages, and people generally stayed with the cooperatives unless economic circumstances were really stacked against membership. Among elderly villagers who looked back to those "comfortable and hopeful days" I detected a strong element of nostalgia.

The High Tide of Socialism

When Mao Zedong launched the "high tide of socialism" in 1956 and pushed the country toward the formation of collectives, also known as higher agricultural producers' cooperatives, the political and economic environment of the peasant producers changed drastically. Model rules for the collectives were laid out by the National People's Congress on June 30, 1956. By November of that year, the party committee in Xinhui County declared they had "thoroughly implemented the socialist transformation of agriculture" and that 99 percent of the peasant households (140,294 in number) had joined the collectives (*Xinhui nongmin bao*, November 4, 1956). In a little less than four months, the 1,210 mutual aid teams and cooperatives in the county were upgraded and restructured. The 925 cooperatives were reorganized into 534 collectives. Only eleven units had fewer than 50 households. Three hundred and seven units consisted of between 100 to 300 households; seven units had over 950 households each; and there were twenty-four cases where an entire township became a collective (*Xinhui nongmin bao*, November 4, 1956). The Huancheng District (*qu*) had 90 cooperatives by about mid-1956. Trial collectives had been operating since March 1956, and the rest were converted by December.[26]

Reaction among peasants and cadres varied. In March 1956, the county newspaper reported that ten trial collectives and eight cooperatives in the Huancheng area had joined a county-wide competition to increase yields. Out of the eighteen units, twelve were from the periurban area. In Mei-jiang Xiang, several hundred households were organized into a single collective, which was subdivided into four production teams. Each team was allocated land and production resources, and had to deliver grain and cash crops to the collective according to set quotas. A complicated system of duties and remuneration regulated the tasks of tending the rice fields, cultivating the cash crops, and other subsidiary activities. Production tasks were assigned work-points. Team members who finished their tasks to the required standard earned the work-points. Palm fields and citrus orchards were allocated to team members who promised to provide an agreed amount of produce in return. Whatever was harvested above and beyond that amount belonged either to the individual or to the work group. After delivering taxes and fulfilling state quotas, the collective's net income was distributed according to the work-points accumulated by each laborer. Households that used to draw income from their contributions of property bickered with those who had strong laborers. Work assignments were challenged and the responsibilities disputed. It was not easy for the rural cadres, as Chen Sheyuan recalled:

It was awful. All households were made to join the collective like a swarm of buzzing bees. There was no prior experimental model or experience. Work teams made up of provincial and prefectural cadres came to supervise us. We had to deliver. We cadres spent everyday calculating work-points for bickering households. We hardly ever saw the fields or the crops. The only saving grace was that we were still concerned with production. (Chen Sheyuan, interview with author, summer 1983)

However, there was a clear element of political self-interest behind the cadres' enthusiasm for production. Meijiang Xiang was cited in the county paper for having "volunteered" a hundred members to help Chakeng and Dadong Xiang during spring planting, thus displaying a spirit of cooperation (*Xinhui nongmin bao*, April 25, 1956). The Number Two Collective in Xianxian Xiang mobilized its members to change the customary *zhenggao* method of rice growing (in which a second crop was sandwiched in between the rows of the first planting twenty days after the transplanting of the first crop) to two full crops, which involved turning over the soil in between the crops. The peasants had to be convinced that, with the larger collectives, enough labor could be mobilized to overcome seasonal constraints and to work the rice fields in a more intensive manner (*Xinhui nongmin bao*, December 25, 1956).

Sometimes ideology was used to further entrenched communal interests. Mobilized to improve irrigation systems, the three periurban collectives of Chengxiang, Duhui, and Qibang dismantled a paved road belonging to Dongjia Collective and appropriated the stone slabs for a floodgate. The water it blocked off damaged some fields in Dongjia and the neighboring Dajiao Collective. One evening members of Dongjia Collective broke down the floodgate. Conflicts flared up among members of the five units. Old community disputes were resurrected in the quarrels, which were complicated by new administrative boundaries. Dongjia had been a populous village in Yuanqing Xiang. Its local bosses had intimidated their neighbors in Xianxian Xiang before the revolution, when they built a fortress for defense. During the dispute over the floodgate, members of the opposing collectives came to blows in a teahouse. Dajiao Collective was caught in a difficult position: it belonged to Dongjia's traditional rival, Xianxian Xiang, which expected its loyalty, but it had also suffered with Dongjia because of the floodgate. The conflict was finally mediated by residents from Xijia Village, a subdivision of Yuanqing Xiang, and Siya Xiang farther west (*Xinhui bao*, June 7, 1957). The incident is revealing because it shows how the increasingly complex economic interests and

traditional community loyalties were crosscut by administrative reorganizations.

The maneuvers of rural cadres are most instructive. In the 1950s collective aggression seemed common enough to be reported in local newspapers, but the party's call for production increases gave a protective covering to such communal tensions.[27] In the name of socialist production, the
cadres mobilized their own newly collectivized communities against others. They were eager to use every possible means to increase the economic
welfare of their members, not only because they could claim a legitimate
and willing following, but also because they gained political credit from
their party superiors in doing so. The cadres were able to manipulate the
floodgate incident to bring the collective's boundaries into conformity with
the traditional social ones, and to establish themselves as the new leaders.
However, cadres' motives were not all Machiavellian. Old Huang Tao
recalled that the cadres in general worked very hard and displayed a sense
of achievement and pride (guangrong gan) when their units did well.

In the townships farther away from Huicheng, the atmosphere was quite
different. Stubborn fruit farmers in Tianlu Xiang were skeptical about the
efficiency of the collectives. Former activists were busy with their own
plots and were reluctant to become involved in collectivization. The outlying farms were larger than those in the periurban areas, and household
labor was stretched. The hastily formed cooperatives had no track record to
show. By October 13, 1956, eighty-one households in Tianlu were still
holding out on their own (Xinhui nongmin bao, October 25, 1956). Persuading them to join was not easy. Numerous mass meetings were held.
With the help of village elders, compromises were finally worked out. For
example, households that pooled their orchards with fruit trees over four
years old into the collective were allowed to keep 35 percent of the harvest,
while the collective bought younger trees outright. For two more years,
income distribution was to be based on the share of property contributed
by each household (Xinhui nongmin bao, October 25, 1956).

Three collectives eventually emerged, but they fought over the allocation of land in Xining Village. Xining was one of the township's eight
cooperatives, formed exclusively of the Liang surname, and it had the best
land. When it was decided that Xining would merge with two other villages to form the Xihua Collective, cadres from Xining united with their
kinsmen to resist the proposal. The Liang had traditionally established
their territorial rights by tracing genealogical ties to a founding ancestor;
other surname groups had never dared settle in the village. The reign of the
local bosses had only reinforced such exclusiveness. During the land reform when land in the village was distributed among lineage members, the

Liang's territorial boundaries were not violated. At most, conflicts arose between strong and weak segments within the lineage community. With collectivization, the Liang for the first time were feeling strong pressure to share village resources with nonkin, which conflicted with many of their cultural assumptions about land rights.

The case of Xining demonstrates that, while land reform and the redistribution of ancestral properties had partly destroyed that aspect of Chinese kinship associated with estates and the political power of the literati, the popularity of genealogy-based territorial rights of settlement remained undiminished. Such cultural assumptions were finally called into question during the "high tide of socialism."

Official Success Stories

With the formation of the collectives, everyone was forced to work harder. The county newspaper reported one success story after another, extolling the efforts of masses and cadres alike. Whereas the cooperatives had aimed at rationalizing resource allocation among households, the higher APCS were expected to do much more. First, they diversified income by organizing work groups to operate small-scale enterprises and to grow cash crops. Second, with a larger pool of capital, the collectives financed technical innovations. Most important of all, they were expected to mobilize labor for land reclamation, dike construction, flood and drought prevention, and more intensive cultivation. The county paper of collectives lists numerous examples of such efforts.[28]

Some cadres were enthusiastic about the results. Xu Wenqing, a city cadre sent to Huancheng district to oversee production management, wrote in the following terms (*Xinhui nongmin bao*, December 10, 1956):

> Since collectivization, Huancheng district has changed its relatively undeveloped farming custom. We have a bumper harvest this year. The district has 50,000 mu of rice, with an average yield of 728 catties per mu, an increase of 118 catties over last year's 612. Production has increased 19.3 percent, that is, by 5.94 million catties. The state has acquired 4 million catties based on the "three fixed" system, plus another 550,000 catties as above-quota grain; the quota was reduced for 2,859 mu of land that were used for roads and dikes. Increased production allows us to set aside 1.5 million catties of animal feed as planned, enough to raise 600 sows, 15,000 chicken, and 170,000 ducks.
>
> In 1955, peasants in the district still practiced *zhenggao* on 20,000 mu of rice

fields, that is, 44 percent of the total. This year collectivization boosted enthusiasm, and *zhenggao* is being replaced by *fangeng* [turning over the soil between crops]. There are also technical innovations: better seed selection, dense transplanting, balanced use of fertilizers. Production has therefore greatly increased.

We had overused commercial fertilizer and had applied pesticides indiscriminately, which raised production costs to 16 yuan per mu. Having learned its lesson, the district now pays close attention to budgeting. This year we accumulated organic fertilizers and adopted preventive pest control. The cost per mu is 8.2 yuan, a decrease of 7.8 yuan from last year. The total cost for grain production dropped 392,714 yuan.

The district pays equal attention to the development of cash crops and subsidiary enterprises, which bring in an income of 254,000 yuan. The year-end distribution shows that except for Chengxi Xiang, which suffered more seriously from drought, and for Meijiang Xiang, where collectives grow mainly citrus, 90 percent of the units have increased their income. Out of the district's 69 collectives, 33 (41.7 percent) have an average household income of over 500 yuan, another 31 have income ranging from 300 to 500 yuan. . . .

Peasants' Complaints

Official success stories were punctuated with loud complaints from peasants against the management to which they were subjected. A major source of friction was the way in which decisions about production were made. As described earlier, the county was under pressure from the provincial government to fulfill its grain quotas. For a district like Huancheng, where cash crops were traditionally grown and subsidiary activities offset the lack of cultivable land, undue emphasis on grain growing, combined with low state prices for grain, cut into peasants' income. When peasants resisted, anxious cadres then tightened control over the planning and management of their collectives. The county newspaper reported numerous examples of cadres overworking the members of their collectives and consequently dampening their enthusiasm.

In the meeting of the People's Political Consultative Committee held in November 1956, a speaker pointed out that collectives had overstressed grain production at the expense of other activities. Meijiang's citrus crop was estimated to have dropped 10 percent. Grain yields did rise, but peasant income did not. Moreover, cadres restricted the subsidiary activities for fear that work on grain would suffer. For example, in the neighboring district of Shuangshui, the 348 households of a collective raised only 137 pigs in 1954; the number dropped further to 126 in 1955, and 74 in 1956.

Private plots where peasants grew vegetables for their own consumption were also abolished. The speaker expressed his worries that if all peasant households had to buy their vegetables, they would not be able to make ends meet; indeed 270 households in the collective had to borrow from the village credit cooperative.[29] As it was, the problems were many. Members of the collectives were punished if they did not fulfill their quotas. Cadres who organized the work would not allow any time for rest and expected their orders to be followed exactly. Women complained that they lacked the time even to do washing and cooking. The men protested that the collectives were equivalent to forced labor (Tan 1956, 25).

The high level of mutual distrust was illustrated by an incident in Meijiang Xiang (*Xinhui bao*, June 10, 1957). During a routine meeting, several members confronted the cadres about the collective's investments. The householders were disturbed that the cadres had not consulted them before investing in a frog farm that cost 1,000 yuan per mu. Collective investment over 500 yuan should have been reviewed by representatives of the masses. Instead, Meijiang's cadres went ahead with the project after discussing it only among themselves. The members' opinion was unfavorable because the investment was large and the return unreliable.

The anxiety of the householders was understandable, because their resources were locked into the collective. With rations, quotas, and marketing restrictions closing in on them, the peasants were finding that supplementary sources of income were becoming closed to them. Their income and well-being depended entirely on how well the collectives were managed and whether the distribution policies served their interests. The high tide of collectivization showed them clearly that rural cadres had their own welfare in mind, for instance, in pushing grain production at the expense of peasant income in order to ingratiate themselves with their party superiors. From the very beginning cadres were known to hold their own meetings where they decided everything before taking matters to members of their collective. In this situation conflict between cadre and masses was unavoidable.

During the formative period of the collectives, when membership was still in a state of flux, peasant households could at least try to influence the political process by threatening not to join. Such tensions are well illustrated in a report in the county newspaper concerning an election of collective cadres in another district (*Xinhui nongmin bao*, October 28, 1956).

Can "democratic election" result in good leadership?
During the upgrading of cooperatives, members had complained about the styles of leadership. Worried that the masses might get confused about the

issues, the party branch planned to nominate candidates for the collective committee whom the masses were expected to endorse in an open ballot. However, before the election started members of the collective raised the following issue with the party branch: "We are not going to approve cadres whom we do not elect." Some households even said: "We will not join the collective until we know who are the cadres."

The party branch must not ignore such warnings from the members of the collective. There was a similar case last year. The Number Seven Cooperative of Weixi Xiang held an election. Originally the members did not select Liang Zhende as the head. However, the party branch ignored the members' opinions and gave their approval to Liang. Subsequently, nobody cooperated with him and work did not get done. Members of the party branch finally came around to seek mass opinion. Members of the Number Three and Number Four Cooperatives then said: "To realize sound production plans one needs sound leadership. We have invested our entire livelihood and welfare in the cooperative. You want good cadres, so do we."

However, the article did not address itself to crucial questions concerning the relation between the masses and the cadres, on the one hand, and the cadres and the party on the other. First, what underlying concerns of the rural cadres prompted them to ignore the opinions of their members? Second, if they were caught between party demands and mass antagonism, what conditioned their course of action? Third, if for various reasons the cadres were able to monopolize decisions and acted against the wishes of the community, what was the basis of their power? Fourth, if the cadres sided with their fellow villagers against party policy, how much flexibility did they have with regard to party discipline? Finally, since there were obvious cases of coercion in the drives to collectivization, why were peasant households unable to resist such pressures?

Losing Ground

From the land reform to the height of collectivization, drastic changes took place in village economies. A centralized party bureaucracy took command over an expanding state sector and severed the ties of private economic interests with the rural economy. Such an expansion of control reduced the flexibility of local structures; at the same time the villages witnessed the creation of a stratum of activists whose function was to assist the party-state in managing rural society according to its priorities.

During the collectivization drives, the cadres who had been recruited in the land reform were joined by another group of activists. While the land reform activists became party members and filled the positions of directors and deputies of the collectives, the new group assumed the posts of leaders and accountants of production teams. The two were joined together by patronage networks as well as by a common political capital expressed in the language of class and socialist construction. However, they found themselves dancing to the party's ideological tunes, over whose composition they had little control. Their role was not easy, for the national leadership, and thus their immediate party superiors, were by no means united in the way they envisaged the direction and pace of the country's transformation. Yet political pressure was intense, as revealed by a party document from Xinhui that outlined the activities of rural cadres (*Xinhui nongmin bao*, June 10, 1956):

> In order to raise enthusiasm and efficiency, the County Party Committee and the People's Committee of Xinhui have made a conscious effort to set the guidelines of work, meetings, and rest for cadres in the county, districts, and townships. The guidelines are as follows. (1) Each day cadres at the county and district administration should spend eight hours at work, two hours in political study, and fourteen hours at rest. Those sent to the rural areas should adjust this schedule flexibly. (2) In principle, township cadres should engage in production for a quarter of each month, and spend 20 to 30 hours on political and literacy studies. (3) Mass meetings in the townships must not exceed two a month; meetings of the members of the collective must not exceed three a month; meetings for team members not more than five a month. None of the meetings should exceed three hours. If the meetings are conducted in the evenings, they must end before 10:30 p.m.; for the meetings of cadres, the time limit is 11 p.m. (4) Literacy classes in the rural areas should be conducted twice a week for two hours.

To focus the efforts of cadres on particular campaigns, the party committee of the county organized training classes at Huicheng. Models were selected and negative cases exposed. Work teams composed of higher-level party cadres were sent to "squat" (*dundian*) in the villages to evaluate the performance of other cadres. The teams were quite successful in persuading disgruntled villagers to report on the misdeeds of cadres. Such evidence was then used to impose discipline. According to the cadres I interviewed, fear of party discipline had been pounded into their heads since the days of land reform. The political struggles between local cadres and those from the South Central Bureau had created a "reign of terror" in the party ranks. The review procedures of the land reform in 1953 and the "campaign to root out counterrevolutionaries" (*sufan*) were fresh in people's memories.[30] So upward mobility through the party ranks was a rather uncertain and risky affair. Joining the party required the patronage of superiors, whose choice was often arbitrary. Chen Sheyuan recalled that he was scrutinized for an extended period because he had been accused by his superiors of displaying political hot-and-cold spells (*leng re bing*).

If cadres found themselves held increasingly accountable to their political superiors, who gave them power but at the same time imposed harsh discipline, they also faced the moral and economic expectations of fellow villagers. Conflicts between cadres and peasant households intensified as the latter, locked into the structures of the emerging collective economy, sensed they were losing control over their own livelihood. Villagers in retrospect agree that the formation of the collectives was a turning point in their relationship to both the party-state and the rural cadres. Before the formation of the collectives, membership in the collective sector was voluntary. Rural markets were restricted but still functioning. Economic mobility involved the customary social networking and ritual enrichment. Though the ancestral estates were divided and the halls turned into village headquarters and schools, festivals and temple fairs continued to draw together people and resources from a broad social and economic landscape. Peasants remembered gathering at ancestral graves during the Qingming festival. They attended *jiao* ceremonies in Hetang, visited the Hongsheng Temple in Chaolian, and watched the elaborate dragon-boat races in Shunde. A variety of local products were exchanged by itinerant traders during these occasions. Households who joined cooperatives dropped out when they felt their interests were not being served. Others chose to remain independent. It was a period of recovery and quiet prosperity after decades of turbulence, and a majority of peasants were quite thankful for what they had acquired and hopeful about the future.

When the collectives were organized, personal autonomy decreased. Peasants were more or less immobilized.[31] Their livelihood in the collectives was overseen by anxious cadres who were not necessarily the best farmers. Along with the peasants' confinement to the collectives came tougher restrictions on rural marketing. Even if they went to the markets, there was little to buy and sell. The best had to be reserved for the state agents. Soon the custom of spending a morning in the markets came to be viewed by cadres as "deviating from collective production work." Cadres' and peasants' concepts about what constituted proper work conflicted. Rural marketing had been an important part of the peasant's household economy, but under party pressure the cadres rejected this activity as superfluous to production. It also became increasingly difficult to confront the cadres, because they monopolized the means to distribute material needs. As the social networks and horizons of the peasants shrank with their confinement to the collectives, the cadres assumed greater importance in determining their livelihood, in shaping their social life, and in exercising political pressure.

Just as the peasants' world was being "cellularized," the party branches in the townships to which cadres belonged became the all-important political cells through which they interacted with the party-state. Many cadres were sensitive to local sentiments and tried at times to cooperate with relatives and friends in order to resist state encroachment. However, their party affiliations held them in a web of political obligations and benefits. Unlike gentry leaders, who were tied to the literati culture but at the same time identified with lineage and community interests, the rural cadres were being identified with a party-state whose interests very often conflicted with those of rural communities. The cadres maneuvered and compromised while their very existence was becoming thoroughly bureaucratized. Powerful though they might be with regard to village life, they were vulnerable to the demands of party superiors, who were the essential sources of their legitimacy.

The dynamics of the collectivization campaigns can be seen as the function of a three-way interaction: between the party-state and the rural cadres; between these state agents, who were held responsible for transmitting party policies, and their fellow villagers, who were confined to collective units; and between an emerging socialist economy at the national level and the rural communities it encompassed. Within a few years of the land reform, the party-state had established its power by creating an army of local agents who not only helped it dismantle the traditional order but also became an essential part of a new power structure governing the daily life of the rural populace. In their eagerness to advance in the party system during collectivization, the cadres felt compelled to uphold the state's priorities. Both cadres and peasants found themselves with less and less room to maneuver as their communities lost ground to the party-state's demands.

CHAPTER 8

The Leap:
Community Bureaucratized

Twenty thousand people marched in Huicheng in August 1959 to celebrate the first anniversary of the establishment of Huancheng Commune
(*Xinhui bao*, September 1, 1959). The euphoria of the previous year still
lingered in the minds of organizers, though food shortages were already
evident. Less than a year before, the rhetoric of socialism had surged to a
frenzied pitch. The Maoist slogan "Socialism is paradise, and the people's
communes are the bridge to it" had assumed the status of holy writ.

What took place in the Huancheng area reflected the national mood at
the time. Following a decision on the *zong luxian* (principal political line),
the country's communization drive was inaugurated in 1958, along with
the Great Leap Forward, a campaign to mobilize all available resources
for the establishment of an agricultural and industrial infrastructure in the
shortest possible time and to share the fruits of this labor with egalitarian
fervor. To achieve these goals, Mao Zedong had promulgated ideological
uniformity and organizational zeal in social and economic life that verged
on military maneuvers.[1] All this was to be accomplished through the faith
of a motivated and unquestioning local leadership, who would draw in
the peasants by personal example. Personal willpower was extolled beyond any reasonable limits as the fuel for the organizational moves. What
Mao envisioned as the all-encompassing commune and the "total" socialist being were to reinforce each other in the defeat of functional
differentiations.

Auspicious trial schemes had taken place during the year. Though faced
with strong opposition from many party leaders, Mao managed to gain
approval for the program from an alliance of leaders in the provinces. Once
the decision to communize was confirmed by the Beidaihe Resolution of
August 1958, party discipline required that the program be fully implemented in the rural areas.[2]

In this chapter I examine the communization movement in the
Huancheng area to show how the already cellularized communities of the
county were further absorbed into the national bureaucratic and ideological power structure engineered by Mao, just as the local economy was

being rapidly transformed by rural cadres. I will also explore the political consequences of this incorporation. Did the state succeed in creating new relationships that forced the peasants to shift their loyalties from family and community to the goals set for the party and the nation? When peasants complied with the demands of their local leaders, what were their underlying political motives? As for the cadres, did their behavior stray increasingly from that traditionally expected of political patrons? Decades before, local leaders had often acquired a measure of wealth, education, and social prestige before their power was recognized and reinforced by bureaucratic office; they were not entirely dependent on the state. The cadres, on the other hand, rose to power through their political activism and class loyalties as defined by the party-state. Did communization augment their political capital and confirm their roles as state agents rather than political brokers?

The Complicity of Huancheng

Comprising 12,115 households and 47,636 individuals, Huancheng Commune was formed in late August 1958 when twenty-six collectives, which were renamed brigades, were merged. Each brigade consisted of several production teams, essentially former villages or cooperatives absorbed into the collectives in 1957. Within the commune, the brigades were administered by thirteen *guanli qu* (management districts), with two periurban townships, Chengdong and Chengxi, placed under the administration of an urban commune in Huicheng. An atmosphere of regimentation prevailed, as these districts were sometimes called battalions (*ying*); the brigades under them, companies (*lian*); and their subordinate teams, platoons (*pai*). However, all but two of the management districts were abolished between 1959 and 1960. The number of brigades grew to twenty-eight. From 1961 to 1965, several other periurban brigades were transferred to the urban commune, and a few from elsewhere were added. The number of brigades in the commune stabilized at twenty-three (as shown in figure 8.1). The commune's boundaries remained basically intact until it was dismantled in 1983, although minor changes took place in between. The commune's nonagricultural population, which was spread out in the periurban brigades, was administratively grouped into a brigade in 1966. Part of a state farm at the southern tip of Tianma was incorporated as Xisheng Brigade in 1971.[3] Tianma Brigade was further divided into six smaller brigades in 1973.

The commune had a total of 79,786 mu of cultivable land at the time of

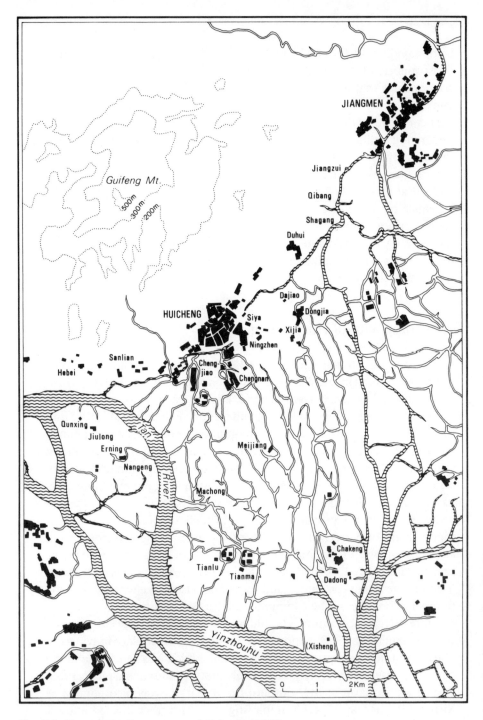

Fig. 8.1. Huancheng Commune and Brigades, 1965

its formation, of which 48,107 mu (60 percent) were rice fields, 16,074 mu (20 percent) were citrus orchards, 7,015 mu (8.7 percent) were palm polders, with 8,591 mu (10.7 percent) devoted to other crops (*Xinhui gongzuo*, October 9, 1958). It was managed by a committee of some twenty cadres, with a political core of party secretaries.

The brigades varied in size, population, and income. The political and administrative core of a brigade consisted of a committee of seven to fifteen cadres headed by a party branch secretary and a brigade leader and his deputies. Each brigade directed the affairs of several production teams. At the lowest level, the post of team leader rotated among villagers who were chosen yearly to organize production and to deal with officials. Team members were to work on and draw income from the land that they had been assigned since collectivization.[4] The brigade cadres also worked on the land that their families were assigned, but for their administrative work they were given work-points whose value was calculated on the basis of a percentage of the team's income.

The brigades operated small-scale enterprises to supplement that income. They looked after former petty traders and craftsmen in the village who were not entitled to income from the teams. The enterprises that operated at the commune level largely took care of the nonagricultural population, numbering from five thousand to six thousand that lived in the periurban brigades and were entitled to a grain ration because they had no land to work on. Chen Shepei, a cadre who helped organize the commune's transport team, recalled that he supervised fifteen men who were making a living in the periurban area by transporting passengers and goods on bicycles. The development of commune enterprises did not stop peasants from seeking work in the city. In fact, many went to Huicheng and to Huancheng Zhen in the chaotic period of commune formation.[5] Liang Song and his wife, both residents of Chengjiao Brigade, had been hired as cooks in the Huicheng Restaurant before communization. However, severe restrictions on urban residence, together with the development of commune enterprises, meant that their children who came of age in the early 1970s were assigned jobs within the commune. Their eldest son, who graduated from the commune's middle school in 1972, was hired by the agricultural machinery factory of the commune. The same applied to several of his schoolmates from the Huancheng Middle School whose parents held jobs in Huicheng. Only upon the parents' retirement were children allowed to take over their jobs, a practice known as *dingti* (substitution).[6] As we will see in chapter 11, the restrictions on urban residence meant that the commune enterprises, which started in 1958, assumed increasing significance in the livelihood of its members. The three-tiered structure of commune, brigade, and team remained stable until the commune was officially dismantled in 1983, though in reality the managerial power shared among the three levels fluctuated with national political trends.

Leadership within the commune was organized in a similar way. Veteran activists of the land reform period either became secretaries of party branches in the brigades or were transferred to the commune administration. Chen Sheyuan of Meijiang, for example, was transferred to the commune office, while Chen Mingfa remained secretary of Meijiang's party branch. Xu Decheng assumed the post of party secretary at Dajiao Brigade. Young activists they had recruited during collectivization were appointed team leaders or became members of the brigade committees. One of their major tasks was to recruit more activists to the communization drive in order to do accounting work for the teams and brigades, to direct production in the fields, and to run the small-scale enterprises, the militia, and the task forces in the construction projects.

Women activists were also in demand, and statistics compiled from local sources seem to indicate that nationwide, women were participating increasingly in collective work.[7] However, they generally worked in the nurseries and the public dining halls and were hardly mentioned when old cadres and villagers related their stories about production in the 1950s. The impression that women were not given many opportunities in commune politics is reinforced by later episodes.[8] An article in the *Xinhui qiaokan* (13 [1964]: 26–27) describes the reluctance of the cadres of a team in Chakeng Brigade to accept a woman accountant assigned to them through the commune. According to the report, the team leader was delighted with the idea that the county had allocated them a graduate of the agricultural middle school of Yashan in Gujing Commune farther to the southeast but was worried that it was to be a woman. The story ended happily, the team pleased with her performance. But she virtually had to achieve superwoman status in order to overcome the prejudice against her. My investigations in the late 1970s and early 1980s also show that, apart from the token woman cadre who took care of population-planning programs and the mediation of family conflicts, and apart from the occasional female "educated youth" sent down to settle in the villages, women played a very minor part in the commune's decision making. An embarrassing incident in my search for women activists took place in 1982. After a visit to the commune's tractor station, I asked the party secretary how many women were employed in their work force of 110. The poor fellow scratched his head for a long time and finally answered, "One." I naively persisted, "What does she do, then?" Someone finally said with a knowing smile, "She's the cook."

Ideological Expectations

In 1958 under the direction of the party committee of the county, commune cadres supervised practically every aspect of rural living. They were
given tremendous power to mobilize the teams' labor and resources. In the
initial months of the campaigns, county officials in Xinhui tried to make
Huancheng a model commune. The department of rural work in the party
committee of Guangdong Province had set general guidelines for the management of communes.[9] To promote the spirit of socialist competition
(*shehui zhuyi jingsai*), the county committee expected Huancheng and its
neighbor, Lile Commune, to exceed these targets. A report of the department of cooperativization (*hezuobu*) in the Xinhui County Party Committee detailed a model for the management of Huancheng Commune in the
same publication.[10] It had to centralize all income. After subtracting production costs, taxes, and capital accumulation, net income was to be distributed in the form of provisions. Grain rations were allotted by the commune on the basis of age grades, with full labor power—that is, males from
16 to 60 years of age and females from 16 to 55 years—receiving the most
grain. The teams operated public canteens that depended on the brigade
for 60 percent of their supplies, and it was expected that 90 percent of the
team members would normally eat in the canteens during the busy seasons
and at least 40 percent during the slack seasons. Apart from grain, the eight
guarantees (*babao*) package included provisions of vegetables and meat,
clothing, living quarters, nursery care, education, medical care, birth and
burial expenses, and miscellaneous living allowances. In sum, the commune centralized production resources and income and assumed the role
of chief provider for its members.

The party committee in Huancheng set up a program for action. They
intended to break the boundaries of the small collective units in the hope
that material resources and specialized skills would be used more efficiently once they were centralized. To support this policy, party leaders
cited the constraints of Chengnan Collective, which had the income to
build a food-processing factory but could not obtain the necessary machines, and wanted to build a new canteen and granary but could not find
the construction workers, while Changhong Collective in the neighboring
township had construction workers whose skills were not fully exploited
because they had been given agricultural tasks.

The party committee also responded to the national call for self-reliance
in grain production with plans for intensive cultivation. Once productivity
improved, party leaders believed that more acreage could be diverted to
cash crops. To achieve the set target of 3,000 catties per mu, which was

raised a few months later to 5,000 catties on paper, the committee urged the brigades to increase the application of fertilizers several times. To improve the technical support for agriculture, the party committee planned to recruit 1,325 workers to start small-scale enterprises such as backyard furnaces, food-processing, and brick and lime factories.[11] The plans were ambitious enough, but the extent to which they were carried out remains unknown.

Practical Actions

A combination of documentary and interview data shows that cadres in Huancheng responded quite eagerly to what was expected of them, while shrewdly using the powers bestowed upon them. The cultural dynamics involved were intriguing, as we see in a visit from Premier Zhou Enlai to the rural district in July 1958, a little more than a month before the commune was formed. This occasion appears to have been an overwhelming experience for the cadres. Expressing heartfelt gratitude, local leaders challenged the neighboring communes to a "great leap for socialism and cooperation." In an open letter to their competitors, which resembled an ancient battle cry, the cadres showed their deference to national leaders in terms that befitted emperors.[12]

> Yesterday was unforgettable. We were blessed with a visit from our beloved Premier Zhou. Moreover, we were most honored and encouraged by his revered personal instructions. He pointed out to us the direction of the leap forward, and made us see the new demands arising out of new situations.
>
> In the past, we were quite happy about our early crop, but could no longer do so after self-examination. Yield had been increased, averaging 550 catties per mu, but it had not reached what the party asked of us. We were determined not to be complacent and to eliminate our conservative attitudes. Our confidence is clad in steel and our bold strides meet no obstacles. With sky-rocketing energies, we vow to become a district with a yield of 2,200 catties per mu. . . . We guarantee that it will top the county. We shall win the red flag from Beijing in order to ingratiate ourselves to Chairman Mao and Premier Zhou.
>
> In order to promote the leap forward, we shall compete with other districts in the entire county. Our soldiers and horses are strong, our generals brave and numerous. . . . We dare to be challenged. Clad in our armor and ready in our formations, we await the battle cry.

Spirits were high. Two months later, the cadres vowed to reach a productivity of 10,000 catties of grain per mu. To obtain such results, they started to count individual ears of grain grown on experimental plots and then to estimate the total yield on this basis (*Xinhui gongzuo*, September 6, 1958). The exaggerations stretched way out of sight.

Skeptics might dismiss the plans as unrealistic or even beyond comprehension, saying that they were mere propaganda drawn up by the commune cadres to please political superiors and to gain control of resources. How far the plans were followed through is debatable, but the interesting questions are why the cadres resorted to such means and how they formed a new political culture in the process. In retrospect, their enthusiasm seems genuine enough. When I interviewed them in the late 1970s and early 1980s, old cadres recalled that they spent days and nights attending conferences and training classes organized by the party committee of the county. They also joined work teams to observe outstanding units in other counties and "to bring back the experiences." Xie Dubing, a cadre in a periurban brigade, gathered together seven of his friends to start a paper-making factory in the commune and tore down part of his house to provide the building material. Xu Decheng of Dajiao Brigade and Xu Wenqing, the provincial cadre who had been with the brigade since 1954, spent weeks repairing dikes with peasants. Xu Decheng recalled sleeping by the roadside for several nights with city students and workers in Jiangmen in the fall of 1958, before setting off for the construction sites the next morning. For three months, he and his wife, who was also a brigade cadre, did not go home. "I was so impressed," he recalled;

> the students and cadres from higher up were all with us peasants in the fields. Indebted to their self-sacrifice, I wanted very much to do my part. We were so motivated. Chairman Mao, the party, the three red flags [the symbols of the Maoist party line], the expected grain yield of 2,000 jin per mu, all looked so unreal but so reachable at once. Everyone talked about these bewildering targets. Possibilities were limitless. The Great Leap Forward swept us off our feet. It was hard to resist. (Xu Decheng, interview with the author, Summer 1980)

Both teams and brigades saw their autonomy to decide economic questions reduced during the height of the mobilization in the autumn and winter of 1958. Every commune member was given a basic wage, with slight adjustments for the brigades' differing production resources. Rations for food and other necessities were also fixed by the commune. Peasants ate at the collective dining halls, to which grain was allocated by the commune cadres. In an effort to free women for labor, children were gathered together at day-care centers. Every household was urged to contribute bricks, furniture, wood, even pots and pans, "to provide raw material for socialist construction."

Until early 1960, the commune was constantly on the honor rolls published in the county and provincial newspapers. In addition to implementing the highly publicized management strategies, which were confirmed by an investigation conducted a year later by county officials (*Xinhui bao*, September 5, 1959), the commune embarked on numerous major construction projects. Bridges, roads, and dikes were built, among them a 12-kilometer motor-road that linked Huicheng to Tianma and Chakeng brigades as well as to the Jinniutou Flood Prevention Gate at the tip of the commune. The road shortened the trip from Tianma to Huicheng from more than an hour through the winding waterways to about twenty minutes by bicycle. The floodgate still stands today and has been vital for controlling the tidal currents that affect over two-thirds of the commune's land. In Chakeng, there was an old saying, "When Jinniu blocks the entrance to the sea, the Jade Horse returns," meaning that if floodwater could be prevented from entering the southern tip of the Huancheng area, a bountiful harvest would follow. With the completion of the Jinniutou Flood Prevention Gate, villagers were persuaded that this would be so.

Small-scale enterprises mushroomed: brick kilns, small-tool repair shops, handicraft concerns, boatbuilding operations, transportation and construction enterprises. Some of the enterprises remained in operation for two and a half decades.[13] Among the major enterprises operated by the commune in 1978, ten were started between 1958 and 1959. Compared to later ones, these had humble beginnings, as shown in table 8.1. Nonetheless, they formed the material bases on which local cadres built up their political capital. As mentioned earlier, Xie Dubing of the Hongxing Brigade organized seven coworkers to start the Huancheng Paper-making Factory with a capital of 200 yuan. He was thirty-one years old at the time. In spite of his being an illiterate former cowhand, his political activism gave him a place in the commune enterprise. In 1965, at the age of thirty-six, he was finally sent to the cadre cultural school for six months. As he told me during an interview in winter 1978, "I took classes full time. I was even given a wage and free meals. Each month of study counted as a year. In six months time, I graduated with a primary school certificate."

In 1966, the factory was praised as a model of self-reliant development. It was reported that the factory had accumulated capital assets of 230,000 yuan and had hired 46 workers in eight years of operation. It also yielded a total of 179,000 yuan to the commune administration as profit.[14] Reliable accounts of the commune show that by 1980 it had an annual production value of 1,116,100 yuan and a work force of 136. Xie remained the party secretary of the factory until he retired in the early 1980s; the growth of the paper-making factory corresponded closely to his own career as cadre.

Table 8.1.   Enterprises in Huancheng Commune, 1958–77

Enterprise	Year of Establishment	Initial Capital Investment (Yuan)
Agricultural		
Agricultural experiment station	1958	2,000
Jinniutou Floodgate	1958	—
Lumber farm	1958	3,000
Livestock and poultry farm	1959	400
Fish hatchery	1959	1,000
Orchard	1970	5,000
Veterinary station	—	—
Industrial		
Transport team	1958	300
Agricultural machinery factory	1958	600
Paper-making factory	1958	3,000
Construction team	—	—
Food-processing factory	1958–59	7,000+
Palm-handicraft factory	1961	3,000
Agricultural machinery station (tractor)	1969–70	27,000
Palm-drying field	1976	33,000
Brick factory	1976–77	400,000

Source: Commune accounts collected during fieldwork.

Li Binglin of the commune's agricultural machinery factory recalled that when he was recruited to the new factory in 1958, he was barely eighteen years old. He had gone to village schools for five years in the township of Nantan, an island off the southwestern bank of Huicheng. In 1953, he had joined a work team to review the land reform in his township and had become an accountant when the collectives were formed. In 1956 he joined the Party Youth League and was transferred to the factory after a three-month training course in the county technical school. Though treated by some town residents as "having nothing but cow dung on his feet," he found his rural skills useful during the hard times following communization. He raised pigs and grew vegetables to supplement the factory canteen fare and was much appreciated. He became the manager of the factory in 1972, and from 1974 to 1978 the enterprise built up a capital of 220,000 yuan and a work force of a hundred or so. It thrived under the political patronage of the Maoist faction in the county's party committee, who heavily subsidized what they saw as self-reliant agricultural mechanization. The factory survived in the post-Mao era by contracting with overseas Chinese merchants to produce small metal parts, with an annual production value of 227,000 yuan and a work force of eighty-seven in 1980. As late as 1983, Li remained the factory manager.

A more visible form of success was in store for Deng Yantang, who joined the commune's newly founded agricultural experimental station in 1958. After graduating from primary school in Huicheng in 1952, Deng joined Chengxiang Brigade for three years and was recruited into the party because of his political activism. In 1953 he was drawn into the countywide campaign to organize youth teams for technical tests. In 1958 his work on rice seedlings took him to the conference on models in socialist agriculture. After the formation of the communes, the county asked every one of its four thousand teams to set up a seedling group to collaborate with the experiment station of the commune. Over fifty varieties of rice seedlings were produced. The station in Huancheng was given 40 mu of experimental plots to be run by peasant activists. In 1964, a seedling developed by Deng, known as the "Nangaoguang," was planted on 700,000 mu in Guangdong and Guangxi, an accomplishment that led to his being cited as the model youth technician of the county. His work attracted enough national attention to warrant a few visits by administrators of the Beijing Agricultural Institute and provincial leaders. As a result, the county gave the station 10,000 yuan to set up a laboratory, as well as an award at the National Science Conference. In 1966, provincial leaders visited Deng's experimental plots in order to establish the ideological point that "peasants can use Marxist dialectics to direct farming," thus making his work legitimate in Maoist terms. Deng and the station to which he was devoted survived many political changes. When I visited the laboratory in September 1977, Deng was still its director and had also been elected as a representative to the National People's Congress.[15]

Public dining halls, nurseries, health centers, and schools also received a good deal of attention. As in other communes, Huancheng's health clinic was founded in 1958, supported by funds from the commune. It became a training center for "barefoot doctors" in the mid-1960s, and has since developed into a hospital with fifty beds, an operating room, and a staff of 116. When I visited the clinic in December 1976, I was told that for a monthly fee of 0.25 yuan and a registration fee of 0.1 yuan, commune members could make use of the facilities, and that the clinic served three hundred to five hundred patients daily.

The network of schools in Huancheng also deserves some mention. Education in the prerevolutionary rural communities had been confined almost exclusively to lineage and community schools. The county's higher education facilities were concentrated in Huicheng and Jiangmen. Accord-

ing to a county report published in 1947,[16] the county had a total population of 630,934 (not including Huicheng and Jiangmen), distributed in
eight districts and seventy townships. There were six middle schools and
technical colleges, with a total of 151 teachers and 1,718 students (1,325
male and 393 female). There were 406 public and private primary schools,
but they were small, with an average of four teachers per school. The total
number of primary school students was 56,605 (37,719 male and 18,886
female). In 1952, the new government nationalized all schools and took
over their finances. Township schools continued to offer some primary
education for village children, but lineage funds were no longer available
for this purpose.

The expansion of the educational system began with the Great Leap
Forward in 1958, when community-supported teachers (*minban jiaoshi*)
were mobilized to work alongside teachers from the state system. The
Maoist orientation in mass education predominated for another two decades. The restructuring of educational opportunities intensified from the
mid-1960s to the mid-1970s through such measures as the shortening of
courses, the establishment of work-study programs, and a general lowering of academic standards.[17] Before 1958, secondary school education had
been concentrated in Huicheng and Jiangmen. A report in *Xinhui qiaokan*
(13 [1964]: 1–5) notes that the entire county had fourteen ordinary middle schools, one teacher-training school, and an overseas-supported middle school. After 1958, the county established fourteen more work-study
middle schools, one of which conducted classes at the senior middle-
school level. By 1964, fifteen more of these schools had been established,
and the total number of middle-school students reached four thousand or
so. The students pursued a three-year course and were expected to accept
rural assignments after their graduation, usually as teachers in the village
primary schools that had sprung up since 1958. In 1964, five hundred
more scheduled classes were established in the villages, boosting the
number of new primary school students that year to 34,000. From 1960 to
1963, the county government also invested in new school buildings to
replace the old ancestral halls and temples that had been used as village
schools. Of the available funds, 573,000 yuan were given to middle
schools, and 823,000 yuan to primary schools.[18] In Huancheng, however,
it was not until 1969 that a branch of the Xinhui First Middle School
became the senior middle school of the commune. Junior middle schools
were established in the brigades in accordance with the Maoist emphasis
on the democratization of education, aimed at providing primary and
junior middle-school education within these units, and senior middle-
school education within the communes. Table 8.2 shows the trend of

Table 8.2. Education and Health Care in Huancheng Commune, 1961–78

Year	No. of Schools	Number of Graduates				Number of Students				Teachers and Staff			Number of Health Care Workers		Participants in Cooperative Health Care
		Total	Primary	Junior Middle	Senior Middle	Total	Primary	Junior Middle	Senior Middle	State-Supported Teachers	Community-Supported Teachers	Staff	Doctors and Staff	Barefoot Doctors	
1961	15	417	364	53	—	6,888	—	—	—	148	54	11	82	—	—
1962	22	526	526	—	—	7,134	—	—	—	148	93	15	77	—	—
1963	22	404	404	—	—	7,270	—	—	—	152	89	12	64	—	—
1964	22	478	478	—	—	8,262	—	—	—	152	102	12	72	—	—
1965	22	497	459	38	—	8,290	—	—	—	152	182	12	73	—	—
1966	22	429	380	49	—	8,320	—	—	—	152	187	6	59	—	—
1967	22	408	360	48	—	7,928	—	—	—	152	217	6	56	—	—
1968	22	412	366	46	—	7,932	—	—	—	152	217	6	57	34	13,080
1969	25	830	745	85	—	8,736	—	—	—	157	230	6	58	64	43,088
1970	25	1,148	932	190	26	9,798	7,422	1,005	371	157	246	6	67	106	45,106
1971	25	1,679	1,243	306	130	10,229	8,027	1,736	465	169	253	6	82	98	44,249
1972	25	1,997	1,286	470	241	10,621	8,454	1,745	422	168	256	6	87	87	45,168
1973	25	1,915	1,089	649	177	10,909	9,113	1,348	448	172	271	8	92	71	47,245
1974	25	1,997	1,282	502	213	11,344	9,297	1,596	451	183	274	8	102	77	48,597
1975	25	2,050	1,279	545	226	11,706	9,185	2,035	456	183	277	9	105	75	48,810
1976	25	2,232	1,342	685	205	11,626	8,654	2,318	604	191	312	11	105	74	48,673
1977	25	2,585	1,456	884	245	11,236	8,128	2,496	613	201	301	11	108	84	48,886
1978	25	2,906	1,631	1,010	265	10,700	7,853	2,282	565	197	305	11	110	80	48,921

Source: Commune accounts collected during fieldwork.

educational decentralization in Huancheng from 1961 on, paralleled by developments in the health care services. When I visited the Huancheng Senior Middle School in December 1976, there were thirty-nine teachers and about six hundred students in two grades. Only a fraction of the commune's junior middle-school graduates continued their education, and fewer than 25 percent were women. Nonetheless, the impact of the educational reforms on the villages was significant. Of the commune's three hundred or so primary and junior middle-school teachers, a hundred were Huancheng's own graduates. Moreover, these schools were the training ground of a new generation of rural cadres. Since the school was operated by the commune from 1969 on, many of its graduates returned to the villages. Seventy percent of the political study classes in the brigades were organized by returning students. Some were instructors in the tractor stations; others were accountants and cashiers. Four became party branch secretaries at the brigade level, and one later assumed the post of deputy director of the revolutionary committee of the commune.

Mass Ambivalence

The late 1950s therefore witnessed the mass mobilization of energy and resources aimed at promoting self-reliance, as local cadres responded to the national call for ideological fervor and practical action. Many cadres, however, were not as enthusiastic in proving themselves to Chairman Mao and Premier Zhou. In a report made one week after the commune was formed, cadres in Tianma were explicitly criticized on this account. The brigade was placed in the low-effort category (*xiayou*) because its members had been slack in the collection and application of fertilizers. Of the 8,741 mu of the late crop of rice, only 70 percent had been fertilized a second time, and only 200 mu were fertilized a third time, despite the fact that seven brigade cadres, including five in the party committee, were supervising the work. The party secretary, who did not belong to the dominant Chen surname group, was not heeded; his deputy, who did, dragged his feet. In one of the teams cultivating 1,373 mu of land, only 116 of its 390 laborers reported to work (*Xinhui gongzuo*, September 7, 1958).

Peasants from Duhui Brigade complained that their wages had gone down since the formation of the commune, although they were repeatedly reminded by cadres that a great deal of the cash income had gone into provisions that peasants did not include in their calculations (*Xinhui bao*, September 1, 1959). However, the report on the trial distribution system of Huancheng Commune (Zhonggong Xinhui Xianhui Hezuobu 1958, 10–

11) acknowledged that some richer households suffered a decrease in income. It cited as examples several households formerly belonging to Chengnan Collective. In 1958, these households expected to receive a per capita distribution of 161 yuan, but instead received only 128. Another example was given in Tianlu Brigade. A man of the former upper-middle-peasant category had been receiving income from the palm fields and fruit trees he had pooled into the collective. In 1957, income for his household of three (with only one laborer) had been 470 yuan. After communization, his income decreased by 113 yuan. The author of the report considered such decreases as normal and expressed confidence that income would eventually rise with better yields.

The Hard Times

The inflated targets for production were hard to reach and even harder to sustain. Euphoria lasted less than a year. Publicly, commune cadres continued to pledge themselves to the "grand victory" (man tang hong) during various conferences on the subject of socialist models (Xinhui bao, January 23, 1960), but even enthusiastic cadres started to worry when a breakdown in production became evident in late 1959. Sensing trouble, the provincial government held a conference for representatives of all levels of cadres. Xinhui County held its own in April 1960. A total of 257 county-level cadres were subsequently sent to the communes to reinforce the faltering rural leadership. Field management, canteens, pig farms, transportation networks, and mechanization were the focus of county cadres' attention (Xinhui bao, April 23, 1960).

The canteens stayed in operation until the end of 1960, but food was by then scarce. Village cooks recall steaming the few grains of rice they could obtain several times to inflate their size. Rice porridge was supplemented with sweet potatoes. Meanwhile the county administration requested that team canteens provide each patron with at least 2 liang (slightly over 2 ounces) of bean sauce a day (Xinhui bao, June 1960). Production incentives for team members were low. Peasants either refused outright to cooperate or merely went through the motions. Tianlu Brigade was faulted for "all kinds of rightist tendencies." The leadership was split; a ploughing team led by a party member refused to speed up its pace, insisting that even if the members could be worked harder, their starving animals could not (Xinhui bao, April 25, 1960). A few months later, after criticizing some village women for not threshing the grain properly, Tianlu brigade cadres saw to it personally that the grain was rethreshed and that the fields were carefully gleaned. To convince team members, they showed them their calculations. If 15 catties of grain were recovered from a mu, then a total of 72,000 catties could be retrieved from the brigade's 4,800 mu of rice, an amount sufficient to supply the brigade with half a month of food (*Xinhui bao*, November 7, 1960). Hunger created some incentive for harder work.

Anxious cadres in Dongjia Brigade asked teams to grow food crops on roadsides and wasteland and to be responsible for providing from 6 to 10 catties of grain a head (or its equivalent in sweet potatoes or other crops) every month. An investigative report (*Xinhui bao*, November 25, 1960) found that Team Number Six did just that and "were able to provide their members with lunches," while leaders in Team Number Two were "unsure of party policy and entertained the idea that food would somehow be shared." By dragging its feet, the second team failed to enjoy these lunches. The real lessons to be learned from the report were that food was scarce and the brigades were finally leaving the teams to fend for themselves. Cadres were anxious, but neither peasants nor animals could be worked any harder. In fact, when the cadres reported to the county that they had exhausted their grain reserves, they were told bluntly that they themselves had to come up with food. As shown in table 8.3, during the communization period the population decreased, production costs increased, and per capita income dropped drastically. Cost as percentage of production jumped from 24.9 percent to 47 percent in 1958, while per capita income dropped from 112 yuan in 1956 to 71 yuan in 1957, 54 yuan in 1958, and 89 yuan in 1959. This trend in fact started as early as 1957, after peasant households were pressured to join the collectives.

In the summer of 1983, when the commune was finally dismantled, Chen Sheyuan of Meijiang looked back with mixed feelings:

> We were all caught in the spirit of euphoria, competing with one another, exaggerating and then believing our exaggerations. The state expected us to deliver, so we pressured the masses. Why did the peasants comply? Well, if they wanted to eat, they had to work; there was no alternative. One could not survive outside of the collective. The cadres expected that the state would take care of them if things went wrong. We had a blind enthusiasm for the ideological power of the party. After all, it gave us what we had thus far; we did not want to let it down. But of course the party was acting on the basis of our exaggerated reports, so we fed each other wrong information that led to unrealistic estimates and much waste. The peasants went along with the wastefulness for a totally different reason. They wanted to get at the resources before the latter were taken by freeloaders. This feeling was particularly strong

Table 8.3. Some Statistics for Huangcheng Commune, 1953–65

Year	Total Output[a] (Yuan)	Cost as % of Output (%)	Per Capita Distribution Income[b] (Yuan)	Growth of Population Entitled to Distribution[c] (%)
1953	6,874,192	29.3	136	—
1954	7,403,611	26.6	148	2.68
1955	6,811,370	25.2	131	3.09
1956	6,462,939	24.9	112	3.09
1957	5,701,457	32.1	71	2.11
1958	6,627,942	47.0	54	2.02
1959	6,860,574	26.3	89	0.59
1960	7,123,972	30.6	103	0.38
1961	6,786,826	29.4	106	2.29
1962	8,496,231	25.8	148	4.22
1963	10,232,746	29.6	129	3.25
1964	7,284,604	39.7	79	2.36
1965	8,502,125	34.9	100	3.60

Source: Commune accounts collected during fieldwork.

[a]Total output includes team and brigade incomes. To facilitate the sale of crops to state agents by households and collectives, the township administration kept records of population, acreage, output per mu, sales of crops to the state, taxes, and estimates of production costs from 1953 on. Team and brigade accounts were even more complete from 1965 to 1983.

[b]Distribution income is what was left after production costs, taxes, collective funds, welfare funds, and so on, were subtracted from total production.

[c]The population entitled to distribution did not include rural residents who earned state wages, such as state cadres, teachers, and overseas Chinese.

in the rich *xiang*. So we ate up our year's grain reserve in three months! Then the hard times came, but the state told us that there was nothing they could do to get us out of the situation. We had to come up with food ourselves. The peasants hated us. Everyone was watching to see who took more than his share of food. The culprits got pretty roughed up sometimes. Even today people bear grudges against fellow peasants who were suspected of having hidden food twenty-five years ago. Cadres were accused of nepotism, given their power over allocation. The hard times lasted until 1961. We rounded up those whose bodies were suffering from severe malnutrition and fed them nutritious foods. On one of the gatherings, the cynical patients "thanked" us and the party for making them so "bloated." We were all losers, including the party. Since the party enjoyed tremendous power to organize people's lives, when things went wrong, people would not blame themselves; they blamed the party and the cadres instead. (Chen Sheyuan, interview with the author, summer 1983)

Winners and Losers

Recent critics in the party have blamed the chaos and wastefulness of this period on the blind fervor of rural cadres, whose "small producers' mentality" is alleged to have dovetailed with the authoritarian but extremely egalitarian Maoist rhetoric.[19] Why were unrealistic policies pushed to such extremes and allowed to incur such heavy human costs before they were revised or abandoned? Assuming that mass disincentives were obvious and that objections were heard, why were they not reported to party superiors in order to shape policy decisions? Finally, why were the cadres as well as the average peasants unable to resist transformations so detrimental to their lives? It is sadly revealing that, although the cadres suffered to some extent with fellow peasants, they continued the legacy of Mao for two more decades, until the party officially admitted the Great Leap Forward and the communization movements to have been tragic mistakes.[20]

It would be difficult to explain away the massive damage incurred during these years by blaming the cadres' blind enthusiasm. Structural reasons were just as important as ideological ones. One must take into account the step-by-step transformations in the configurations of power that isolated rural communities, as well as the changing perceptions of that structure. Ideologically, the party-state had gained precedence over potential challengers such as the landlords, industrialists, and dissenting intellectuals. Independent local newspapers had been closed down since the land reform.[21] By the time of the "Three Anti" and "Five Anti" campaigns of 1952, those progressive intellectuals who had stayed with the party had been purged. The Jiangmen incident, in which members of the Democratic Alliance were persecuted, was a typical instance of the suppression of differing points of view. The replacement of educated cadres by peasants and workers at the local level, and by military cadres from the north at the level of the provincial administration, helped the party redefine political authority based on class prerogatives. The purging continued in the *sufan* campaigns of 1955 and 1956, followed by the antirightist campaign of 1957. These were interspersed with the antilocalism campaigns aimed at leading Cantonese cadres in the provincial government.

In the economic realm, the land reform dislodged the local bosses and the corporate estates, severing the ties between town and country. Although kin and community affiliations proved more durable, the completion of the socialist transformation of industry and commerce in 1956 enfolded the rural communities within an emerging state sector. Meanwhile, the townships and villages were transformed from within, as peasants found themselves increasingly confined to collectivized units. The formation of the higher APCs in 1957 implied further tightening of state control over agricultural production and commerce, diminishing the range of livelihoods available to the rural populace.[22] The reduction in alternative channels of mobility made peasant livelihood more dependent on cadre performance, just as the cadres were growing more dependent on a party organization that by the late 1950s had established an ideological monopoly.

In sum, the rural cadres and peasants hardly had a chance to recover before they were mobilized for the Great Leap Forward and the communization drive. Class rhetoric reached a feverish pitch during the land reform movement; socialist rhetoric reached its own boiling point in 1958. Complying with the expectations of the party state, the rural cadres built up the commune economy, and with it their political capital. In so doing, they further enmeshed the livelihoods of fellow peasants in the state system. The "three red flags" (sanmian hongqi), symbolically representing the Maoist line in communization, became a means for the rural cadres to invoke political authority. As late as 1977 and 1978 when I started fieldwork in Huancheng, Chen Mingfa, Xu Decheng, and old peasants such as Uncle Yong and Uncle Luan constantly quoted "Chairman Mao's three red flags" in our conversations. The phrase had clearly assumed a tremendous significance for them. The peasants may have participated in the land reform and collectivization drives for various reasons, but their actions changed their situation as well as that of their communities. The drama of 1958 vividly demonstrates the power of a consolidated bureaucracy over its rural cadres, the corresponding power of the cadres over the peasants, and the dominating effects of a party-state over rural lives and landscape. But how could such a structure have emerged without a touch of complicity on the part of cadres and peasants?

CHAPTER 9

Complicity and Compliance

Practically every old cadre I talked to in Huancheng Commune agreed that "life could not have been better" from the time the pieces of the shattered commune economy were picked up in late 1961 until 1964, when the Siqing (Four Cleanups) movement bore down on them. They considered this short interlude a golden era in their thirty-five-year careers, surpassing even the apparent boom of the 1980s. What they left unsaid were their reasons for this opinion: that they continued to enjoy the class legitimacy conferred on them by the Maoist vision, and that, compared to the ideological rigidity of the previous period, they had room to maneuver within the bureaucratic structure guaranteed by the politics of Liu. For once they were able to see themselves as the comfortable brokers between the state and their fellow peasants in a period of ideological relaxation.

However, from the standpoint of the average villager the best times were entirely different. The villagers' golden era was the early 1950s, before the beginning of large-scale collectivization, and the 1980s, when the party-state made a conscious effort to disengage itself from the economy and society. These differing views highlight not only the precarious position that rural cadres had occupied as managers of the local economy and society, but also the changes in their situation in relation to the larger state structure. In this chapter I trace events from the end of the communization movement through the Cultural Revolution in order to illustrate the ways in which the party-state, itself a center of political conflict at the time, penetrated local society through an increasingly factionalized corps of cadres.

Winds of Moderation

Revisions of the communization program were introduced in 1960 and became very obvious by the end of the year.[1] As soon as the winds of moderation began to be detected, brigades in the Huancheng Commune initiated certain changes. Meijiang Brigade, for example, changed its dis-

tribution policy in a series of stages. In April 1960, it reduced direct provisions of food and raised the proportion of income given as wages; in
October, it eliminated free medical care. By December, 70 percent of its
members' income was in the form of wages (*Xinhui bao,* December 3,
1960). Chengnan Brigade introduced the system of *san bao yi jiang* (three
contracts, one bonus), whereby the teams guaranteed the brigade a delivery of grain based on an allowance of production costs and then received a
negotiated number of work-points for the year-end distribution of income.[2] Yields that exceeded the negotiated amounts were retained by the
team as a bonus. Twenty percent of this bonus was kept by the teams for
welfare services, but the rest was distributed to households in proportion to
the work-points accumulated by their members (*Xinhui bao,* December 11,
1960).

Tianlu Brigade, on the other hand, took a big step backward. As early as
April 1959, its cadres were debating how much autonomy the teams
should have. The Tianlu Brigade's four thousand members were organized
into twenty-eight teams occupying eight villages. The centralized allocations of food and services had been chaotic, but the cadres were reluctant to
delegate power to the teams. The cadres' three fears (*san pa*) were aptly
summed up by an article in *Xinhui bao* (December 5, 1960).

> Last year, the brigade cadres debated the issue of team autonomy. Some of
> them expressed their three fears. First, they were afraid that once the teams
> developed on their own, their interests would conflict with those of the larger
> collective and thus hamper brigade development. Second, they were afraid
> that the teams might misallocate labor, thus failing to fulfill their contracted
> crop deliveries. Third, they were afraid that once the teams expanded their
> economic bases, they would refuse any mobilization from the center, thus
> providing problems for the leadership.

It was clear that these cadres were concerned about losing the economic
bases of their political control. Nevertheless, incentives were such a serious
problem at the time that the party committees of the county and commune
finally sided with the teams. For the early crop in 1959, Tianlu installed the
san bao system in the production of grain, palm, and seventeen other
items.[3] The results were convincing to those who had pushed for team
autonomy. An average of 550 catties of grain per mu was harvested in the
late crop, which meant that after delivering the required procurement
quotas to the state, each member retained an average of 41 catties per
month for consumption, only 9 catties short of what the villagers considered a normal amount for monthly consumption. In 1960, the brigade
extended the contracts to roughly thirty other crops. A "four fixed" system

(*si guding*) was added, guaranteeing the teams the autonomous use of a fixed amount of land, labor, cattle, and tools for three years. Procurement quotas for the crops were reduced, and the entire amount produced above quota was kept by team members themselves. The process was not without disputes and negotiations. Teams had challenged the initial "four fixed" allocations by claiming that the land-to-labor ratio on which it was based was not accurate enough, that the allocated land was too scattered, or that the proportion of mature polders to younger alluvial fields was not reasonable. After the terms were finally settled, member households took greater initiative in the upkeep of these resources. The Xihua team, for example, constructed a flood prevention gate for its rice fields. Member households also reclaimed 10 mu of sandbanks and planted sweet potatoes, eggplants, bananas, and papayas on the dikes. Xining, the village dominated by the Liang surname group, secured the best land in the brigade. Its member households diversified their crops by adding beans and sugarcane to grain production while working hard on their private plots.

Worried that peasant households would not meet the grain procurement quotas, some brigade cadres remained ambivalent about the changes until the production results became clearly positive. Chen Mingfa, then party branch secretary of the Meijiang Brigade, recalled,

> I was not sure of the moves of my superiors in the county, but as a party branch secretary, I felt obliged to implement party policies. Fellow villagers welcomed the changes but were fearful. After our superiors pressed us long enough, we decided to set our own example. I took the lead in working in the private plots and made my family sell the vegetables in the village market. We felt like fools because a couple years ago we were driving peasants away from those same markets. Even my own uncles and cousins ridiculed us for promoting communism (*gong chan*) in the beginning of the year and contract production (*bao chan*) at the end. However, even though they were harsh on us in words, people began to do things, and the village suddenly bustled with activities. (Chen Mingfa, interview with the author, summer 1980)

County policies that permitted flexibility in the procurement and pricing of grain, sugarcane, and citrus were favorable to Huancheng Commune. For example, when it was ruled that certain sweet potatoes, beans, and oil seeds could be substituted for grain in the procurement quotas, teams in Tianlu planned a spring crop. They estimated that if they obtained a normal harvest from the 1,934 mu of secondary food crops, the brigade could substitute this amount for 557,995 catties of its grain procurement quota, leaving four extra months of grain for the brigade's approximately four thousand members (*Xinhui gongzuo*, February 15, 1962:1–3). The county government also took the initiative in reviving cash crops for export. The county commercial department, for example, arranged with the banks to set aside 6,000 to 7,000 yuan specifically for loans to brigades in Huancheng to grow vegetables (*Xinhui gongzuo*, January 30, 1964:3–4). Early in 1964, the provincial government publicized its plans to revive the citrus crop. With a baseline of 25,000 mu in 1961 (of which Huancheng held 8,000 mu), acreage for citrus in Xinhui was to increase 4,000 mu per year starting with 1963. Grain quotas for the converted acreage were correspondingly reduced by some 500 to 700 catties per mu. Fruits produced above the quota were at the disposal of the growers. They could sell the produce in rural markets, offer it to the state agents at above-quota prices, or exchange it for fertilizers.[4] Chen Mingfa recalled that in 1963, citrus from his family's own gardens was sold in the rural markets for 2.80 yuan per catty, an extremely high price.

Crop diversification does not seem to have affected grain production, which peaked in 1963. Echoed by others, Uncle Ye and Old Liang insisted that the bumper crop was due to *"tianshi, dili, renhe,"* a harmony of the natural elements and human spirits. Commune accounts show that collective income increased 21 percent from 1961 to 1963, not including the substantial income that households earned from their private plots as well as from poultry, handicrafts, and petty trade.

The three-tiered ownership structure of the commune now existed in form only. The teams were reduced in size, consisting basically of close relatives engaged in mutual aid. Responsibility for production returned to the level of individual or small groups of households, which made all decisions regarding production and distribution as long as they paid taxes and delivered the agreed-upon crops to state agents. Peasants were quite willing to sell to the agents because high prices had been set for the major crops. But for the crops produced above the quota, they preferred to sell in the thriving rural markets.

Who Came Out Ahead?

Ironically enough, the cadres found themselves enjoying their apparent loss of political control and were actually doing better than their fellow villagers. They no longer had to spend long arduous hours negotiating with team members over the allocation and calculation of work-points or interfering with the peasants on their private plots and in the rural markets. They continued to see to the payment of taxes and crop procurement, but the required items were no longer in short supply. In fact, the cadres had become the unobtrusive brokers between state agencies willing to pay and villagers eager to produce crops for sale. A decade of nationalized industries and commerce had turned the state sector into an important supplier of fertilizers, seeds, machinery, consumer goods, and credit. The cadres had their share of political clout and economic leverage with factories and offices in the county capital. As a result, they also became the middlemen between state factories and peasant households who needed industrial goods. Their connections with the state sector allowed them to create a system of patronage in the villages, embodying a combination of formal authority associated with the party bureaucracy, and the informal power of the market, community, and kin networks. The cadres' ability to take advantage of the autonomy granted to local economies rested on their privileged access to the party bureaucracy and the state industrial sector.

Juggling with the intangible political authority of the party, the cadres used the organizational means within their grasp to build local political power for themselves. While at the national level the political winds changed their course and velocity, rural cadres calculated their assets and liabilities. They were quite unable to control the national ideological tunes, but they improvised upon them to their own advantage. From the time of the land reform, veteran activists had recruited their successors in the various campaigns. They struggled against one another during party purges, but they also learned to share power.

During the fifteen years of socialist transformation, the peasant activists had toed a fine line. In the early 1950s, they had tried to balance the interests of the party with those of the community. Concerns for kin and community, benevolent leadership, and moral authority continued to be expressed in political dialogues. However, when the economic autonomy of local society shrank after collectivization, the cadres' ability and willingness to draw on traditional resources decreased correspondingly. Since communization, they had been using the apparatus of the party-state to build up their political capital, sometimes at the expense of their fellow villagers. Their strategies involved a system of evaluation that had become inaccessible and incomprehensible to the peasants. On the other hand, the peasants were performing their own calculations in order to make the best of their situations. Together, cadres and peasants changed the rural communities from within. Tables 9.1 and 9.2 outline the general development of the commune and its brigades under the management of the cadres from the early 1960s on.

One may wonder whether the rural cadres can be equated with the traditional gentry, as Schurmann (1968) and Shue (1985) have implied. Madsen (1984) has argued that the "Communist gentry" was alive and

Table 9.1. General Statistics for the Brigades and Teams, 1962–82

Year	No. of Brigades	No. of Teams	Population[a]	Brigade and Team Economy Total Output (Yuan)	Total Costs (Yuan)	Collective Reserves (Yuan)	Welfare Reserves (Yuan)	Taxes (Yuan)	Per Capita Distribution Income[d] (Yuan) Team and Brigade	Team Only
1962	28	231	39,110	8,496,231	2,189,627	503,523	128,758	562,710	148	—
1963	28	213	40,050	10,232,746	3,029,512	1,081,369	132,633	—	129	—
1964	23	213	41,498	7,284,604	2,894,021	485,787	116,508	586,059	79	98
1965	23	184	42,701	8,502,125	2,974,070	467,751	137,765	649,820	100	115
1966	23	184	43,973	9,411,958	2,724,748	810,215	147,439	645,262	119	124
1967	23	183	44,829	10,134,773	2,861,474	774,499	187,244	648,684	129	121
1968	23	183	46,631	10,138,675	2,658,631	746,967	380,583	622,576	126	110
1969	23	182	47,293	9,845,310	2,769,521	618,255	343,453	602,428	117	104
1970	24	182	48,276	9,415,660	2,759,985	551,729	253,919	632,064	109	110
1971	24	187	50,399	10,322,957	2,894,992	573,830	300,535	616,631	119	111
1972	29	187	50,894	11,441,150	3,685,338	627,843	315,550	638,767	122	108
1973	29	190	57,698	12,444,744	3,960,155	563,104[b]	302,529	649,143[b]	—	120
1974	29	190	52,466	13,663,108	5,047,627	900,423	361,339	672,455	—	97
1975	29	190	53,096	11,978,105	4,431,113	688,711	318,633	707,169[c]	—	101
1976	29	190	53,362	13,460,099	5,265,728	770,377	326,792	720,072	—	146
1977	29	190	54,088	17,028,214	5,607,503	1,268,174	476,684	708,227	—	126
1978	29	189	54,836	16,173,509	6,285,829	718,101	384,082	769,767	—	119
1979	29	189	54,220	17,008,093	7,991,514	577,686	379,475	680,676	—	175
1980	29	189	54,602	26,654,836	13,351,754	603,050	509,262	1,029,047	—	187
1981	29	191	54,976	29,137,051	14,623,938	736,338	518,535	1,108,505	—	431
1982	29	191	55,437	51,181,692	25,175,854	529,190	369,574	1,390,937	—	

Source: Commune accounts collected during fieldwork.

[a] The population here does not include those who were on the state payroll or from the market town, who totaled around 6,000.

[b] For the years 1973–82, contributions from the brigade level of ownership were missing from the figures on collective and welfare reserves.

[c] From 1962–75, the figures for taxes did not include taxes paid by brigade enterprises.

[d] These figures are recorded in commune accounts. They only roughly correspond to what can be calculated from the production figures. It is difficult to obtain the exact number of commune members who are actually entitled to distribution; this may explain the discrepancies. Team income does not

well up to the Cultural Revolution. Apart from the matter of semantics, one should be cautious about linking the cadres to the gentry in terms of their functional requisites. In the 1960s the party cadres differed from the gentry in several distinctive ways; their power over fellow villages and the sources of their authority were of a very different nature. Though the imperial officials maintained a formal, organizational distance from the gentry elites, the latter nevertheless commanded multiple, overlapping sources of authority. Their power was integral to the cultural reproduction of kinship, community, popular religion, and literati networks, as well as being firmly ingrained in the historical consciousness of the peasants. The cadres, on the other hand, were tied to a single political source of legitimacy: the party and its revolutionary programs. They came to prominence with a national state obsessed with establishing unanimity for its policies and committed to turning cultural reproduction into a matter of political organization. The process of sinking the party's political roots into the rural communities was painful, as was shown by the moral dilemmas of the 1950s. Nevertheless, the communization movement demonstrated the cadres' willingness to follow the party at tremendous cost. Once they were established in bureaucratic positions, the cadres also displayed resilience in maintaining entrenched interests, as shown by their comfortable circumstances in the early 1960s. However, as later events would demonstrate, these powerful positions could become insecure. Veteran cadres conceded that they could weather most political storms, although they could not prevent the storms' outbreaks. From 1964 on, the nature of the storms became increasingly incomprehensible.

The Impending Storm

The golden period of the early 1960s did not last long. An ideological battle was brewing among the nation's top leaders; the schism between the political factions of Mao Zedong and Liu Shaoqi was widening. Mao Zedong was alarmed at how economic liberalization had swept the country. Liu Shaoqi, then head of the state, was amenable to a relaxation of ideological control, but he also valued a hierarchical party organization. Mao was uncomfortable with both. To him, market orientations aggravated class differences and dampened socialist consciousness; a party bureaucracy with the power to defend its entrenched privileges contaminated the vanguard and the revolution. The struggle with Liu was a life-and-death issue as far as Mao's vision of socialism was concerned.[5]

Table 9.2. General Statistics for the Brigades, 1962–82

		1962			1966		
Brigade	No. of Teams	Population	Grain Yield (Catties per Mu)	Per Capita Income (Yuan)	Population	Grain Yield (Catties per Mu)	Per Capita Income (Yuan)
Jiangzui	1	311	842	—	346	1,150	103
Qibang	5	743	866	—	864	1,258	91
Shagang	1	199	1,024	—	233	1,255	144
Duhui	11	1,764	902	—	2,064	1,122	108
Dajiao	8	1,211	824	—	1,297	828	85
Dongjia	16	3,855	878	—	3,855	924	93
Xijia	6	892	832	—	1,010	878	82
Ningzhen	6	997	1,094	—	1,192	1,176	138
Siya	5	776	1,044	—	870	1,091	113
Chengnan	11	2,081	1,014	—	2,409	1,154	137
Meijiang	12	3,019	909	—	3,417	1,002	126
Chengjiao	7	1,490	886	—	1,764	897	80
Sanlian	4	548	806	—	650	1,180	115
Hebei	5	698	875	—	802	1,152	118
Qunsheng	7	1,431	1,057	—	1,599	1,140	137
Jiulong	8	1,148	889	—	1,295	1,093	129
Erning	5	734	1,082	—	842	1,105	134
Nangeng	4	650	1,026	—	751	1,192	148
Machong	2	396	850	—	443	1,234	125
Tianlu	8	4,361	855	—	4,731	1,186	147
Tianma							
Ercun	3	461	757	—	—	1,022	—
Sancun	6	1,086	799	—	—	990	—
Sicun	7	941	798	—	7,226	957	118
Wucun	9	1,788	934	—	—	1,023	—
Liucun	4	1,067	964	—	—	1,075	—
Qicun	4	787	889	—	—	997	—
Xisheng	5	—	—	—	—	—	—
Chakeng	12	3,984	959	—	4,338	1,013	127
Dadong	7	1,343	843	—	1,485	1,021	160
Danwei	—	6,364	—	—	6,502	—	—

Source: Commune and brigade accounts.

Note: Danwei population figures include the residents of the market town, cadres, and employees of commune enterprises who were given a grain quota from the state or collective.

	1972			1976			1982	
Population	Grain Yield (Catties per Mu)	Per Capita Income (Yuan)	Population	Grain Yield (Catties per Mu)	Per Capita Income (Yuan)	Population	Grain Yield (Catties per Mu)	Per Capita Income (Yuan)
375	1,055	194	421	1,171	278	434	1,319	770
1,030	1,122	135	1,116	1,142	92	1,166	1,102	288
309	1,067	145	332	1,050	174	334	1,371	738
2,478	977	123	2,675	955	108	2,763	1,103	342
1,458	808	82	1,555	718	81	1,610	1,016	522
4,346	843	93	4,491	864	81	4,812	1,100	450
1,180	880	71	1,243	740	80	1,393	1,071	495
1,384	1,000	132	1,450	923	103	1,494	974	262
990	956	114	1,082	890	140	1,115	1,046	537
2,694	1,022	152	2,827	969	128	2,840	1,152	501
3,777	834	84	3,906	846	87	4,010	886	328
2,054	919	92	2,144	806	101	2,205	1,002	402
786	1,015	113	846	1,065	117	883	1,137	402
962	1,049	101	1,010	1,028	91	1,065	1,202	257
1,841	872	116	1,912	849	102	1,939	1,133	337
1,408	818	111	1,444	844	101	1,425	1,036	459
981	902	112	1,048	808	83	1,072	1,174	334
835	902	132	885	988	138	893	1,110	297
496	805	112	501	836	99	494	1,135	464
5,364	1,101	150	5,645	1,018	119	5,939	1,132	418
—	907	—	663	789	71	694	1,100	264
—	809	—	1,488	924	96	1,579	998	545
8,115	764	110	1,303	749	77	1,445	1,065	401
—	794	—	2,456	869	81	2,500	1,097	262
—	868	—	1,466	730	94	1,556	1,074	382
—	829	—	979	657	66	970	1,290	278
1,138	1,158	142	1,222	1,174	96	1,289	1,257	237
4,646	909	115	4,845	879	88	4,961	1,188	406
1,645	751	100	1,652	884	121	1,677	852	469
6,743	—	—	6,723	—	—	6,572	—	—

Clouds gathered over the prosperity of the villages as Mao launched the Socialist Education Movement at the end of 1963. The Central Committee of the party issued a series of directives about an overhaul of rural leadership. Known as the "First Ten Points" (May 1963), the "Later Ten Points" (September 1963), and then the "Revised Later Ten Points" (September 1964), these documents reflected sharp cleavages among the national leaders.[6] In selected rural communities, the Maoists used the campaigns to promote their version of socialism, which was to rest on a corps of reinspired cadres. The political agenda was not hidden: the Maoists intended also to root out those "who had gone astray" by following the Liuist party line.

Mao's campaign emphasized that the ideological relaxation had allowed new class differentiation to take place. A rich-peasant mentality had begun to undermine long-term socialist goals. People had forgotten the class struggle, and Mao asserted that party cadres who were supposedly the vanguard of proletarian class interests had been corrupted by the privileges they had accumulated and now lorded over the peasants. In this way cadres had joined ranks with former class enemies (landlords and rich peasants) to subvert the socialist system. The moral leadership that Mao had hoped for needed revitalizing.

While the storm was brewing, Xinhui County conducted an investigation of the conflict of interest between the collective and the private sectors in two of Huancheng's brigades, Tianma and Dadong. The political message was made explicit: The problems of renewed class differentiation had their source in the collective economy itself, and for this the cadres were responsible. The report on the inquiries showed that the county leadership was concerned about the continued class differentiation within the brigades.[7]

The report brought out the fact that in neither the collective nor the private sectors could the poor peasant households catch up with the richer ones (see table 9.3). It went on to blame the situation on the selfish motives of some of the richer peasants; their possession of technical skills, savings, and tools; and their ability to make use of social and market networks. The report cautioned that these qualities made them oppose socialist transformation. During the collectivization drives of 1956 and 1957, fourteen of the eighteen upper middle peasants in Liucun of Tianma remained independent until they finally joined the commune in 1958. In the early 1960s, they fulfilled only 40 percent of their team responsibilities. They complained about energy expended on rice production and insisted on distribution according to labor inputs since they often had greater numbers of able-bodied laborers in their households. They also accumulated many

Table 9.3. Class Differentiation in Selected Brigades, 1964

Class Status	No. of Households	Per Capita Income (Yuan)	Per Capita Daily Work-Points	Above-Production Bonuses (Yuan)	Grain Bartered for Fertilizer (Catties per Household)
1. *Liucun Team Number 4, Tianma Brigade*					
Poor and lower middle peasant	26	89.7	3.22	20.4	165
Middle peasant	7	90.6	3.63	23.4	181
Upper middle peasant	8	95.8	3.32	25.0	270
Landlord	4	130.8	4.37	28.9	283
2. *Team Number 5, Dadong Brigade*					
Poor and lower middle peasant	29	112	3.08	21.5	—
Middle peasant	5	108	3.45	27.0	—
Upper middle peasant	3	149	4.10	36.0	—
Landlord	2	128	4.00	24.0	—

Source: Xinhui Gongzuo, August 12, 1964, 1–6.

Note: Statistics are available only for a sample of the households: in the first case, 45 out of 56 and in the second, 39 out of 47. The category of rich peasants is not mentioned in the report. I suspect that they are included in the landlord category.

work-points on the side. One upper middle peasant made full use of his
social networks in Huicheng and Jiangmen by running errands and getting
supplies for the team. In one year, he earned 1,049 work-points. Another
one, skilled in tending palm and citrus, netted 1,398 points in the same
period. When orchards were auctioned out to households in 1962, the
upper middle peasants had the resources to win the bidding. In one of the
polders, for example, 6.42 mu out of a dike measuring 11.47 mu were
obtained by three middle and upper middle peasants.

Because the allocation of land was based on labor skills and capacity,
poor-peasant households generally received less land. The report gave the
example of an upper middle peasant whose peanut patch was three times
the size of that of an average poor-peasant household. Similar problems
were found in the contracting for the use of boats. The report cautioned
that a liberalized, market-oriented economy and a system of production
responsibility based entirely on rewards to skilled labor favored upper
middle peasants' interests over those of the poor peasants. The dissolution
of the collective economy and increased social differentiation were issues
of which rural cadres should take note, the report advised. They involved
"a struggle between two political lines" (*Xinhui gongzuo* [July 24,
1964]:6). Records in Dongjia Brigade show that investigations were carried out there too. A comparison of the amount of savings and loans taken
from the brigade's credit cooperative clearly demonstrated the economic
superiority of the upper middle peasants (see table 9.4).

To channel the renewed concern for the class struggle, Mao insisted on a
different kind of work team. The teams were to be composed of people

Table 9.4.   Class Differences in Savings and Loans, Yuanqing Cooperative,
Dongjia Brigade, 1962

	Team Number Six		Team Number Two	
Class Status	Average Savings per Household (Yuan)	Average Loans per Household (Yuan)	Average Savings per Household (Yuan)	Average Loans per Household (Yuan)
Poor and lower middle peasants	72.85	39.60	87.45	40.95
Upper middle peasants	176.80	32.60	128.20	22.50
Rich peasants	77.00	32.60	90.00	33.30
Landlords	30.00	14.60	38.00	35.50
Others	27.00	28.00	57.00	33.00

Source: Brigade accounts collected during fieldwork.

with reliable class backgrounds who would not approach political problems in an ad hoc manner. It was obvious that Mao hoped through the
work teams to develop a new rural leadership consisting of young activists
willing to upset the status quo. Their weapon in the struggle was the
language of class and revolution; but this time the target was the party
bureaucracy itself.

However, the Liuist faction countered Maoist attacks by diverting the
attention of the campaigns to the corruption of the cadres and to a reasser-
tion of party discipline. Instead of focusing on party leaders as Mao had
intended, the campaign was directed to attack all rural cadres indiscriminately. Xiao Siqing (the Four Small Cleanups campaign) was conducted at selected villages in the summer and fall of 1963, allegedly to
stamp out corruption. In 1964 the campaign was extended to the entire
countryside. Without much sense of what was brewing on the national
political scene, commune and brigade cadres in Huancheng joined work
teams from the county to "struggle against cadre corruption" in neighboring counties. When they returned, they were surprised to find themselves
the targets of attack. During the height of the movement in 1964, the party
committee of the county rounded up all the rural cadres from its twenty-
one communes. For several weeks they were confined in compounds in
Huicheng, where they attended political study sessions and were required
"to reflect on their mistakes in isolation." Each commune was assigned a
quota of fines. Cadres were instructed to report on their own corruption
and to pay back the amounts they had acquired. Lin Qing, then a member
of Tianlu Brigade's party committee, looked back on the experience with
unabashed cynicism.

> Except for a few deputy team leaders who remained behind to take care of the
> technical matters of production, all the cadres in Tianlu, including the accoun-
> tants and cashiers, were rounded up and sent for political study, forty-four in
> all. We were kept in the compound of the Cultural Palace in Huicheng. For the
> best part of a month we were made to study party documents and write
> confessions. I even had to confess how many free movies I had attended, and
> how many pieces of sugarcane I ate while working in the collective fields. I
> was fined 46 yuan but refused to pay. Many cadres were scared stiff. If we did
> not have enough cash, we had to pay the party back with our personal belong-
> ings, such as watches and furniture (valued at a very low price, of course!).
> Telling myself that the whole episode was a farce, I took the opportunity to
> take a good look around in the city. Some cadres felt so humiliated that they
> refused to resume their posts afterward. (Lin Qing, interview with the author,
> summer 1983)

Ye, a former land reform activist who assumed the post of party secretary in Tianlu in 1958 at the age of thirty, was expelled from the party and demoted. He ended up as an ordinary worker in Huicheng. County officials accused him of not cooperating with the campaign and therefore made an example of him. It was clear that the campaigns were used to settle personal grudges. Tianlu was considered rather "backward" as far as its enthusiasm for communization was concerned, and some commune and county officials felt that the brigade secretary had made them look bad. Ironically, the brigade leader, then forty years old, who was subjected to as much criticism as Secretary Ye was, replaced him and basically held the post until he was transferred to the brick factory of the commune in 1978.

Chen Sheyuan told a similar story:

> I was already working at the commune office then. They made me pay back 42 yuan for free meals and free movies. To think of it, an occasional meal after evening meetings at the brigade canteen was no big deal. I had a 60-yuan watch, but the party valued it at 20 yuan, so I refused to give it up. Huang Tao was fined 230 yuan, having been accused of receiving extra work-points that made up his wages. I think it was only fair that he took the work-points because in 1962–63 his fellow villagers were earning 2.8 yuan a day.[8] Some cadres were so fearful that they lay awake at night, and our superiors claimed that it was a sign of guilt. I slept well and was then accused of not having done enough self-reflection. When we returned home, the work teams mobilized the masses to criticize us. It was vicious. In previous rectification campaigns, the matter was largely confined within the party. This time, all hell broke loose. Many charges were ways for the masses to settle personal accounts with us. We had no respect left for one another. The campaigns seemed so unnecessary. I think the party work teams targeted the wrong people, diagnosed the wrong disease, and prescribed the wrong cure. (Chen Sheyuan, interview with the author, summer 1983)

Most cadres I interviewed in Huancheng agreed that the Siqing movement had been personally devastating. Two cadres committed suicide, and a few lost their posts. For most cadres the movement had come as a total surprise. They had been comfortably off. As described earlier, the Maoist rhetoric of the 1950s had made them politically powerful. At the same time, their affiliations with the Liuist bureaucracy had given them access to scarce state resources. In a traditionally commercialized area, ideological relaxation meant that the cadres could also tap the resources of the thriving rural markets and so get ahead of fellow villagers. It was the best of both worlds. However, the Siqing movement upset the comfortable balance. They were afraid and angry at the party for the harsh disciplinary actions it was taking. It troubled them that the influence they had built up over years could be destroyed so easily by the same organization that had given it to them in the first place. The most worrisome aspect of the campaign, however, was the realization that unprecedented political struggles were brewing among the national leaders and that the cadres were mere pawns in the drama.

Politicized Patronage

At the same time that rural cadres were being sucked into the political whirlpool surrounding their party superiors, they were confronted with internal rifts that their earlier maneuvers had created. Lin Qing observed that villagers who held personal grudges against the cadres for their misdeeds during the "three bad years" (1959–61) joined the work teams and attacked with a vengeance. Young men from the village who had felt left out in the period of prosperity came forward to claim their share of the resources. By the early 1960s, everyone had become aware that ties based on kin and community were effective means to get ahead only if they were attached to cadre patronage. Cadre positions and their associated access to scarce resources had become a sought-after prize among the young and the ambitious.

In 1965, the Maoist faction in the national leadership gained momentum. Calls for ideological purity appeared frequently in the official papers and reached a feverish pitch in the following years. In the villages, the loosely organized production teams were tightened up once again, and market flexibility was reduced. Brigade cadres were called upon to supervise the changes, but they had to tolerate the presence of new activists recruited by the work teams during the Siqing movement. The new recruits came from within the brigades and soon became subject to the patronage of the older cadres once the work teams had left. It was on the recommendation of the older cadres that they became the new heads of production teams and members of the Party Youth League. Moreover, the brigade cadres themselves were part of the patronage network of the broader commune.

Every major campaign imposed from above brought with it a new group of cadres. Cadres who shared common recruitment criteria and political experiences with the older leaders were actively sought out. In meetings at the commune, veterans of different campaigns settled political and personal matters among themselves. Items for negotiation ranged from commune subsidies and investment, to the distribution of grain quotas and the grooming of successors. Patronage based on kin and community ties was a familiar concept from the past, but connecting it to the party's political priorities to form a hierarchical leadership structure in the commune was probably one of the most effective means for the party to influence the rural communities from within.

The ability of cadres to survive the economic retrenchment and the Siqing movement and to endure attacks by both the Maoists and the Liuists demonstrated their resilience. As a group, the rural cadres consolidated their positions in relation to the ordinary peasants and held onto their privileged access to resources. Initially, the older cadres had seen in the necessity of absorbing younger competitors into their ranks nothing but unavoidable compromise. Yet in doing so they further buttressed the power of the patronage network and confirmed the value of party affiliations. When conflicts of interests arose among brigade cadres, they would seek out patrons at the next higher level of the commune party organization to mediate between them. However, the increasing polarization of the national leadership in the mid-1960s destabilized the patronage system. When the influence of county and commune patrons changed with shifts of the political wind, their power of mediation became uncertain, and their motives unpredictable. When conflicts among cadres became irreparable, the villagers took sides with whoever best served their economic interests and moral expectations.

Factions and Pawns

When tabloids denouncing leading party cadres first appeared in Guangzhou and Huicheng, cadres at Huancheng Commune saw the writing on the wall. Their agonizing experiences with work teams during the Siqing campaign were barely behind them. Some members of the Party Youth League, together with city youths who had been relocated to the rural areas, revived the study of Mao's works that had started with the arrival of the work teams during the previous two years. A flood of party documents carrying conflicting messages followed. By June 1966, newspaper editorials had reached an almost hysterical pitch. The gathering storm was all too clear to the anxious observers in the commune.[9]

In Huicheng, the county party headquarters were only a half-mile away across the bridge from Huancheng. Daily crowds of young students and workers paraded the streets in support of Mao. They fiercely accused each other of supporting "capitalist roaders" (zou zi pai) in the party hierarchy. When one after the other county officials began professing their political stands in mass meetings, commune and brigade cadres were pressured to do likewise. Chen Sheyuan recalled:

> We quoted Chairman Mao, read party documents, and made public statements about the class struggle, but we all belonged to the General Faction [*zong pai*, meaning supporters of the party status quo]. I was the writer of tabloids in the commune office. We could cover the whole city with tabloids. The county party committee initially asked us to go through the motions and conduct self-criticism sessions. So we did, and we found no ideological disagreement among us. Then the banner faction [*qi pai*, meaning Maoists, or the rebel faction] accused the established party cadres of being counterrevolutionaries. Some young students in our secondary school were incited by rebels in the city to put up posters against us. There was one hanging in the main street, at least 30 feet long, pointing to some as "capitalist roaders." (Chen Sheyuan, interview with the author, summer 1983)

In September 1966, the county party committee was finally forced to "step aside" (*kao bian zhan*). Competing Red Guard factions, claiming the correct class origins or expressing ardent loyalty to Mao, battled with each other and imposed their own rules of behavior on Huicheng and Jiangmen. Members of the city's transportation department sought refuge with their vehicles at the commune across the bridge for fear of sabotage by rival factions in the county capital.[10] Since Huancheng was situated at the southern edge of the two cities, commune cadres nervously organized their militia to prevent the fighting from spilling over into commune territory. The main street of the commune was connected to the southwestern part of Huicheng by a bridge, which became the central point of contention between pro-Liu and pro-Mao factions in the city. Maoist rebel Red Guards stood at the head of the bridge and harassed women coming into town to do their marketing. Married peasant women in Tianma and Tianlu often wore their hair up; the young rebels cut their hair off, accusing them of continuing "feudal customs." It was quite a sight, Chen Sheyuan recalled, to see these women crying and cursing the students, who were dead serious in their acts. Other incidents seemed equally ridiculous to Chen. He said that a teacher in the commune who was giving lessons on personal hygiene cautioned students that shirt collars (*ling*) and sleeves (*xiu*) were most easily soiled. Because of the pun on the words for collar and sleeve, city rebels incited commune students to denounce the man for "blaspheming Mao the Great leader" (*lingxiu*).

Peasants in Huancheng generally had little patience with the Maoist rebels. Students in the commune school once cooperated with the Red Guards and staged a sit-in in front of the commune headquarters to protest the treatment of a student. Peasant militia in Chengjiao Brigade situated near the commune headquarters stormed the sit-in and beat up the students. The commune called in army units at Niuguling south of the commune[11] to help the peasants "teach the rebels a lesson." Another incident revealed similar attitudes. A group of Red Guards from Huicheng had taken a truck from the army base at Niuguling. Driving through the commune, they crashed into a bridge. Villagers left the wounded rebels by the roadside. To them, the Red Guards were outsiders, troublemakers from the opposing faction, who did not deserve sympathy.

It seems that the peasants' political orientation was largely shaped by their cadres. At the beginning of the Cultural Revolution, the commune leadership had made it clear that denouncing party secretaries was an act against the party. The commune militia, which sided with the army units at Niuguling, was on the alert against "outside agitators." The young activists who had been recruited into the established patronage network in 1964 were by no means radical followers of Mao. On the contrary, they were intent on defending their newly acquired positions. Residents of the market town who were educated workers at the commune enterprises chose not to associate with any faction and called themselves the "faction of the free spirits" (xiao yao pai).

The political rituals of self-criticism and of pledging loyalty to Mao were nevertheless performed. In every brigade Party Youth League members had been instructed to organize Mao study sessions from the beginning of the Siqing movement. They became the activists whom the city rebels sought out to mobilize the peasants in mass meetings. An uncle of Chen Mingfa in Meijiang recalled in 1983 that he watched his nephew make token self-criticisms with indignant embarrassment, and that the designated "revolutionary successors" performed their duties with obvious awkwardness. Chen Mingfa himself admitted that they eventually performed the "loyalty parade" (zhong zi wu), recited Mao quotations, and studied Mao's works. The group that suffered most in the villages were the former landlords and rich peasants. Their class labels reduced them to the state of perpetual political scapegoats. They were paraded around and roughed up whenever party superiors made rural cadres go through the motions of the class struggle.[12]

The handful of rebel activists were city youths who had been assigned to work in the rural areas in the early 1960s. Some of them were of middle class origins and especially anxious to establish political credit by showing loyalty to Mao. Peasants identified these activists as those who joined with students from the commune school to vandalize family altars, burn temple objects, and harass women wearing traditional attire. "They were simply a nuisance," said Lin Qing in his most dismissive mode.[13]

Under pressure from the county political factions, the commune administration finally stepped aside at the end of 1966. An interregnum committee composed of the *san jiehe* elements (young activists, militia, and representatives of the poor peasants) was set up. They formed the core of the Cultural Revolution Small Group, which was entrusted with conducting political criticism. Xu Decheng and Huang Tao, for example, became mass representatives at the commune level because of their poor-peasant class status and were put in charge of the commune militia as well. The class credentials of these new activists were no different than those of the party cadres. In Tianlu the interregnum committee was headed by an old man of the Feng surname. He was a figurehead of the Poor Peasant League who deferred completely to the party cadres. According to Lin Qing, "whenever the commune activists came around, we would gather around and criticize one another a little; then we went back to work."[14] It seems that the mass representatives and the cadres covered up well for each other.

Though relative calm prevailed, brigades in the periurban areas did encounter more rebel activities when city Red Guards were involved. In one mass meeting, the party secretary of Dongjia and his brother, who was in charge of brigade finances, were accused of having constructed a feudal kingdom (*fengjian wangguo*) for themselves. Urged on by city Red Guards, village youths gave them a beating. Fortunately, according to Cheng Mingfa, the violence never got out of hand, because a deputy party secretary of the commune, who was a native of Dongjia, had returned to the brigade after the commune leadership was dismantled. Out of respect for him, the city youths restrained their zeal.[15] There was another, structural reason for the relative calm in the commune and brigades. When the revolutionary committees at the national and the provincial levels were set up in 1968 and 1969, the Maoist faction did not succeed in acquiring dominant positions. The military often sided with party cadres against what they considered rebel mass representatives. The revolutionary committees at each level directed the administrative reorganization of the next lower level. So one finds that by the time the commune and brigade committees were reconstituted, most of the important posts were filled by supporters of the status quo.

In February 1968, the revolutionary committee of Xinhui County was established (Xinhui Xian Dang'anguan 1984, 33). A few months later, Huancheng Commune created its own revolutionary committee. The assignment of positions resembled nothing so much as a game of musical chairs: old cadres switched posts in the new committee. Chen Sheyuan was good with his pen and was therefore assigned to the political work section. Xu Decheng and Huang Tao, who had been given the power to organize the militia during the interregnum period, remained as its heads.

The militia was nicknamed the "107 militia": the 7 symbolized the hoe, the *0* stood for the hat, and the *1* was the bamboo pole, the three major possessions of a peasant. The appointment of Xu and Huang was an example of the commune's creative compromise with county politics. The two men satisfied radical class criteria: they were of poor-peasant status, and they qualified for the label of mass representative because they were not state cadres. They were in fact brigade party secretaries loyal to the old status quo.[16] I got the impression that the militia under Xu Decheng was used defensively to prevent the fighting in Huicheng from spilling over into the commune. In other parts of China, such as the periurban areas of Guangdong, as described by Hai Feng (1971), and in Guilin, as described by Hua Linshan (1987), the militia was used by the army to attack Red Guard factions in the cities. A cadre in Dongjia mentioned that its militia was mobilized to fight the "radicals" in Jiangmen.

Though the Cultural Revolution officially came to an end in 1969, the party committee in Xinhui County was not reconstituted until late 1970. The membership of the new party committee in Huancheng overlapped with that of the commune revolutionary committee. The party committee had consisted of twenty-eight members ever since its establishment in 1958. The new committee in 1970 replaced fourteen members, including the party secretary, who was transferred to a neighboring commune. A few state cadres from neighboring communes assumed the posts of deputy party secretaries. The six brigade cadres who had been mass representatives (*qunzong daibiao*) returned to their posts in the brigades. Figures 9.1 and 9.2 show the important positions in the party committee and the commune revolutionary committee.

Only three of the twenty-eight member party committee were "outsiders," and of these two came from Guangzhou. The reason for this was that the county party committee demanded that the candidates for the commune committee be under twenty-five years old, with a senior middle school education and with no overseas connections. "It was not easy for us in the commune to find candidates with such qualifications," recalled Chen Sheyuan during an interview in 1983, "so we had to make do with the two youths from Guangzhou. Fortunately, the family of one was originally from Xinhui. We made them members of three groups in one day. In the morning they were made commune members, in the afternoon they became party members, and in the evening they were elected members of the party committee."

The commune revolutionary committee consisted of the twenty-eight members of the party committee, plus six brigade members who were mass representatives. There were six directors, the head of the commune and his

```
                    Party secretary
                    ─────────────────
                    4 deputy secretaries
─────────────────────────────────────────────────────────────
    Party and          Agriculture        Finance         Industry
    Mass Work                             and Trade

*Party Organization*

*Propaganda*

*Political Work*

*Public Security*

*Health*

*Education*

*Women's Affairs*

*Legal Work*

*Militia*
```

Fig. 9.1. The Party Committee in Huancheng Commune, 1970–79 (28 members), out of which 13 members formed an executive committee. They were served by a Party Committee Office doing clerical work.

five deputies. Except for one mass representative (who happened to be the cadre for women's affairs in Chengnan Brigade), the other directors were also the five party secretaries in the commune. They ran the various administrative offices. The heads of these offices were often members of the revolutionary committee. Only three came from outside Xinhui County.

In the brigades only a handful of rebels emerged. Village youths seldom went outside the commune to foment revolution. The ones who did so were promptly promoted to commune committees and then beyond. There was Feng Rui of Tianlu, who graduated from the senior middle school attached to the commune in 1965. She joined a Red Guard faction in Guangzhou and upon her return volunteered to direct the brigade's broadcasting station. The brigade leadership promptly recommended her for the commune's party youth training camps. Subsequently she became a party member and a member of the party committee. In 1976 she was promoted by the commune to the county Women's League, and ended up as a cadre at the provincial Women's League. With larger issues to deal with, she was safely out of the way.

On the surface, it seemed that nothing drastic had changed in Huancheng Commune. Nevertheless life did not go on as before. The bases

Director
Four deputy directors and Six mass representatives

Office of Finance and Trade	Office of Commune Enterprises	Sections for: *Public Security* *Militia* *Youth* *Women's Affairs* *Education and* *Health* *Civil Affairs*	Section for Agriculture

Fig. 9.2. The Revolutionary Committee in Huancheng Commune, 1970–79 (28 members of the party committee, plus 6 mass representatives from the brigades)

of political power and the principles of political struggle changed substantially in the wake of the Cultural Revolution. As political tensions subsided, the ideological and factional struggles left a lingering chill. The dissenting voices at each level of the reconstituted party and government committees found patrons at the next level up in the party hierarchy. Since 1968, educated youths had been sent down from the cities to "settle" in the villages.[17] Under the wing of their radical patrons in the commune and county party organizations, many of these youths had been recruited to the party branches. Their presence perpetuated factional fights, with repercussions all the way from the national leadership down to the villages and factories. When rural cadres could no longer ignore the factional splits among their party superiors, their own united front with new recruits started to crack.

Once formal institutional structures had been fractured too much to be reliable, political decisions began to rest less on established standards of bureaucratic behavior and more on individual interpretations of whatever official ideology was emanating from the party center. This tendency, coupled with the fact that the military and mass representatives shared the political stage at every administrative level and could don political caps (*dai maozi*) just as easily as the cadres, had the effect of politicizing everyone's life. From complaining about the grain quotas to showing personal favors, a range of otherwise petty and private concerns was raised to the level of "wrong political attitudes and counterrevolutionary activities."[18] If an opponent arbitrarily decided to use such incriminating evidence, one's career could be jeopardized. According to the cadres I later interviewed, not only did they find public denunciations personally trying, they also feared dismissal from their posts, the reduction or withholding of wages, the freezing of their savings in the banks, and even imprisonment. What the peasants feared most was the withholding of grain allocations and the threat of "expulsion from the collective" (*kaichu chushe*). With few other ways of making a living and the state's virtual monopoly of the grain trades, the threat of expulsion from the brigade was an effective weapon for cadres to keep peasants in line.

It is worth comparing such threats with expulsion from lineage membership during the prerevolutionary era. The withholding of ceremonial pork by the lineages was only a symbolic gesture, because culprits whose rights of settlement and tenure had been denied eventually wandered off to be absorbed into other villages. In the 1970s, the household registration system and the grain rations in the cellularized collective units made life more difficult for peasants who happened to be expelled. It was hard to be accepted elsewhere outside the proper bureaucratic channels. Everyone started to watch what he said and how he behaved. Consequently the peasants heeded the ideological messages of party superiors more closely than they might have wished. In a sense, peasants' lives were dominated by ideological battles over which they had little or no control. Sticking closely to whatever political rhetoric had been adopted by one's immediate superiors became a necessary though precarious way of navigating the stormy political waters. Patronage and clientage among the cadres and peasants were clearly observable, but they were exercised within an overarching structure of dependence and served to incorporate the clients into the state system rather than to protect them. Mao had placed tremendous responsibility on the rural cadres as well as bestowing on them the power to transform rural lives. But the cadres' relationship to the ideologically rigid party-state gave them little room to maneuver as patrons to fellow villagers.[19] State power was exercised and experienced through this structure of dependence, which came to dominate practically every sphere of life.

CHAPTER 10

The Paradox of Power

The Cultural Revolution created an extremely volatile political situation. Mao and Maoism became the ultimate ideological authority on the basis of which opposing factions in the party fought one another.[1] During the 1970s, political rhetoric nationwide shifted left and right, reflecting intense ideological struggles among Mao's radical associates, the old cadres who reemerged with the organized party, and the military. Each time a faction flexed its political muscle, conflicts rippled down from the party and the government bureaucracies through their networks of patronage.

From the movements of Red Guards, the violence in the factional fights, the mass public meetings against the party cadres in the cities, the reorganization of schools and factories, and the epistemological debates in the anti–Lin Biao and anti-Confucius campaigns in the early 1970s, one may form the impression that the political battles were confined to the urban industrial sectors and the intellectuals. However, one should not underestimate the amount of actual fighting that spilled over to the periurban areas in 1968, as described by Hua Linshan (1987) and Hai Feng (1971). Nor can one disregard the rhetoric used to promote the Dazhai model and the pressure it exerted on the rural cadres. Dazhai not only symbolized the Maoist line of agricultural development in its emphasis on self-reliance and egalitarianism, but was also shrewdly used as a political weapon by the factions between 1964, when it first emerged on the ideological scene, and the early 1980s, when it was finally discarded.[2]

In retrospect, officials admit that the pursuit of this model caused irreversible damage in many areas. Recent official pronouncements should be viewed with some skepticism as attempts to discredit the similarly radical policies of the Gang of Four and their followers. One may also wonder how much the policies were actually followed through. After all, local cadres were known to have occasionally paid lip service to the ideas of their superiors. In fact, party officials in Xinhui repeatedly accused rural cadres of dragging their feet in the implementation of policy and had alerted work teams to this problem.[3] However, it is clear from commune accounts and interviews that the cadres in Huancheng complied with most of the ideological extremes, although in the eyes of their party superiors they might not have done enough. The areas most seriously affected were grain procurement, cash crops, the agricultural infrastructure, and the system of production responsibilities.

Assuming that rural cadres were no longer as naive or as ideologically motivated to promote socialism as they were in the 1950s, one wonders why they followed Maoist directives so closely in the 1970s and thus antagonized fellow villagers, a predicament not entirely in their best interest in a politically charged environment. I would argue that the presence of a new generation of local activists within the factionalized party bureaucracy made it difficult for cadres to maintain a united front against the impositions of their superiors. The "pawns" who worked for the other faction could not always be counted on to cooperate in local manipulations. The status of state agent had brought its holder power and privilege, but it also locked him in untenable positions. The very structures of power that the cadres had built also victimized them. The Siqing campaigns and the upheavals of the Cultural Revolution had made the cadres painfully aware of the accusing fingers of their party superiors; disgruntled villagers who allied themselves with outside agitators made things worse. Cadres therefore toed ideological lines closely to save their positions.

The question that logically follows is, Why did the cadres try to preserve their positions at such costs? Was involvement in the party structure so vital to them that they could see no better alternative? Similarly, why were the anger and anxiety of the peasants so intensely focused on these cadres? In the following sections I try to address these questions by describing the leadership structure that existed in Huancheng Commune during the radical decade from the mid-1960s to the mid-1970s, its interactions with the party committee at the county level and with the work teams who "squatted" in the villages, and the major policies pursued by the cadres and their political consequences in local society.

A New Generation of Rural Cadres

If the political dynamics of the commune in the 1960s and 1970s were created by a factionalized and vulnerable rural leadership, it is important to analyze the character of some of the major political actors. The following are selected profiles.

Feng Guopei and Liang Chenghou of Tianlu Brigade were both from the poor-peasant class. Their education did not extend beyond the primary school level. At the end of the Siqing campaign they were recruited into the

Party Youth League, and became active in the Cultural Revolution Small Group in the teams.[4] In the wake of the Cultural Revolution, they were made members of the party and were selected to be team leaders. In 1976, they joined the brigade's party branch committee, which had nine members. In 1979, when the old secretary was transferred to the commune, Liang took his place, and Feng became his deputy. They were both thirty-four years old. A year later, Liang was transferred to the commune office to manage the cash crop production, and his post was filled by old Lin Qing.

Though old cadres continued to dominate Tianlu Brigade's party committee, young cadres were being groomed to succeed them. As mentioned earlier, Feng Rui was among the first group of students who graduated in 1965 from a branch of the Huicheng First Middle School attached to the commune. After having been involved with Red Guards in Huicheng, she joined the commune party committee in 1976 and was later transferred to the provincial Women's League. Ye Yunyi graduated from a technical middle school and joined the party branch committee at the age of twenty-two. She was then recruited to work in a county factory. Four of her contemporaries remained in the brigade as of 1982. Feng Shi, the militia captain, joined the party branch committee in 1976 at the age of twenty-five. Feng Tian, Ye Yu, and Zhang Fa became team leaders. In 1982, they were in their late twenties and early thirties.[5]

A similar generation of young cadres emerged in Dongjia Brigade. Liang Ronggen of Dongjia took the fast track. In 1966 he was the secretary of the Party Youth League and became an active figure in the Cultural Revolution Small Group in the brigade. When the old secretary refused to resume his post in 1970, Liang, a twenty-two-year-old party member, was elected to the party branch committee and then appointed to be its secretary. He kept this post until 1983. Dongjia had a relatively young leadership among the brigades in Huancheng. In 1980, seven of its nine members had been recruited in the early 1970s. They had attended junior middle school, and their average age was thirty-seven in 1982. Only six out of its sixteen team leaders were over forty years old; the rest were around thirty-five years old and had attended junior middle school.

In Meijiang Brigade, the eight-member party committee was dominated by older cadres. Chen Mingfa was its secretary from 1958 to 1968. Chen Mingjian, a known radical, ruled from 1968 to 1974, but Mingfa's pal, Chen Mingzhi, took over as secretary from 1974 to 1983. Three younger cadres were being groomed for leadership positions. The brigade leader from 1975 to 1983 was from the militia and had joined the party in the early 1970s. The deputy party secretary, Chen Lairen, was recruited into the party in 1970 at the age of twenty-one after participating in the construction of the hydroelectric station on Gudou Mountain at the border of Taishan and Xinhui counties. He was later assigned to oversee youth, militia, and propaganda work. From 1975 to 1983, he was the deputy party secretary in charge of brigade enterprises. Chen Mingjian was the infamous one. He was a junior middle school graduate. In his early twenties, he became a team leader and was given charge of the Party Youth League. He made friends with Li Chaolun of the Chengnan Brigade, who was a mass representative of the county party committee. Chen Mingjian attached himself to the county's Maoist factions and experienced a "helicopter ride." From 1968 to 1974, he was the political boss of Meijiang. Complaints from fellow cadres caused him to be transferred to the commune's cultural center in 1974 and a few years later to the clothing factory of the commune. In 1982, he was charged with the crime of using the factory as a cover for smuggling, and imprisoned.

This generation of cadres emerged in the mid-1960s. Their numbers grew during the 1970s as they assumed leadership posts in the brigade enterprises. Most continued to hold onto their positions in the early 1980s. Table 10.1 shows a sample of their number and positions in selected brigades in 1980. Table 10.2 shows the average ages of the party branch secretaries and the heads of brigades in 1980.

The Changing Structure of Commune Leadership

How did the nature of leadership and the structure of power change with the maturing of these cadres? In 1982, Huancheng Commune had around fourteen hundred party members out of a population of 60,000.[6] Twenty-five percent of the party members were selected to be representatives in the party congress. Of the twenty-eight members of the commune party committee, the secretary and four of his five deputies were appointed by the party committee of the county and approved by representatives from the commune without much fanfare. So changes in leadership occurred largely according to the will of the county party committee. The first party secretary held his post for ten years. As described in the previous chapter, the interregnum administration during the Cultural Revolution lasted only a brief time. Chen Wenyu, the first party secretary assigned to the re-organized party committee, held the position from 1970 to August 1981. When Chen was transferred to the county government, he was replaced by a young secretary from Qibao Commune in the western part of the county. The thirty-seven-year-old secretary stayed for only a year and went on to become the county's deputy secretary for agriculture. A forty-year-old

Table 10.1. Leading Cadres in Selected Brigades, 1980

Cadre Position	Dongjia		Chengnan		Tianlu		Sancun	
	Age	Education	Age	Education	Age	Education	Age	Education
Party branch secretary	34	Jr. middle	34	Jr. middle	52	Primary	48	None
Brigade leader	40	Sr. primary	40	Jr. middle	54	Primary	32	Sr. primary
Finance and trade	57	Primary	58	Primary	47	—	52	Primary
Enterprise	40	Jr. middle	34	Primary	40	Sr. primary	46	Sr. primary
Cash crops	36	Sr. primary	35	Primary	55	—	—	—
Militia	33	Sr. primary	24	Jr. middle	31	—	—	—
Security	34	Sr. primary	40	Jr. middle	37	—	—	—
Women's affairs	57	Sr. primary	28	Primary	29	—	38	Sr. primary
Propaganda	32	Sr. primary	46	Primary	37	Sr. primary	35	Jr. primary

Source: Interviews by author.

Table 10.2. Ages of Leading Brigade Cadres, 1980

Brigade	Party Branch Secretaries	Brigade Heads
Meijiang	51	33
Nangeng	33	29
Qunsheng	32	49
Chengnan	34	40
Chengjiao	33	44
Machong	43	27
Dajiao	29	29
Jiangzui	49	49
Shagang	55	39
Qibang	31	49
Duhui	41	26
Ercun	29	49
Sancun	48	32
Sicun	31	49
Wucun	36	51
Liucun	29	49
Qicun	39	34
Chakeng	33	51
Dadong	29	35
Xisheng	35	49
Dongjia	34	40
Xijia	31	50
Siya	41	52
Ningzhen	53	36
Tianlu	52	54
Hebei	47	51
Sanlian	55	54
Jiulong	45	49
Erning	34	—

Source: Interviews by author.

cadre from the county's agricultural bureau took over the vacated post. However, the elections in 1980 created a storm in a teacup. When the four appointed deputy party secretaries were "approved" by party delegates in the commune, three out of the four were not elected by mass representatives to the commune management committee.[7]

To assess the commune leadership from the late 1950s the early 1980s, one can divide the cadres into three broad categories based on their age and education and the time of their recruitment. The first generation were the veterans of the land reform and the collectivization campaigns. In the early 1980s, they constituted 60 percent of the cadres in the commune. They were over fifty years old, and many of them had old-style village-school educations or had attended adult literacy classes after the revolution. Some were brigade cadres transferred to the commune administration in the 1970s. The second group were recruited from the mid-1960s to the mid-1970s. They constituted 25 percent of the cadres, and were between thirty and forty years old. They had attended first the village schools and then technical junior middle schools when education was decentralized in 1958. The third category constituted 15 percent of the corps of rural cadres. They were in their twenties, had a senior middle school education, and were members of work teams during the Basic Line Education campaigns of the mid-1970s.[8] From 1976 to 1982, the commune groomed seven of these cadres for leadership positions.

In the brigades, the distribution of these groups of cadres was different. Only about 40 percent of the land reform veterans remained. When these cadres were transferred to the commune administration, the middle age group, which constituted about 45 percent of the corps of cadres, became the most active. The remaining 15 percent were under thirty years old.[9] Though the younger cadres were apprentices under the patronage of the veterans of the land reform, they were recruited according to different criteria and experienced a different political environment—one in which the position of cadre was powerful in relation to that of the ordinary peasant, but vulnerable due to the factional fights involving his superiors. They learned to read carefully between the lines.

The Reach of the County Authorities

The changes in the commune's leadership structure reflected a decade of intensive efforts by county authorities to control the villages. An analysis of the reports written for internal circulation among cadres reveals the interesting dynamics among the three levels of leaders.[10] Even in a year such as 1974, when the influence of the Gang of Four had ebbed, the party committee of the commune reported that it had organized 260 classes and had prepared 3,400 activists for the numerous political campaigns, in particular, the anti–Lin Biao and anti-Confucius campaigns and the Basic Line Education campaign. Numerous work teams were sent by the county to the villages. The work teams "squatted" in the villages and mobilized disgruntled peasants to report on commune and brigade leaders.

Huancheng Commune encountered its share of the official criticism.

One of the reports accused the leaders of not taking grain production seriously. The commune responded by sowing an additional 620 mu of rice to reach a total acreage of 41,812 mu, and in doing so forced the peasants to uproot 528 mu of cash crops, reduced the size of 128 dikes, and reclaimed 30 mu of land occupied by brick kilns. It also confiscated 180 mu of land that had been used improperly and disciplined a hundred or so households which had been raising poultry privately. About 402 individual entrepreneurs were returned to the teams (*Xinhui tongxun* [August 1, 1974]:1–4). In an area where half the cultivated land had traditionally been used for growing cash crops and where 20 percent of the population had engaged in one form of nonagricultural occupation or another, the relatively low number of delinquent acts cited by the report reveals how thoroughly the state had already restructured the rural economy.[11]

Other reports criticized selected brigades. After "squatting" in Meijiang for nine months, for example, the county work team found that the brigade duck farm had secured a contract from a state factory to raise 4,000 ducks. The cadres had received 6,000 yuan worth of feed and 1,300 yuan of fees and had divided the sum among themselves. The work team therefore organized a meeting of the poor- and middle-peasant representatives and severely chastised the cadres, who denied any knowledge of the contract. The cadres were also accused of having allowed more than sixty individuals to engage in private work outside the village and of being reluctant to accumulate organic fertilizers (*Xinhui tongxun*, June 6, 1974: 1–3). In the same year, criticisms of the leadership of Chakeng, Dadong, Xijia, Wucun, Qicun, and Hebei brigades were also published (*Xinhui tongxun*, March 17, 1974: 1–4).

These political exercises were not pleasant, as revealed by former members of the work teams.[12] The work teams followed five steps in denouncing the rural leaders. For a brigade with a population of two thousand, a work team of eight or nine members would be sent. After settling in, the team would seek out those with grievances, a tactic not unlike that of the land reform, and then confront the cadres. A few individuals would be selected for severe public criticism and punishment. This was known as "killing the chicken in order to scare the monkey" (*shaji jinghou*). The team members were expected to do field labor, but, according to the young villagers I interviewed, they had neither the motivation nor the stamina. Before leaving the village, the work team made a summary of its findings. The cadres considered the work teams threatening and "a real pain in the neck." Angry peasants in Tianma who did not want their cash crops trampled under had chased away young work team members with sickles and hoes. Generally, work team members from the commune who had families in the rural areas were considered more sensitive to people's feelings. Those from the county units with no ties in the villages were usually the most inflexible, and therefore hated and feared. Cadres accused them of unnecessarily aggravating entrenched factional conflicts among villagers and of making them report on one another. Ironically, these were the same tactics on which the older cadres had founded their careers. In the summer of 1983 Uncle Ye and Old Liang remembered their ambivalence: "The world had made a full circle back. We called it retribution."

From the mid-1960s to the early 1980s, a tenuous front of rural cadres faced the demands of their factionalized party superiors. According to Hong Yung Lee, the post–Cultural Revolution leadership at the national level comprised four groups of entrenched interests: those who had been purged but intended to make a comeback, the old survivors, those who had risen to power during the turmoil, and the Maoist rebels. Representatives of each group could be found in the major power hierarchies of the party, the military, and the government. Policies in the decade of the 1970s lurched left and right depending on the level of conflict or cooperation among the different groups. The strategies employed by rural cadres to cope with pressure from the party and the demands of the peasants shaped the political dynamics of the period and produced distinct perceptions of state power. In the following sections I describe the major policies implemented in Huancheng Commune by the rural cadres under the shadow of this political factionalism, and evaluate the effects of the policies on society and economy.

Grain Procurement

Grain procurement was a very sore issue for both cadres and peasants. The county set goals, according to which the commune would plan its acreage and estimate yield and total production. Quotas for the grain tax, the compulsory sales, and the above-quota sales were all based on these targets. However, the commune, as tables 10.3 and 10.4 show, tried to avoid the quotas by manipulating production figures. For most of the years after 1961, it reported a lower estimated yield per mu, on the basis of which the procurement quotas were calculated. This meant that even if the commune planted less grain, it might still have an actual harvest large enough for the government grain stations.

Table 10.5 shows that grain procurement for the commune peaked around 1969 and fell only slightly through the following decade. The increase was associated with the policies of Lin Biao, at the time Mao's heir

Table 10.3. Grain Production: Planned Acreage and Output

Year	Acreage (Mu)	Yield per Mu (Catties)	Total Estimated Yield (Picul)
1961	45,499	904	411,419
1962	44,701	915	409,786
1963	42,162	1,150	484,760
1964	39,218	902	353,675
1965	40,025	974	389,985
1966	39,732	1,072	425,863
1967	38,446	1,063	408,647
1968	39,727	979	388,943
1969	44,406	963	427,784
1970	45,100	882	397,879
1971	44,049	987	443,577
1972	43,950	964	423,528
1973	43,100	962	414,806
1974	43,425	1,075	466,786
1975	43,503	922	401,153
1976	42,879	963	413,074
1977	48,660	1,252	546,690
1978	44,099	1,008	444,354
1979	43,198	1,030	444,759
1980	42,803	1,198	504,180
1981	38,254	942	360,230
1982	38,622	1,116	431,102

Source: Commune accounts collected during fieldwork.

apparent, who mobilized the nation in preparation for a defensive war. To meet the large grain quota set against projected population increases and stable yields, the commune increased its acreage of winter wheat as a third crop after the double-cropping of rice.

Such efforts put a great deal of pressure on the commune's traditional cash crops and vegetables. As shown in table 10.6, taro, other root crops, and spring vegetables, which were extra sources of income for the peasants, were largely replaced by winter wheat. Citrus acreage was cut in half, and harvests were poor (see table 10.7). An independent study conducted by the county government in the early 1980s made similar observations.[13] It placed the problem of citrus growing in Huancheng in the context of citrus production in the county as a whole. As described in chapter 2, the citrus crop in Xinhui had a long history. The independent study claimed that, in 1936, acreage devoted to citrus in the county totaled around 60,617 mu, with a yield of 1,298,327 picul. There were thirty-five whole-

Table 10.4. Grain Production: Actual Acreage and Output

Year	Yield per Mu (Catties)	Acreage (Mu)	Total Yield (Picul) Collective	Private
1961	951	43,512	409,912	3,749
1962	952	43,228	407,253	4,125
1963	1,207	40,200	477,592	7,764
1964	835	37,931	352,227	2,514
1965	1,001	39,105	389,527	1,764
1966	1,096	39,007	425,564	1,989
1967	1,103	37,374	410,419	1,807
1968	1,012	38,963	392,899	1,555
1969	987	44,137	434,286	1,162
1970	912	44,653	404,133	3,267
1971	1,017	44,198	445,534	4,184
1972	989	54,495	426,846	2,281
1973	984	42,610	417,508	1,901
1974	1,098	43,067	471,026	1,947
1975	938	43,300	403,865	2,187
1976	979	42,627	414,407	2,723
1977	1,270	43,345	546,901	3,620
1978	1,020	43,804	445,388	2,473
1979	1,045	43,009	442,709	6,653
1980	1,194	42,594	497,453	11,001
1981	956	38,149	361,208	3,370
1982	1,128	38,529	432,680	1,967

Source: Commune accounts collected during fieldwork.

sale citrus merchants in Huicheng and Jiangmen, who sold the fruit to Guangzhou, Foshan, Shanghai, Macao, and Hong Kong, and another twelve fruit-processing factories. The crop suffered partial destruction during the Japanese occupation but revived in the early 1950s. From the mid-1950s on, the crop declined.

During the peak of ideological relaxation in 1962, Tao Zhu, then provincial party secretary, proposed to revive the crop. From 1963 to 1966, the provincial government gave the county interest-free loans amounting to 340,000 yuan, an additional 95,950 tons of chemical fertilizer, and an annual quota of 10,000 to 20,000 picul of organic fertilizer. For 1963 and 1964, it allocated 50,000 picul of rice for communes whose land was devoted to citrus. However, these efforts were discontinued when Tao Zhu was purged during the Cultural Revolution and the Maoist faction branded the citrus growing as "capitalistic."

The same study claims that political uncertainties discouraged produc-

Table 10.5. Grain Procurement and Consumption for Huancheng Commune

Year	Grain Quota (Picul)	Actual Delivery		Percentage of Quota Met (%)	Above-Quota Sales (Picul)	Procurement per Mu (Catties)	Per Capita Grain Consumption Allowances (Catties per Month)
		Grain Levies (Picul)	Grain Sales (Picul)				
1961	—	—	—	—	—	—	38.1
1962	171,236	59,198	112,038	100.0	4,252	405	40.3
1963	161,265	63,809	97,202	99.8	40,751	502	36.6
1964	180,211	65,619	79,655	80.7	14,338	421	38.0
1965	200,198	66,739	98,552	82.5	1,488	426	38.9
1966	187,436	65,970	110,210	93.5	21,728	507	43.8
1967	191,498	61,840	75,394	71.7	23,493	430	41.0
1968	189,390	61,983	71,833	70.6	4,518	355	37.5
1969	221,248	65,168	128,618	87.6	5,123	351	33.3
1970	220,796	62,590	100,451	73.8	5,912	378	36.0
1971	191,077	64,006	107,885	90.0	9,399	410	39.1
1972	168,199	64,607	79,323	85.6	7,355	349	39.1
1973	—	—	—	—	—	—	—
1974	168,519	64,450	96,913	95.7	9,166	396	45.0
1975	168,092	56,966	64,396	72.2	4,740	291	37.9
1976	167,822	56,697	57,280	68.5	3,626	276	37.8
1977	168,140	62,578	104,025	99.1	12,009	411	44.4
1978	—	—	—	—	—	—	—
1979	172,335	133,394		77.4	—	310	39.0
1980	173,476	172,076		99.0	—	404	43.0
1981	125,011	122,634		98.0	—	321	34.7
1982	133,276	132,722		99.5	—	344	41.0

Source: Commune accounts collected during fieldwork.

Table 10.6. Secondary Crops, Huancheng Commune, 1961–78

Year	Winter Wheat (Mu)	Taro (Mu)	Other Root Crops (Spring Harvested) (Mu)	Spring Vegetables (Mu)	Summer Vegetables (Mu)	Autumn Vegetables (Mu)
1961	5,082	1,965	1,887	2,558	1,893	2,422
1962	1,034	1,455	1,621	3,425	2,384	1,989
1963	393	1,306	901	1,175	1,802	749
1964	719	2,121	1,558	2,229	2,840	1,562
1965	261	3,260	2,204	2,118	6,527	2,664
1966	2,950	1,463	2,184	1,876	6,890	2,414
1967	1,101	624	1,082	1,099	3,770	2,109
1968	2,798	985	1,728	1,450	2,699	2,066
1969	2,231	569	365	663	1,549	891
1970	3,344	571	148	959	1,385	777
1971	6,621	715	561	1,125	1,586	928
1972	8,430	794	884	682	1,455	759
1973	10,559	889	480	905	1,752	1,193
1974	6,803	472	170	1,089	1,859	998
1975	9,481	517	748	1,411	892	876
1976	12,205	607	287	1,427	1,863	1,265
1977	18,396	373	225	1,540	1,753	1,304
1978	21,347	364	259	1,523	1,302	1,313

Source: Commune accounts collected during fieldwork.

Note: These crops are grown interspersed with the major crops and after the late crop of rice is harvested. From the early 1970s on, the production of winter wheat outpaced all other crops except summer vegetables.

tion teams from making long-term investments in the crop and that the low price set by state agents, together with their allocation of fertilizers based on output, created a vicious cycle (Xinhui Xian Nongye Quhua Bangongshi 1983, 291).

Despite the emphasis on grain production, the commune continued to fall short of meeting the grain quotas, nor could its per capita allowance for grain consumption satisfy local expectations of 50 catties per month. The pressure exerted on the brigades was uneven. Old cadres in Tianlu Brigade were less successful in negotiating lower quotas, which led them to con-clude that "honest old folks always lost out to the sharp-tongued in the periurban brigades." However, they realized that Tianlu and Tianma bri-gades supplied nearly 60 percent of the commune's grain sales. If they chose not to cooperate, the commune cadres would have been in trouble.

Table 10.7. Major Crops as a Percentage of Total Cultivated Area, 1961–82

Year	Total Cultivated Area (Mu)	Rice (%)	Peanuts (%)	Sugarcane (%)	Citrus (%)	Fan Palm (%)	Other (%)	Fish Ponds (%)	Private Plot (%)
1961	65,295	66.7	1.8	2.1	11.3	9.9	4.6	—	3.6
1962	65,100	66.4	2.3	2.9	9.7	10.0	3.0	—	5.7
1963	64,778	62.1	4.1	4.5	10.0	10.0	4.9	—	4.4
1964	64,713	58.6	3.6	6.4	12.6	10.1	4.7	—	4.0
1965	65,145	60.0	4.2	4.5	14.2	10.8	3.0	—	3.3
1966	65,560	59.4	3.8	4.7	13.8	11.5	4.0	—	2.8
1967	66,719	56.0	5.9	5.5	12.3	13.3	4.8	—	2.2
1968	66,755	58.4	4.0	5.8	11.9	13.5	4.3	—	2.1
1969	67,165	65.7	3.1	6.1	7.4	14.0	1.7	—	2.0
1970	66,874	66.8	3.8	5.8	5.7	14.2	0.4	—	3.3
1971	68,494	64.5	3.9	5.9	6.8	14.0	1.7	—	3.2
1972	68,623	63.2	4.1	7.6	6.9	14.2	0.9	—	3.1
1973	68,495	62.2	4.2	7.8	6.7	14.3	1.7	—	3.1
1974	68,572	62.8	3.7	7.8	6.6	14.4	1.6	—	3.1
1975	68,418	63.8	3.7	7.7	6.8	14.2	1.3	—	3.0
1976	67,930	62.7	3.8	7.8	6.5	13.9	2.2	—	3.1
1977	67,780	63.9	3.7	7.9	6.1	13.2	2.0	—	3.2
1978	67,861	74.6	2.7	7.8	6.2	13.1	1.5	0.72	3.1
1979	67,648	63.5	7.5	7.8	6.4	12.9	—	0.72	3.2
1980	67,818	62.8	7.4	9.0	5.5	12.6	—	0.70	3.3
1981	67,739	56.3	7.4	14.0	5.6	12.5	—	0.88	3.3
1982	67,434	57.1	8.7	12.6	6.1	12.3	—	0.89	2.4

Source: Commune accounts collected during fieldwork.

Note: Grain, peanuts, sugar cane, citrus, and fan palm were sold to state agents. The category under "other" includes tropical fruits, taro, sweet potatoes, seasonal vegetables, and so on.

Caught in this trap, the commune had to negotiate hard to make the two brigades comply with the assigned quotas.

At times, with the tacit approval of their associates in the commune, cadres in Tianlu cheated on the county cadres. In 1975, when the peasants were urged to plant grain intensively, the cadres asked them to apply the intensive method only in the fields bordering the commune highway. When county officials accompanied by commune cadres came to inspect, they were shown only those fields. However, the trick did not always work, Lin Qing claimed. There were "internal spies" who reported to their patrons in the commune or in the party committee of the county. The fate of the party secretary of Tianlu during the Siqing movement was well remembered by his colleagues. As described earlier, Secretary Ye was accused of not cooperating with the work teams. He was subsequently dismissed from office, expelled from the party, and "reduced to an ordinary worker." His fate was considered a tremendous loss of face.

Even with room to maneuver, the quotas were considered burdensome. Not only did they increase the older peasants' anxieties over food security, but they also cut into their cash crop incomes. These two concerns created tensions between commune and brigades, among brigade leaders, and between brigade cadres and peasants. When the commune's quota was distributed among its brigades, brigade cadres often quarreled over who should bear the greater responsibilities. Brigade accounts shows that Tianlu consistently bore the heaviest grain quota. Well-connected Chengnan got away with the least (see table 10.8).

When the grain procurement quota started to rise in the mid-1960s, reaching its height in 1969,[14] the brigades nearly drained their grain reserves. For Chengnan Brigade, 1,000 picul were added to the 1966 quota of 2,578 picul, an increase of 38.7 percent. Four thousand picul were added to Dongjia's 17,272 picul, an increase of 23 percent. Tianlu, which already had a heavy quota of 29,196 picul, was able to increase production by only 3,000 picul, an increase of 10 percent. The county then fixed the higher quotas as the targets for following years.

To avoid the stigma of "not taking grain as the basis," a common accusation from the Maoists, cadres either forced their teams to reduce grain consumption or made villagers uproot their cash crops in order to make room for grain cultivation. Both strategies were extremely unpopular among the peasants, who were already anxious about their grain reserves.

The tension was deeply felt in the periurban brigades where handicrafts and petty trade had been traditional sources of income but also where the cadres were more eager to toe the party line. To prevent the peasants from taking time away from grain production, the cadres from Dongjia allowed

Table 10.8. Grain Quotas for Selected Brigades, 1966–82

Year	Chengnan		Dongjia		Tianlu	
	Quota (Catties per Mu of Rice)	Monthly Grain Consumption Allowance (Catties per Person)	Quota (Catties per Mu of Rice)	Monthly Grain Consumption Allowance (Catties per Person)	Quota (Catties per Mu of Rice)	Monthly Grain Consumption Allowance (Catties per Person)
1966	177	35.3	480	36.9	642	40.8
1969	246	—	591	—	708	—
1979	149	41	392	36	469	38
1982	143	39.5	397	32	326	48
Percent change 1966–82	(−19%)		(−17%)		(−49%)	

Source: Brigade accounts collected during fieldwork.

them to raise at most ten chickens. Cadres from Chengnan collectivized the production of individual palm handicrafts, forbade private sales, and awarded the workers work-points. Another periurban brigade, Hebei, was chosen by the radical faction in the county party committee as a political model. The party secretary was a twenty-six-year-old teacher with a junior middle school education who sided with the Maoists. Five work teams were sent into Hebei by the county in 1975. They destroyed the brigade's major cash crop, watercress. Villagers I interviewed in 1983 recalled that during the reign of this secretary, every item that generated a profit became "capitalist activity." "It was not enough for them to trample the crops under, but they dragged us in it." The old party secretary from Meijiang, Chen Mingzhi, also complained that the tangerine crop suffered a decline from 1958 on. Efforts were made in the early 1960s to revive it, but the politics of the Cultural Revolution only made matters worse. Tangerine acreage in the brigade dropped from 2,800 mu in the late 1950s to a mere 400 mu in the late 1970s. "Peasants were angry," Chen said during a 1983 interview, "but what else could we do with a large grain procurement quota? Did we not want to eat?"

The relative susceptibility of the brigade cadres to ideological pressures from the county in the 1970s is further illustrated by the ways they juggled the figures for the procurement quotas, production yields, and peasant consumption. Chengnan, Dongjia, and Tianlu brigades presented three different types of response. The cadres in the Chengnan Brigade were able to keep their quotas to a minimum during the 1960s, but in the 1970s a young party secretary who had sided with the Maoists felt obliged to respond to the pleas of the radicals for more grain.[15] From 1966 to 1982, the quota for Chengnan decreased only 19 percent. The brigade fulfilled these quotas by lowering the amount distributed for peasant consumption. Instead of the usual 50 catties per adult per month, cadres often allocated only 35 to 40 catties to the peasants and sold the rest to the state.

Tianlu, on the other hand, had had a large quota since the 1960s. However, it was able to resist further increases in its quota because the cadres, as they put it, "were not ashamed to be ideologically backward." Except for the jump in procurement in 1969, which affected every brigade one way or another, the quota for Tianlu actually decreased by 49 percent from 1966 to 1982. Furthermore, the cadres kept the consumption allowances above the commune average even if it meant not meeting the quotas.

Dongjia Brigade was the worst off. The young party secretary felt ideologically obliged to accept a large quota. Its grain quota decreased only 17 percent during the 1970s. The brigade never had particularly high yields, and its consumption allowances for the peasants were kept at 32 to 36 catties per person. Even then it could not fulfill the quotas. In fact, the party secretary was suspended from his post in 1975 because of the brigade's poor delivery, as the peasants agonized over the small margin of security.

Production and Labor Management

Since collectivization, different systems of production responsibility had been tried. In the mid-1950s, the party committee of the *xiang* directed collective agricultural production. Even during the height of the communization movement, the *xiang* (renamed brigades) remained the most important unit for policy implementation. Except for a short period of radical mobilization in 1958, the dominant mode of distribution in Huancheng was the *san bao yi jiang* (three guarantees, one bonus). After the radical mobilization of the communization period, when team resources were often used without compensation, the autonomy of the teams to use the resources they had been assigned was finally guaranteed in 1961 by the "four fixed" (*si guding*) system. Each team was assigned a fixed amount of land, agricultural machinery, animals, and labor power. The size of the teams was reduced and private plots were revived. The decollectivization trend continued in the beginning of 1962, when Liu Shaoqi and his associates advocated the *san zi yi bao* program (three freedoms, one guarantee), whereby private plots were expanded, rural markets were revived, enterprises were allowed to control their own profits and losses, and production contracts were made with households. Political relaxation encouraged some former rich peasants and landlords to attempt to reclaim land and tools confiscated from them over a decade earlier.

These "capitalist tendencies" in Huancheng and other communes were used by the Maoist faction in the county government at the beginning of the Cultural Revolution to discredit political enemies. Under pressure, the commune cadres restored the three-tiered ownership system, with the team as the basic accounting unit. This system remained intact until the early 1980s.[16] In the three-tiered ownership system, team members earned income from the land assigned to the team. Team leaders drew up annual production plans and divided their laborers into work groups. For the tasks completed, each laborer was given a number of work-points. Work-points accumulated throughout the year as agricultural tasks were performed. The team sold its crops to the state agents and subtracted production costs and taxes from its gross income. Some funds were also set aside for welfare and investment. The value of a work day was then calculated by dividing net income by the total number of work-points accumulated by all the team members. Each household received what its members earned in kind as well as in cash, distributed twice yearly. Households that overspent were given a minimal ration, but the amount was debited against their future earnings. The availability of social services depended on how much the team was willing to set aside as collective funds. In Huancheng, the teams' welfare fund averaged 3 to 5 percent of their annual gross income. They also set aside 10 to 13 percent as investment funds.

For labor management, the teams adopted several methods to determine the work-point value of various tasks. Piece rate was the most common. Each agricultural task was assigned a certain number of points. Laborers who finished their tasks to the required standards were awarded the points. However, determining the work-points for specific tasks involved complicated technical calculations. Peasants and team leaders bickered over whether ploughing a field earned more work-points than weeding it. Team leaders were accused of nepotism if they assigned jobs that required less physical effort to relatives and friends. Production standards became problematic when laborers rushed through their tasks to make more time for other work. Villagers with whom I talked in the early 1980s generally agreed that the value of their work-points suffered because of sloppy work and low yield. Team leaders who had to assign and inspect the work considered their jobs troublesome and thankless.

The *san bao yi jiang* system resolved these difficulties somewhat by linking effort with productivity and reward. Work groups were assigned tasks with set quotas for yield and costs. The work-points they received depended on how well they met the targets. Bonus work-points were given for yields that exceeded the targets.[17]

A third method was the system termed the "democratic evaluation of work-points" (*minzhu pingfen*), which was adopted during the height of the radical period. Brigade cadres were obliged to implement it despite its unpopularity among the peasants. Each laborer was assigned a labor grade with work-points attached. The physical strength of each laborer was considered, but the number of work-points could be raised or lowered according to the team's evaluation of the individual's political attitudes. The practice was also known as "fixed points flexibly evaluated" (*sifen huoping*).

This method of evaluating work and income was highly politicized, subjective, and arbitrary. The difficulty of putting this system into practice is vividly illustrated by what took place in Tianlu Brigade. Tianlu was the largest brigade in Huancheng after the breakup of Tianma Brigade in 1973. In 1966 it had 4,731 members and a total cultivated area of 8,239 mu. The land-to-man ratio was 1.74 mu per capita, higher than the commune's average of 1.5 mu. The brigade was divided into eight unusually large teams. The largest had 810 residents; the smallest, 302. Although the accounting unit remained at the team level, the teams were subdivided into twenty-eight work groups, which were assigned different production responsibilities. As described earlier, Tianlu had dragged its feet during collectivization. By the time of the Cultural Revolution, brigade cadres began to feel ideological pressures more strongly. They resisted certain policies, such as the above-quota grain procurement. The leadership was more divided on the question of production management. The old cadres had no choice but to toe the ideological line, since they could not present a united front among themselves when facing party superiors. Tianlu started *minzhu pingfen* in 1967 but reverted to the piece-rate system in 1969 (when the party branch committee was reorganized with the old cadres). A year later, another radical upsurge in national political affairs prompted the brigade to adopt the program, only to drop it again in late 1972. For a brief period in 1973 and then from late 1975 to mid-1976, *minzhu pingfen* was promoted. After mid-1976 a "three fixed" (*san ding*) system was adopted. Ling Qing held that the system was no different from the "three guarantees" (*san bao*) system. Cadres used a different term just to avoid any association with Liu Shaoqi.

Chengnan Brigade faced similar circumstances. The brigade started to decollectivize in 1962 but restored team accounting in 1966. Piece rate continued. The brigade adopted the "democratic evaluation of workpoints" in 1967 and 1968. As in Tianlu, "women cried and men fought." Brigade cadres reverted to the piece-rate system in 1969 with the tacit approval of the commune cadres, but the brigade restored the "democratic work-point evaluations" again in 1972 and 1973. The cadres tried to reintroduce piece rate in 1973 but were accused in a mass meeting of the commune of "following the Liu Shaoqi line." They did not raise the issue of contracts until 1977.

The radical program and the successive policy reversals left unpleasant memories among peasants and cadres. Lin Qing commented skeptically:

> At first, we instructed our team leaders to hold an evaluation meeting once a year, but relatives and friends quarrelled over attitudes and ridiculed one another over labor worth. Nobody ever felt that he had had a fair evaluation. Some of the masses were embarrassed to claim too much, but became angry when fellow villagers did not give them enough credit. Others whose labor capabilities were doubted made a big fuss. The ones who talked loud and intimidated others got the most. We tried secret evaluations but people were suspicious of one another. The team leaders finally made the work groups do the evaluations. Some met once a season, then once a month, once a week,

and even once every three days. Nobody wanted to be stuck with a low value
for any extended period. Women cried and men fought. Feelings were hurt
and production was practically paralyzed. (Lin Qing, interview with the author, summer 1983)

The negative social and economic effects of the radical program were felt
by everyone in the brigade. The question remains as to why the brigade
cadres adopted the program time and again.

"Gather Enthusiasm to Bring Transformations"

In an effort to conform to the spirit of Dazhai, Huancheng Commune was
commissioned by the county party committee to undertake an ambitious
project: the construction of a network of dikes and a 12-kilometer highway. The project was not without merit. The commune is situated on a
floodplain. In the 1950s the collectives had built small reservoirs to regu-
late the flow of the river that meandered through the commune area.
During the Great Leap Forward, the flood-prevention gate at Jinniutou was
built to control the tides that surged in from the Ya Men inlet. In the 1960s,
eighteen electric pumping stations were installed to drain periodic floodwater from the fields. However, with the water level barely 16 centimeters
below the surface, crops often rotted at the roots.

In 1972, eighteen thousand members of the commune worked for a
month to dredge the numerous waterways. The method they used was
locally known as "closing the gate to beat the dog" (*guanmen dagou*): they
closed the flood-prevention gate, pumped the water out, and dredged the
riverbeds. However, rapid sedimentation blocked the narrow waterways
within a few years. The highway-dike project planned to replace the existing waterways (see figure 10.1) with a network of irrigation and drainage
canals (as shown in figure 10.2). Engineers estimated that with electric
water pumps they would be able to drain floodwater out of the area within
two hours and that they could lower underground water by 60 centimeters. The finished project would control the flow of water in 12,000
mu of land.

The party committee and eight brigades involved with the first phase of
the project resisted by appealing to their patrons in the provincial government. However, the Maoists in the county party organization wanted to
"break the small peasant mentality." "Big change comes only with effort"
(*da gan chu da bian*), they insisted. In December 1975 the commune started
work on the project (see figure 10.3), expecting it to be completed by

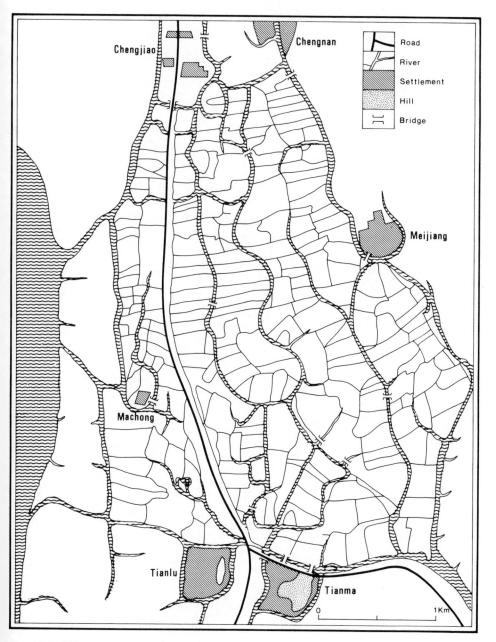

Fig. 10.1. Old Waterways in the Huancheng Area

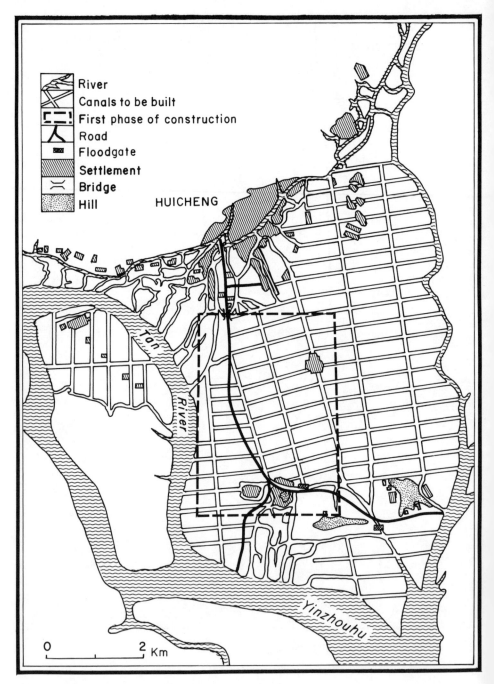

Fig. 10.2. The Plan for the Highway-Dike Project, 1975

spring planting. The brigades were unwilling to participate because the project encroached on their manpower. The eight brigades whose land was directly involved felt a financial strain as well. Not only were they responsible for part of the expenses, but also once their old dikes were leveled, team members lost their fruit trees. Reluctantly, a task force of 18,000 worked for six and a half days to dig the main canal, followed by another of 17,500 who worked for seven days to dig the tributary canals. Ten days before the Chinese New Year, 22,500 peasants filled the old waterways and flattened the fields. The commune used 500,000 yuan from its accumulated funds, while the county contributed a mere 57,000 yuan.[18] The brigades absorbed all the labor costs.

However, the project received neither the electricity nor the pumps it needed from the county. Peasants who relied on their small cargo boats complained that familiar waterways were blocked. Soil erosion occurred on the new dikes where fruit trees could not be replanted in time. The rest of the project was abandoned. As a commune cadre described it, "the project was a big, expensive, uncoordinated disaster in ecological and political terms; it hurt the energies and the finances of the commune and benefited only the vanity of county cadres. Such was the spirit of Dazhai." When asked why they allowed an unrealistic project to squander precious commune resources, the cadres uniformly expressed the fear of being reprimanded by party superiors. It seems to me that by the mid-1970s the cadres were holding on to their positions at all costs.

The Development of Brigade Enterprises

In the early 1970s, the brigades started to develop small-scale enterprises in response to the Maoist call for self-reliance and local ingenuity. Intended to serve agriculture cheaply, the enterprises could take the form of grain mills, oil presses, machine- and tool-repair workshops, and palm handicrafts and wine-making concerns. Some of the enterprises could subcontract with county industries to engage in the chemical processing of machine parts, clothes-making, and the recycling of industrial waste. The brigade cadres considered the latter ventures the most desirable because they were the least restricted by weather or agricultural conditions. They required little capital but introduced industrial know-how and discipline to the workers, and their profits were high.

The periurban brigades were particularly well connected to the county industries, and their nonagricultural workers badly needed employment. Nonetheless, team leaders were reluctant to give up their laborers; they

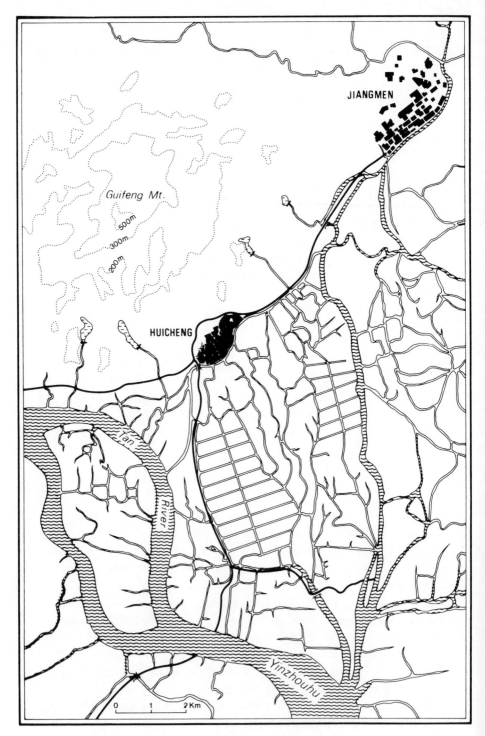

Fig. 10.3. The Highway-Dike Project—The Parts Completed

and their party superiors were wary of nonagricultural activities that might disturb grain production. Intensive methods of agriculture and construction projects placed seasonal strains on the teams' labor supply. From the start, the enterprises lured away the younger, better educated workers from the teams. On the other side of the coin, cadres in charge of the enterprises that secured contracts with county factories or with the state export corporations complained loudly when their workers were called back to the fields to meet agricultural schedules.

Conflicts also occurred between brigade cadres and workers, as well as among team members, over the issues of recruitment and wages. The experience of the Dongjia Brigade illustrates some of the problems. Dongjia's development of enterprises had been the highest in the commune since the 1970s. Industrial wages distributed by the enterprises were higher than the agricultural income distributed by the teams. Aspiring workers accused team and brigade cadres of favoring friends and relatives in the recruitment of workers. In 1976, when radical politics prevailed, the cadres calculated work-points for the enterprises on the basis of the value of the work-points in the teams. This measure was supposed to put an end to the fierce competition among team members for enterprise jobs. However, it succeeded only in creating conflict among the enterprise workers who came from different teams. Brigade cadres in charge of these decisions again found themselves accused of favoritism and unfairness.

Thus, while brigade cadres (in particular the younger generation of cadres) had acquired enough power at the brigade level to distribute favors to fellow villagers, structural problems of recruitment and wages caused by the ideological concerns of their party superiors triggered bitter conflicts. Such conflicts sharpened during the reign of the Maoist radicals, when opportunities outside of the collective sector were not readily available. Secretary Liang in Dongjia remembered that industrial jobs were fiercely contested and defended by whoever had gained access to them. The development of brigade enterprises in Huancheng Commune and its political paradoxes will be described in greater detail in the chapter 11.

The Transition to Brigade Accounting

A corollary of the Dazhai model was the transition from team to brigade accounting. The goal of this policy was to raise the socialist content in the collectively owned agricultural sector and to reduce differentiation among the teams.[19] Surprisingly, Sancun Village, which was made a brigade after Tianma Brigade was split up in 1973, made the transition to brigade accounting in 1978. The 1,532 residents of the single-surnamed community were divided into six teams, which grew grain and sugarcane. A few of the villagers engaged in handicrafts or petty trade. The brigade's average grain yield barely reached 900 catties throughout the 1970s. In 1977, the brigade had an annual per capita income of 146 yuan, the commune's median. The teams were even in size, but the income of the richest team was one-third more than that of the poorest (1.20 yuan vs. 0.84 yuan per workday).

The brigade cadres were proud of their enterprises, whose fixed assets were valued at 60,000 yuan. The enterprises employed 63 team members. Sancun's agricultural machinery station and grain mill served local needs at the same time as they accepted contracts from Huicheng. The brigade operated a twine-making factory, which sold its products to factories in Zhongshan County.[20] The brigade's chemical-processing workshop looked promising. When it began operating in 1976, the brigade invested 30,000 yuan and hired 13 young women with junior middle school educations from the teams. Contracts were secured through a personal contact, a technician in the County Electrical Machinery Plant in Huicheng. The enterprises created employment for the team members and income for the brigade. With expectations of further growth, the brigade cadres felt that they were accumulating collective assets, which were considered prerequisite for the transition to brigade accounting. In 1977 income from the enterprises constituted 30.3 percent of the total income of the teams and brigade. The growth of the brigade enterprises led cadres to expect that, despite disparities among the teams, the pooling of brigade and team incomes would continue to yield an average workday value of 1.50 yuan, 0.30 yuan more than that of the richest team. Commune cadres studying the possibility of switching to brigade accounting believed that the poor teams would find the proposal attractive and that the rich teams would at least reluctantly go along with the idea.

The transition to brigade accounting in Sancun was abruptly imposed by the county and commune administrations. From "nourishing the idea among peasant masses" to final approval from the county party committee, the process took exactly a month. The county party committee had its own reasons for promoting the change. The Gang of Four had barely been ousted from power. Under the leadership of Hua Guofeng, a series of "Learn from Dazhai" conferences were held nationwide. Radical associates of the Gang of Four continued to influence the national leadership, but it was clear to insiders that Hua's position was not secure. Some county officials decided to play it safe by upholding the Dazhai spirit in a limited way. They picked a few less well known brigades to apply Dazhai-inspired policies. If the experiments turned out badly, their superiors would not notice. But if Hua or the Maoists managed to consolidate their positions, these mini-models could be turned to political advantage. I asked a county official at the time whether it had crossed his mind that peasant livelihoods might be jeopardized or that villagers might resist. His reply was, "We have to convince the peasants that they are doing this for the country's future. They come from good classes and should maintain a good consciousness. After all, the county administration has important production resources at its disposal. We can make the transition easier with compensation."

Under pressure from the county and the provincial administration, the commune party secretary actually "squatted" in the brigade to oversee the transition. He had recommended Sancun to the county officials because he believed its predominantly young group of cadres would comply with policies more readily. Early in 1978, the brigade proceeded to centralize all the teams' land, machinery, and other production resources. Cash and grain reserves were taken over with promises of future compensation. Teams with greater collective resources loudly protested this outright confiscation. A few months later, the brigade relented by granting the teams the autonomy to control their own land, machinery, and animals, but the collective funds were never returned.

The brigade planned overall production. It contracted with the teams under the *san ding* system. Once a team fulfilled the set quota on yield and costs, it was given a number of work-points. The brigade gave bonus work-points to the teams that delivered above-quota yields. A second level of contracting applied between the team and its work groups. If the work groups produced above the fixed targets, they were given bonus work-points by the team.

The brigade pooled the income from the agricultural sector and from its enterprises to determine the value of a workday (an equivalent of 10 work-points). The members of the brigade received one uniform value for the workday; but, depending on the number of work-points they managed to accumulate for their labor efforts, they received different incomes. For example, if the value of the brigade's workday was 1 yuan, a team that accumulated 20,000 work-points would receive 2,000 yuan. If its production was 10 percent above the set quota, it received 2,000 more work-points, or 200 yuan. The value of a workday for the team would become 1.10 yuan.

However, brigade income did not rise as expected. Extra expenses incurred during the transition kept the amount for distribution small. The value of the workday dropped from an average of 1 yuan to 0.89 yuan in 1978, and 0.79 in 1979. Three teams out of six could not meet the set quotas in the first year, and two more joined their ranks in the second year. The brigade enterprises were also unexpectedly affected by nationwide industrial retrenchment, which diminished the brigade's sources of contracts. As shown in table 10.9, the enterprises were able to maintain their income level, but the brigade cadres virtually exhausted the funds accumulated by the enterprises in the previous years in order to keep team incomes at a reasonable level. This was not a popular remedy. The teams that met their production quotas complained that the brigade cadres were squandering scarce resource on freeloaders. Per capita agricultural income dropped from 131 yuan in 1977 to 128 yuan in 1978, and to 116 yuan in 1979. The unstable brigade economy confirmed the fears of the already skeptical peasants and fueled new anxieties at a time when individuals were already sensitive to the undercurrents of national power struggles. In 1980 the brigade quietly reverted to team accounting, with the tacit approval of commune cadres.

In the eyes of ordinary peasants, the experiment was merely one more example of the cadres' lack of judgment and sensitivity to the interests of fellow villagers. However unwilling the brigade cadres may have been to undertake the task, they quickly yielded to the county officials for political reasons. The speed with which the change in accounting was implemented demonstrated the power that the brigade cadres held over the lives of the villagers.

Power Is Its Own Enemy

In the wake of the Cultural Revolution, new dimensions in national politics reshaped the relationship between the rural cadres and the party bureaucracy. In Huancheng a new generation of activists became part of the organized political scene. A highly factionalized party bureaucracy allowed them to turn against old patrons. In a decade when factional fights were conducted in the name of political ideals, such as the importance of class consciousness and the future of socialism, it appears that the authoritarian political tradition prevailed. The rhetoric of the dictatorship of the proletariat, power seizure, the concept of *dang quan pai* (the faction in power)—all took on the force usually associated with a monopolizing political hierarchy. Rebellion against authority was apparently motivated by ardent loyalty to authority, be it Mao's or that of the party bureaucrats. Powerful patrons like Mao were elevated to superhuman stature. Revolt against leading political figures in the party hierarchy paradoxically reinforced their importance among those involved in the struggle. It seemed that rebellion was occurring under the shadow of its ideological opposite.

Moreover, as the power to promote or condemn became increasingly dependent on one's adherence to rhetoric, politics became more subjective

Table 10.9. Enterprise Performance of Sancun Brigade

Year	Total Population	Total Enterprise Workers	Number of Enterprises	Total Output of Enterprises (Yuan)	Value of Fixed Assets (Yuan)	Per Capita Agricultural Income (Yuan)	Per Capita Income Distributed (Enterprise Income Added) (Yuan)
1977	1,509	63	4	156,214	60,904	131	146
1978	1,532	98	6	169,841	74,391	128	149
1979	1,553	102	(merged)	147,753	7,388	116	131
1980	1,564	98	9	193,481	—	135	196
1981	1,571	107	7	103,448	24,640	209	242
1982	—	35	4	105,300	15,500	—	545

Source: Commune and brigade accounts.

Note: Whenever there is a discrepancy, I have chosen the brigade figures. The differences have been minor.

and volatile. Direct ideological weapons partially replaced organizational power. Armed with these, the cadres extended the power of the party-state to the most private corners of people's lives, including their own. Except for a few youths unrealistically committed to "the revolution," it was clear to all that the target of the struggle as well as the prize sought was a powerful party bureaucracy and its entrenched privileges. Catering to divided party superiors who had connections among local dissidents, the commune and brigade cadres, both young and old, maintained a precarious united front. Though they continued to dominate the "recollectivized" rural economy, as leaders they had less room to maneuver. Most cadres chose to comply with the political rules in order to keep their status.

With livelihoods for the common peasants frozen in the teams and brigades, and with agricultural production and the distribution of income impeded by the fluctuating policies that the cadres felt obliged to impose, the conflicts between ordinary peasants and cadres intensified. A great deal was at stake. How the collective economy was managed affected the peasants' livelihood in an all-encompassing way. Complying with their patrons' ideological positions was of the utmost importance if the cadres were to keep their privileged positions. The peasants found the cadres conforming more and more to the party line, but there was little they could do to correct the imbalance of power. The peasants had been silent partners in the transformation of the countryside from the start. In using their class status to claim the fruits of the revolution and to gain access to scarce resources, the majority of the peasants had paid lip service to the ideals and goals of the party-state.[21]

"We lost either way," Chen Sheyuan said of the decade:

> If we pressed the masses, they complained, refused to cooperate, or cheated. When we yielded to their wishes, they said to us: "We are in this game all together; don't give us lessons about socialism or claim moral superiority over us." Our superiors handed us party policies left and right. Every time we followed, we had to justify the new positions. After a few times, we were left with no credibility. We dared not speak so loudly because we were unconvinced about the policies as well. When our superiors pressed hard, we at least made everyone go through the motions. The hypocrisy was clear to all. It was a drama of the absurd, with us both actors and audience.

Among the younger cadres, the enthusiasm of the Cultural Revolution had degenerated into a lingering skepticism. Chen Sheyuan continued:

> During the time that Lin Biao was in power, we were instructed to guard against the people with overseas connections; but this meant that all of us in

the Pearl River delta were automatically suspect. Then all of a sudden, Mao's heir apparent became a villain. When Lin Biao's conspiracy and death was transmitted to us in an emergency cadre meeting at the commune headquarters, we were wondering how to break the news to the masses. Our worries were quite unwarranted, because the masses did not seem to care. Then *pi Lin pi Kong* [the anti-Lin Biao and anti-Confucius campaign] began. We conducted meetings to study party documents. The educated youths were the only ones who could interpret the newspaper headlines. Old men reminisced about the feudal past and lamented quietly that colorful performances of traditional operas had disappeared. Young people on the other hand wondered why a silly old man called Confucius had gained national attention. Our womenfolk complained that the evening meetings left them no time for household chores, and they stopped coming after a while. The masses were concerned about the campaigns only because they knew that whenever rhetoric intensified, we cadres would be pressed to implement even the most unpopular policies, and that hurt their economic interests. Being a cadre was a privilege as well as a stigma. We commanded the distribution of scarce resources, but the masses had little good feeling for us. (Chen Sheyuan, interview with the author, summer 1983)

If cadres were disillusioned, so were many peasants. Such feelings are reflected in an unusual outburst from an articulate peasant in a periurban brigade:

The cadres talked politics and we bore the consequences. I remember the beginning of the campaigns when we were forced to take out all the ancestral tablets and burn them. The landlords had the hardest time. What they had retrieved after the land reform and had saved was then taken away and ground into dust. Whatever remained of the village temples was smeared over with mud and concrete. This was to "destroy the four olds!" Why disturb the gods and ancestors further? They were helpless anyway; they could not even save themselves. Only old women in the village went to them; but the young rebels would not leave them alone. Politics made people heartless.

Then there was the perpetual problem of grain quotas. After 1969, the cadres became very anxious. Secretary Zhang led a group of members of the Party Youth League to our team to uproot vegetables, saying that we should be growing winter wheat instead. I heard that Chakeng Brigade allowed their villagers to grow a maximum of 2 feet of sugarcane! The cadres also came around and confiscated palm fans that our womenfolk made at home, accusing us of engaging in capitalistic activities. The women cried and the men swore. That evening we uprooted a few vegetables in our private plots and hid our chickens and ducks. People did not act with feeling [*meiyou ganqing*] anymore. We were angry, but we did not dare to contradict the cadres. The team leaders were sympathetic, but what could they do? They were not party members.

Some people said that the cadres too had their share of being bashed around in the campaigns, but let's face it, they were able to use power more readily. If an official decided not to like you, he could make life so difficult. He held all the seals [official stamps] that controlled your livelihood, and it was up to him to interpret the political messages as well as your actions. So we had to butter him up. You see the nice brick house of Secretary Ma. Does he deserve it? The important fact is that we built it for him. It took one seal for a cadre to send a cousin of mine to the jungles of Hainan Island, but it took seven seals and seven years to bring him back. Who could we appeal to? They were all in it together. When we brought the matter to the commune committee, they told us that it was party policy to send down educated youths. Was it party policy that cadre children were not to be sent away? When we appealed to the county labor management office, it referred the case back to Secretary Ma. Politics was personal and arbitrary, and bureaucrats were the best at it. (Li Song, interview with the author, summer 1983)

In the midst of skepticism and sullen compliance, a generation of peasants and cadres came of age.

CHAPTER 11

The Paradox of
Self-Reliance

A central theme of China's rural development has been industrialization: the creation of small-scale enterprises in the communes and brigades. The Great Leap Forward in 1958 marked the beginning of the movement to industrialize the countryside, but it was not until the early 1970s that the small-scale enterprises were consciously integrated into the industrial sector. The institutionalization of these enterprises was tied to the Maoist concern for narrowing "the three disparities": those between the city and countryside, agriculture and industry, and mental and menial labor.

The movement toward rural industrialization, however, placed major emphasis on the self-reliance of the enterprises. Mao believed that the small-scale enterprises would serve agriculture better than the centralized state industries. They were closer to the areas where their services were needed. They were in a better position to exploit local talent. While the state invested its scarce resources in urban industries, the rural enterprises would grow at their own pace with input from the villages. This strategy of "walking on two legs" was considered flexible and economical. It would neither strain national resources nor ignore the rural population. Although some connections were established with the urban industrial sector in the transfer of technology (Sigurdson 1977; American Rural Small-Scale Industry Delegation 1977), the Maoist emphasis on local resources gave the development of rural enterprise a cellular focus.[1]

The fledgling enterprises were not spared the consequences of political factionalism. As with the Dazhai model, they became ideological weapons for both the Maoists and their opponents. The Maoists insisted on self-reliance, on making the enterprises serve local agriculture exclusively, while their opponents stressed the enterprises' potential to "develop productive forces," that is, to increase income, to accumulate capital, and eventually to join the state industrial sector. The commune and brigade enterprises in Huancheng grew in this politically charged environment. The cadres tried to resolve the ideological differences to their own advantage. The commune and brigade administrations operated their enterprises with the aim of providing employment for their team members and ac-

cumulating capital. The commune could then use its new resources politically to narrow the disparities among the teams and the brigades through a
selective allocation of funds and materials. Economic assets would serve as
political leverage. When the rural enterprises grew larger, they would need
more institutional support from the county government, enhancing the
political leverage of the state sector. According to the cadres' optimistic
calculations, economics and politics would not be mutually exclusive.
Rationalizing the situation in this way, the cadres in Huancheng hoped to
make the best of circumstances. As shown in table 11.1, the proportion of
Huancheng's income that derived from the enterprises rose rapidly during
the 1970s.

One would expect that the enterprises would have provided the rural
cadres with numerous opportunities to score points with both the state and
the community. There was even some talk at the time that the enterprises
would create autonomous bases from which the commune and brigade
cadres could maneuver against the demands of the state (see table 11.2).
However, the development of the rural enterprises created its own paradoxes. Because economic growth was tied to a factionalized bureaucratic
structure of power, success could also become a political liability, as the
painful experience of Sancun Brigade demonstrated.

The Politics of Competitive Advantage

Compared with other communes in Xinhui County, Huancheng was considered above average in its enterprise development. It ranked second
among twenty-one communes in the early 1960s but dropped to the tenth
place in the mid-1970s. By 1979 it had regained third place. Table 11.3
compares Huancheng's enterprise development with that of other communes in Xinhui for 1980. The commune thrived on the enterprises that
were tied to the town industries and commerce, such as the processing of
local crops for the urban and export markets. The cadres successfully
secured contracts from the state enterprises in Huicheng and Jiangmen.[2]
But this source of growth was vulnerable to the policy fluctuations that hit
the commune's urban patrons from time to time. In the decade from the
mid-1960s to the mid-1970s, the Maoists often pressured state enterprises
to "cut the tails of capitalism." Managers of some state factories in
Huicheng reported that they would respond to such pressure by cancelling
their contracts with the communes.[3] The Corporation for Daily Consumption Goods in the county, for example, which had contracted with

Table 11.1.   The Growth of Commune Enterprises
in Huancheng

Year	Output[a] (Yuan)	Profit[b] (Yuan)	Net Capital Assets[c] (Yuan)	No. of Workers[d]
1958	181,800	—	—	—
1959	477,800	—	—	—
1960	1,199,100	—	—	—
1961	917,300	—	341,800	—
1962	770,900	—	250,400	—
1963	1,075,900	—	232,300	—
1964	1,000,900	—	254,100	—
1965	1,038,600	151,700	277,600	—
1966	1,289,100	218,200	277,200	473
1967	1,567,400	220,600	299,000	—
1968	1,437,000	126,300	274,100	511
1969	1,973,600	309,900	222,800	602
1970	1,785,200	253,900	401,600	627
1971	1,928,200	156,700	434,900	637
1972	2,612,200	176,100	406,400	920
1973	2,855,600	297,000	692,800	774
1974	2,655,200	339,300	954,200	741
1975	2,619,200	257,800	1,176,200	825
1976	3,373,500	297,100	1,211,000	1,101
1977	3,844,100	286,600	1,945,500	1,431
1978	5,016,900	532,100	2,009,300	1,418
1979	5,101,600	425,400	2,080,800	1,355
1980[e]	5,477,700	560,881	—	1,185
1981[f]	3,363,500	451,031	—	1,392

Source: Commune accounts collected during fieldwork.

[a]From 1961 to 1966, output figures for the transport team and the construction team are missing. From 1961 to 1972, output figures for the agricultural enterprises are missing.

[b]Profits of agricultural enterprises are not included here. Those were experiment stations which yielded very little profit.

[c]Capital assets of agricultural enterprises are missing between 1961 and 1972.

[d]From 1966 to 1971, the number of workers in agricultural enterprises is missing. In 1972, the large jump in the number of workers is due to 194 workers in agricultural enterprises being added to the accounting. The same applies to the year after.

[e]The figures include industrial enterprises only.

[f]The figures include industrial enterprises only, and apply to the first 6 months of 1981. The planned annual output was 6,859,000 yuan.

Table 11.2.   A Comparison of Commune, Brigade, and Team Output

Year	Total (Yuan)	Team (%)	Team and Brigade (%)	Brigade (%)	Commune (%)
1958	6,809,742	—	97	—	3
1959	7,338,373	—	93	—	7
1960	8,323,072	—	86	—	14
1961	7,904,126	—	88	—	12
1962	9,267,131	—	92	—	8
1963	11,308,696	82	—	9	9
1964	—	—	88	—	12
1965	9,540,725	79	—	10	11
1966	10,701,058	83	—	5	12
1967	11,702,173	81	—	6	13
1968	11,575,675	81	—	7	12
1969	11,818,910	74	—	9	17
1970	11,200,860	76	—	8	16
1971	12,251,157	75	—	9	16
1972	14,053,350	68	—	13	19
1973	15,300,344	66	—	15	19
1974	16,318,308	72	—	12	16
1975	14,597,305	69	—	13	18
1976	16,833,599	65	—	15	20
1977	20,872,314	69	—	13	18
1978	21,190,409	58	—	18	24
1979	23,491,893	56	—	22	22
1980	33,368,869	50	—	33	17
1981	36,997,271	44	—	39	17
1982	—	—	—	—	—
1983	—	—	—	—	—
1984	—	—	—	—	—
1985	—	—	—	—	—
1986	130,000,000	46	—	31	23

Source: Commune and brigade accounts collected during fieldwork.

Huancheng's paper-making factory, was condemned by the Maoists in the early 1970s for "profiteering."

Despite political vicissitudes, the enterprises in Huancheng grew steadily. As shown in chapter 8, the enterprises established in the 1950s and the 1960s required little initial investment. Their production capacities were small, and they placed only limited demands on local raw material and labor. Their technological requirements were also low, and their ties to state industries were few. Because of their inefficiency, they were dropped when state agencies streamlined their operations during periods of eco-

Table 11.3. Industrial Development: Comparisons of Huancheng and Other Communes in Xinhui County, 1979

| | | | | | Selected Trades | | | |
Commune	Total Output	Steel Processing	Stone Quarry	Brick Making	Boat Making	Silicone Quarry	Palm Handicrafts	Paper Making
Shuangshui	6,954,500	388,300	36,400	313,600	207,500	965,700	596,300	—
Gujing	5,924,400	1,295,500	1,489,100	240,800	18,800	244,500	—	—
Huancheng	4,349,800	—	—	298,100	—	—	1,233,100	1,011,200
Lile	3,676,400	632,200	—	64,400	214,100	—	1,158,000	—
Shadui	3,503,100	1,191,500	236,000	61,000	—	818,400	—	—
Daao	3,417,500	985,200	—	260,700	71,600	—	193,300	—
Daze	3,288,800	577,200	154,000	77,000	142,300	—	61,800	—
Yaxi	3,211,000	—	41,900	171,100	—	722,200	—	—
Siqian	3,179,100	—	—	58,600	—	—	661,500	—
Duyuan	2,901,600	—	—	—	—	—	—	—
Sanjiang	2,893,000	—	—	27,200	102,400	—	639,400	836,000
Hetang	2,774,300	—	—	96,400	114,800	—	—	—
Tangxia	2,350,900	—	119,000	22,000	111,000	—	177,800	—
Luokeng	2,228,200	—	—	43,400	23,400	—	—	—
Muzhou	2,102,500	—	—	397,900	158,500	—	304,300	—
Qibao	2,079,700	—	—	—	47,200	—	—	487,100
Xiaogang	1,903,400	—	—	—	55,900	—	240,600	440,000
Yanan	1,146,200	—	—	93,300	52,700	—	—	—
Niuwan	677,000	—	27,200	—	—	—	113,600	—
Yayu	96,600	—	—	—	—	—	—	—
Total	58,658,300	5,069,900	2,103,600	2,181,200	1,320,200	2,800,800	5,377,700	2,774,300

Source: Xinhui xian sheban qiye jingyan xuanji, compiled by Xinhui Xian Shedui Qiye Guanliju, 1980, 1–4.

Note: Total output for Huancheng Commune is smaller than in table 11.1. The probable reason for this discrepancy is that some new enterprises and the agricultural enterprises are not included in the county figures.

nomic retrenchment, and were readily abandoned when their urban contractors were under ideological fire from the Maoists. By the early 1970s,
however, the commune had built large-scale enterprises partly with its
own savings and partly with county funds, because the county government wished to secure some decentralized bases for agricultural mechanization. These enterprises, such as the agricultural machinery factory and
the brick factory, stabilized their production and maintained close ties with
county-level factories. With heavier investment and consequently more at
stake, the commune found political fluctuations more disruptive than before, while it was also harder for the county government to dismiss these
enterprises on either political or economic grounds.

In the early 1980s, the commune operated nineteen enterprises, which
fell into two broad categories, agricultural and industrial. The commune
Office for the Management of Commune and Brigade Enterprises (hereafter Commune MCBE Office) oversaw the financing, planning, and labor
management of all the enterprises. In the 1970s, old cadres from the brigades tended increasingly to be appointed as secretaries in these enterprises. Chen Mingfa was recruited to the commune administration in 1973
and became the director of the Commune MCBE Office when it was formally established in 1976. In the same year, Xu Decheng was assigned as
director of the agricultural machinery station.

There were five agricultural enterprises: a veterinary station, a fish
hatchery, a lumber farm, an agricultural experiment station, and an orchard. Except for the orchard, which was set up in 1970, the other enterprises had been operated by the collectives and were taken over by the
commune in 1958. Their function was to provide the teams with seeds and
veterinary services and to improve cultivation techniques. They came into
existence through a series of political campaigns. As described in chapter 8,
the agricultural experiment station was set up in 1958 to promote soil
improvement, pest control, and crop protection. The station technician,
Deng Yentang, became a hero in the Foshan Prefecture after he developed
several new varieties of grain. By the mid-1970s, he was responding to the
radicals' calls for new strains of winter wheat that could withstand sub-
tropical climates.

The commune fish hatchery was established in 1959 with ten employees. It was unable to meet the commune's demand for fish, let alone
produce a surplus. The commune orchard, established twelve years later,
had to be subsidized to the tune of 10,000 yuan a year. When political
dogma relaxed in the early 1980s, the commune leadership tried to make
these enterprises self-supporting. In 1980, for example, the fish hatchery
was breeding fish for markets in Huicheng and Jiangmen. Similarly, the

orchard started producing mandarin oranges and tangerines for the export corporations in Huicheng. The commune lumber farm employed 160 workers and produced bamboo, jute, pine, and oranges for the commercial departments in the cities. The commune's veterinary station raised poultry for export to Hong Kong.

The industrial enterprises, numbering fourteen in 1980, were less peripheral to the commune economy.[4] These enterprises differed from the brigade enterprises as well as from one another in terms of their production requirements and marketing potentials, their technical sophistication, their employment capacities, and their need for institutional support from the county. They provided a variety of industrial environments and were affected by different political campaigns.

The industrial enterprises can accordingly be grouped into three broad categories. The first category consisted of agricultural machinery stations, grain mills, oil presses, and small brick kilns. They provided cheap and readily available services to local agriculture. Their operations were small, and their technical requirements simple. They employed only a few workers, and their profits were minimal. The second category consisted of factories that processed local crops for the urban and export markets. The commune's palm handicraft factory and the palm-drying field were typical examples. Although their technical facilities were simple, they thrived on a sophisticated handicraft tradition and needed substantial institutional support from the county's commercial departments. They depended directly on local agriculture for steady supplies of palm leaves. They hired many workers, mostly women, and earned sizable profits for the commune. The third category consisted of enterprises that produced machine parts or took on additional processing work for state factories. Because the production of their urban contractors was within state plans, these enterprises could count on quotas of valuable industrial raw material at state prices. For example, the paper-making factory obtained highly sought after chemicals from the Corporation for Sugar and Paper Products in the county. Unlike factories whose production was not within state plans and whose supply of raw material could be cut short, the agricultural machinery factory had obtained stable quotas of steel and coal. This category required the highest technical sophistication and demanded strict industrial discipline of its workers. Their production capacities were large, and they brought large profits for the commune. Because of their relatively cosmopolitan orientations, their jobs were highly sought after by the nonagricultural residents of the commune.

Huancheng's periurban location meant that even those of its enterprises most directly related to agriculture catered to the urban markets. For ex-

ample, the commune's agricultural machinery factory contracted with
factories in Huicheng to process machine parts rather than to produce
agricultural implements for the brigades. The construction team built
houses for the County Housing Authority instead of pigsties, bridges, and
canals in the villages. The transport team was reluctant to transport seeds
and fertilizers for rural clients at discount rates. The commune's brick
factory, built in 1976, was the largest and the most modernized in the
county. It depended on the county's Materials Supply Bureau for fuel.
With an annual production of ten million bricks a year, it aimed to meet
the needs of the entire Huicheng-Jiangmen area.

This urban focus encouraged the enterprises to maintain links with the
industrial and commercial units of the county. By the late 1970s, these ties
had been formalized. Each commune factory was assigned a "matching
unit" (*duikou danwei*) in the county administration. The agricultural machinery station, for example, was matched with the County Agricultural
Machinery Corporation, which set the station's standards of services and
charges, supplied it with necessary machine parts, and trained its mechan-
ics. The commune palm-handicraft factory received production quotas
from the County Native Products Export Corporation and the County
Palm-Handicraft Factory. Even the most locally oriented factory, the commune grain-processing factory, found its prices set and supervised by the
County Bureau for Food Grain.

These economic relationships contradicted the Maoists' view that rural
enterprises should serve local agriculture in a self-sufficient manner. As
expected, during the reign of the Maoists in the 1970s, commune enterprises in Huancheng were singled out by the county party committee as
examples of "having deviated from the tracks of agriculture" (*zhinong
zhuangui*). At times, commune cadres were urged to trust mass spontaneity
and local ingenuity; long-term planning was considered suspect. Egalitarian remuneration systems were tried, and rural clients received generous subsidies. The county government set strict limits on enterprise expansion just in case it interfered with the labor needs of agriculture. During
peak seasons, factory workers were sent back to work in the fields to the
dismay of their urban contractors.

Huancheng Commune has tried to balance its geographic advantage and
political vulnerability by developing enterprises that can withstand a variety of political climates. Though their origins were humble, Huancheng's
rural enterprises did not start from scratch. Local handicrafts had existed
before the revolution. Handicraft workers and small traders were organized into cooperative units from 1953 to 1956. During communization,

efforts to establish self-supporting enterprises intensified. Out of the fourteen industrial enterprises in Huancheng, five were established around
1958. The paper-making factory, for example, was formed when Xie Dubing and seven of his friends used straw, scrap cloth, and pressed sugarcane
to produce 50 catties of paper a day. The fifteen members of the commune
transport team were laborers who transported passengers and goods between Huicheng and the villages by pushcart and bicycle. To set up commune enterprises, the cadres relied on the skilled technicians and resources
from the villages. However, by the early 1960s, the political climate no
longer favored these enterprises. As early as 1959, Tao Zhu, the leading
cadre in Guangdong at the time, criticized the "leftist deviations" of the
Great Leap Forward (Vogel 1969, 262). At a provincial party committee
conference on rural work in October 1960, he outlined the program for
economic retrenchment. In the rush to dismantle the collectives, workers
and raw materials from the enterprises returned to the rural teams. Manager Li of the agricultural machinery factory remembered how discouraged
he was:

> When the peasants were released from the collectives, they wanted their
> resources back. My factory was stranded. On the other hand, the technical
> experts from the county factories looked down on us. They said we had
> nothing but cow dung on our feet and refused us help. They took one look at
> our paper factory and said that it would not survive unless we installed their
> 8,000-yuan copper paper-press; but we had no capital. Our agricultural ma-
> chinery workshop sent away twenty-three of its thirty workers. We were too
> poorly equipped to secure contracts. (Li Binglin, interview with the author,
> winter 1978)

After a period of cutbacks in the early 1960s, some commune enterprises
were revived during a general recovery in the rural economy. The county
government even helped the grain mill to buy two motors; the transport
team invested in a few tricycles. A palm-handicraft factory was set up in
1961 to process fans for export. The county government "sent down"
(xiafang) some old palm-handicraft workers from Huicheng to the commune as "technical backbone" (jishu gugan) and assigned a quota of charcoal fuel for the new enterprise. The period of the Cultural Revolution
produced no upheavals for commune enterprises in Huancheng. Despite
the fact that Mao called on the peasants in 1966 to establish small-scale
enterprises when conditions permitted (Riskin 1978, 86), Huancheng established no new enterprises. However, the commune promoted the paper
factory as following Mao's ideal for self-reliance. Piece rate and bonuses

were abolished, and work discipline deteriorated in the general political confusion. Cadres in the enterprises were not harassed; as Manager Li explained, "we were not high enough in the administrative hierarchy."

In the early 1970s, factional fights did trickle down to commune enterprises, which faced serious problems in planning, incentives, and work discipline. Political messages from the county officials were mixed. Calls for the promotion of local ingenuity also stressed the need for high-quality production and rational integration with the state industrial sector. Demands for increased production through agricultural mechanization were punctuated by attacks on "profiteering motives," "capitalist management styles," and "overemphasis on productive forces." As in agricultural policies, enterprise policy in the commune fluctuated left and right, showing that anxious cadres were toeing ideological lines closely. In 1969, the commune's agricultural machinery station was set up with aid from the county as part of a general program to develop agricultural mechanization. In 1971 it merged with the commune's agricultural machinery factory to conserve resources. However, the move was criticized by the county as "deviating from the tracks of serving agriculture" (zhinong zhuangui), because machinery in the consolidated factory was also used for urban contracts. By early 1973 the factory had been split into two. The agricultural station was ordered to plough fields for the teams, and Xu Decheng was appointed director.

As the national political atmosphere became even more radical from late 1975 to late 1976, minute management problems were elevated to the level of political principles. "Manager Li was known to have a bad temper," a worker in the agricultural machinery factory told me, "so when he attempted to tighten labor discipline, some young fellows would get restless and accuse him of paying undue attention to the productive forces, or of applying the bureaucratic guan, ka, ya [to control, to block, to suppress]. "We avoided responsibility to keep out of political trouble," Cheng Mingfa recalled in the summer of 1980. "The Commune MCBE Office put its investment plans on hold, because we did not want to be accused of profiteering. Workers were bored with political study. Absenteeism was high, as the young fellows encouraged one another by saying, 'Who cares! You get 36 yuan if you work, you get 36 yuan if you don't.' " In 1978 young workers in the agricultural machinery factory told me rather cynically that they welcomed political study. "It takes us away from the shop floor. If peasants do not show up for work, they lose work-points; but we spend all our time sitting around in political classes and are paid all the same. Why not take a rest? That has been our attitude. If Manager Li complains, we tell Uncle Fa [Chen Mingfa] that Li is a technocrat."

A Bureaucratic System of Support and Control

From the times of the Fan Palm Guild, the corporate estates, and the academies, the cultural and commercial institutions of Huicheng had undergone a profound transformation. In the name of helping the rural economy, the urban state factories, the commercial departments, and the party committee of the county had imposed an elaborate system of bureaucratic control on the countryside. In the decade of the 1970s, the government supervised four major branches of economic administration, represented by the Planning Committee, the Department of Finance and Trade, the Department of Industry and Transport, and the Department of Agriculture. Under each division were bureaus that oversaw specialized corporations and factories. All these county units played a role in supporting commune and brigade enterprises. The County Planning Committee approved the allocation of production materials for commune enterprises if their contracts were fell directly or indirectly within state plans. The Department of Finance and Trade issued low-interest loans and located sources of contracts for the enterprises. The Department of Industry and Transport supervised the corporations and factories that contracted with the commune enterprises. The Department of Agriculture gave technical aid to the commune's agricultural enterprises. By and large, it was up to the County Bureau for the Management of Commune and Brigade Enterprise (hereafter County MCBE Bureau) to coordinate the network of support and control.

The County MCBE Bureau was established in June 1975 with ten staff members. It survived the fall of the Maoists and continued to thrive under the short reign of Hua Guofeng. By December 1978, its staff had multiplied by six to become a mini-bureaucracy.[5] The bureau controlled the commune enterprises in several ways. It reviewed proposals from the communes on the basis of their technical capacities, their profitability, and their requirements for raw materials. It then sent its assessments to the Planning Committee for approval. Projects requiring an initial investment greater than 10,000 yuan had to obtain approval from the prefectural administration. Cadres in the County MCBE Bureau insisted that the procedure was designed to ensure a balance between the state and collectives as well as among the communes. The bureau appears to have made full use of its powers, because numerous examples of unsuccessful applications can be cited. Huancheng Commune once proposed establishing a wine factory. The County MCBE bureau rejected the proposal, claiming that the quality of the wine could not be properly controlled. However, commune officials were aware of the fact that the county bureau was under pressure from county-level wine factories in Huicheng, which would not tolerate competition. A proposal for a dry fruit and vegetable factory at the commune was discouraged as late as 1980 for similar reasons. The bureau did not reject these proposals outright; commune cadres were told that if they stopped supplying the county factories with fruit, they would lose their quotas of fertilizers. Fearing that the brigades and teams would object to such reductions, the commune officials dropped the plans.

The bureau did provide services, however. Huancheng's paper-making factory, for example, produced paper for the Corporation of Daily Consumer Goods of the county. It received a quota of charcoal fuel from its contractor at 7 yuan per ton. The rest it bought through other channels at 9 yuan per ton. The County MCBE Bureau intervened on the commune's behalf to make the corporation buy the paper at a slightly higher price as a form of subsidy to the commune factory. Contracts obtained through the county bureau also made it easier for the commune enterprises to obtain low-interest loans from state banks. If an enterprise produced goods for export, the bureau helped negotiate with the export corporations.[6] The county-level bureaus provided protection for the commune enterprises. To cope with fluctuations in market demand and the constant need for new designs and technology, the Bureau of Foreign Trade acted as a first-level buffer. It accepted foreign contracts and assumed the responsibility for negotiation and compensation if problems arose. The County MCBE Bureau acted as a second-level buffer by controlling the assignment of contracts to the commune enterprises. If products were returned, it found domestic markets for them. If export-oriented production facilities became idle, the bureau helped the commune enterprise switch to other activities. In an institutional environment where private networks had been destroyed, the bureau assumed unparalleled importance for the communes.

In general, the County MCBE Bureau was eager to provide the institutional support for commune enterprises. The more indebted the commune administrations were to the bureau, the more political muscle it could flex. An efficient network of institutional support could easily be turned into an effective means of control. Commune cadres in Huancheng knew this all too well. The only defense they could muster was to seek out friends in the county administration to mediate on their behalf. Many county officials had commune connections of various sorts. Either they had been members of work teams in one political campaign or another, or they were natives who had since been transferred to the county administration. Some of the county cadres, whose relatives needed housing or whose children could not avoid being sent down to the countryside, had pressed the commune to accommodate them in the periurban brigades. Well-connected old commune cadres took calculated risks in acceding to such requests.

Old Niches Recreated

The golden age of the commune enterprises was the decade of the 1970s, in which they became an integral part of the commune economy. Output from the commune's enterprises constituted 22 percent of the total commune output in 1979. The enterprises provided social mobility for the cadres and commune members. However, the new work environments generated political tensions as well. Two types of commune members were most involved with the changes: old brigade cadres who had been transferred to the commune enterprises as leaders, and young, educated residents of the market town who made up the bulk of the work force.

As shown in table 11.4, brigade cadres were transferred to the commune enterprises through the decades of the 1960s and 1970s. In the early 1970s Maoists in the county administration insisted that the newly established commune enterprises be headed by cadres of poor peasant origin in order to ensure that they served agriculture wholeheartedly. As described earlier, Chen Mingfa was among the first of the brigade party branch secretaries to be transferred. Barely forty years old in 1969, he was assigned to the commune hospital. He accepted the promotion but found nonagricultural work difficult. His initial introduction to commune-level work lasted only seven days. He felt totally out of place, away from the rural environment in which he had maneuvered with confidence. Instead of respectful peasants, he was confronted with technicians and young workers who looked down on his peasant appearance. He found the daily schedules inflexible and the political stakes uncertain. "It was like being a river shrimp thrown into the sea," he recalled during a conversation in the summer of 1980. "The water tasted strange and I had no idea what the currents were like. Each day at the hospital seemed endless. I felt so anxious that the commune finally sent me home." Despite his reservations, he was again called upon to join the commune enterprise office in 1973. He became head of that office in 1976, a post he kept until 1982.

Xu Decheng, the old party secretary of Dajiao Brigade, made similar comments on his change of work. He became the head of the agricultural machinery station in 1973. He adjusted more easily than Chen because the main task of the station was to plough fields. He and his tractor drivers

Table 11.4. The Background of Leading Cadres in Commune Enterprises, 1981

Enterprise Head	Age	Previous Posts	Year Transferred to Commune Level
Commune enterprise office	51	Meijiang PS	1976 (1969, commune hospital)
Commercial office	52	Dajiao L&PS	1981 (1973, agricultural machinery station)
Transport team	50+	Chakeng PS	1980
Agricultural machinery station	33	Chakeng Brigade	1980
Paper-making factory	54	Hongxing Brigade	1958
Construction team	50	Chakeng L	1978
Food-processing factory	50+	Yongan Brigade accountant	1958
Palm-handicraft factory	48	Sanlian PS	1979 (1975, agricultural experiment station)
	57	Qibang PS	1981
Agricultural machinery factory	41	Nangeng	1958
Palm-drying field	62	Dajiao L&PS	1976
Brick factory	40	Duhui accountant	1976
Printing factory	—	Siya PS	1979 (1976, veterinary station)
General palm products factory	44	Sancun PS	1981
	60	Chengnan Brigade	1981
Clothing factory	50	Duhui PS	1981 (1979, paper factory)
	39+	Meijiang PS	1980 (1974, commune cultural station)
Agricultural experiment station	50	Dajiao L&PS	
Lumber farm	—	Renyi Brigade	1978 (1975, livestock and poultry farm)
Livestock and poultry farm	50	Xisheng Brigade	1979 (1977, fish hatchery)
Fish hatchery	47+	Xijia PS	1979 (1976, market town)
Orchard	56+	Chakeng Team L	1967

Source: Interviews by author.

Note: PS = Party Branch Secretary; L = Brigade Leader.

were in touch with the villagers. "It took me three years to adjust," he admitted.

> It was easier if old pals were transferred together. Zhou Yi, my partner of a decade in Dajiao, became the head of the palm-drying ground in 1976. We met for morning tea often and looked back with amusement at our circumstances. We finally sank our roots in the commune. My family remained in the village. I went back once or twice a month to help out in the private plots. The rest of the time I spent in the commune headquarters. There were enough of our old pals around. (Xu Decheng, interview with the author, winter 1978)

By the mid-1970s, more old cadres were being transferred to the industrial enterprises. The official explanation for the appointments was that the retiring cadres could no longer carry their weight in the fields. Underlying the transfers, however, was an unspoken political objective: the Maoists were more than happy to remove the old cadres from their bases in the villages. As they were absorbed into the commune-level economy, with its urban focus, they were pulled away from the rural scene. The administration of the brigades could then be monopolized by younger cadres who had been recruited during the Cultural Revolution and whom the Maoists in the county government considered potential allies. These cadres might not differ from the old cadres in their political assumptions. Nevertheless, they did not share the same networks because they came of age in a different political period. When old cadres were physically removed from the brigades, the younger leaders were left on their own to face the peasants without the mediation of their former patrons.

The commune enterprises faced another set of problems. The rural background of the semiliterate older cadres manifested itself in their management style. They valued learning by experience and were wary of the young technicians and their education. Young workers, for their part, were not pleased to be denied access to senior positions. They complained that the factories were run according to "the rule of the elders" and that the cadres valued only workers who were compliant and personally loyal.

There was some correspondence between the cadres' expectations and the type of workers they recruited. The enterprises that required manual labor (such as the brick factory, the construction team, and the transport team) and those that processed local crops (such as the grain mill, the palm-drying ground, and the palm-handicraft factory) recruited the majority of their workers from the villages. At the end of the 1970s, around five hundred of them were employed in the enterprises. They were called *yigong yinong* (worker-peasants). Such status meant that they relied on their teams for grain rations, though the factories paid them wages. They maintained close ties to their families in the villages; they were often sent back to the teams to help during the peak agricultural seasons, and they maintained private plots. They were predominantly young males.[7] The palm-handicraft factory employed a larger number of older women from Chengnan, Siya, Ningzhen, and Chengjiao brigades. Though it expanded its work force from 116 in 1974 to 167 in 1978, the recruits were principally younger women who had barely finished junior middle school. They looked upon their work as a source of income, not of mobility. In my conversations with a sample of them in the summer of 1978, they showed little interest in commenting on things beyond their daily personal lives. In a sense, the rural cadres who made the transition from field to factory succeeded in recreating their niches in the commune-level economy.

New Horizons

Tables 11.5, 11.6, 11.7, and 11.8 compare workers' backgrounds in various commune enterprises. The palm-handicraft factory represents the more traditionally managed enterprises; its workers tend to have rural backgrounds and orientations. The paper-making factory and the agricultural machinery factory are more city-oriented and more technologically advanced; their workers are better educated and share a more cosmopolitan outlook.

Among the commune enterprises, the paper-making factory and the agricultural machinery factory faced special problems in labor management. Both enterprises catered to the urban markets. They had acquired the technical competence to attract urban contracts and had recruited the best educated young workers from the commune's nonagricultural population. Eight-five percent of the workers in the agricultural machinery factory were males in their twenties, whereas 70 percent of the workers in the paper factory were young women who had attended junior middle school and in some cases graduated from the commune senior middle school. Their families also worked in the commune or county enterprises.

These workers came of age during the political turmoil of the 1970s. They enjoyed the best the commune could offer, but their desire for social mobility was frustrated by the static character of the rural collective sector. They were given all the ideological education of the Maoist era, but the socialist system they knew was, according to some, discriminatory, authoritarian, and arbitrary. They were skeptical about politics, but, to the dismay of their elders, fully capable of exploiting the rhetoric of their time.

Table 11.5. Profiles of Workers in the Huancheng Commune Palm-Handicraft Factory, 1978

Name	Sex	Age	Years of Work	Educational Level	Residence	Marital Status	Employment before Entering Factory	Employment of Relatives
Chen	F	40+	12	None	Market town (formerly of Siya Xiang)	Married	Individual and collective palm handicraft	Daughter: educated youth in Xinhui Labor College; Son: machine worker; 3 daughters in school
Chen	F	30+	8	Primary	Market town (formerly of Siya Xiang)	Married	Commune hotel	Husband: county irrigation station worker; Brother: commune construction team; Mother and sister in agriculture

Source: Interviews by author.

Table 11.6. Profiles of Workers in the Huancheng Commune Agricultural Machinery Station, 1978

Name	Sex	Age	Years of Work	Educational Level	Residence	Marital Status	Employment before Entering Factory	Employment of Relatives
Tan	M	29	3	Senior middle	Qunsheng Brigade	Married	Brigade electrician	Agriculture
Liang	M	39	10	Primary	Dongjia Brigade	Married	County tractor station	Agriculture

Source: Interviews by author.

Table 11.7. Profiles of Workers in the Huancheng Commune Paper Factory, 1978

Name	Sex	Age	Years of Work	Educational Level	Residence	Marital Status	Employment of Parents	Employment of Other Relatives
Huang	F	21	7	Primary	Market town	Single	Father: barber in Huicheng	Brother: Huancheng transport team (mechanic) Brother: county agricultural tool factory Brother: state farm in Doumen County Sister-in-law: county palm-handicraft factory
Lian	F	26	7	Junior middle	Market town	Single	Father: county electrical appliance factory Mother: printer in market town	Brother: county fertilizer factory Brother: commune agricultural machinery factory Brother: county photography office Sister: county textile factory Sister: educated youth in Tangxia Commune
Lai	M	25	7–8	Senior middle	Market town	Single		

Source: Interviews by author.

Table 11.8. Profiles of Workers in the Huancheng Commune Agricultural Machinery Factory, 1978

Name	Sex	Age	Years of Work	Educational Level	Residence	Marital Status	Employment of Parents	Employment of Other Relatives
Liang	M	25	6	Senior middle	Market town	Single	Father: cook in Huicheng	Brother: cook in Huicheng Sister: commune lumber farm Sister: junior middle school Brother: senior middle school
Hong	F	23	3	Senior middle	Shuangshui	Single	Father and Mother: brigade school teachers	Sister: Niuwan Commune hospital pharmacy Brother: senior middle school Brother: senior middle school
Qun	F	22	2	Senior middle	Market town	Single	Father: overseas; Mother: market town printing	Brother: senior middle school
Yu	M	43	20	County technical school	Dadong Brigade	Married		Wife: commune supply and marketing cooperative Children: all in primary school

Source: Interviews by author.

They made their feelings known by slacking off at work and by daring to struggle against their superiors.

Unlike the worker-peasants whose primary allegiance was to their respective villages, young workers in the two factories maintained many ties with each other. They were residents of the commune's market towns; they had attended the commune's only senior middle school and often had graduated in the same class. Through the labor management office at the market town, they were recruited to the factories together. The factories provided many opportunities for interaction. The management organized evening technical classes and field trips to county factories. The Party Youth League conducted political study groups and recruited members through social activities such as outings, visits to revolutionary sites, sports, and games. Activists were sent to political training classes in the city and to the villages. In the 1970s, the activists were members of the work teams for the Basic Line Education campaigns. In fact, they were being groomed as future cadres in the enterprises. Their stake in the factories was high. However, the arbitrary, personal, and authoritarian styles of old factory leaders thwarted their progress. To show their defiance, young workers in the agricultural machinery factory brought their complaints against Manager Li directly to the Commune MCBE Office.

A few workers' profiles may help to convey the social and political ethos of the commune as the young generation faced its dilemmas. Liang Daxin was a model technician in the agricultural machinery factory. When I met him in 1978 he was twenty-five years old. Both of his parents were cooks in a restaurant in Huicheng. He graduated from the commune senior middle school in 1972 and became an apprentice in the agricultural machinery factory a month later. The factory quickly discovered his aptitude and sent him to several machine-tool factories in Huicheng for short-term training. By 1975 he was promoted to technician. He and an older employee trained twenty apprentices, teaching evening classes once a week. He gained a reputation as an expert in lathe work after he and a few friends in the factory organized a research group on technology. As a member of the factory's Party Youth League, he became a representative in the management committee of the factory.

His problems started in 1977 when he was admitted to a technical college in Huicheng. His parents wanted him to have the education, hoping that it would lead to his being transferred to one of the state enterprises in Huicheng. Manager Li refused to release him from the factory. Party cadres also reminded him of his political duties to the commune. It was obvious to Liang and his peers that the factory was unwilling to lose a good technician and was therefore applying political pressure on him. He stayed on, but agonized over the fact that Manager Li subsequently used his influence to transfer a relative of his own to a county factory.

One day in 1979, the county government office unexpectedly handed out visa applications for those who had relatives in Macao. Liang happened to pass by the county government offices and, without giving it much thought, took one of the forms home to show his father. Liang knew he qualified because he had a younger sister in Macao. His family urged him to leave. His mother's brothers were in the food business in Macao and could set him up. Life might be rather unsettled for a while, they thought, but it would be better than the endless political uncertainties that were draining all their energies. Moreover, as the eldest son, he might also pave the way for his younger brothers.

The factory was shocked when Liang applied for an exit visa, and Manager Li strongly opposed the idea. Chen Mingfa of the Commune MCBE Office finally intervened. He understood the young man's feelings. Liang had been a conscientious worker and a solid Party Youth League member, Chen asserted, so the commune should approve his application if he promised to use his economic connections for the good of the commune once he settled overseas. Hesitant at first, Liang by that time had become preoccupied with going abroad. The application took a long time to process. Impatient with the delays, he took a chance and smuggled himself to Hong Kong, becoming one of the 400,000 emigrants to settle there in the late 1970s.[8]

Huang Youfen, Liang's classmate and friend, was less fortunate. A good technician, he was also well regarded at the factory. However, in 1979 national economic retrenchment shut off the factory's usual sources of state subsidies and contracts.[9] When there was only enough work for four months, Manager Li finally asked the workers to fend for themselves. Huang was disillusioned for many reasons. As a member of the Party Youth League, he had been sent to cadre training courses. In the mid-1970s, he and a few others had been organized as a political work team to "squat" in the countryside, to "discipline brigade cadres," and "to guide peasants in socialist education." He recalled that when the team insisted on uprooting cash crops, angry peasants had threatened to "axe them to pieces." He had been naive but full of political enthusiasm at the time. Conditions at the factory strengthened his decision to leave the system altogether. In late 1979, he tried to reach Hong Kong by sea but was caught before he could reach the coast. Together with many such prisoners, he was kept at near starvation for half a month. He watched the weaker ones perish. Then, to his great surprise, he was returned to the commune and only slightly humiliated. The factory gave him back his job, although he was no longer asked to participate in the activities of the Party Youth League. By then he no longer cared. He felt betrayed by the political system he grew up with as much as by his own ambition. "I rotted with the system," he told me bitterly.

Brigade Enterprises: Cellular Development

Though commune enterprises in Huancheng employed the nonagricultural population, jobs in brigade enterprises were exclusively reserved for the villagers. The development of brigade enterprises in Huancheng was uneven. Table 11.9 compares industrial development in selected brigades. Donjia Brigade, for example, was the pride of the commune in the 1970s. Tianlu Brigade, by contrast, had little to show until the 1980s. The imbalance is easy to understand. Tianlu Brigade's land area was large, and its team leaders were reluctant to release young male workers from the fields. Brigade cadres who were anxious about grain procurement sympathized.

Table 11.9. Enterprise Development, Selected Brigades

	Dongjia				Chengnan			
Year	Output (Yuan)	Net Income (Yuan)	Number of Workers	Value of Fixed Assets (Yuan)	Output (Yuan)	Net Income (Yuan)	Number of Workers	Value of Fixed Assets (Yuan)
1969	—	—	—	67,200	—	—	—	—
1970	153,215	81,591	109	84,268	—	—	—	—
1971	140,263	76,027	143	98,988	—	—	—	—
1972	145,458	69,933	138	121,203	—	—	—	—
1973	143,652	63,953	138	136,633	—	—	—	—
1974	159,882	87,928	169	171,319	50,770	19,821	93	—
1975	153,748	83,247	172	187,099	81,745	38,190	110	—
1976	274,668	174,137	250	250,277	123,286	56,933	125	—
1977	401,722	237,627	375	330,621	170,420	76,086	207	—
1978	487,642	255,654	481	433,026	204,357	101,854	202	—
1979	738,351	308,889	506	487,959	198,533	124,899	175	—
1980	1,889,535	947,077	649	853,228	325,186	192,798	98	210,500
1981	2,427,585	856,047	662	1,043,228	305,639	179,019	183	156,455
1982	2,473,000	376,000	698	750,000	422,000	77,100	229	269,000

Source: Commune and brigade accounts collected during fieldwork.

Moreover, Tianlu had traditionally geared its marketing activities toward Sanjiang and Shuangshui, market towns farther away from the industrial complexes of Huicheng and Jiangmen. State discrimination against private marketing had sharply limited the economic activities of these towns. Hence peasants in Tianlu perceived few opportunities for themselves outside collective agriculture. For them, livelihood under the old cadres was tolerable. Unless the weather was particularly bad, grain production was maintained at a high level. Despite Maoist complaints about cash crops, the brigade contracted with the state corporations in Huicheng and Jiangmen to sell sugarcane and tropical fruits. Neither the peasants nor their leaders were enthusiastic about the unfamiliar industrial enterprises. Lin Qing argued that, even if the brigade transcended its conservative outlook, self-imposed or otherwise, it would be difficult to compete with brigades such as Chengnan and Dongjia. Tianlu's traditional parochialism remained an obvious liability.

Tianlu's agricultural enterprises in the 1970s included a pig farm; a work team that grew fruits, palm, and melon; and a seedling station. In 1977

	Sancun				Tianlu		
Output (Yuan)	Net Income (Yuan)	Number of Workers	Value of Fixed Assets (Yuan)	Output (Yuan)	Net Income (Yuan)	Number of Workers	Value of Fixed Assets (Yuan)
—	—	—	—	—	—	—	—
—	—	—	—	—	—	—	—
—	—	—	—	—	—	—	—
—	—	—	—	45,041	31,000	90	31,000
—	—	—	—	60,531	37,000	106	36,400
—	—	—	—	89,451	52,000	118	41,280
48,496	30,064	52	28,000	76,702	46,700	118	49,160
73,725	29,948	55	60,174	116,439	67,800	116	49,160
156,214	99,168	63	60,904	78,425	35,911	84	51,000
169,841	108,933	98	74,391	97,708	56,913	88	71,200
147,753	93,683	102	7,388	156,489	67,810	162	92,600
193,481	55,936	98	—	180,223	105,415	180	75,000
103,448	1,696	107	24,640	1,220,318	314,944	506	109,629
105,300	19,500	35	15,500	2,044,500	350,200	325	451,600

these groups hired a total of twenty-seven workers. The brigade's industrial enterprises, consisting of village crafts and services left over from the 1950s and 1960s, were no better. They provided little employment or income for the brigade members. In 1977, workers in the enterprises constituted only 1.47 percent of the total brigade population. Enterprise output represented only 9.6 percent of the brigade and teams' total output in 1979, and 8.6 percent in 1980. A vicious cycle developed, with team members reluctant to work in the enterprises because their wages were below those of agriculture. It was not until 1981, when political reforms were underway, that Tianlu caught on to enterprise development. It established a large refinery for local sugar and organized labor groups to work at construction sites in Huicheng and Jiangmen. In 1981, 8.6 percent of Tianlu's population was engaged in such enterprises.[10]

The development of brigade enterprises in Chengnan and Dongjia was different. Like Tianlu, Dongjia was a large, multi-surnamed brigade. Situated midway between Jiangmen and Huicheng, Dongjia had once been the center of a larger Yuanqing Xiang and had held a daily market attended by peasants from Dajiao and Xijia Xiang. Villagers used the numerous waterways to transport their goods to the cities. In 1977, the brigade built a paved road linking Dongjia to the major county highway, which shortened the bicycle ride to the two cities to ten minutes.

Compared to that of Tianlu, Dongjia's agriculture was not particularly productive. Its land-to-man ratio was median in the commune. Its grain production hovered around 900 catties per mu in the 1970s. Dongjia never successfully revived its traditional orange crop, but palm handicrafts and petty trade remained popular. Dongjia had a variety of agricultural enterprises, some of them in operation since the 1950s, that catered to both local and urban markets. For example, the brigade orchard sold 30,000 catties of lychee fruits a year to Hong Kong through the export corporations in Huicheng. Its palm fields supplied 10,000 yuan of fan palm to the commune palm-drying field. Dongjia also ran an impressive variety of industrial enterprises. Using expediters who were well connected with the commercial departments, the brigade secured contracts all over the delta. The brigade had its usual grain mills, oil presses, brick kilns, and agricultural machine-repair shops, catering particularly to its teams. It also produced small parts and took up chemical processing for county factories. By the early 1980s, the small-parts workshop was producing metal moldings and had developed its own brand of metal locks. Its embroidery workshop had secured contracts from the export corporations in Huicheng and was employing over a hundred women workers to sew children's pyjamas. As early as 1977, 8.2 percent of its population was working in the enterprises.

Enterprise development in Dongjia forced the brigade to secure institutional ties with extralocal administrative units. In the 1970s the permission of the County MCBE Bureau was necessary for its expediters to travel beyond the commune. It also relied on the County Materials Bureau for the allocation of scarce fuel and metal. To finance its expanded enterprise, the brigade borrowed heavily from the commune credit cooperative and from the state bank. In 1979, it took advantage of the first signs of liberalization to sign a contract with a Hong Kong factory, whose owner was a native of Dongjia, to process small metal parts. The output of Dongjia's enterprises reached 44.4 percent of the brigade's total agricultural and industrial output in 1979, and 58 percent in 1980.

However, Dongjia's successes generated unique problems for its cadres. The brigade initially recruited young women for light industrial jobs. Only a handful of the 134 workers in the embroidery workshop were men. Factory management was entrusted to a retired cadre. A few work-group leaders set production targets and wages. Two types of women made up the work force. The older ones, who wanted only seasonal work, had little education or career ambition. From my talks with them, I could see that they were not interested in how the factories were run as long as work-group leaders "cared about people's feelings" (you renqing). They did not bother with further training. The younger group of women were in their late teens and early twenties. Many had a few years of primary or junior middle school. Usually single, they were expected to help in family chores. Occasionally they shopped and watched movies in town with coworkers, but village and family remained the center of their social world. They cared more about wages than the older women and were more motivated to learn new skills. They viewed visits to town factories as exciting social outings rather than as vital steps along a career track.

The small-parts workshop stood out as the brigade's pride and hope. Its workers were all men in their twenties who had attended or graduated from the junior middle school in the brigade. A few technicians had taken short-term training courses at state factories in Jiangmen. Young workers generally considered the factory the first step in getting out of the fields. They were eager for the higher industrial wages and did not hide their ambitions of becoming skilled technicians. If the brigade factory prospered, perhaps the commune or collective enterprises in town would notice and recruit them. In the late 1970s and early 1980s, the metal workshop (molding and lock-making) took the lead in output and profits among the brigade's various enterprises.

Young brigade leaders who replaced the old cadres during the 1970s were eager to build up the economy. If the enterprises expanded, they would be able to use offers of employment and funds as political leverage with the teams. Their efforts came to the attention of the county authorities, who were quite willing to make Dongjia a model. If party superiors happened to be keen on production, Dongjia had the figures to show. If the Maoists were calling for self-reliance, Dongjia could always boast how its enterprises utilized local ingenuity. Through the County MCBE Bureau, Dongjia received crucial allocations of production materials and contracts.

However, wage disputes in the enterprises show how the cadres' susceptibility to ideological pressure damaged their relationships with the workers. Up until late 1976, workers in brigade enterprises were given work-points whose value was calculated after all costs, taxes, and collective investment funds were subtracted from total output. From late 1976 to 1978, the brigade adopted a Maoist remuneration system under pressure from the commune and county MCBE offices. The value of work-points was no longer calculated on the basis of brigade enterprise income. Instead, the average income of the five richest agricultural teams (out of sixteen) was used as a standard. The rationale behind this move was to narrow the gap between enterprise and agricultural income so as to reduce competition among team members for industrial jobs.[11] The move demoralized the workers from the most productive teams because the value of their work-points dropped in relation to that of other teams. When the wages of less productive teams were subsidized, other workers protested. They felt that they were doing similar types of work, but were being penalized for their team membership. One way or another, the workers all felt they were being cheated in the name of the collective. Workers in the metal workshop protested most loudly. Disagreement and lack of cooperation finally forced the brigade cadres to restore the old system of remuneration in 1979. With the enterprises generating nearly 50 percent of the brigade's total output, the cadres could not afford prolonged labor conflicts.

This episode illustrates a dilemma for the brigade. The cadres were concerned about the enterprises because they were vital political capital. For the average member, successful enterprises meant higher wages and escape from back-breaking labor in the fields. For young male workers, the metal workshop represented one of the few paths to upward mobility. But prosperous enterprises also meant that the cadres had to ingratiate themselves with commune and county-level patrons and respond to their ideological priorities, a situation which eventually bred new conflicts within the brigade.

Self-Reliance: Credit and Liability

The history of enterprise development in Huancheng Commune thus created a series of paradoxes. The commune's periurban location gave it a strategic advantage for dealing with state industries in Huicheng and Jiangmen. As the enterprises expanded in scale and number, their operations became more dependent on the urban industries and the commercial departments of the county. Prosperity generated its own vulnerability: during the radical political campaigns, when urban industries were pressured "to cut the tails of capitalism," contracts with the rural enterprises dwindled. During periods of political moderation, when industries were streamlined in the name of economic rationality and efficiency, the technologically cruder rural enterprises were the first to be dropped. In the 1950s and 1960s, when the enterprises were still peripheral to the commune economy, policy fluctuations did not affect peasant livelihood significantly. However, by the 1970s, when income from the enterprises constituted over 20 percent of the total commune income, any change in their operation had a greater impact.

Both commune and brigade cadres considered the enterprises an economic asset. They could negotiate with the resources, distribute favors to fellow villagers, and build up their own credibility. But economic success also required that cadres pay more attention to policy fluctuations that affected their urban patrons, and these shifts were quite beyond the cadres' control. Sancun Brigade is a clear case of this type of political vulnerability. County officials used the success of its enterprises to push for the transition to brigade accounting. They promised contracts and subsidies, but when industrial retrenchment set in, Sancun received nothing. In the meantime, team members bore the economic consequences and cadres paid the political price.

Another paradox involved the workers in the enterprises. The commune and periurban brigades thrived on subcontracts from urban industries. To meet their technological standards, they recruited the most educated, articulate, and ambitious workers. A new generation, with a different self-image and different aspirations, emerged on the commune's social landscape. They had a stake in the enterprises, but the volatility of the collective economy continually frustrated their hopes. And frustration turned into skepticism in the late 1970s. These workers posed a new and real political challenge to the cadres in the commune when the cellular structures of the collective economy began to unravel in the 1980s.

A final paradox concerns the relationship between the commune and brigade leaders. At the same time that brigades were developing their enterprises, the commune administration was expanding its own. From 1969 to 1979 six new enterprises were established, while the work force increased from 602 to 1,355 and production value increased threefold. In order to provide politically reliable leadership to these enterprises, old

brigade cadres were transferred to the commune, altering the power structure of the brigades. Old cadres who had risen to power during the 1950s
and were entrenched in the personal networks of their communities found
themselves preoccupied with political developments in the industrial and
commercial departments of the county. The transfer of these older cadres
broke whatever personal ties the commune-level cadres might have had
with the brigades. During political campaigns, ideological pressures were
applied directly to the new brigade leaders because the old cadres were out
of touch. Thus, instead of fostering solidarity among the units within the
commune, the commune and brigade enterprises created divisiveness and
isolated their leadership. The informal networks of patronage were dis-
rupted and often discredited. Self-reliant enterprise development made the
brigades more cellular yet at the same time more vulnerable to external
political pressure and internal dissent.

Industrial growth in the commune and the brigades brought in new
actors and expanded social horizons. A young generation of educated,
articulate workers with a stake in the collective units became alienated
because of the system's structural flaws. Though their disillusionment had
crystallized by the late 1970s, they did not speak out, because the cadres
continued to monopolize the commune economy and politics. There were
few alternatives for the young workers. Clearly, they complied with the
system; many of them were active in the Party Youth League branches. It
was not until the early 1980s, when the decollectivization drives initiated
at the national level undermined the cadres' cellular power base that the
tensions building up in the commune burst into the open.

The emerging private repair workshop in Huicheng. (1981)

One of the first signs of liberalization: the People's Bank of China in Huicheng offering bonuses for savings accounts. (1981)

Mother and child in their best
at a day-long birthday banquet
in Huancheng. (1982)

The revived dragon boat races on the river separating Huicheng from Huancheng
Commune. (1980)

A busy daily market in Huicheng. (1982)

A revived daily market in Tianma. (1987)

The pantheon of deities inside the Tianhou temple at Yuanjiacun, Chakeng. (1987)

A renovated Tianhou temple at Yuanjiacun, Chakeng. (1987)

Lanterns from the faithful hang inside the Hongsheng temple at Chaolian. (1986)

Village children in their colorful daily clothes, Chaolian. (1986)

The rejected in an age of reform: migrant-beggar on the streets of Huicheng. (1982)

The Mo lineage hall complex in Huicheng succumbed to the forces of modernization. (1986)

CHAPTER 12

State Involution

The Third Plenum of the Party Central Committee in December 1978 confirmed the demise of the Maoists as well as the intention of the new regime to decollectivize the rural economy. At first the reformers experimented on new systems of production responsibility only in selected areas. When positive results became evident in the early 1980s, implementation of the new systems was accelerated in the rest of the country.[1] The reforms released the vast economic potential of the Pearl River delta, which had a long tradition of highly specialized agriculture, sophisticated rural marketing, entrepreneurship, and labor mobility.[2]

In Xinhui, decollectivization formally started in 1983. Daze Commune served as a trial model in August. The commune party committee relinquished some of its power to the management committee. An amalgamated corporation was set up to handle economic affairs. By October, the administrative reorganizations, which aimed at breaking the monopolistic power of the party committee, had extended to all the other communes. Communes were renamed rural districts (*qu*), and township (*xiang*) government and village (*cun*) committees were then set up to replace the brigades and teams. The entire process was completed by March 1984.[3] The system of household registration that determined who was entitled to obtain state grain rations continued, but the rural population previously confined to the villages was allowed to seek work in the numerous towns in the county. Grain and other restricted commodities reappeared in rural markets.[4] The township and village cadres were responsible for administering contracts and supervising tax payments and the state procurement of crops, but they no longer managed agricultural production. This task reverted to individual households, which were given a share of the land and tools previously held by the teams. Commune and brigade enterprises were converted to independent units, and their management was auctioned off to the highest bidder, not necessarily commune members.

In September 1983, Huancheng Commune became a rural district with 20 townships and 86 villages. Three small brigades, Jiangzui, Qibang, and Shagang, formed a new township, Sanxing Xiang. Chengjiao and Machong brigades together formed the Chengjiao Xiang. Tianma Xiang reverted to its former composition when its six brigades were reunited as one township (Xinhui Xian Dang'anguan 1984, 36–57). By late 1986, the Huancheng rural district was officially designated a market town (zhen). Because of the government's intention to revive market-town economies, its enterprises were allowed tax exemptions and preferential credit.

One would expect that both the peasants and the cadres in Huancheng welcomed the economic reforms. The area had all the prerequisites of a specialized and commercialized agriculture that the reforms aimed to revive: easy and cheap water transportation; proximity to large cities, and therefore access to supplies, markets, and technical information; and abundant overseas contacts. An atmosphere of hopeful prosperity prevailed. Uncle Ye and Old Liang, together with many others, happily claimed that the 1980s reminded them of the hopeful days in the early 1950s. "Call it a second liberation," they announced to me when I visited in the summer of 1987.

In this chapter I will focus on the changing social landscape of the commune as it responded to the national call for economic liberalization. A crucial question is whether state agents with entrenched interests have been able to tolerate a diminished role in the management of the rural economy. To put the question another way, if each individual takes for granted the state power that so effectively penetrated daily life, and therefore embarks on his or her entrepreneurial adventures with skills acquired to cope with such power, to what extent can the state be said to be disengaging itself from society? Do the reforms signify "a second liberation" or "state involution?"[5]

Decollectivization in Huancheng Commune

Decollectivization came to Huancheng only gradually. The cadres were apprehensive, as were the peasants. Encouraged by the more flexible procurement and pricing policies in 1980, several brigades drastically reorganized their cropping patterns. As shown in table 12.1, Dongjia and Tianlu converted several rice fields to orchards, sugarcane, and palm fields.

Commune leaders promoted the changes. Though the grain quota for the commune remained at 16.9 million catties a year, other crops could be substituted for grain. Out of an average yield of 10 tons of sugarcane per mu, growers were obliged to sell only 3.3 tons to state agents. The rest could be used to substitute at the rate of a ton of cane for a picul of the grain quota. The difference in the prices of the two commodities meant that the

Table 12.1.   Cropping Patterns in Dongjia and Tianlu Brigades

(Percent of Total Cultivated Area)

Year	Rice	Sugarcane	Palm	Peanut	Citrus	Lychee	Fish Ponds	Private Plots
Tianlu Brigade								
1966	55.2	3.3	16.4	10.9	18.8	—	—	3.0
1978	66.1	9.0	17.2	3.6	2.4	1.3	—	—
1979	62.9	9.3	16.6	6.3	6.9	—	—	3.1
1980	60.3	10.0	15.9	6.0	5.4	—	—	3.2
1981	55.2	14.3	15.6	6.4	7.7	—	—	3.3
1982	57.9	11.9	14.4	6.8	10.8	—	—	3.0
Dongjia Brigade								
1966	62.2	5.3	6.1	6.2	13.0	—	1.3	2.7
1978	66.6	8.7	7.6	3.3	12.6	—	1.3	—
1979	65.5	8.2	7.0	6.0	12.0	—	—	2.7
1980	65.6	9.5	6.8	8.2	11.0	—	1.2	2.8
1981	59.5	10.9	7.1	11.9	10.8	—	1.3	2.8
1982	59.6	15.2	7.2	8.6	9.4	—	—	1.8

Source: Commune and brigade accounts collected during fieldwork.

brigades made more money selling sugarcane than they could selling grain. By the mid-1980s, the commune even allowed villagers to meet part of their procurement quotas with cash and then bought grain from other provinces to make up the balance for the required state quotas. A deputy party secretary in the commune told me that in 1986 the commune spent over 1 million yuan to buy grain from Hubei at 32 yuan a picul, and argued that it was worth the effort. The total value of the brigades' and teams' output reached 90 million yuan in 1986, compared to 13 million yuan in 1979 before the reforms were implemented.

However, when the reforms were initiated, reactions were mixed. Old peasants such as Uncle Luan and Old Yong in the Chengnan Brigade were anxious. They had known poverty and were more tolerant of the short-comings of the socialist regime. As they said to me, "We had seen worse times when we had no legitimate claims to anything. We were counting on the collective to see to our old age, but now we are left on our own." This reaction was especially common among households with few laborers. They knew they could not compete on an equal footing with others. After many years of complying with the policies of the party, they felt abandoned.

The households with younger and stronger members were enthusiastic about the reforms. In a typical family, the young men would leave for Huicheng and Jiangmen to work on construction sites and at short-distance hauling. In the cities they relied on relatives and school friends for support. In their absence, farm work fell heavily on the shoulders of the elderly, women, and children. Some households refused to take the land allocated to them because it came encumbered with the responsibilities for grain delivery. Instead, they left the area for opportunities in neighboring counties.[6] In 1982, 35 percent of the labor force of Dongjia commuted to Huicheng and Jiangmen despite objections from the cadres. A few households left for Doumen County to go into the fish-raising business that catered to the Hong Kong market. There was a trace of desperation in the activities of rural youths. Past political experience taught them that economic liberalization might not last, so they decided to "gamble with their livelihoods" (*panming qu gan*) in order to generate some reserves before another campaign confronted them. Young residents in the periurban townships took bolder steps. Earlier waves of emigration made it possible for entrepreneurs to make contact with their friends in Hong Kong and Macao and create new social networks. The emigrants have become a major source of information on markets, credit, technical know-how, and employment opportunities.

Brigade cadres shared the apprehension of the old peasants and felt betrayed by the party they had served in the past decades. Many older cadres retired in 1982 when the number of cadres in the commune was trimmed. They found themselves too old to make good use of the land allocated to them. The collectives they had built and profited from disintegrated in front of their eyes. As one cadre said bitterly, "During the land reform in the 1950s, we took the land from the landlords and bullies, and now the peasants, with the approval of the party, are taking the land from the collectives. The efforts we put in to transform the countryside just vanished. We have made a full circle back" (interview with the author, summer 1983).

Those who had been appointed party branch secretaries in the mid-1970s became the most outspoken opponents of the reforms and openly clashed with young entrepreneurs who were clamoring for the division of collective assets. Not only would these cadres lose the most because the collective economy that had given them power was unraveling, but the party reformers were also using them as scapegoats for past mistakes. However, they did not lose everything. When pressure from party superiors could no longer be avoided, they started dismantling the collective by allocating the best resources to their own households. They were able to get away with this because the average peasants, whose experience had taught them never to stick out their necks before the political dust had settled, did not challenge the cadres immediately.[7] Nevertheless, the efforts of party reformers to recruit a new group of skilled young entrepreneurs to replace them in the rural power structure only reminded the rural cadres that, however sheltered they had been from local opinion, they were highly dispensable in the eyes of the party.

It is not too difficult to understand the mixed reactions of the rural populace to the reforms. Even if one assumes that the state's penetration of the countryside was limited, it would still be naive to expect that, once administrative restraints were removed, the native entrepreneurial spirit would reassert itself at once. Three decades of socialist government created communities with unique internal structures that related to the state institutions in various ways. Having internalized the power of the state, the peasants cautiously marshalled their resources to find an uneasy niche within the changing political environment.[8]

The experiences of Dongjia and Tianlu brigades[9] bring out the conceptual issue of state involution at a stage of rural reforms that extends at least to the mid-1980s. The two brigades encompassed large, multi-surnamed townships, but differed in their major crops, their sources of income, their distance from urban centers, and their leaders. The responses of the cadres and the peasants in the two communities contrasted sharply. In the 1980s, Tianlu underwent a well-paced transformation. Income rose; young laborers did not migrate out of the villages at any alarming rate, although labor groups arranged through the brigade to work in the cities. Morale was high. Dongjia, however, virtually fell apart as a community. Team members demanded change before the cadres were ready to act. Although brigade accounts show that only thirty-seven laborers engaged in contract work outside the community, many young males went to Huicheng or Jiangmen on their own. Twenty percent of the households in 1982 produced less than the amounts they had negotiated with the teams. Cadres and peasants accused each other of mismanagement and irresponsibility, and generally did not cooperate. The two brigades are too near each other for us to be able to attribute the difference in their responses to the reforms to geographical factors alone. In the next section, I examine the administrative history of the two brigades for an explanation of their different development.

The Enthusiasm of Tianlu Xiang

Tianlu is situated at the southern tip of Huancheng Commune, 6 kilometers from Huicheng. It was the largest brigade in the commune. In 1979, it had a cultivated area of 8,253 mu and a population of 5,780. The land-to-man ratio was 1.43 mu per capita, putting it above the commune's average of 1.25 mu. By 1982 its population had reached 5,927, but cultivated area did not expand. Its eight teams were unusually large, with an average of 735 persons. Though the teams were the basic accounting units, work responsibility had always been set by the work groups, which numbered twenty-eight.

The residents of Tianlu were considered hillbillies by their neighbors. The social networks of Tianlu were tied to the marketing community of Shuangshui farther south. Its women wore the traditional black attire. A stable corps of cadres exchanged posts among themselves for several decades and remained in their positions as late as 1983. When I visited Lin Qing in the summer of 1987, he was still the party branch secretary.

The brigade's major crops were rice, sugarcane, palm, peanuts, citrus, and lychees. Tianlu's rice yields averaged above 1,000 catties per mu, and each mu of sugarcane yielded 7 to 8 tons. Team income varied. In 1977, when the weather was good, the richest team produced a collective income of 192 yuan per capita and the poorest, 143 yuan (the commune average was 146 yuan). In 1981, the collective per capita income ranged from 294 yuan to 186 yuan (as shown in table 12.2).

Since the major crops were all under contract to be sold to the state, the peasants were concerned about procurement quotas, market restrictions, and state prices. In return for fulfilling the quotas, the brigade received quotas of fertilizers, machinery, and insecticides, which had not been read-

Table 12.2. Per Capita Team Income of Tianlu Brigade

Year	Average	Highest Team Income	Lowest Team Income
1966	118	—	—
1976	119	137	104
1977	171	197	143
1978	134	150	114
1979	122	148	96
1980	190	218	160
1981	240	294	186
1982	418	—	—

Source: Commune and brigade accounts, and interviews.

Note: These figures represent collective team income. They do not include income from brigade enterprises, private plots, and individual sideline activities.

ily available through private channels since the 1950s. The brigade had devoted over half its land to grain production, but a relaxation of the grain quotas in the 1980s enabled it to grow more sugarcane. The cadres calculated the advantages of growing sugarcane as follows. A mu of land produced 10,000 catties of sugarcane, which yielded 1,300 catties of raw sugar. The government at the time allowed the brigade to substitute 1 catty of sugar for 1 catty of the grain quota. Since sugar prices were higher than grain prices, 1 mu of sugarcane yielded an income of 270 yuan with production expenses of 20 to 30 percent, whereas income from a mu of grain was about 154.7 yuan with production expenses of 35 to 40 percent. From a mu of sugarcane, peasants could earn 190 yuan, compared to 90 yuan from a mu of rice.

The cadres juggled with quotas, acreage, and prices to arrive at the highest possible income within the limits set by the government when the reforms were introduced. Their first step under decollectivization was to a system of production responsibility known as *lian chan dao zu* (output linked to the work group). The teams planned overall production and allocated resources and quotas to the work groups. Each group then distributed its share among its households. Individuals received work-points after finishing the tasks. The work group kept track of total production. Whatever the groups produced above the quotas was retained and distributed to the members in the form of work-points. If the group could not meet the team's target, it had to make up the difference. The team calculated the value of the work-points after total output from all the work groups was pooled.

In 1981, the production responsibilities for sugarcane and tangerine were given directly to the households. Soon afterward, in January 1982, six of the eight teams assigned responsibility for all crops to individual households. The system was known as *lian chan dao hu* (linking output to households). Team leaders set output targets based on the total yield in the past three years. The brigade no longer guaranteed a minimum grain allowance for peasant households. For delivering the agreed amount of crops from the resources they were allocated, the households received work-points. They could sell their above-quota produce to the team for extra work-points, or they could sell it in the rural markets. The value of work-points continued to be calculated at the team level. The system of *da bao gan* (total production responsibility) was not implemented until the commune was dismantled in the autumn of 1983. *Da bao gan* abolished both the work-points and distribution at the team level.

In 1980, the peasants of Tianlu got a pleasant surprise when the government raised the price of major agricultural commodities. The price of sugarcane rose from 1.9 yuan to 2.4 yuan per picul. The sugar refineries also began offering a 30-fen (cents) rebate per picul. Fan palm could be sold freely in the rural markets, though the state agencies remained the major buyers. The prices for fan palm rose from 4 fen to 6 fen per stalk. Processed fans brought 12 fen each. For the brigade which produced an average of seven million palm fans a year, the price changes meant an increase of over 100,000 yuan in income. The same applied to its annual production of 10,000 picul of lychee fruits when state prices were raised from 25 yuan to 40 yuan per picul.

On the whole, the transition to the new responsibility systems produced few complaints. However, one wonders why the brigade stalled on *da bao gan* until it was absolutely unavoidable in late 1983.[10] The issue becomes clearer if one understands how the brigade members perceived their relationship with the state sector: what crops they needed to grow, how the crops were sold to the government, and the degree of their dependence on the state sector for supplies. At the heart of the matter was grain production. While most people welcomed the reforms, many were unwilling to bear responsibility individually for growing grain. Rice cultivation requires a well-coordinated labor force. In a multiple cropping area, overlapping seasons inevitably produce labor shortages. If the brigade parcelled out all its land to individual households, the quotas of grain for personal consumption could not be guaranteed. In the early 1980s, no one was ready to dissociate himself from the state system of supplies because the revival of rural marketing was as yet uncertain. So long as the government continued to restrict the sale and price of grain, those who accepted household responsibility for its production could only count on an increase in labor needed, an uncertain rise in productivity, a loss of collective security, and a marginal increase in income at best.[11] In the two teams whose labor force was stable, the members actually demanded to stay together. The other six teams distributed their land and production responsibilities to the households while preserving the team as the accounting unit. In this instance, the households received two allotments of land: one called *kou liang tian* (land providing grain for peasant consumption), and the second called *zeren tian* (responsibility land) from which the households delivered the negotiated amounts to the team. The team sold the grain to the government agents and calculated the value of work-points. The responsibilities for grain production were thus shared.

However, the peasants were happy to assume total household responsibility for cash crops, which required less coordinated effort. The prices set for these crops were high. Since production targets were based on a regional average, the high yields in Tianlu boosted incentives. Peasants aimed for a large surplus above the quotas. They stayed with the team to secure the guaranteed sales to the state at increased state prices and sold their surplus privately in the rural markets.

High crop prices and expected increases in output encouraged the peasants to continue participating in the township's agricultural activities. Brigade leaders estimated that in the summer of 1982 around 17 percent of Tianlu's residents were commuting to the county capital as day laborers. The commuters were "adventurous young men" who had finished work in the fields. Older men and women stayed in the villages to engage in secondary occupations. Relative stability in agricultural production meant that the teams could count on meeting their quotas and maintain the value of their work-points. This in turn induced villagers not to break with the collective. The collective still provided basic security, yet allowed the young to explore new opportunities. For the peasants of Tianlu, this was the best of both worlds.

The Woes of Dongjia

Dongjia was the second largest brigade in Huancheng Commune. In 1979 it had a cultivated area of 5,565 mu and 4,631 residents. The land-to-man ratio was average: 1.2 mu per capita. The brigade was subdivided into sixteen teams, the largest of which had more than 400 members and the smallest, 160. The brigade was considered periurban, situated halfway between Huicheng and Jiangmen. A paved road built by the brigade in 1977 connected the brigade headquarters to the county road.

The major crops were similar to those of Tianlu: rice, citrus, sugarcane, palm, and peanuts. However, Dongjia devoted more land to rice and mandarin orange than to palm, and its grain yields were not as high as those of Tianlu—about 900 catties per mu. It harvested an average of 6 tons of sugarcane per mu. Processing palm leaves and drying mandarin orange peel were important sidelines for the villagers. As shown in table 12.3, its teams' incomes were lower than those of Tianlu. In 1976, before the brigade enterprises were generating substantial wages for the team members, Dongjia's average per capita income was only 80 yuan per year.

Young cadres in the mid-1970s turned the industrial enterprises into an important part of the local economy. From then on, wages from brigade enterprises added an average of 40 yuan to per capita income. By 1977, annual per capita income had grown to 149 yuan. In 1982 the enterprises employed 698 workers, with a total output of 2.5 million yuan. Since

Table 12.3.   Per Capita Team Income of Dongjia Brigade

Year	Average	Highest Team Income	Lowest Team Income
1966	93	—	—
1976	80	117	58
1977	119.5	147	81
1978	91	—	—
1979	105	120	70
1980	176	226	110
1981	163	219	102
1982	282	367	195

Source: Commune and brigade accounts, and interviews.

Note: These figures represent collective team income. They do not include income from brigade enterprises, private plots, and individual side-line activities.

industrial wages were higher than agricultural wages, team members competed fiercely for jobs in the enterprises.

Unlike Tianlu, Dongjia had a young leadership recruited largely during the Cultural Revolution. Even before that, Dongjia had had its share of radicals. Its older cadres were activists from the period of the land reform, who toed the party line closely. The brigade had served as a trial site (*shidian*) for political campaigns. During the Cultural Revolution, the Red Guards had beaten up old cadres at the mass meetings. The young brigade leaders had created a great deal of bad feelings in the 1970s when they pushed for grain production, cut cash crops, forbade household handicrafts, and implemented the democratic evaluation of work-points.

At first, the cadres were skeptical about introducing the new responsibility systems, but when the official newspapers began referring to the policy changes, the peasants started clamoring for the division of land. The cadres finally responded by assigning production responsibilities to the households. Large machinery was kept by the teams and managed by technicians, who received work-points for contract work. The accounting unit remained at the level of the team, where income was pooled and the value of work-points was calculated on the basis of collective net income. The village's young men were already drifting into the cities at an alarming rate. The cadres divided the land and imposed production responsibilities in the hope that the households would at least deliver their quotas before they struck out on their own. However, some households refused even to take the land. They gave up their grain allowances and shunned the meager services that the brigade offered. Within the first year of the transition, 20 percent of the households failed to meet their quotas. The peasants blamed the cadres for setting unrealistic goals. Household also bickered over the use of public space for drying and storing grain. Whatever communal spirit remained was further damaged by a flood in the following year. Nobody wanted to repair the broken dike. The brigade cadres finally drafted all enterprise workers and made each household volunteer one laborer for the necessary repairs.

Despite the lack of community feelings, few members of the brigade wished to adopt the total responsibility of the *da bao gan*. It is tempting to blame the woes of Dongjia on the cadres who had pursued radical policies at the expense of ordinary peasants and to suggest that when national policies eroded the basis of their power, the villagers spitefully ignored their wishes. Such feelings were certainly expressed, but the peasants of Dongjia could not afford to make decisions based on spite. As in Tianlu, their strategies had more to do with the brigade economy and its connections to state structures. Since the prices for grain remained low relative to cash crops, households seldom devoted their full resources to its production. They produced just enough for their own consumption and for their share of the team's quota. What were their alternative sources of income? Some grew sugarcane, but Dongjia's yield was only average, and some peasants complained about the arbitrary decisions of the sugar refineries. Although fan palm and citrus could now be sold privately, the peasants worried about the long-term investments of three to five years these crops required. In the early 1980s, the average peasant was not willing to take great risks.

The towns offered most attractive opportunities. A relaxation of control over the movement of peasants meant that they could use their old urban networks to engage in petty trade or seek odd jobs in Huicheng and Jiangmen. Their needs dovetailed nicely with those of the town enterprises, which were under increasing pressure to assume responsibility for their own bottom lines. The enterprises were willing to take on the cheaper temporary laborers, who were more eager to work than their own employees and who did not demand fringe benefits. The urban enterprises thus undermined the interests of Dongjia's own enterprises. A few years before, the cadres could draw laborers from the teams and send them back to the fields during busy seasons. Now not only were their workers leaving, but their best technicians were defecting to city jobs. Although the urban enterprises did not necessarily offer better wages, the prospect of the privileges enjoyed by the urban state sector drew the young technicians from the villages. Jobs at the lower end of the urban hierarchy, such as hauling and construction, were relatively well paid.[12] In many households, all the young men worked in the cities, while the women and older men took care of the fields. Realizing that agricultural production would be adversely affected by this strategy, most households chose to stick with team-level accounting in order to spread the risks.

In evaluating peasant strategies in the early 1980s, one can hardly discount the influence of thirty years of socialist government. The peasants in Dongjia and Tianlu were responding to historical realities that their actions had helped create. Each peasant household had to plan its strategy in this period of economic liberalization, taking into account a powerful but arbitrary state whose agents were still able to defend their entrenched privileges. Under these circumstances, peasants either avoided making long-term investments or took speculative, short-term employment at the lower end of the urban labor market. Neither strategy was in their best economic interest; neither had been intended by party reformers. The situation should remind us of how difficult it is for the party-state to disengage itself from the economy and society, even when it has the best intentions of doing so.[13]

The Revival of Market Towns and Rural Migration

As the production responsibility systems gained momentum in the villages, market towns where rural migrants congregated also underwent drastic changes. Since 1983, the government has promoted the revival of market towns as part of its overall reform program. Its purpose has been clear: it believes that the rapid specialization of peasant production in recent years calls for an institutionalized environment for exchange. The labor surplus caused by a better managed agriculture also needs employment. To prevent an influx of rural migrants to the cities, the revival of market towns has been regarded as an urgent necessity (*Renmin ribao*, April 10, 1983; June 5, 1984). In Guangdong, the market towns targeted for promotion were the headquarters of former communes. Huancheng Zhen was one such town.

G. William Skinner (1964) has highlighted the dynamic interaction between market towns and their rural hinterland in late imperial China. The rural-urban linkages described in the earlier chapters of this work show that spirit at work in the Huancheng area at the turn of the century. However, forty years later, the area was dominated by local bosses in an era of political turmoil, a situation that caused Fei Xiaotong, the Chinese anthropologist, to mourn the loss of the symbiotic relationship between market towns and their hinterland, and to predict that the paralysis of market towns would force rural communities to become self-defensively autarkic (Fei 1948, 16–32). Thirty years of socialism did not restore any positive interaction between town and country. The persistent under-valuation of agriculture by the government slowed rural growth and investment (Lardy 1984). Because of the antiurban and anticommodity bias of the Maoist party line (Solinger 1984), market towns suffered a decline instead. Their populations remained low. Artisans with specialized skills were dispersed to the surrounding rural communities, as were educated youths. Under the Maoists, commodity production and rural trade were severely restricted and politically stigmatized. The only productive activities in the market towns were the commune enterprises, whose fate fluctuated with each policy change in Beijing rather than with the demands of local or regional markets. Agriculture remained self-contained, as did social and political interactions among the peasants. Commune and brigade leaders became local bosses who controlled production, distribution, and communication. The peasants were given few incentives and few opportunities for advancement.[14]

After 1983, the national leaders decided to reverse the situation. Peasants were allowed to settle in the market towns, although they could not obtain grain rations (*Renmin ribao,* April 23, 1983). At the same time, the collective enterprises in the market towns were given the autonomy to recruit and hire on their own terms. The reviving market town economies therefore attracted not only small traders but also migrant workers from the villages. These young migrants were the best educated and most articulate and ambitious group in the rural sector. They entered into competition with their peers in the market towns, who had better educations and industrial training. These two groups fueled the economic revival of the market towns. A few observations on Huancheng Zhen and Huicheng will shed some light on the transformation of these towns.

One summer afternoon in 1983 I was eating lunch at the Overseas Chinese Hostel in Huicheng. The restaurant had installed air-conditioning and was packed with people. Young waiters in white shirt and black tie, a style copied from Hong Kong, moved swiftly. Their service was extraordinarily different from that of the previous years. Moreover, the range of customers as well as the interactions between customers and waiters were very interesting. Many of them were the same young migrant workers whom I had seen earlier in the morning waiting at the bridge between Huancheng and Huicheng for their daily contract work. Although they were temporary workers, they seemed happy to pay for a good meal, and the waiters appeared courteous for a change. A few years earlier, peasants from neighboring communities who were visiting overseas relatives would sit uneasily at the same tables. The waiters would either ignore them or throw their dishes in front of them to show disdain. The old prejudices seemed to have disappeared.

The migrant workers I saw were categorized as "those who had left agricultural work but remained members of their villages" (*litu bulixiang*). They were not entitled to commodity grain, because their families had claimed land in the villages. Many commuted as day laborers. As noted earlier, the young men of Dongjia and Chengnan had started coming to town even before the collectives were dismantled. Their social connections in the town enterprises were strong and included relatives of brigade members, classmates from the commune secondary school, and former business contacts in the handicraft and fruit trades. Young peasants from Tianlu and Tianma, who could not compete with their more highly skilled peers for jobs in the urban enterprises, performed heavy physical labor, even when they were employed by factories in Huancheng Zhen or Huicheng. Except for a few technicians, most would not learn industrial skills.

In the periurban communities, many workers in the commune enterprises of Huancheng had been "released" from their factories. The commune enterprises had gone through a rather unsteady period in the early 1980s. State subsidies that once sustained the inefficient agricultural machinery factory were withdrawn. Local paper and fan palm became unmarketable when the tastes of newly affluent rural customers changed. When the commune tried to auction off the enterprises, nobody even made a bid. The commune's agricultural machinery station in 1982 nearly closed down for lack of contracts, and the workers were asked to fend for themselves. As a result, market-town youths in Huancheng who had hoped to get jobs after they graduated from school suddenly found life uncertain. However, they did not see the situation as negative. They harbored a few grudges, but were otherwise prepared to take advantage of the new political conditions before the pendulum had time to swing back.

Huang Youfen had just reached thirty in 1982 and was now married and the father of an infant son. The disgrace of his unsuccessful attempt to emigrate to Hong Kong had been forgotten. He did not quit his job as a technician in the agricultural machinery factory but started what he termed "legitimate moonlighting."[15] First, he and a few coworkers took orders from clients to make metal gates. Most of their contractors provided the metal, but the group also managed to find scrap materials in nearby factories. Manager Li allowed them to use idle machinery for a small fee. This type of work depended a great deal on personal contacts and favors, and Huang's years at the commune factory put him ahead of the game.

Second, he and his father-in-law, who had retired from the County MCBE Bureau, started a quail-breeding business. They sold both eggs and the birds to the restaurants in town. In 1983 he got in touch with Liang Daxin, the classmate and coworker who had left for Hong Kong, in order to find a secondhand motor-tricycle from Hong Kong. Huang needed the vehicle to expand his quail business to the neighboring counties, where the demand and the prices were higher. He convinced Liang to invest in the tricycle and buy into the enterprise.

Huang hoped to involve Liang in an even more ambitious project. Liang had been an apprentice in a restaurant for several years and had obtained temporary residence in Hong Kong. The recent liberalization in China allowed him to travel back to Huancheng. With two more friends from the commune, they planned to set up a bakery with imported machinery in order to make Western-style breads, cakes, and snacks. Their operation was to be a fast-food service catering to the workers in the area who could no longer afford a two-hour lunch break. Liang's brother, who had recently assumed the post of accountant at a new guest house in Huicheng, could secure wholesale contracts on his own, though his parents' business contacts in the food trade were also valuable.

Money Talk

The major actors in this period's explosion of economic energies were a young generation who came of age during the past two decades of political turmoil. Like the peasants in Tianlu and Dongjia who reacted ambivalently to the total production responsibility system, their choice of employment reflected obvious political considerations. These young people avoided long-term commitment to entrepreneurial plans and investments. They continued to attach themselves to commune factories but watched for opportunities to work on the side, a tactic known among them as *chaogeng* (moonlighting). As Huang Youfen put it, "everyone tries to make a quick buck and then sit tight for the next political reversal."

It was not until late 1983 that the new generation started to make longer-term plans and investments. These strategies involved the use of social ties, a knowledge of market rhythms, a keen sense of political leverage, and an urgent need to explore new networks. By 1987, economic liberalization seemed to be taken for granted. Nobody would deny that the reforms had brought welcome changes. Everyone was working much harder; affluence and upward mobility were common phenomena. "Money talk" dominated family dinner conversations as well as business meetings in Huancheng Zhen. Although it may have taken only ten years to destroy what it took the party-state thirty years to achieve, still the government's presence continues to be felt in every entrepreneurial strategy.

Looking ahead, we must ask whether the decade of reforms has triggered social processes in rural China that could lead to a point of no return. Will rural migrants, who have adjusted to the pace of work in the emerging market towns, be forced to return to their villages when officials in the urban sector find their resources strained? How can market-town youths who have made long-term investments in urban enterprises and find themselves increasingly involved in the technical and social networks of Guangzhou, Hong Kong, and Macao protect themselves against the traditional official ambivalence toward such networks? The 400,000 emigrants who entered Hong Kong legally and illegally between 1978 and 1980 (among them Liang Daxin) made adjustments of a different kind. Their stories are nonetheless interwoven with those of their friends and families in rural Guangdong.

Political Talk

For the party leadership, some pressing problems remain. By abandoning the middle-aged cadres who dominated the villages in the 1970s, the party had hoped to make room for a new generation of leaders from the ranks of the young entrepreneurs emerging on the social scene. But if entrepreneurs continue to thrive under economic liberalization, will they seek party affiliations? If they do not, how will the party be able to function in the rural sector, which is rapidly developing independent economic resources? Will the party be able to reestablish control if necessary? In fact, the party organizations in Huancheng have not done too badly by their own criteria. A series of party rectifications from 1982 to 1984 removed most of the unpopular cadres in the rural townships. Those who had maintained relatively good relationships with fellow villagers were kept on. Lin Qing of Tianlu Xiang was one such example.

The *qu* leadership was also overhauled. Old "commander" Xu was reassigned to the rural district's amalgamated corporation (*nong-gong-shang zonggongsi*) after the agricultural machinery station disbanded. Chen Sheyuan, head of the commune office, became a consultant to the basic construction office. Chen Mingfa, disgraced in a corruption case in 1982, was brought back to manage the new hostel and restaurant complex. All but one of the deputy party secretaries were retired. Yuan Dewei, a schoolmate and friend of Liang Daxin and Huang Youfen, employed in the county legal department, returned to serve as deputy party secretary. Another schoolmate, Zhang Deman, who had obtained the equivalent of a college degree in the county cadre school, was made party secretary of the neighboring Hetang District. Other assignments bolstered the district's new political network. A young commune secretary, whose post in Huancheng was transitional in 1981, became the county's deputy secretary for agriculture. A young lecturer in the county cadre college who was good friends with Liang Daxin, Huang Youfen, and Yuan Dewei became the county's first party secretary.

Shrine Talk

Elderly friends seem happy that many villages have revived their communal shrines. Surprisingly enough, young factory workers are also enthusiastically visiting sites where particular trees or boulders are believed to have special powers. When asked to explain these rituals, they admit that they do not know much about them. It is difficult for them to have faith in the deities, some of whom have literally disintegrated in their hands, but they feel that it will not hurt to copy what others are doing. If there happen to be spirits, one should at least appease them. If the spirits decide to bestow grace on them, all the better. If the charms do not work, nothing is lost. One cannot count on anything these days, they say. The pilgrimages constitute enjoyable social outings, if nothing else.

Several of the temples in the area have been restored. The Hongsheng Temple in the neighboring Chaolian District was reopened with a 500,000-yuan donation from the Chaolian Native Place Association in Hong Kong. The district government used half the money to build a park in front of the temple and the other half for a major road. The temple's patrons considered this a reasonable compromise. The birthdate of the deity was a busy occasion in March 1987. The faithful flocked from overseas as well as from surrounding villages. Activities were organized by the temple association in cooperation with the tourist bureau of Jiangmen. There was no parade of the deity, but the bureau held a waterborne tug-of-war for schoolchildren in front of the temple, and overseas patrons were feasted.

In Huancheng, the few temples I visited were small "do-it-yourself" affairs. A group of village women at Yuanjiacun in Chakeng Xiang restored the old Tianhou Temple. The pantheon of deities behind the veils was most incongruous in its humble settings. Though the self-appointed temple manager, a forty-year-old woman, could not distinguish one deity from another, she was pleased to report that members of the neighboring Liang lineage visited the temple occasionally. I was sadly amused at the fact that, in her enthusiasm to show me the gods' images, she climbed on the altar barefoot and drew back the mosquito nets in front of them, which, according to an old temple manager in Tianma Xiang, is extremely improper. The Beidi Temple in Tianlu Xiang was restored in an old garage behind the marketplace by another group of village women who put together 6,000 yuan. Apart from the fact that only half the garage was roofed, one could enter the small room only through a side door. This was what the gods had to settle for. After all, according to my friends, they were fortunate to have the temples restored at all.

Ancestral halls, the other traditional centers of popular rituals, remained dilapidated buildings used by factories and village schools. Rural residents under fifty knew little of their history and symbolic significance. My attempt to identify a large hall next to the focal ancestral hall of the Lu lineage in Chaolian was a case in point. What remained of the tall stone pillars and carved wooden beams that had withstood the Red Guards' attempts to destroy it in the 1960s suggested that the hall had been a rather important center for the Lu lineage community. After I had painstakingly described the building, perplexed villagers finally asked, "Do you mean the shoe factory?"

It is difficult to summarize the decade of reforms in Huancheng Commune. Its cellular and frozen existence has changed dramatically. There is obvious excitement at the new opportunities. Old networks have been revived, traditional customs have been restored with new improvisations, and hopes for the future are high. Yet amidst the enthusiasm I detect a certain ambivalence. At the end of a visit in the summer of 1987, I had dinner with a group of old friends whom I had known for ten years. Liang Daxin happened to be back for a visit to the parents of his future bride, whom he met in Hong Kong. It was therefore a particularly meaningful and happy get-together. We rejoiced at the obvious prosperity of the community. We mourned the loss of Xu Wenqing, who died in 1979. We marveled at the rise and fall of Chen Mingfa. We joked with Huang Youfen about his entrepreneurial adventures, and we discussed everyone's careers during the last decade. Finally I asked the question that was uppermost in my mind. "Granted that the reforms have brought changes you hoped for, could you have resisted them if you had wished to?" Yuan Dewei, the young deputy secretary, finally broke the silence. "I suppose not," he said quietly.

CHAPTER 13

Agents and Victims

Collective ownership means that the collective "owns" us peasants as well as the resources we work with. The cadres who control the collective then do whatever they please with our lives. They behave no differently than the local bullies we heard so much about in the "recall bitterness" accounts of our fathers. However, the strongmen of the 1930s and 1940s had no legitimate claim on the peasants, who regarded them as excesses of the traditional society. The cadres, on the other hand, enjoy total authority given by the socialist system. Chairman Mao once said that the scriptures were good, except that from time to time they had been recited by monks with crooked mouths. I wonder about these scriptures; it seems that they have distorted the mouths instead. (Anonymous interview with the author, summer 1982)

Judging from this candid comment by a former member of the Party Youth League in his late twenties, it would be hard to deny that the party-state has penetrated deeply into rural society.[1] But the reach of the state created its own paradox. During the land reform in 1950, the young peasant activists recruited by the Chinese Communist Party strongly attacked the local bosses in the name of the revolution. Three decades later the accusing fingers of a bitter and disillusioned young generation raised under socialism were pointed at them. Furthermore, while the peasants could condemn the local strongmen of the 1940s yet still preserve their respect for the traditional order, the peasants who denounced the rural cadres in the 1980s had begun to question the very principles that had given the cadres a central place in the Chinese countryside. The socialist system and its agents are experiencing a crisis of legitimacy because of their very power to induce compliance.

It is incorrect to conclude that the socialist state was unable to transform society as much as it hoped to from the evidence that traditional kinship, community, and religious functions have reemerged in the 1980s. One cannot expect the rural population as a whole to look back on the prerevolutionary period with nostalgia and hope for a return of the "good old days." Except for elderly villagers who have some emotional ties to the past, the majority of the peasants have neither the experience nor the memory of those times. The features of traditional village life that scholars see being revived in the 1980s—from popular rituals to the territorial identity based on communal and kinship ties—differ substantially in form and meaning from their counterparts in the past. The history of the delta involves centuries of community- and lineage-building, the development of marketing networks and multitiered contract tenancy, and the creation by upwardly mobile local elites of multiple centers of power that linked town to country.

The dominant imperial values and ideas that had percolated down to the villages despite the state's negligible administrative presence withstood severe challenges during the demise of the Qing dynasty in the first part of the twentieth century. A new cast of local strongmen emerged on the political scene, but the cultural perceptions of power and authority were not fundamentally changed. As I have tried to show, the highly cellularized villages of the late 1970s were products of the Maoist revolution.

Three decades of Communist rule stripped away the power base of the former elites and modified the traditional affiliations in rural social life. At the same time, new political conditions inculcated different assumptions about power and authority. The land reform destroyed the economic foundation of the lineage organizations; collectivization turned rural communities into component cells within the state sector. The communization movement incorporated the rural cadres into a tight bureaucratic network, whose legitimacy was tested and strengthened through successive ideological campaigns. A reorganized agriculture, decentralized educational and health care systems, and the development of self-reliant local industries— all served to breed new generations of political cadres. These leaders, acting more as state agents than as political brokers, redefined social hierarchies and standards of behavior in the name of class, revolution, and socialism, and established the power of the party-state in the daily lives of the villagers. The state's presence became a major factor in the social and economic institutions of these rural communities, for it came to determine the villagers' acceptance of and resistance to the political order in which they found themselves.[2] To understand the historical images that people in Huancheng draw upon, their present moral dilemmas, and their strategies for the future, we must take into account the evolution of this postrevolutionary system of power, which was a fact of life at least until the early 1980s.

In view of the outburst of entrepreneurial energies accompanying the liberalization of social life today, one must avoid overemphasizing the power of the state. The issue is how to conceptually incorporate the administrative history of the socialist state into today's political situation. Cut off from the past and lacking faith in the present, how will the young rural residents of the Pearl River delta face the future? Ru Zhijuan, writer who deeply senses the Chinese peasants' ambivalence, has commented on this dilemma:

> The Chinese peasants have been the most accepting and content. Since the land reform, was there ever a single door that lacked the couplet "Listen to Chairman Mao, follow the Communist Party"? They were able to endure hunger and cold and worked on their land from dawn to dusk. This was their greatest happiness. When the liberation war began, when their land was threatened, they stood by the liberation army, and gave their properties and lives. . . . It was not mere rifles that won the war, but the blood and sweat of the people and their will. After the revolution, they continued faithfully. It was collectivization, communization, the public canteens, deep ploughing, dense planting, chopping down fruit trees to make way for grain and to fuel the backyard furnaces. . . . They have complied, endured hardships, yet their days were not any better. So what lay ahead? . . . My head swelled, and a deadly serious question confronted me, and that was, if our party, our country experienced another war, would the peasants stand by us in the struggle just as they did before? I raised the question in order to confront the issue. After much debate and turmoil, my answer was no.[3]

What saddens her is precisely the paradox of power.

State-Society Articulations

State power and human agency are not mutually exclusive. If cultural meaning is a vital part of the historical process, a key task for students of state agrarian societies is to identify and examine the multiple factors that create culture and social change. If subordination is so total that it shapes even the spheres of resistance and strategies for negotiation, how can one meaningfully interpret the aspirations of either the upward mobile or the powerless?[4] For anthropologists who respect the need for "bringing the state back in" (Evans et al. 1985) and at the same time wish to emphasize local initiative, the task then is to see how state goals and popular morality interpenetrate each other through human agents.[5]

With these concerns in mind, I have argued that the priorities of the various state systems could not have penetrated local society had it not been for the initiative of the ambitious individuals who actively pursued the symbols of power recognized by the state tradition. Cultural status reinforced the power of the local elites. Combined, the symbolic and material attributes of power conveyed a quality of permanence and universality. In imperial times, power was associated with landed wealth, lineage organizations based on patrilineal descent, community solidarity, the etiquette of arbitration in guilds and academies, and literati culture. In the decades after the revolution, it became identified with class rhetoric, loyalty to the socialist state, and party discipline. At the same time that these concepts were transforming rural life, they were being exploited by self-interested local groups for various purposes.

These forces continue to influence the way in which people view their past and present, and give existing conditions a distinct local flavor. Nevertheless, in both the pre- and post-revolutionary periods, local leaders demanded compliance and commitment from those under their control and thus incorporated their communities into the larger structure of power and authority. All were accomplices to their own encapsulation.

However, the situations of the gentry elites and the rural cadres differed greatly. Dealing from multiple bases of power in their communities with an administratively weak state, the local elites in the delta of the late Qing had a great deal of freedom with which to develop the local economy, to acquire power and the symbols of authority, and to resolve social tensions built up in the process. Political brokers rose and fell, but the legitimacy of the imperial paradigm they promoted continued well into the mid-twentieth century. The rural cadres, on the other hand, rose to power not only in a much more cellularized rural society, but also through a single source of legitimacy: the party. With strong organizational and ideological pressure needed to induce compliance, the party-state gave its rural agents much less room for maneuver. The structure of dependence obliged the cadres to push even the most unrealistic policies upon the villagers, so that within a matter of decades, a unique set of social tensions and political liabilities was created. These tensions permeated every level of government and society. In this inquiry, I have focused on the situation of the cadres, caught between peasants and party, but actively pursuing their strategies of self-interest.

Rethinking Chinese Anthropology

This volume represents ten years of study. I conducted field research in the Pearl River delta in a period marked by tremendous social, political, and economic changes. I remember a nine-hour bus ride in 1976 from Huicheng to Guangzhou, 110 kilometers away. It was cheap then, 1 yuan

25 fen. The bus conductor, however, had to run down to the river every hundred meters or so to fill a leaking water tank. The ride could not even be considered a test of patience. The passengers sat there quietly and accepted the situation. Today the road is full of speeding minibuses owned by young drivers yelling at the top of their lungs to attract passengers. I remember visits to peasant homes, where Mao occupied a place on the family altar, and, despite all the "redness" displayed in conversations, life seemed colorless. Today, cousins come to blows at family grave sites over matters of inheritance. Elderly villagers, whom I would have expected to be sympathetic to the revival of popular religion, complain that the rituals are being vulgarized by the extravagance and ignorance of their new adherents. Young practitioners of these cults tell me that they do not care whether a deity is black or red, so long as it delivers. Their lack of knowledge about traditional culture is just as alarming as their disillusionment with socialism.

Just as the former Party Youth League member whom I quoted doubted the political scriptures he had been taught, I too have increasingly wondered about my academic assumptions. If I raise the matter of the analysis of "traditional" society in a study that concentrates on south China in the postrevolutionary period, it is because I believe one cannot follow the current situation without an understanding of the earlier society. Major paradigms in Chinese anthropology—G. William Skinner's regional systems analysis, Maurice Freedman's lineage paradigm, and Arthur Wolf's studies in religion and ritual—have provided valuable insight into Chinese culture and society. In thinking through this study, I feel the urgent need to integrate as well as to advance these paradigms.

The fact that little justification is needed to adopt a regional approach to social history is largely due to Skinner. He divides China into nine macroregions, each having undergone cycles of growth and decline at different periods of Chinese history. He makes the point that the political history of dynastic events, a topic that so preoccupies historians, must be seen in terms of the inherent structures of these macroregional systems, which derive from their fundamental economic activities. He has also been at pains to show that these systems and their component parts provide the basis for social communities, parapolitical systems, and culture-bearing units. Therefore, it is important to see how Skinner constructs the model of regional systems.

Each macroregion is internally differentiated and functionally integrated, with a regional core continuously drawing in the resources of the periphery. The growth and decline of these physiographic economies depend on how well people have exploited the material environment with a

given technology, based on cost-distance calculations. The region's economy also depends on the state's ability to ensure political and fiscal stability
and to administer its affairs efficiently (1985a, 281). In an earlier article,
Skinner argued against the image of the static, closed corporate rural community, stressing instead the cyclical opening and closure of community
boundaries as Chinese peasants responded to the vicissitudes of the wider
administrative and economic environments (1971).

In examining Huicheng and its rural hinterland, as well as the larger
regional system of the delta of which Huicheng forms a part, I pointed out
that development did not conform exactly to Skinner's model. Economic
calculations are important, but they are not confined to the level of market
exchange. Politics is also important, but official functions are interwoven
with the cultural strategies of local social groups. The power structures of
the area were shaped by the accumulation of wealth in Huicheng, by
community- and lineage-building in Huancheng, and by the political aspirations of numerous merchants and scholar-officials in the guilds, academies, and community temples. By focusing on the class politics and cultural
strategies for the control of local society from initial settlement to growth
and decline, I am not denying the validity of Skinner's functionally integrated regional system. However, the logic of market exchange based on
cost-distance calculations, as well as the demands and the administrative
provisions of the state, must be seen in the context of social institutions
whose cultural repertoire in itself embodied the constant interpenetration
of state and society at many levels. Social differentiation and cultural
exclusion entered into economic calculations at the local level, just as the
state brought its administrative and political powers to bear on a matter as
mundane as tax collection. Skinner provides a valuable, formalist conceptual model through which to view the evolution of Chinese society and
history, but if we are to understand the dynamic aspects of the political
process, we also need to examine specific social institutions and cultural
phenomena that embody relationships of dominance and subordination.
Unless we consider the broader picture and identify entrenched interests
and affiliations, the problems of analyzing the region's transformation in
the postrevolutionary era become bewildering.

If power, material and symbolic, is integral to the formation of a regional
system, what has been the dominant institution of social life? Freedman's
lineage paradigm offers us a valuable conceptual supplement to Skinner's
market-oriented macroregion. Freedman identified the lineage community as one of the most important social institutions of south China (1958,
1966), defining it as a nucleated settlement of agnates tracing unilineal
descent from a founding ancestor, tied together by substantial ancestral

estates, and expressing its solidarity through periodic rituals at ancestral graves and in ornate ancestral halls. The imposing presence of the lineage community was enhanced by genealogies compiled by educated members, who claimed descent from imperial officials in centuries past, and by the number of scholar-officials it could boast among its recent members. From the genealogies and evidence on the establishment of the estates, Freedman also observed that asymmetrical segmentation took place continuously in the lineages' development. Branches without descendants or estates eventually dropped out of sight. Freedman assumed that lineage formation in southeastern China depended on a combination of factors: a frontier environment needing defense, a river delta requiring large-scale irrigation, and rice cultivation, which permits a substantial accumulation of wealth. Lineage organizations achieved the cultural ideal of patrilineal kinship when all material factors were present.

What I observed in Huicheng and the Huancheng area seemed to fit Freedman's paradigm well in many ways. Documentary sources show that from the Ming period on, Huicheng's major lineages accumulated land from the surrounding sands. They dominated the regional political economy not only through a multitiered contract tenancy system, but also by controlling the thriving trade in grain, fan palm, and citrus. With their genealogies and ancestral halls, their patronage of community temples, and their alliances with other elites in parapolitical organizations, they created power relationships that penetrated the outlying rural areas. But I have reservations about the applicability of Freedman's model to the origin and function of lineages in the Huancheng area. The genealogies of most of the major lineages in the delta claim ancestors who came from the central plains during the southward movement of the Song dynasty. However, it is known that historically native populations and later the Dan fishermen inhabited the maturing delta before massive land migrations. David Faure (n.d.-2) argues that it was in response to the imposition of a certain tax in the Ming period that the local populations of Guangdong re-sorted themselves into the Yao or the Han, depending on whether or not they paid the tax. The sedentary agriculturalists eventually achieved cultural dominance in the expanding Chinese state, whereas the Yao preserved their tribal organizations in the hills in northern Guangdong.

The Dan fishermen of the Huancheng area may have been involved in a parallel situation. My own investigations in Tianma Xiang suggest that although the Chen lineage built thirty-odd ancestral estates, a few halls, and even compiled a genealogy in the 1920s, their myth of origin, their dress, and religious rituals point to their roots as Dan. The Chen insisted that two villages in their township inhabited by people of mixed surnames belonged to this ethnic stock. "But we are Han. We have ancestral halls and written genealogies," they declared. Could the highly differentiated lineages in the Huancheng area have originated with the upwardly mobile members of the native population, who separated themselves from what they now referred to as the "non-Han peoples out in the sands?" If this was the case, did the elaborate lineage organizations and their rituals offer frontier settlers a social structure and practices that the economy of the sands made necessary and possible, as the Freedman paradigm suggests? Or were they cultural devices that local populations used to exclude others as they merged into the larger polity?

Assuming that cultural contact means interpenetration, what was the nature of the Han Chinese culture that evolved in south China? In the realm of Chinese religion, Freedman asserted that "with the exception of prophecy and ecstasy, every religious phenomenon to be found among the common people of China was susceptible of transformation into belief and rites among the cultivated elite" (Freedman 1974, 39). Given this possibility in the religious sphere, how should we interpret the elite-commoner distinctions embodied in the evolution of lineage organizations in the delta?

The process through which local groups transformed themselves into a supposedly elitist institution that originated in the larger polity is shown by the uncharacteristic development of the focal ancestral halls at the very beginning of community formation. The Wubentang in Tianma Xiang is a case in point. Though not endowed with vast estates, this lineage hall served as a "political umbrella" apparently to express the territorial concerns of the locally powerful. Its managers acted as the large contractors of corporate estates in Huicheng and as second-level landlords to lineage members. The Wubentang became the township's political front for dealing with vexatious tax collectors and official functionaries, though its managers did their fair share of encroaching on weaker members. It was the major patron of the community's annual *jiao* (community exorcism) ceremonies and was closely linked to the community temple, the granary, and the school. All these developments occurred before substantial internal lineage segmentation had taken place. The lineage, though poorly endowed, acted much more as a community-level institution than is suggested by Freedman's model of lopsided lineage segmentation, which is characterized by the establishment of corporate estates by branches within the major lineage. In the process of segmentation, the lineage, its hall, and its managers became as much involved with questions of class and local community as they were with the local descent group. It may be that the genealogical umbrella was originally created to include households of differing descent, or that segmentation resulted, as the genealogies claim, from a process of growth and fission from a single ancestral core.

Whatever the case, we should recognize, as Faure has suggested in his study of lineage formation in Hong Kong (1986), that settlement rights and territorial control are at the heart of lineage politics. A preoccupation with the operations of a system of patrilineal descent may blind us to other aspects of these social affiliations equally meaningful to the rural population. In other words, the local lineage organization can be seen not only as a response to tensions within the kinship realm that can lead to segmentation, such as problems related to inheritance, but also as a response to the political-jural demands of the overarching state system and to the maturing of the regional economy. By studying the lineage organizations of the Huancheng area, we may gain a clearer understanding of the history of migration and cultural fusion in south China. In addition, by examining the ways in which kin, class, community, and state were interwoven in the lineage organizations, we may be better equipped to decipher the puzzling reactions of these social units when they came under attack after the Communist revolution.

State and society interpenetrate not only at the level of material and institutional relationships. It is relatively easy to evaluate the "successes" or "failures" of the Chinese revolution by measuring productivity or by counting incidents of cooperation or resistance to the demands of power-holders. But what the revolutionary experience has meant to those involved—how power is perceived and felt—cannot be quantified. If we accept that meaning and its symbolic expressions are often private and ambivalent as well as public and concrete, and that these aspects intertwine in observable behavior, the question remains as to how to "deconstruct" behavior in order to understand its multiple meanings and motivations, that is, the human aspects of the interpenetration of state and society.

In this line of thinking, the works of De Groot (1892–1910) and Granet (1922) on popular rituals and beliefs have been invaluable. Wolf (1974) shows how the supernatural categories of gods, ghosts, and ancestors in popular religion replicate the imperial bureaucracy, unwanted village vagabonds, and senior members of one's descent line in the physical world, and illuminate the peasants' perceptions of power, affinity, and social distance.[6] Ahern (1981) has extended this conceptual scheme by viewing rituals as the means for practitioners to learn and communicate about power. In doing so, it is of utmost importance to ground rituals in the histories of the local communities. If power is at stake, we have to consider the questions of who is entitled to compete for it, the bases on which the rivals make their claims, the purposes for which they are claiming the power, and how they convey their claim. Watson (1985) uses the development of the cult of the Empress of Heaven in south China to clarify the process by which local groups adopted rituals to promote their own upward mobility in a state system whose authority was being carried down to the local level by the same means. Similarly, my analysis of the Hongsheng cult in Chaolian tries to show how community- and lineage-building from the Ming period to the twentieth century was reflected in the transformation of a deity for overseas traders and travelers into a community patron.

I have tried to show in the first part of the study how cultural institutions, social identity, and the changing local configurations of power associated with a maturing regional economy joined to form a specific historical consciousness as well as to accommodate diverse political strategies. I applied a similar analysis to political rituals in the postrevolutionary era. The struggle against the local bosses during the land reform, the mobilization of the Great Leap Forward, and the upheavals of the Cultural Revolution, as described in the later chapters, all had their symbolic aspects. Though policies fluctuated left and right, rural cadres and villagers alike were increasingly compelled to participate in the political dialogue of socialism.

Observers of the resurgence of popular rituals in the Chinese villages today may conclude that tradition is being restored. On closer examination, the worship of gods, ghosts, and ancestors will be seen to have taken on a very different meaning for contemporary practitioners. Peasants in traditional China believed in a supernatural power structure that interacted with the material world to which they belonged. If a deity failed, the believer did not cease to believe in the authority the deity symbolized. Appeals to deities expressed faith in a culturally defined system of power. The "revival" of popular rituals today does not entail the same perceptions of power on the part of the faithful. If a deity fails, believers tend to blame the atheist state power that suppressed religious activity for decades. To me, the contemporary popular rituals express a lack of faith in both the supernatural and material power structures, and a pervasive sense of alienation among the practitioners. These cultural fragments paradoxically show the extent to which popular beliefs have been affected by the Marxist state.

In sum, to see the analytical connections between the political economy and cultural change, we need to combine the approaches developed by Skinner, Freedman, and Wolf, among other. To analyze the evolution of local society in the Huancheng area, we need to understand trade and commerce in terms of the development of regional marketing systems, lineage- and community-building, and religious rituals. In addition, we need to study the evolving local power structures to which the various political actors in the local stage gave their compliance and their complicity.

In writing this ethnography, I do not pretend to present every aspect of this complex region. In my ten years of fieldwork, I have been classified as student, compatriot, professor, party agent, as well as friend and sympathizer. What I absorbed were responses to my presence in the commune, shaped by the painful unraveling of ideological assumptions as much as by the semiconscious efforts of friends to balance what I should know and what I was politically obliged to know. But the changing nature of our interaction over the years provided the meaning I was looking for. I came to know elderly villagers such as Uncle Liang and his friends, who insisted that the land in their communities was owned by the lineages of He the Minister and Mo the Eunuch. I made friends with old cadres such as Xu Decheng, who admitted that "the three red flags of Mao" swept him off his feet; Lin Qing, who declared that the grain procurement quotas were "utterly damnable"; and Chen Sheyuan, who remembered the Cultural Revolution as "the drama of the absurd." I sympathized with Huang Youfen, who had participated in earnest in the loyalty dances for Mao during the Cultural Revolution and came to the conclusion a dozen years later that he and the socialist system had nothing left to offer each other. I sensed the hopefulness of the young party secretary, Yuan Dewei, who spoke proudly of the embankment and the wide motor-road in Huicheng as goals for modernization in the 1980s. At the same time, I appreciated the subtle nostalgia of the elderly historians who showed me around the county capital and pointed to the invisible line of ancestral halls at the southern gate of the city that long ago succumbed to the forces of socialism. Their stories and those of many others form the narrative of the people who were both agents and victims, accomplices in a process of change they named revolution.

Notes

Prologue

1. This was only a few months after the radical followers of Mao Zedong were removed from power in the national government.

2. The commune had a three-tiered structure of collective ownership. The teams (basically small villages) received their income from the land they were given to work on. The brigades and commune ran small-scale enterprises. The government planned to gradually raise the level of accounting from team to brigade and commune in order to reduce differences.

3. See my essay, "Doing Fieldwork in Rural Guangdong: The Virtues of Flexibility," in Thurston and Pasternak (1983), 143–61.

4. The Pearl River delta was dotted with single-surname communities whose wealthy members had built halls for the collective worship of ancestors. There were halls (*citang*) dedicated to the founders of specific lineage segments in a particular community and used by their members. There were also the apical ancestral halls (*da zongci*), often dedicated to a remote founder of a senior line. These halls were often established in cities, and membership and contributors to its estate were not restricted to demonstrated genealogical links. More on lineage organizations in chapter 3.

5. When I started fieldwork in the Huancheng area, I relied for information on old people to whom I was introduced by the commune cadres. It was clear that these were "safe informants"; one of them belonged to a household chosen for outsiders to visit (*kaifang hu*). However, as years went by, I developed my own network of friends and steered away from the official connections. The cadres' initial reserve toward me also wore off. A more relaxed political atmosphere in the 1980s made the cadres less selective about the people they chose for me to interview. Though I found the content of our conversations somewhat restricted for the postrevolutionary era, the narratives about life in the Republican era or during the Japanese occupation rarely adhered to the official line. Eventually, I was invited to dinners and birthday or wedding banquets, where people were too absorbed in the occasion to develop a conscious political distance.

6. Dazhai is a brigade in north China promoted in the early 1960s by Mao as a model for self-reliant development and egalitarianism.

7. Reinhart Bendix notes that the making of nation-states involved a restructuring of authority from religious sanctions of kingship to authority in the name of popular sovereignty. However, the shift has not always involved popular participation. See a discussion of the relevance of this idea in nineteenth-century Japan by William Kelly (1985).

303

8. Compared with traditional elites who enjoyed multiple bases of power and authority granted by the imperial state and local communities, rural cadres were more directly dependent on party affiliations. Their predicaments and their changing relationships with fellow villagers show how the party-state transformed rural communities as it consolidated its control over societal resources and ideology.

Chapter 1. Introduction

1. I have adopted the phrase "the reach of the state" from Shue (1985). I follow the conventional definition of a state as a system of legitimate power, an administrative body to exert such power, and an arena for contest and arbitration about power. Power is the capacity to induce compliance by force or persuasion; it does not have to be overtly contested and applied in a formal political realm, but can be pervasive in everyday human relationships (Foucault 1977). Authority is understood as legitimized power when the ability to obtain compliance of others becomes a right (Bendix 1978). See the introduction to Duara (1988), and Kelly (1985) for similar discussions.

2. See Alitto (1979), Marks (1984), Thaxton (1983), Perry (1984, 1985), Duara (1988), Chen Yung-fa (1986), Madsen (1984), Rankin (1986), Shue (1988), Mann (1987), Yang (1959), and Parish and Whyte (1978).

3. See Sun (1983) on the imperial tradition embedded in what he terms the deep structure of contemporary political culture.

4. See Yang (1959) and Parish and Whyte (1978) for various interpretations of the Chinese family in transition based on research on south China. From discussions with Myron L. Cohen and Deborah Davis, I feel that family dynamics is an extremely important area of analysis for understanding cultural continuity and change during China's decades of social and political engineering. However, because of limitations in the data I have collected, I cannot treat this level of analysis in any depth. I can only hope to compensate for this omission in my future inquiries.

5. Serving as patrons, according to Shue, did not stop them from being abusive to their peasant clients, an observation that matches my own in rural Guangdong. Richard Madsen (1984) categorizes this type of leader as a member of the Communist gentry and as Communist rebel, who dominated the villages at least up to the Cultural Revolution.

6. See Shue (1988) for a thorough theoretical summary of the different approaches to the reach of the state in China. She emphasizes that local initiative has had a substantial place in shaping state-society relations in the Maoist era.

7. The literature on lineage organizations in south eastern China is vast. For more detailed analyses of their dynamics and variety, see Freedman (1958, 1966), Baker (1966), J. Watson (1975, 1977, 1982), Potter (1970), Faure (1986), Strauch (1983), and R. Watson (1985).

8. I use the term to mean properties held by lineages, charity organizations, temples, academies, and merchant associations. They were generally managed by an elected body dominated by the wealthy and the politically active.

9. In Xinhui County, the annual ceremonies performed in the academies and the Confucian Temple in Huicheng, in the merchant-dominated Dilintang Temple festival on the southern bank of Huicheng, and in the Hongsheng Temple of Chaolian

Xiang off the coast of Jiangmen were quite dazzling in their display of wealth, literary culture, social networks, and political influence. From the late Ming period on, it was not unknown for scholars in the delta to achieve positions in the metropolitan officialdom. For a full treatment of the concept of "the cultural nexus of power," see Duara (1988). I appreciate his discussing the concept with me.

10. For example, the records of tax accounts (*hu*) upon which the county tax officers relied to collect taxes and levies remained unchanged since the early Qing. Yet during the ensuing centuries, descendants of members registered under the accounts multiplied, branched off, or perished. Properties under their names also changed hands.

11. I share this idea with Hong Yung Lee, who studied national party organizations.

12. Political brokerage is a central concern in the works of anthropologists and political scientists. See the works of Bailey (1969), Barth (1959), Asad (1972), Blok (1974), Swartz (1969), Eisenstadt and Lamarchand (1981), Vincent (1971), Gellner and Waterbury (1979), Gluckman (1969), and Scott (1977).

13. See Michael (1964), Ho (1962), Balazs (1964), Chang (1955), and Lau (1975).

14. It is nevertheless important to distinguish among cadres at different levels of rural administration to understand the reach of the state. No one would deny that there were conflicts of interest between the political center (*zhongyang*) and regional administrations (*difang*). Scholars of contemporary China have made great progress in specifying which levels had the power to resist the party's central control. For example, scholars recognize that cadres in county governments had considerable freedom in interpreting policies from the center (Wong 1985). Therefore, accusations of local resistance often reflected conflicts between different levels of government administration rather than between state and society. This study focuses on cadres at the level of the township (*xiang*, equivalent to brigades in Guangdong), because I believe their dilemma best captures the changing relationship between state and society in China's turbulent decades of rural transformation. I translate the unit *xiang* as township despite the fact that it does not entirely convey the complexity of rural organization. A *xiang* in the delta was a large village, often with more than a thousand residents, or a cluster of villages supporting a market center and having several thousand members.

15. Xu Wenqing, for example, was the only "intellectual" in Huancheng Commune, a unit of 60,000. He became director of the office of the commune, which handled voluminous documents every day, but was not a member of the political leadership. Chen Sheyuan, whose few years of village education taught him the much-needed skills of accounting, was not allowed to join the Poor Peasant League at the time of the land reform because "he was not poor enough."

16. Being party members, brigade cadres established long-term relationships with the state, which team leaders did not have. Unlike commune cadres, brigade cadres were seldom subject to administrative transfer. Their income and the well-being of their families were tied to the rural collectives.

17. See Siu, "Reforming Tradition: The Politics of Popular Rituals in Contemporary Rural China," presented at a conference on popular thought, October 1987.

18. See Siu, "Socialist Peddlers and Princes in a Chinese Market Town," *American Ethnologist* 16. 2 (May 1989).

19. See Abrams (1982), Giddens (1979), and Bourdieu (1977).

20. This is expressed by Geertz (1984) in his reflection on the debates that have continued to rage since the publication of his *Agricultural Involution* (1963). See also Tambiah (1985) on the connections between culture, thought, and social action.

21. This idea came from William Kelly.

Chapter 2. Historical Geography

1. See *Xinhui xianzhi* (1840), *Xinhui xiangtuzhi* (1908), *Chaolian xiangzhi* (1946), and the genealogies of the He lineage in Huicheng, the Zhao lineage in Sanjiang, the Lu lineage in Chaolian, the Zhang lineage in Haoshang, and the Chen lineage of Waihai.

2. Chaolian Xiang was administratively part of Xinhui County until the mid-1970s.

3. For a detailed description of these ferries and the peasant mobility associated with them, see Yu Ziliang (1986).

4. South China, as treated in this work, corresponds largely to the macroregion known as Lingnan in G. William Skinner's regional systems analysis (1977).

5. Hongsheng, the temple's major deity, was popular in the Pearl River delta as the protector of long-distance traders and travelers. See chapter 4 for more detailed descriptions of the cult's origins. The complex was the political center of Chaolian Xiang.

6. See *Chaolian xiangzhi* (1946). I obtained rubbings of the stone tablets during field trips to the Chaolian Hongsheng Temple in 1986 and 1987.

7. The area identified today as Huancheng included parts of Guide Du of Chaolian Si, Chaoju Du of Shacun Si, Huairen Du of Niuduwan Si, and parts of the periurban districts.

8. The townships in the First District were Chengnan Xiang with fourteen *bao*, Yuanqing Xiang with twelve *bao*, Huairen Xiang with ten *bao*, Shenhuan Xiang with twelve *bao*, Tianma Xiang with nine *bao*, Tianlu Xiang with nine *bao*, and Renyi Xiang with seven *bao*. The two townships in the Second District were Upper Xianxian Xiang with fifteen *bao* and Jiaotou Xiang with sixteen *bao*. See *Xinhui xian xingzheng quyu yange cankao ziliao*, compiled by Xinhui Xian Dang'anguan (1984).

9. The Huancheng area is situated at the western edge of the Pearl River delta. The Pearl River system, the largest in south China, is made up of four major tributaries—the Xi, Bei, Dong, and Liuxi rivers—and several lesser tributaries—the Tan, You, Gui, Sui, and Zeng rivers. The system has been characterized historically by a heavy flow, a long period of high water with several torrential peaks each year, a high silt content, and numerous tidal confluence points (*Nongyezhi* 1:8–14). The different directions of the tributaries—combined with seasonal changes of the flow due to monsoons, typhoons, and tides—created a complex and variable river system for the delta population. Today, the Xi River is still the largest component of the Pearl River system. It carries 80 percent of the total volume of water, with high water starting around the end of March and ending in September. An average of five torrential peaks occurs during this period, each lasting from five to twenty days, causing flash floods in its lower courses (Sun et al. 1959, 9–10). Though treacherous at times, the river is vital for transportation in the western part of the Lingnan

macroregion. However, the river carries an average of over 75 million tons of silt a year (*Nongyezhi* 1:12). Ocean currents and tides during winter months rush into the numerous inlets at the mouth of the river, slow the river flow, and accelerate sedimentation.

10. *Chaolian xiangzhi* (1946) describes how diking efforts have allowed two full crops of rice to be grown since the mid-Ming period.

11. I found a stone tablet from a temple during a field trip to Xiaolan market town. On it were inscribed the names of eighteen military colonies (*weisuo*), each centering on a temple dedicated to a legendary military figure, Guandi. One of the colonies was the Xinhui Suo. The administrative boundaries of the two counties shifted several times in the centuries, probably because of the development of new sands.

12. I agree with Faure (1986, 173) that these were not frontiers in the conventional sense, because the expanding delta was situated in a regional core (as defined in Skinner's regional systems analysis) and was developed with capital from institutions in the towns and cities. The same applies to the Yangzi delta.

13. The warlord and Republican regimes in the twentieth century continued the futile efforts, creating special administrative offices to oversee land registration and tax collection, and to supervise crop protection forces (Qiu 1941, 15–27).

14. The method was common in areas of Guangdong and Fujian where land was abundant and labor was in short supply (*Nongyezhi* 5:18–19).

15. See *Donghai shiliusha jishi,* compiled by the major landlords in Xiangshan (Guangzhou Xiangshan Gonghui 1912).

16. See Zhang (1948) and Liu Bogao (1963a).

17. For the political economy of the sands in the delta in general, see Nishikawa (1985), Wu Qingshi (1962), *Nongyezhi* 5, Huang Yonghao (1987), and Ye Shaohua (1965). Ye's analysis (1965, 13) of the large contractors of Mingluntang (a government-sponsored academy) shows that they were not necessarily natives of Dongguan County; they owned local banks and shops in Guangzhou, and operated granaries and rice mills in Shunde and Panyu counties. By placing their granaries in a part of Shunde County where cash crops were grown, they made full use of price fluctuations in the grain markets. They also turned their resources into a form of usury for those who relied on them for seed and grain advances. By the late Qing, the grain trade was no longer monopolized by Guangzhou. Instead, the opening of ports in the delta decentralized the trade to many of its market towns.

18. In the local system, each shi of grain weighs about 150 catties.

19. See *Chaolian xiangzhi* (1946) on gentry and merchant patronage of the Hongsheng Temple festival.

20. Information in this section was drawn from He (1965a) and a personal interview with him in 1986. For an official evaluation of citrus production, see Xinhui Xian Nongye Quhua Bangongshi (1983, 289–98).

21. He Zhuojian estimates that 85 percent of the peel was collected from the periurban townships of Huicheng and Jiangmen.

22. The descriptions of palm growing and its associated trade are based on the following accounts: Ye and Xu (1963), Guan (1983), and He Zhuojian (1965b). The documentary sources were supplemented by interviews with He Zhuojian and another local historian, Li Anzhi. Both have written articles for the *Xinhui wenshi ziliao xuanji.* See also *Xinhui xiangtuzhi* (1908), *Xinhui xianzhi* (1840), Guangdong

Jiansheting Nonglinju Nongqing Baogaochu (1936), and Huanan Chengxiang Wuzijiaoliu Zhidao Weiyuanhui (1952). I had the opportunity to read some documents from the land reform period that examined the fan palm enterprises in detail. That information matches the local historian's reports.

23. From around 1911 to 1923, there were 50 or so palm-drying enterprises in Huicheng and about 110 fan-processing workshops (Guan 1983, 5).

24. For example, the Gugang *zhan* (enterprises) in Chongqing served as the headquarters for the Sichuan group that encompassed seven enterprises; Lianzhu *tang* (corporation) of the Hankou group and the guild for the Shanghai group were both associated with the Guangdong Huiguan (native-place association) in these large cities. The Lianyi *tang* (corporation) of the Zhenjiang group also functioned within the Guang-Zhao Gongsuo (an association for Guangzhou and Zhaoqing merchants), with a membership of thirteen long-distance traders.

25. See Skinner (1977) on regional systems analysis. The delta supported a dense population. According to the statistics presented in *Guangdong jingji nianjian* (The economic yearbook of Guangdong), 1941, the population in the delta was 355.8 per square kilometer in 1934, a period of relative peace. This figure is an average of six counties in the delta—Nanhai, Panyu, Zhongshan, Shunde, Dongguan, and Xinhui. The population density of six counties from the periphery (Qujiang, Qingyuan, Nanxiong, Yingde, Fogang, and Wengyuan in northern Guangdong) contrasts sharply with that of the delta, averaging 71.5 persons per square kilometer in 1934. Population figures are also presented for the years 1938 and 1939. Like the compiler of the economic yearbook, I think the 1939 figures reflect the situation before the Japanese occupation rather than after. If these figures can be trusted at all, they indicate an interesting trend. From 1934 to roughly 1938, the population density of the delta increased 42.6 percent to 507.4 persons per square kilometer, whereas that for northern Guangdong dropped 7.1 percent to 66.4 persons per square kilometer. It seems that during peaceful times, the disparities between the core and the periphery were aggravated because of the influx of resources and people into the core. The figures in the following years are too fragmented and unreliable to show whether the population dispersed to the regional periphery, though economic historians of Guangdong have estimated that the delta lost one-third of its prewar population (see Sun et al. 1959, 13).

26. Xinhui, Taishan, Kaiping, and Enping were the major suppliers of overseas emigrants from the mid-nineteenth century on. These counties were collectively known as Siyi (Sze-Yap, the Four Counties).

27. See *Xinhui wenshi ziliao xuanji* 12 (1983), a special issue on preliberation local industries in Huicheng.

28. In this sector, both overseas Chinese interests and local capital competed with the provincial government. In the 1930s, Chen Jitang, the warlord of Guangdong, promoted government-run industries. In the vicinity of Guangzhou he built a cement factory, two modern sugar refineries, a chemical fertilizer plant, paper mill, and a caustic soda factory. However, his programs were interrupted by the war and by the general political chaos that accompanied the Japanese advances in the late 1930s. See Xie (1980) on the development of industries under Chen Jitang. See also Guangdong Gongshang Fudaochu Gongshangbu (1948), Zeng (1942), and Wu Wanli (1947) on the general economy of Guangdong in the republican period. An invaluable but confusing source is the *Guangdong jingji nianjian*

(1941). For a concise description of the various types of local and regional banks and the nature of their businesses in Guangdong in the first half of the century, see Zhou (1962, 20–41).

29. The hall was dedicated to the founder of Chen surname group in Tianma, whose father and grandfather supposedly were members of a Chen surname group in Shitou to the north of the county capital.

30. See *Siyi huaqiao daobao* 6–7 (1941): 67.

31. See Zhonggong Xinhui Xianwei Xuanchuanbu (1960), 2:19–20, on the rise of Zeng Huan.

32. There are numerous sources on the rural economy of Guangdong during the first half of the twentieth century. The Republican regimes as well as scholars based at Zhongshan University conducted many studies on land and tax policies, and on peasant economic conditions. Among the best known are Chen Hanseng's *Landlord and Peasant in China* (1936) and Chen Ta's *Emigrant Communities in South China* (1939). Some useful Chinese sources include *Guangdong tudi liyong yu liangshi chanxiao,* written by Chen Qihui in the 1930s and published as nos. 50 and 51 of a collection of manuscripts edited by Xiao Zheng in 1977; *Guangdong quansheng tianfu zhi yanjiu,* written by Lin Shidan in the 1930s and published as no. 4 in Xiao Zheng (1977); and the two volumes of *Guangdong nongye gaikuang diaocha* put out by Guoli Zhongshan Daxue Nongke Xueyuan in 1925 and 1929.

33. See the local debates on the transformation of the fan palm industry published in a volume entitled *Zhengming kuaibao,* edited by the Industry Commerce League of Xinhui County in 1957. See Xinhui Xian Nongye Quhua Bangongshi (1983), which outlines county plans to restructure cropping patterns around certain specialized crops and laments the destruction of major cash crops in favor of grain cultivation in the previous decades. As early as 1957, the periodic market schedules, which had traditionally given the rural economy the maximum room for maneuvering and provided village social life with its basic rhythm, were fixed on the first and sixth days of the month for the entire province. The new simultaneous schedule cut the attendance of rural markets, which also had the effect of shrinking the social networks based on these periodic markets.

Chapter 3. Social Cells

1. The Dan were a mobile group who lived on boats and made their living by fishing and transporting goods along the southeastern coast and on the rivers. In the delta, many of them were also seasonal tenant farmers. Their customs differed from those of the settled Han population, who looked down on them as culturally inferior.

2. On the issue of the interaction between government and local society some historians have argued that by the late Qing rural society was quite sealed off from formal administration. Wakeman (1966, 1975a) and Kuhn (1975, 1979) stress the increasing importance of the local gentry in community affairs as well as its role as mediator between the government and local community from the mid-nineteenth century on. They describe the frustrations of the government in its attempts to make the rural gentry act according to its moral ideals. Their works paint a picture of a rural China led by "local bullies and evil gentry," who used community self-

defense corps and lineage organizations to prey on neighbors, and cheated both the state and their metropolitan patrons. During this period, sporadic and large-scale rebellions occurred, abetted by the antistate sentiments fostered by secret societies, general rural militarization, and frequent feuds (Hsieh 1974; Wakeman 1966). These phenomena could be interpreted as characteristics of dynastic decline and crisis, when the administrative capacities of the imperial state were disintegrating and communities turned inward for their own protection (Skinner 1971). From the work of Alitto (1979) and Huang (1985), one may conclude that the trend reached its chaotic climax during the first half of the twentieth century when a majority of the peasants had become impoverished and local warlords had carved out their spheres of control and preyed on the countryside.

However, others have argued that neither the Qing state nor the Republican regimes lost as much control over society as this account suggests. Susan Mann's study (1987) of tax farming illuminates a renewed effort by the Qing state to collect more taxes. She emphasizes that the state was a force that local merchants, however powerful, had to come to terms with. Focusing on regional elites, Schoppa (1982) and Rankin (1986) argue that merchant activism and politicization were stimulated by the attempts of Republican leaders at state-making and nation-building. Roger Thompson's study (1988) of the transformation of local opera organizations into tax-collection agencies in Shangxi reveals a heavy-handed Republican government attempting to create a new rural power structure to facilitate state intrusion. Duara (1987) goes even further by stating that attempts by the Republican regimes to extract revenue had the effect of creating entrepreneurial state brokers who accumulated resources at the local level. What he described as state involution is not unlike the portrait of Sicily painted by Anton Blok (1974). In fact, Sicily's tortuous introduction to the modern world in the first half of the twentieth century suggests a similar situation: an agrarian state, in its attempts to control local society in its transition to modernity, created a climate of lawlessness and violence.

3. Presumably the He ancestral trust owned the land at Tianma and Tianlu at an earlier time and lost the land rights to residents in these townships. From a report of the local bosses in Tianma in Zhonggong Xinhui Xianwei Xuanchuanbu (1960), it would seem that the rights were lost as late as the Republican period. See also articles on the He ancestral trust by He Zhuojian (1963) and Ye and Tan (1985a, 53–54).

4. See Xinhui Xian Xinhui Shuyuan Xi'nan Shuyuan Dongbei Ju Changchan Zhengli Weiyuanhui (1946). The academies were set up by wealthy local residents who had acquired academic degrees by passing the civil service examinations. They donated land and money to set up trusts in the name of these institutions and elected a managerial body from among their own ranks. Income from the trusts was used to promote education among local scholars who could claim common descent as well as communal affiliation with the founders. Rituals were performed to celebrate the birthday of Confucius and other patron deities. The Dongbei Public Bureau was set up by the Qing government in cooperation with the wealthy local residents in response to peasant unrest connected with the Taipings in the mid-nineteenth century. Educated elites were appointed to organize militia for self-defense against the rebels. The estates held by the bureau were donated partly by the county government and partly by the local leaders themselves. Their income

was used to finance militia operations. See chapter 4 for a more detailed analysis of the institutions and their estates.

5. The Wanqingsha between Dongguan and Xiangshan counties, the Donghai Shiliusha between Shunde and Xiangshan, and Xihai Shibasha between Xiangshan and Xinhui were notable examples of marshland reclaimed during the last two centuries. See the section on the sands in *Dongguan County Gazetteer* (1922); *Donghai shiliusha jishi* (1912) and *Donghai shiliusha wushiyunian de tongshi* (1912) by Guangzhou Xiangshan Gonghui; Wu (1962, 72–89); "Zhongshan shatianzhi" by Liu Zhiliang, in *Zhongshan wenxian* (1948) 2:75–88. Since this chapter was written, I have come across an article by Robert Eng (1986) that examines the issue of institutionalized and secondary landlordism in the sands using very similar source material.

6. A gentry-led institution in the county capital of Dongguan that supervised education.

7. This is a common phenomenon in frontier settlements, as noted also by Myron L. Cohen for Taiwan and by Fu Yiling for Fujian.

8. For other incidents, see Huang (1987) and Eng (1986).

9. I was told by local cadres that brick houses were not built in the villages until the 1970s. Local peasants seemed to have resisted the idea of a permanent, more centralized settlement. It is true that many of the local peasants were originally migrant fishermen who farmed only part of the year. This local custom may also have had its origins in the estates' system of land ownership and their methods of tax evasion. Wu (1962) asserts that institutional landlords, such as the Minglun-tang of Dongguan County, specifically forbade tenants to build brick houses in the sands. The appearance of a less than permanent settlement allowed the estate managers to claim that the land had not matured enough to incur tax duties.

10. In a different paper I present an account of the chrysanthemum festivals organized by elites in Xiaolan, Xiangshan County, during the nineteenth century as an example of such cultural manipulation (Siu 1988).

11. A particular settlement pattern arose in the sands because of the way the crops were cultivated. After the dikes and polders were constructed, farmers lived at the site of the former *weiguan* (which existed for security purposes) and ventured out to the fields only during the times of planting and harvest, where they built temporary sheds to live in. This practice was known as "stringing out cultivation" (*diaogeng*). The crops harvested from these extensive areas were brought by the grower-entrepreneurs to the *weiguan* settlements before being transported to brokers in the market towns. In time, the former *weiguan* developed into oversized outposts that were connected directly to urban centers. There were few other substantial settlements around. Even today one hears peasants refer to themselves as those living "over here" (indicating the thriving centers) and those living "out there" (indicating the sands).

12. Freedman described the various lineage organizations as a continuum. His accounts of the highly differentiated lineages in Guangdong and Fujian were given a great deal of attention by scholars such as Baker (1966) and Potter (1970). Other scholars, such as Cohen (1969), Ebrey and Watson (1986), Strauch (1983), Pasternak (1969), Gallin (1966), and Chen (1984), describe different aspects of kinship organizations. Strauch (1983) stresses the importance of analyzing different forms of lineage communities not as basically short-term, unstable organizations striving to reach the highly stratified, corporate ideal, but as social phenomena related to a

combination of historical circumstances. Resting on a historical argument, J. Watson (1982) aptly points out that the frog-in-the-well perspective of anthropologists often blinds them to the fact that agnatic descent became a dominant principle of social organization only after the Tang dynasty and as the result of changes in elite ideologies. Therefore lineage organizations should be analyzed as social phenomena limited in historical time and place.

13. The idea of the *xiangzu* (lineage community) espoused by Fu Yiling in his work on rural Fujian stresses territorial concerns underlying descent-group formation. A good combination of Fu's concept of *xiangzu* and the concept of village community popularized by Japanese scholarship is summarized in Mori Masao (1986).

14. As Faure puts it: "The history of the settlement at a village by an ancestor was the justification whereby villagers exerted their rights to natural resources within what they considered to be their territories. These rights included the rights to build houses within or near the village, to gather fuel on the hillsides, to open land for cultivation, and sometimes also to bury the dead. In short, settlement rights included rights on land that had not been privately claimed, except by the village as a corporate body. . . . The recognition of these rights should also introduce a totally new dimension into the discussion on stratification in rural China, for the difference between the villager who enjoyed settlement rights and the outsider who did not would hardly have been smaller than that between the landlord and the tenant" (n.d.-1, 3).

15. See Freedman (1958, 46–50) on lineage segmentation in China. According to Freedman, a Chinese lineage does not adhere to a fixed chronology. When new generations are added between the founder and a present generation, families continue to redefine themselves in relation to recent ancestors. Every male member starts a line (*fang*) whose descendants form a lineage segment (see also Chen 1984 for different interpretations of *fang*). Wealthy men either leave part of their properties to an already established ancestral trust, or set up a new one for their immediate ancestors. When members of a segment are united economically and ritually by estates, the segment acquires a structural focus and permanence. A rich lineage is often characterized by a high degree of segmentation because its members are able to set up trusts for their immediate ancestors.

16. These halls represent two types of kinship organization. They can be the ritual and economic centers of higher-order lineages, which are corporate bodies linking several localized lineages whose members trace descent to a common ancestor. This was often done, as described in the Chinese anthropological literature, when lineages sharing a surname "invented" a genealogical union at some point in the remote past in order to foster alliances for economic or political purposes. See Freedman (1958, 70), Baker (1968), and Faure (1986). There are also halls and estates established mostly by merchants, encompassing members of a single surname who do not necessarily demonstrate common descent. In some anthropological literature, these are considered "clans." See Ebrey and Watson (1986) for a discussion of these categories.

17. Ancestral halls dedicated to remote founders and having an inclusive membership were not uncommon in rural Guangdong; but Qu Dajun in the late 1600s pointed out their humble origins, showing that commoners rather than the literati

were their founders (Faure 1986, 143). I call these halls "focal ancestral halls" because they were not the same as apical ancestral halls in the cities; at the same time, their membership was not narrowly defined along genealogical lines. See also Faure (1986) on the differences between the official type of ancestral halls whose buildings displayed ornate architecture and whose membership included families with official titles, and those that grew out of bedchambers in commoner households. In the Huancheng area, the latter were known as *shushi* (study chambers).

18. See Eberhard (1962, 62–63) for a translation of the recorded episode from the Wu lineage genealogy in Xinhui. For similar records, see *Xinhui xianzhi* (1840), *Xinhui xiangtuzhi* (1908), *Chaolian xiangzhi* (1946), the records of the He lineage of Lujiang (1870), the records of the Mo of Huicheng (*Nanmen Mo shi zupu*, 1921), and the records of the Chen lineage of Tianma (1923).

19. See *Danmin de yanjiu* by the late Chen Xujing on the Dan (1946). See also the three volumes on the Dan in Guangdong compiled by Guangdong Sheng Renmin Zhengfu Minzu Shiwu Weiyuanhui (1953). For the fishing communities in Hong Kong, see *Through Other Eyes* by the late Barbara Ward (1985).

20. See the lineage genealogy of the Zhao of Sanjiang.

21. See Liu Bogao (1963a) and Lin Datian (1984). Lineage communities to the southwest of the Huancheng area were also notoriously belligerent around the turn of the century. Among them were the Chen of Shanzui and Tianhulang, the Yuan of Tangang, and the Ye of Zhoukeng. Together they pitted themselves against the Lin of Luokeng, who subsequently mobilized an alliance of seven surnames. Help was sought from as far away as the Zhao of Sanjiang in the east and the Li of Qibao to the north. From 1882 to 1919, the two sides fought numerous times over territorial and water rights, over the control of sites for markets and temple fairs, and, most important of all, over the collection of the skeletal levy in the sands. County officials from Huicheng intervened periodically by pressuring village and lineage leaders to negotiate peace, by imposing harsh fines on both sides, by shutting down ancestral halls and local temples that had been used as centers of political mobilization, and by direct military suppression. Still, entire villages were burnt, and more than four hundred villagers are reported to have perished. See Chen Xiangheng (1963, 11–20); a journal entitled *Tangang xiang zazhi* (1937); and Chen Ruojin (1964, 16–20).

22. The descriptions are based on articles by Chen Zhanbiao (1984, 1–4) and Jia Mu (1964, 126–29). The accounts are supplemented by interviews of villagers in Chakeng. On my last visit in the summer of 1987, I discussed local history with three elderly men of the Liang surname in their seventies and eighties.

23. The story is intriguing. The island was probably used as a shelter by coastal fishermen. Does it contain clues to ancient conflicts between Han migrants and Dan fishermen, the former pushing the fishermen from their coastal niches as well as incorporating some of them into their communities?

24. For a description of the Red Turban uprising in Guangdong, see Wakeman (1966). See also historical materials on the Taipings in Guangdong compiled by Chen Zhoutang (1986).

25. They have been referred to in Liang Qichao's writings more or less as bond servants, a phenomenon not uncommon in the county. They were organized into a production team after collectivization in the late 1950s. Others might have been

former Liang lineage members driven out to the sands. See also J. Watson (1976, 1977) and Ahern (1973) on the status of these bond servants in Hong Kong and Taiwan, and Ye (1983) on their status in Huizhou.

26. To explain why some of the lineage communities in the New Territories did not have ancestral halls, Faure (1986) argues that some of them must have started as dependent households attached to large lineages and were not allowed to have their own halls.

27. In my visit to Chakeng in the summer of 1987, it was pointed out to me that the present village headquarters was originally the Beidi Temple. Though it was rebuilt in the 1950s, the main pillars of the temple, on which were carved the names of the members of the Liang surname who had donated them during the Qing dynasty, still stood at the front entrance.

28. The original founder of the village migrated from Chakeng. Old inhabitants of Chakeng claimed that he was the younger brother of their original founder.

29. Elderly villagers insisted that ancestral estates of the different surnames would finance only their own lineage rituals.

30. During a movement to create a local administration in the early Republican period, village or township council offices were set up by the government.

31. The Chen surname groups worshipped the fisherman Guo as their benefactor (engong) because they claimed he brought the wife of Chen to the area and helped her settle down. Chen Kao was a popular local deity. He was believed to be a native of Shitou who acquired Daoist wisdom and became a guardian against evil spirits. I found him worshipped in Tianlu Xiang and Chaolian Xiang as well as in the neighboring county of Zhongshan.

32. Historical documents mention the involvement of the fishermen households (Dan hu) in the reclamation of the sands. See Dongguan xianzhi (1922), Qu (1700), and Nishikawa (1985).

33. This was probably characteristic of the way local cultures and people became part of the Confucian state system. An anthropologist in Zhongshan University, Pan Xiong, spent years tracing the ethnic origins of the delta Cantonese. He was of the opinion that many of the genealogies of delta lineages were so poorly fabricated that he could tell they were of Dan origins. Most of the ancestral halls they built were for remote and legendary ancestors. The Hu surname group of Shunde has been cited as an example in Guangdong Sheng Renmin Zhengfu Minzu Shiwu Weiyuanhui (1953, 9).

34. See "Mani cun Wubentang jiagui" in the lineage genealogy of the Chen (1923).

35. These three deities were very popular in south China. The Tianhou Temple was probably connected with the Dan population.

36. See Baker (1968) and Faure (1986) for similar observations in the New Territories of Hong Kong.

37. See Hayes (1977) for a discussion of a similar phenomenon in Hong Kong.

38. See also Meskill (1979) on the Lin of Wufeng for similar processes of mobility for a pioneer family in Taiwan.

39. As mentioned earlier, a member of the seventh generation of the Chen lineage in Tianma had acquired official honors during the first year of Qianlong (1736) and moved into Huicheng. The ancestral estate set up in his name consisted of land properties in the sands in and around Tianma. One of his descendants

compiled the Chen lineage genealogy, which includes the history of the seven generations in Tianma. See *Chenzu Shipu* (1923).

Chapter 4. Cultural Tissues

1. See Wakeman (1966) and Kuhn (1971) on the rise of the local gentry in connection with the organization of the local defense corps (*tuanlian*). I use the term "gentry" or "literati" with reservations because the group is so amorphous. By the mid-nineteenth century, the local elites I refer to were not those with higher academic degrees (such as the provincial graduates or higher) or metropolitan political connections; instead, they passed lower-level examinations, were aspiring scholars, or had purchased titles with no official assignments.

2. The description of the Xi'nan Academy is based on the following sources: *Xi'nan shuyuan quantu* (1921) and *Xinhui xi'nanfang shenshi renminglu* (Liang 1919).

3. See *Lujiang He shi shiyuan* (1870).

4. In the summer of 1986, I saw the two largest ancestral halls being torn down. From the ruins of the Li ancestral hall one could see that it had three layers of halls and two courtyards. From the ruins of the Mo ancestral hall near the southern gate of the city, one could detect elaborate interior archways.

5. The interaction of a range of social groups and of the state and popular cultures in the ritual arena appears to be a standard feature of Chinese popular religion.

6. The historians are He Zhuojian and Li Anzhi, who are in their sixties and seventies. I was rather surprised that several of the teachers and librarians with whom I made friends (in their late forties and early fifties), along with the manager of the Overseas Chinese Hotel, could not identify the Mo ancestral hall that was torn down in the summer of 1986. For a detailed street map of Huicheng in the early twentieth century, see the one redrawn from an old map by Xinhui Xian Huicheng Zheng Jiance Weiyuanhui (1925).

7. See Ye and Tan (1985a) and *Lujiang He shi shiyuan* (1870) on the distribution of the land of the He estate, named He Wenyi Gong Tang. Wenyi was an honorific title bestowed upon He Xiongxang by the Ming court after his death.

8. This was not peculiar to the ancestral estates in Huicheng. Ye and Tan (1985a, 1985b) have associated the rise of specific lineages in the delta with wealth they accumulated from the sands. Notable examples of growth include increases of the He lineage estate of Panyu County from 14 mu in 1578 to 16,409 mu in 1718, and to 56,575 mu in 1920 (1985a, 26).

9. See Wu (1962, 72—89) for the general land tenure arrangements in the delta's sands.

10. See Ye and Tan (1985a, 49—50). From 1818 to 1892 rent per mu ranged from 14.2 to 38.7 catties. Except for the two years from 1839 to 1840, when rent deposits averaged 29.6 catties per mu, the rest of the years averaged 60 catties per mu.

11. See Wu (1962) and Qiu (1941) on the problems in Guangdong's sands.

12. This might explain why peasants in such a densely populated area continued to practice the labor-saving method of *zhenggao*.

13. In reading the accounts of corporate estates in Huicheng, I found rent in kind

a negligible form of payment. Ye and Tan (1984, 1985a) also assert that from the mid-Qing on, cash rents were common for the delta's ancestral estates as a result of commercial developments.

14. See Li Yuncheng Tang (1905) and Li Zhichen (1921).

15. For the rise and fall of the merchant militia, see Mai and Huang (1965). Descriptions of the palm trade and the guild are drawn from He (1965b) and Guan (1983), supplemented by interviews with local historians in Huicheng and cadres who had seen written reports on the guild during the land reform. The ten sub-guilds and associations under the Fan Palm Guild owned a total of 277 mu of land (263.5 mu of rice fields and 13 mu of palm polders) spread out over five districts and nine townships. The guild acquired its first piece of land during the sixth year of Xianfeng's reign; the last, in 1929. The average rent per mu was 73 catties of grain a year, under contract with large contractors, many of whom were themselves managers in the subguilds and associations. In the Huancheng area, the guild owned land in Shenhuan, Chengnan, Yuanqing, Xianxian, and Duhui Xiang.

16. See *Gangzhou gongdu* by Nie Erkang (1867). See also a description of the event by Susan Mann (1987).

17. See the association rules of the Heqing Hui of the Fan Palm Guild (Kuishanhang Heqinghui huigui 1885).

18. This occurred in Tianlu and Tianma, which were situated in the more recently reclaimed sands, and in Meijiang closer to Huicheng, where palm was grown. The problems with cash rents were also related to me by former landlords in neighboring Xiangshan county. One former landlord in Xiaolan, Xiangshan County, who owned polders and rice fields before the revolution, told me he lost 20 mu of land because the cash rents which he had negotiated with local strongmen became worthless. His tenants were able to buy up the land within a year or two.

19. I suspect that at the time the Dongbei Public Bureau was formed in the mid-nineteenth century to manage local defense, the memberships of the academy and the public bureau overlapped. With its estates and paramilitary power, leaders in the Dongbei Public Bureau (referred to as the *jushen,* or bureau gentry) came to dominate the political discourse in the northeastern part of the county centering on Jiangmen.

20. The third division in the county was Chaolian Si near Jiangmen. Each was supervised by a police intendant.

21. See Grimm (1977) for the functions of the academies in Guangdong in the late imperial period. Kandice Hauf informed me in personal communications that the nature of the academies changed from the Ming to the Qing dynasties. By the late Qing, they were geared more toward pubic education and were more popular than elitist.

22. See *Xi'nan shuyuan quantu* (1921).

23. The Qing government abolished civil service examinations in 1905, but by 1904 the Xinhui Public Office for Education had already been set up to promote new-style schools. See He Zhuojian's article in *Xinhui wenshi ziliao xuanji* (1985) 17:6–19, for the history of the relationship between the academy and the new-style schools. The membership directory, *Xinhui xi'nanfang shenshi renminglu,* was complied by Liang Zaoquan in 1919.

24. Gangzhou was a historic name for Xinhui County.

25. See *Xinhui shuyuan gongding changji ji guanli zhangcheng* (1928) and *Choujian*

Xinhui shuyuan jingxinlu (1927). The following was also based on an account compiled by the Wenshi Ziliao Bianjizu in *Wenshi ziliao xuanji* (1964) 2:30–36.

26. A native of Xiaogang Xiang in the southwestern part of the county, Liang had a purchased title. His father, Liang Guoshi, had been a powerful figure in the Gangzhou Academy a few decades earlier. They lived in a *jinshidi* (the residence of a metropolitan graduate), a way for wealthy locals to flaunt literati connections.

27. See Wenshi Ziliao Bianjizu (1964, 30). The towering academy now shares the landscape with numerous modern hotels and office buildings. It is used as a hostel for the Xinhui First Middle School and as a recreation center.

28. This account is based on Liu (1983) and Huang Lun (1983).

29. See *Guangdong Gangzhou shangfu zhangcheng quanjuan* (1911). See also an account of the project by Lin Qichang (1985).

30. The feuds had involved alliances between several surname groups. Among the protagonists were the Chen of Shanzui and the Lin of Luokeng, southwest of the Huancheng area. See an article by Chen Xiangheng (1963) on the feuds that continued intermittently from 1882 to 1919. The Yuan of Tangang were drawn into the fights and their village was destroyed.

31. See the journal *Tangang xiang zazhi* (1938). David Faure generously loaned me the minutes of the meetings of the trustees of the Tangang Xiang Association for the years 1936, 1945, and 1946.

32. According to a document of the Liu Maofeng Agricultural Corporation (1932), leaders in the village committee of Hengtou (near Niuwan to the west of Huicheng) in 1932 secured the consent of the lineage elders to put out the community's wasteland to contract for reclamation. The contractor was a Maofeng Agricultural Corporation, whose shareholders were all surnamed Liu. There were seventy-two individuals and twenty-one lineage segments holding shares. Twenty-five of these invested over 500 yuan to obtain membership on the board of directors. The corporation secured a tenure of thirty years from the village council with a plan to reclaim the wasteland. Profits from the agricultural enterprise were to be divided between interests paid to shareholders (70 percent) and management fees (30 percent). The interesting point about the power dynamics within the enterprise was that the council of elders relinquished control to the village council, an administrative extension of the Republican governments; real power was in the hands of the founders of the corporation, all of whom were members of the village council, and all of whom, except for one, were elected to the board of directors.

33. For a brief history of the different militarists in Xinhui who collaborated with the provincial warlords, see an article by Chen Zhanbiao (1985).

34. For information on tax collection in the Pearl River delta during the late imperial period, see Liu (n.d.) on the Ming, Katayama (1982), and Ye and Tan (1985b).

35. See Ye and Tan (1985b) for such practices among ancestral estates in the Pearl River delta during the Qing.

36. This was suggested to me during a conversations with Susan Mann, G. William Skinner, and David Faure in March 1987. For commodity tax collection in Xinhui, see Mann (1987).

37. See Chen (1936), Feng (1962), Wu (1962), Qiu (1941), and Lin (1977) on the numerous surcharges imposed in Guangdong during the Republican era. See also

Qin (1983) on the provincial finances of Guangdong in the Republican era, and
Zhao (1986) on the levies in Xinhui.

38. See Wu (1962, 85) on tax collection in the sands in Guangdong.

39. Wu (1962, 80) listed an example of their strategies. At the time, an average
rent per mu of sands was 12 yuan. The contractor advanced the following payments
per mu for his landlords: a land tax of 29 cents, an alluvial levy of 35 cents, a crop-
watching fee of 50 cents, and a self-defense fee of 30 catties of grain, which, when
converted to current grain prices, amounted to 5,760 yuan. After subtracting the
rent of 12 yuan, the corporate landlord ended up owing its contractor 5,749 yuan
per mu. Since areas rented in the sands were vast, the debt skyrocketed.

40. See the genealogy of the Mo of Huicheng (*Nanmen Mo shi zupu* 1921).

41. See Lun Haibin (1982).

42. See Silverman (1979) for a summary of the three views. On rituals as cultural
texts, see Geertz (1973) and Forster and Ranum (1982). Chinese anthropology is
rich in studies of popular beliefs and rituals. A. Wolf (1974) argues that rituals not
only reflected social boundaries and family tensions, but also cultural understand-
ings of the hierarchies of power and the proper etiquette for dealing with the
imperial bureaucracy. The supernatural roles of gods, ghosts, and ancestors mir-
rored the major social categories of government officials, strangers, and kin. Ahern
(1981) elaborates the notion of an interactive corporeal and spiritual world by
seeing ritual practice as a way of learning and communicating about power. An
emphasis on the dialogic quality in the symbolic meaning of rituals does not mean
that the voices exert equal force. Echoing J. Watson (1985, 294), I think it is easy for
anthropologists to undervalue the play of power when they focus on the collective
participation in rituals. European cultural historians have examined popular rituals
as arenas for political articulation. See Davis (1965), Thompson (1974), and Sabean
(1984). For an anthropological study, see Taussig (1980) and Comaroff (1985). For
a similar focus in Chinese studies, see J. Watson (1985) and Ahern (1981).

43. See Weschler (1985) for an exemplary study of state rituals in the Tang
dynasty in which power was transformed into authority. For other anthropological
studies, see Kertzer (1988) and Geertz (1980).

44. See Faure (1986) on the shrines. See also "Shu 'sheyi'" by Ning Ke (1985).
The authors argue that village settlements sprang up around earth shrines and that
the administrative unit of *li* (neighborhood) in the Ming dynasty was an accom-
modation to these locally defined entities.

45. See *Gangzhou xingqibao* 6 (1925): 40.

46. Town-based religious sects and secret societies also maintained chapters
among the rural underclass. Wakeman's (1966) account of the "party purges" by
warlord regimes in Xinhui after the 1911 revolution stresses the widespread activities of brotherhoods and secret societies. Because of the vastness of the topic, I
am unable to give it adequate treatment here.

47. See Yang (1961) for a general statement about such interaction in Chinese
religion. See J. Watson (1985) on the association between the increase in state
authority in south China and the development of the cult of the Tianhou from 960
to 1960. See also Siu (1987) for a discussion of how popular rituals before and after
the Communist revolution came to reflect different perceptions of power and
commitment.

48. Most of the descriptions of the Hongsheng Temple are taken from *Chaolian*

xiangzhi (1946). See also *Nanhai shenmiao* (Long Qingzhong et al. 1985) and Tanaka (1981) on ritual and theater in the temple festivals of south China.

49. During several trips to the temple in 1986 and 1987, I observed that the stone
tablets are being preserved at the side of the temple. However, the chisel marks left
by the Red Guards seem less damaging than the fumes from a nearby candy factory
in operation today.

50. The hierarchy among the major lineages shifted in time, according to their
history of settlement, population, communal wealth, and the literati achievements
of their members. My mother, whose father and uncles migrated from Nanhai
County to Chaolian, remembers that as members of a weak surname, Fu, some of
her cousins joined an established lineage of the Ma surname by abandoning their
own in return for rights to cultivate the land controlled by the Ma. The Ma surname
group had lived in Chaolian for a long time but was facing a decline in its numbers.

51. See Faure (1986). He quotes Barbara Ward as describing similar occasions in
the New Territories of Hong Kong. See also Law and Ward (1982) for Chinese
festivals.

52. This is very similar to Duara's notion of ritual superscription in his study of
the Guandi cult, which he uses to explain cultural continuity and change. I enjoyed
the opportunity of discussing such notions with him in personal communications.

53. *Gangzhou xingqibao* 6 (1925): 40.

54. See an account of the temple festival by Li Anzhi (1982b). The above descriptions are also based on an interview with Li.

55. See Ch'u (1962) and Hsiao (1960).

Chapter 5. The Reign of Local Bosses

1. The term comes from the Chinese domino game. A *tian* (heaven) combination
of domino chips commands the highest score. A *di* (earth) combination contains
two red dots. The image of *da tian er* meant local bosses dominating particular
territories. See the article by Li Langru and Lu Man (1962, 1–19). See also an article
by Ye Shaolin (1965, 33–47).

2. This work depicted a group of 108 social bandits who resisted imperial officials. They were familiar figures in Chinese popular culture.

3. See Duara (1987), Rankin (1986), and Alitto (1979).

4. Long Jiguang, a trusted ally of the leading warlord, Yuan Shikai, in Beijing,
ruled Guangdong from 1913 to 1916. When Yuan died in 1916, he hurriedly transferred his allegiance to the central government. However, an alliance of militarists
from Guangxi, Yunnan, and eastern Guangdong defeated him. From 1916 to 1920,
under Lu Rongting, military commanders from Guangxi dominated provincial
politics and finance. They mortgaged practically every asset that Guangdong had.
Their activities were described by Liao Zhongkai, who was later the director of the
province's financial department. According to Liao's findings, the items mortgaged
included the land tax for Panyu and Nanhai counties, the tobacco and liquor levies,
and the surcharges on animal slaughtering (*tujuan*) and on prostitution (*huajuan*);
also mortgaged were the cement factory, the mint, the telecommunications bureau,
the former customs and prefectural offices, the Nanhai and Panyu county offices,

government land, the Guangzhou-Sanshui Railway, and the Navigation Bureau. See a long article by Qin Qingjun in *Guangzhou wenshi ziliao* (1983) 29:13. See also *Guangdong caizheng yaolan* by Guangdong Sheng Zhengfu Caizhengting (1929) for a detailed description of the various taxes in the province. From 1920 to 1922, local commanders regained power. Though a combined force under Sun Yixian (Sun Yat-sen) started a national campaign against regional warlords, several commanders in Guangdong managed to carve out their own spheres. The persecution of Communists by Jiang Jieshi (Chiang Kai-shek) in 1927 threw Guangdong politics into further confusion. The province regained some stability under the warlord Chen Jitang, who independently ruled Guangdong from 1931 to 1936. However, in 1936 his own officers sided with Jiang Jieshi in Nanjing to topple him. From then until Guangzhou fell to the Japanese military in the winter of 1938, Guangdong was ruled by a succession of administrators sent by Jiang Jieshi.

5. The above descriptions of provincial finance are based on Qin (1983, 46–74). He acknowledges that it is difficult to estimate all the taxes and surcharges, but the periodic efforts of financial officers to eliminate tax excesses give some indication of the size of the tax burden. He estimated from the provincial statistics that from 1937 to 1940 about 6,000 items of county and municipal taxation were dropped. In 1942, 292 more items were cancelled (1983, 57). Other desperate efforts to increase revenue included taking over provincial reserves, mortgaging government revenue and properties, and printing money at will. Taxes levied by the central governments included customs and salt duties. Guangdong provincial government relied heavily on opium and gambling levies as well as on commercial taxes and local surcharges. Local militarists controlled these revenues and manipulated them in the financial markets. Qin describes the foreign-dominated financial market of Guangdong as one big casino.

6. Some local historians argued over the political issues underlying the project. See comments and replies made by Mo Shizhong (1986) and Chao Lian (1986).

7. For a detailed description of Guangdong's tax collection structure in the sands, see *Guangdong caizheng yaolian* (1929, 203–34).

8. This was the organization under Sun Yixian responsible for the political revolution against the Qing dynasty.

9. Wakeman's study of rural Guangdong in the mid-nineteenth century describes how the activities of the secret societies increasingly diverted peasants' loyalties from kin and communal ties (1966, 117–125). See also a study of the secret societies with anti-Qing tendencies by Xiao I-shan (first edition 1935, reprinted 1986).

10. Long Jiguang, who sided with Yuan Shikai, also regarded some of the bands as rebels and expelled them from the delta (Li and Lu 1962, 7).

11. See the article on the political history of the Jiangmen-Huicheng area by Chen Zhanbiao (1985, 23–40).

12. See Li and Lu (1962, 1–19). The societies included the Guanglong Tang in Nanhai County with over a thousand members; Tianshun Tang, which consisted of an alliance of members from Shunde, Nanhai and Panyu counties, also with over a thousand members; Longsheng and Fuhu Tang with an estimated nine hundred and seven hundred members, respectively, from Nanhai and Shunde; an alliance of local bosses that dominated Zhongshan County with over two thousand members; and another group of a thousand or so gathered at the Xinhui-Taishan border.

13. See Li and Lu (1962, 12–13). See also various issues of *Zhongshan wenshi ziliao* containing articles on these military adventurers and their maneuvers in provincial politics. See Alitto (1979) for the national picture.

14. Much of the information on Zhao was taken from a personal account by He Jitang (1986).

15. The document recorded a total of one village with a population of 1,479 as a peasant activist base in 1927, seven villages with a total population of 2,475 as anti-Japanese bases, and three villages as anti-Japanese guerrilla zones involving a total of 1,773 residents. All the villagers were situated in relatively isolated hilly areas. The data was presented in Guangdong Sheng Lao Genjudi Jiance Weiyuanhui Bangongshi (draft 1959, 252).

16. Many of the descriptions in this section are based on the following accounts: Li (1982a), Yu (1982), Lun (1981), Liu (1963b), and Liu Yousheng (1981). They are confirmed by interviews with villagers in the surrounding area.

17. For a horrifying account of how some of the unemployed elements of Huicheng were recruited by the Japanese to become the initial group of collaborators, see Liu (1981, 37–39).

18. The periodic market schedules for some of the major townships in the rural vicinity of Huicheng were Daze (second, fifth, and eighth day of the month), Shuangshui (fourth and ninth), Huicheng (first, fourth, and seventh), and Jiangmen (second, fifth, and eighth).

19. For the wartime monetary situation in Guangdong, see also *Guangdong gedi jingji diaocha* by Guangdong Sheng Yinhang Jingji Yanjiushi (1941, 5).

20. Food shortages were particularly serious in 1943. Both Liu (1981) and Lun (1981) describe cannibalism in Huicheng that they had either heard of or seen. Lun records that a butcher and a woman accused of slaughtering young children were arrested and shot by the Japanese army.

21. Yu (1982) states that armed bands under the local bosses of Tianma and Tianlu posed as resistance forces. They wore uniforms bearing words such as "loyalty, righteousness, and bravery," and demanded various payments from the peri-urban villages.

22. During the early years of the republic, merchants in Huicheng had financed a militia. After it was disbanded in the early 1930s, the merchants kept the arms. They reorganized self-defense units immediately before the Japanese occupation. See Yu (1982, 21).

23. Villagers in the Huancheng area have told me what they saw and heard about these local bosses. The accounts match those recorded by Yu (1982, 24), and Lu (1965, 48–65) on Zhao Qixiu and Zhou Hanling. See also descriptions in *Xinhui xian tugai yundong ziliao huibian* (1960).

24. These townships were Duhui, Qibang, Jiangjui, Dongjia, Xijia, Siya, Dajiao, and Ningzhen. See Yu (1982, 23).

25. It was most probably a realignment of spheres of control under various local bosses, as indicated by the insistence of my elderly friends that one of the villages (Ercun) was "swallowed" by two local bosses in the township.

26. This information was obtained from a report of the township council of Tianma in Zhongxin Guomin Xuexiao Chuban Weiyuanhui (1948, 24–27).

27. The military convened a conference at the end of October 1945 to coordinate the campaigns for Guangdong and Guangxi. See *Guangdong fengyun*, compiled by

Nanzhong Tongxunshe Ziliaoshi (1947, 2–3). They included the regular army, the regional security forces, the self-defense corps, and the reinforced local police.

28. This was reported in Zhongxin Guomin Xuexiao Chuban Weiyuanhui (1948).

29. See Nanzhong Tongxunshe Ziliaoshi (1947, 35–41) for the prices of these positions and the expected income and fringe benefits.

30. Nanzhong Tongxunshe Ziliaoshi (1947, 4–22). Security forces were given the power to kill Communist sympathizers on the spot. A KMT commander openly declared that for each hundred killed, they were bound to hit a few "communist bandits" (4–5). See also *Guangdong Siyi qiaobao* (1947–49), a monthly published in Hong Kong by the overseas Chinese of the Siyi area, which contained news on the four counties.

31. See *Guangdong Siyi qiaobao* 10 (1947): 37.

32. See the report by Zhang Yang, *Guangdong Siyi qiaobao* 16 (1948): 15–17.

33. The feud was also reported in articles by Lu (1965, 55), Liu (1963a), and Lin (1984).

34. Numerous incidents were reported in *Guangdong Siyi qiaobao* 16 (1948); 22 (1949).

35. See *Guangdong Siyi qiaobao* 16 (1948): 31. The quota for Xinhui County for the second half of 1948 was 1,119 recruits.

36. See *Xinhui xian tugai yundong ziliao huibian* 2 (1960): 157–58. The city poor were also rounded up and taken to recruitment stations; the phenomenon was widely known as "the pig raid." "Pig" is a colloquial term for recruits. See also *Guangdong Siyi qiaobao* 28 (1949): 56–57. For a description of the military recruitment stations in Guangdong, see an article by Zeng (1962, 146–58). The military service was notorious for the corruption of its officers and the abuse of new recruits, see Zha (1962, 159–71).

37. See *Guangdong Siyi qiaobao* 10 (1947): 37–38.

38. An investigative report by members of the county assembly found conflicts between the procurement agents and the peasants. In Duyuan Xiang, north of Huicheng, peasant representatives complained that the government pressed for the payment of taxes dating back to 1935; peasants in Xiaogang Xiang, southwest of Huicheng, protested that groups of uniformed men stationed themselves in the township for the ostensible purpose of supervising the grain procurement and demanded 600,000 yuan from the village to cover their living expenses. The report concluded that the weaker communities, lineage segments, and poor peasant households bore most of the burden. See an article by Ba Lei, "Mianlin siwang de Xinhui nongmin," in *Zhongguo nongcun banyuekan* 1 (October 1946): 24. Given the leftist leanings of the journal, the size of the payments may have been exaggerated. However, the article does illuminate the nature of the abuse by petty functionaries and soldiers.

39. *Guangdong Siyi qiaobao* 18 (1948): 9.

40. *Guangdong Siyi qiaobao* 22 (1949): 20.

41. See a summary of these activities by He Dayun and Zhao Gongqing (1981) and He Dayun (1983). Their information corresponds with that of Li and Hong 1952 despite the fact that the authors write from opposite ends of the political spectrum.

42. See the article by Lin Datian (1986).

43. See Chang Gong et al. (1950, 46). They listed schools from Heshan, Kaiping, and Changsha. I saw none from Huicheng.

44. Wen Zhiyu asserts that the merchants organized the defense corps to keep order in the city around July and August 1949, when retreating Nationalist troops were passing through (1983, 88). The alliance planted their trusted personnel in the corps.

45. In a private conversation in 1987, Hong Yung Lee and I agreed that the first wave of party members in Guangdong were more educated and came from wealthier families than those in the north. The northern Communists were poor peasants from the old liberated areas who were largely motivated by material promises. The class background of the pro-Communist intellectuals in Guangdong and their contacts with Nationalist officials became political liabilities during the early years of the revolution, particularly during political purges such as the "Three Anti" and "Five Anti" campaigns in 1952 and the *sufan* campaigns in 1955 and 1956. In the Jiangmen-Huicheng area, the most notable victim of the purges was Wen Zhiyu, a former member of the Jiangmen City Work Small Group and chairman of the Jiangmen Business League. He was accused of espionage and corruption in 1952, put on trial in a mass meeting, and sentenced to a labor camp in northeastern China. The above information is taken from Li and Hong (1952).

46. See Yun Han (1980, 216–28) and Peng (1980, 229–42) for the military maneuvers in the Siyi area. See Lu (1965, 48–65) on the activities of Zhou and his rival, Zhao Qixiu.

47. Li and Hong (1952, 12).

48. Li and Hong (1952, 20).

49. According to unofficial estimates, the raid on the Huancheng area and two other districts in the county yielded over five hundred machine guns, twenty thousand rifles and pistols, and over a dozen cannons (Li and Hong 1952, 18).

Chapter 6. Understanding Revolution

1. Theories explaining the Chinese Communist seizure of power are summarized by Lyman Van Slyke in the foreword to Chen (1986) and elaborated in the introduction to the book. Some scholars argue that the CCP successfully exploited peasant nationalism for its own purposes (Johnson 1962); others see revolutionary potential in the needs of the peasants aroused by the political work of the CCP (Selden 1971); another group focuses on the organizational effectiveness of the party; and a fourth group relies on the notion of a "moral economy" to explain how Communist actions dovetailed with the peasants' communal ideals (Thaxton 1983).

2. For studies of pre-1949 rural mobilization by the CCP, see Hinton (1966), Crook and Crook (1959), Thaxton (1983), Selden (1971), Chen (1986), and Marks (1984).

3. Ralph Thaxton (1983), for example, has made a valiant attempt to argue that in its guerrilla bases in the Taihang Mountains the CCP was successful precisely because its programs dovetailed with the peasants' longing for a return to traditional morality. However, the merciless destruction of the leadership in Chen Vil-

lage as a result of higher-level party politics in the 1970s has also been vividly documented (Madsen 1984).

4. For a detailed study of such a dialogue in the late 1960s and early 1970s in rural south China, see Madsen (1984).

5. See Meisner (1967, 237). The article was published in six parts in a periodical in Beijing between December 1925 and February 1926.

6. This is the analysis put forth in Meisner's thorough analysis of Li Dazhao's intellectual history. See the chapter on peasant revolution (1967, 234–56) and pp. xii–xiii.

7. See the party's class policies in *Decisions concerning the differentiation of class status in the countryside*, which includes two important articles, "How to analyze class status in the countryside" and "Decisions concerning some problems arising from agrarian reform." These were published in 1933 and revised by the Central Committee of the Chinese Communist Party in 1948. See an analysis and a translation in Selden (1979). For Mao's views on the countryside, see *Mao Zedong nongcun diaocha wenji* (1982).

8. The literature on Mao's political philosophy is enormous. For concise expositions, see Schram (1969), Wakeman (1973), Starr (1979), and Wilson (1977). For an analysis of party debates on issues of class, see Kraus (1981).

9. For thorough studies of such history, see Selden (1971) for the Yenan period when many class policies were formulated. For the use of the language of class in Chinese historiography, see Harrison (1968). For ideology and organization in the postrevolutionary period, see Schurmann (1968) and Meisner (1986). For a documentary history, see Selden (1979). For studies on women, see K. Johnson (1983) and Stacey (1983). For a documentary history on the treatment of intellectuals, see Lin, Hai, and Chen (1978).

10. Ye Jianying and Fang Fang, the first and third party secretaries of the South China Branch of the party's Central Committee, collaborated and clashed with Tao Zhu, who became a major opponent of "localism." The statistics are taken from *Guangdong qingkuang huibian*, compiled by the Zhonggong Zhongyang Huanan Fenju Zhengce Yanjiushi (1950).

11. This meant basically land rent.

12. See his speech made to the delegates of the first Provincial People's Congress in the fall of 1950 (Guangdong Sheng Tudi Gaige Weiyuanhui 1950a, 27–37). For the treatment of emigrant households, see "Guangdong sheng tudi gaige zhong huaqiao tudi chuli banfa" (Policies for handling the properties of overseas Chinese during land reform in Guangdong), in the same volume (1950b, 16–17). For the debate on the rich-peasant economy in other parts of China, see the writings of Chen Yun and Deng Zihui.

13. See a reprint of the editorial in *Nanfang zhoubao* 1, 1 (1951): 5–6.

14. Guangdong was one of the six provinces under its jurisdiction. Guangdong's party leadership was under the South China Branch of the South Central Party Bureau. Dong (1953, 11) quoted Deng's speech from *Changjiang ribao* (December 27, 1950).

15. See Li (1985, 45–53). See also the article by Wen Zhiyu after he was rehabilitated in the early 1980s (Wen 1983). Apart from Wen Zhiyu, other notables who were disgraced include Ma Shu, the head of the county government, who was dismissed on charges of corruption in April 1952; Li Jinbo, a former member of the

county assembly and later secretary of the central administration office, who was jailed after the Jiangmen incident; Yu Jingbo, a former member of the Democratic Alliance and later head of the Construction Office in the Xinhui county government, who was arrested in 1951; Lin Shudeng, a former member of the county assembly and member of the Democratic Alliance and later head of the Business Enterprise Office in the county government, who was allegedly returned to his native village and shot; and Zhao Meiyou, former headmaster of Gangzhou Simplified Teachers College, member of the Democratic Alliance, and later head of the education office in the county government, who was convicted of espionage and shot. The above information is taken from Li and Hong (1952).

16. See *Fan fengjian* (1952). See also Li and Hong (1952) and Xinhui Xian Chengxiang Lianluo Weiyuanhui Lianluochu (1952). For evidence of excesses in other areas of the delta, see Guangdong Sheng Tudigaige Weiyuanhui (1951, 17, 32, 58, 60).

17. The figures for Dongjia are taken from brigade records examined during fieldwork. The figures for Tianlu are based on interviews with cadres who were responsible for the land reform in Xian Village, which had about six hundred residents at the time. The class composition of Xinhui County can be found in the appendix of *Xinhui xian tugai yundong ziliao huibian* (1960). The landlord and rich-peasant categories seem to have been smaller in Tianlu than in Dongjia and the county in general (the county average was 7.1 percent according to 1952 statistics).

18. One of the ways the party got around the complexities of land ownership was to rule that households be classified on the basis of the proportion of their income derived from the labor of others during a period of three years before the land reform.

19. Faure (1986) argues that rights of settlement in a village were just as important as the ownership of land to a peasant's livelihood.

20. In the area, households were labeled small rentier if they owned and rented land that exceeded by up to 200 percent the legitimate per capita ownership of 1.5 mu.

21. The document distinguished emigrants who used resources earned from overseas to buy land in their native villages (forty-eight households) from native landlords whose family members had branched into overseas operations (nine households). The former were treated more leniently. See Xinhui Xian Chengxiang Lianluo Weiyuanhui Lianluochu (1952).

22. The following information on the land reform campaigns in Huicheng and its vicinity is based on interviews with old cadres, supplemented by documentary evidence. Two documents I relied on in particular are *Fan fengjian* (1952) and a report drawn up by the Xinhui Xian Chengxiang Lianluo Weiyuanhui Lianluochu (1952). Other sources include *Xinhui wenshi ziliao xuanji*, vols. 1–22, and *Xinhui xian tudi gaige ziliao yundong huibian*, vols. 1 and 2. For statistical information for the six provinces under the party's South Central Bureau, see *Zhongnanqu yibaige xiang diaocha tongji biao* (Zhongnan Junzheng Weiyuanhui Tudigaige Weiyuanhui Diaocha Yanjiuchu 1953). For statistical information for the entire province, see *Guangdong qingkuang huibian* (Zhonggong Zhongyang Huanan Fenju Zhengce Yanjiushi 1950) and *Guangdong sheng geming lao genjudi jiben qingkuang tongji zhiliao* (Guangdong Sheng Lao Genjudi Jiance Weiyuanhui Bangongshi, draft 1959).

23. The same land reform document lists a total of 7,560 households and 27,030 residents in Huicheng at the time of the land reform in late 1950. Out of the total,

1,794 households with a population of 9,409 were categorized as having "property relationships of a feudal nature." Apart from emigrant landlords and small rentiers, the households were further divided into landlords (447 households), landlords with commercial interests (78 households), and commercial and industrial entrepreneurs with landed interests (27 households). See Xinhui Xian Chengxiang Lianluo Weiyuanhui Lianluochu (1952, 1).

24. These dispatches were often used to describe typical problems in a wider area, though a certain amount of exaggeration was to be expected. See Xinhui Xian Siqu Tugaidui (August 3, 1952).

25. Accusations against local bosses in other townships carried similar undertones of vengeance. See *Xinhui xian tugai yundong ziliao huibian* (1960), in which episodes of the struggle meetings in Tianma, Meijiang, Duhui, Nantan, and Dadong Xiang are described. "Who killed my entire family? It was bully X. Now the Communists help me avenge my grievance. He must pay this blood debt with his own blood!"

26. This was a common problem in Guangdong. Party directives from the South Central Bureau spoke of the "blind spontaneity and violence in struggle sessions" in the provinces under its supervision (Guangdong Sheng Tudigaige Weiyuanhui 1951, 15, 74, 127). The party blamed these problems on the inexperience of party cadres who relied on the "brave elements" (ibid., 77) and an article in *Nanfang ribao* (July 6, 1951) explicitly addresses this question. It states:

> The so-called mass opinion is that of a minority of brave elements who have deviated from proper mass consciousness. Cadres who believe them to represent mass opinion commit commandism and tailism. They have been allowed to claim back rent payments since the reign of Guangxu. Landlords of various standing are indiscriminately attacked. Small rentiers and widows are not given due attention. People were tied up and beaten. They have treated wrong experience as the correct policy. (Dong 1953, 24)

27. See Li and Hong (1952, 39–43). The authors take a strongly anti-Communist attitude toward events. They gathered the information from refugees in Hong Kong. Despite such potential bias, their information is concrete and detailed; it contains not only the names of victims, but also their age, occupation, the accusations made against them, and the sentences they received. I have found a similar document for neighboring Zhongshan County.

28. See Yang (1959) for similar observations in Guangdong. See Crook and Crook (1959) for a report on a north China village.

29. This was a crude categorization. Under each category more refined distinctions were made to fit local situations. For example, poor peasants who became better off during the interregnum between the Communist takeover and the land reform were classified as new middle peasants. See Zhongyang Renmin Zhengfu Zhengwu Yuan, "Guanyu huafeng nongcun jieji chengfen de jueding" (Decisions concerning the differentiation of class status in the countryside), in *Tudigaige cankao ziliao xuanbian* (1951, 29–50).

30. For example, in the periurban villages where vegetables were grown for the urban market and where farming households shared the frequent tasks of weeding, watering, and marketing the crops with hired laborers, it was difficult to determine the percentage of labor inputs.

31. Interviews with old peasant activists echoed documentary evidence from

other areas of Guangdong; see *Tugai fucha gongzuo chankao ziliao* (Reference materials for review work of the land reform), edited by Yuezhongqu Tuweihui Xijiang Tugai Gongzuozu (January 21, 1953), 3:7; see also (February 11, 1953) 6:3–5.

32. The activists and their leadership styles could be distinguished in terms of their distance from urban centers. In the periurban communities, the brave elements predominated. They combined the qualities of what Madsen describes as Communist rebels with a strong dose of opportunism. In the communities farther from town, the activists fitted Madsen's categorization of the Communist gentry, whose communal ties were overriding.

33. See Perry (1984) and Anagnost (1985).

Chapter 7. Losing Ground

1. The five enlarged townships were Tianma, Wuhuan, Chengnan, Chengdong, and Chengxi (Xinhui Xian Dang'anguan 1984); see also *Xinhui bao* (January 7, 1957): 1.

2. For the country in general, the rules for organizing the peasant associations were announced in July 1950. By November 1951 there were 88 million members (Zongyang Weiyuanhui Shejikaohe Weiyuanhui 1953, 44). Though middle peasants were allowed to join, the leadership of the associations was reserved for the very poorest, whom the party trusted as class allies. The association was supported by a militia.

3. The topic has been well studied. For different aspects of the socialist transformation of agriculture, commerce, and handicrafts, see Lardy (1983), Lippit and Selden (1982), Shue (1980), and Oi (1983) for grain procurement policies; Solinger (1984) for commerce; and Parish and Whyte (1978) for social conditions. For Chinese sources, see the three volumes of *Zhongguo nongcun de shehui zhuyi gaochao* (The high tide of socialism in the Chinese countryside), edited by Zhonggong Zhongyang Bangongting (1956); the three volumes of *Guomin jingji huifu shiqi nongye shengchan hezuo ziliao huibian,* edited by Zhongguo Kexueyuan Jingji Yanjiusuo (1957); and *Zhongguo nongye hezuohua yundong shiliao,* edited by Shi Jingtang et al. (1957). For transformations in commerce, see *Xin Zhongguo shangye shigao 1949–1982,* edited by Shangyebu Shangye Jingji Yanjiusuo (hereafter cited as Shangyebu 1984). For handicrafts, see *1954 nian quanguo geti shougongye diaocha ziliao,* compiled by Zhongguo Kexueyuan Jingji Yanjiusuo Shougongyezu (1957). A good statistical source is the *Zhongguo nongye nianjian* (1982–84), published annually by Zhongguo Nongye Nianjian Bianji Weiyuanhui. Chen Yun, known as the economic czar of the new China, is considered to be author of the new socialist economy. Though he favors market incentives and the protection of private plots for peasants, he is a strong advocate of centralized planning. See a translation and analysis of Chen Yun's writings in *Chen Yun's Strategy for China's Development,* edited by Nicholas Lardy and Kenneth Lieberthal (1983).

4. See Whyte and Parish (1984) on the government's efforts to create a congenial environment for the urban proletariat.

5. A great deal of the information used in this section was obtained from the volume compiled by Shangyebu (1984, 1–128). See also Solinger (1984).

6. See "Gongxiao hezuoshe bishu guance wei nongye shengchan fuwu de fang-zhen" in Renmin ribao (July 26, 1954). The article was published in Nongye shehui zhuyi gaizao wenji (1955).

7. According to Shangyebu (1984, 8), the state commerce system supplied the cooperatives first and gave them discount points. For example, in 1950 the cooperatives were given discounts off wholesale prices as follows: cotton cloth and vegetable oil, 2 percent; coal and charcoal, 6 percent; salt, 5 percent; and grain, 3–4 percent. In 1951 the range of commodities was extended and the discount rate was increased: cotton cloth, 7 percent; rice, flour, and other grains, and salt, 7 percent; sugar, coal, and charcoal, 8 percent; and kerosene, 12 percent. Furthermore, the cooperatives could obtain long-term and short-term loans from the Bank of China at interest rates 10 percent lower than those for other enterprises. New cooperatives were exempt from income tax for a year, and their sales tax was reduced by 20 percent.

8. See Li (1954, 8–9, 19–20) on higher grain prices paid by private merchants in other provinces.

9. The following descriptions were taken from his article in Xinhui wenshi ziliao xuanji (1986) 22:44–52 and from a personal interview with him in September 1986.

10. He quoted from "Huicheng zhen gongshanyehu 1956 nian jiben qingkuang tongjibiao", compiled by the Industry-Commerce League in December 1956.

11. See a series of government documents concerning the grain policies: Zhongyang Renmin Zhengfu Zhengwuyuan (November 19, 1953), "Guanyu shix-ing liangshi de jihua shougou he jihua gongying de mingling" (Directives on the planned purchase and supply of grain). See also editorials from Renmin ribao, "Liangshi jihua shougou he jihua gongying shi zongluxian de yige zhongyao zucheng bufen" (The planned purchase and supply of grain is an important part of the general policy line), March 1, 1954; "Jiaqiang liangshi shougou zhong de jingji gongzuo" (Strengthen the economic work on the procurement of grain), November 30, 1953; "Jiaqiang liangshi shougou zhong de zhengzhi gongzuo (Strengthen the political work on the procurement of grain), November 23, 1953; and "Liangshi tonggou tongxiao dui nongmin de haochu" (The benefits of unified purchase and sale of grain for the peasants), November 17, 1954. These documents are edited in a volume entitled Nongye shehui zhuyi gaizao wenji (1955). See also Liu (1957).

12. See Liu (1957, 55). See also "Nongcun liangshi tonggou tongxiao zanxing banfa" (Provisional rules for the unified purchase and sale of grain in the countryside), Article 28. The policy directive was revised for Guangdong Province as "Guangdong sheng 1956 nongcun liangshi tonggou tongxiao shishi xize," and reprinted in Xinhui nongmin bao, June 13, 1956. See Article 14 for the adjustment of purchase quotas.

13. See Dang Xiangmin (1956).

14. The figures are taken from Xinhui xian nongye quhua baogaoji (1983, 292).

15. See Xinhui Xian Renwei Bangongshi (June 1958) 1:31–32. Documents from 1958 should be treated with some caution because of their overwhelmingly political tone. However, what they describe corresponds with the general impression of the bureaucratic problems I was able to get from the cadres I interviewed. In many parts of the country peasants had similar complaints about having to queue up for

days to register, weigh, grade, and store what they were selling. The purchasing stations were accused of withholding state funds and arbitrarily issuing IOUS (Li 1957, 13–18).

16. See Chen Jiangtian (1956, 13).

17. See "Guangyu fangkuan shichang guanli de gexiang caoshi" (On various policies for relaxing market restrictions) in *Xinhui nongmin bao,* November 4, 1956. The first group of policies applied to grain and peanuts under unified purchase and sale by the state. The second category applied to live pigs, cattle, cowhide, used copper, tin and steel products, rubber, jute, silk cocoons, sugarcane, and palm leaves. This group of products had to be sold to the state at fixed prices. Private traders could sell only to state agents. The third category applied to young poultry and piglets, fish, oranges, preserved turnips, garlic, tobacco, and orange peel. Peasants were allowed to sell the portion they produced above the state quotas. However, they could not sell at prices higher than those fixed by the state. Moreover, producers who intended to trade such goods over long distances had to obtain permission from the market management offices. The free-trade category included local fresh fruits, vegetables, palm and bamboo handicrafts, and game. By March 1957, the Guangdong Provincial government had added live pigs to the category of unified purchase and sales (*Xinhui bao,* March 13, 1957).

18. See *Xinhui nongmin bao,* December 10, 1956. See also a speech by another leading cadre, Gan Weiguang, entitled "Guanyu shiying shangye de shehui zhuyi gaizao wenti de fayan" (Addressing the problem of the socialist transformation of private commerce, November 1956, 18–20), in which he addresses the problem of the county's small traders and outlined the party-state's difficulties in incorporating them into the state commercial networks.

19. Chen Yun and Deng Zihui favored the use of market mechanisms, some private trading, and autonomy for production in households. Mao disagreed. See Lardy and Lieberthal (1983, Introduction).

20. Peasants traditionally exchanged labor for the use of draft animals and tools among themselves. The Communists built on these arrangements while trying to change some of the more unequal terms of the exchange. For example, in a cattle-labor exchange between two households, the owner of the ox usually had an advantage because labor was cheaper. For labor gangs, the leader-contractor (*baogong tou*) dominated the distribution of wages. See Shi et al. (1957) on the different forms of traditional exchanges, largely in north China.

21. See "Guanyu nongye shengchan wuzuo hezuo de jueding" (Decisions on agricultural cooperativization) by the Central Committee of the CCP. A draft of the document was issued to party committees at every administrative level for trial implementation starting in December 1951.

22. Among the regions, the number of cooperatives in Huabei (north China) was planned to increase from 6,186 to 12,400; in Dongbei (northeast China), from 4,817 to 10,000; in Huadong (east China), from 2,301 to 8,300 or more; in Zhongnan (south central China), from 527 to 3,600; in Xibei (northwest China), from 302 to 700 or more; in Xinan (southwest China), from 59 to 600 or more. See "Guanyu fazhan nongye shengchan hezuoshe de jueyi" by the Central Committee of the CCP (December 16, 1953). The document was published in a collection entitled *Guanyu fazhan nongye shengchan hezuoshe de jueyi jiqi youguan wenjian,* edited by Zhongguo Gongchandang Zhongyang Weiyuanhui (1955, 13–31).

23. For general discussions of conflicts of interest in the cooperatives, see also Wan (1956).

24. The county newspaper reported in 1956 that 738 cadres from 638 units had been trained for five days before spring planting (*Xinhui nongmin bao,* March 21, 1956).

25. The villages ranged in size from four hundred to nearly a thousand residents. The largest one, Xian, was divided into two cooperatives. *Xinhui nongmin bao* (October 25, 1956) indicated that there were nine cooperatives, but cadres in the township said there were only eight.

26. See *Xinhui nongmin bao,* April 25 and December 10, 1956.

27. Perry (1984) has remarked on the rise in collective violence in the 1980s after the reforms, and attributes this trend to the maneuvers of cadres who were trying to hold on to their positions as the reforms were undermining their power. In the 1950s, the strategy was not a defensive one on the part of cadres.

28. *Xinhui nongmin bao,* October 10 and 25, 1956; November 4, 1956; *Xinhui bao,* December 26, 1957.

29. See Tan Xingyue (1956, 24).

30. In Guangdong, party cadres accused of coming from bad class backgrounds or of having associated with the earlier regimes were disgraced and imprisoned. Some are even said to have been executed. A degree of secrecy developed around the party. Activists claimed that even the members of the work team did not know who the party members were until they were invited to join political study classes in preparation for membership.

31. See Whyte and Parish (1984) on the restrictions on urban residence. In 1954, when grain rations were established, the population was divided into agricultural and nonagricultural households. Regulations in 1958 further restricted movements. By 1960, the number of peasants who could enter the urban areas was negligible.

Chapter 8. The Leap

1. The militarization of social life was very evident during the entire Maoist era, and especially during the Great Leap Forward and the Cultural Revolution. In the recent decade of reforms, the martial tone has quickly faded from everyday vocabulary.

2. See party documents and debates in Selden (1979, 381–431). From August to September 1958, the percentage of participating households jumped from 30 to 98 (1979, 79). In his introduction, Selden shows that, in the beginning, communes corresponded to townships, with 20,000 to 25,000 members on average, and constituted the lowest administrative level. In 1962 the team became the basic accounting unit, with approximately 20 to 35 households collectively working and drawing income from the land allocated to them. In 1963, the communes were reduced in size to an average of 8,000 or so members; the total number of communes nationwide jumped from 26,000 to 74,000. Selden asserts that the commune corresponds to a standard rural marketing community. In the 1970s, there were around 50,000 communes with an average membership of 13,000 to 16,000 (1979, 77). However, communes in Guangdong were generally larger. They corresponded to the district (*qu*) rather than the township (*xiang*) level of administra-

tion. In 1961, the population of Huancheng totaled 42,574. By 1979 it had grown to 60,181. Other communes in the delta that I visited had populations that ranged from 20,000 (in Taishan County) to over 100,000 (Xiaolan Commune of Zhongshan County). A brigade in Huancheng corresponded to a township, with an average population of 1,500. The largest, Tianma, had a membership of 6,082 in 1961, followed by Tianlu with 4,213 members, and Dongjia with 4,206 members. The smallest, Jiangzui, was a village too isolated to be grouped with others. It became a brigade with 321 members. The same applied to Shagang with 185 members.

3. The farm consisted of undiked river-marshes left over from the land redistribution under the land reform. Dan fishermen and migrant laborers had settled there, and it was one of the poorest areas in Huancheng.

4. When the cooperatives were formed in the mid-1950s, members handed over their properties to the units. A certain amount of swapping was arranged by township cadres to centralize the land so as to make production work easier. When the collectives were formed, the cooperatives were organized into teams. Another round of land swapping and allocation took place if the cooperatives merged or split up to form new teams, as in the case of Tianlu Xiang. These activities invariably created a great deal of conflict. Accusations of favoritism and corruption against the cadres were rampant. See also Chan, Madsen, and Unger (1984) for similar observations in another south China village.

5. According to an article by Mu Fu (1984), who quotes statistics published by the government in 1983, city and market-town population increased during the commune years. Some people were sent back to the rural areas during the economic retrenchment of the early 1960s. From then on, urban residence was severely restricted. See Whyte and Parish (1984) on rural-urban tensions and the party policies developed to deal with them. For a general assessment of the development of the urban sector, see the articles by Tang and Ma (1985) and Chan and Xu (1985).

6. For age-specific employment opportunities and intergenerational relationships, see Davis-Friedmann (1983).

7. Selden (1979, 82) compiled a table from *China's Economy and Technology* (Kojima) to show that, in 1957, 60 to 80 percent of rural women joined the work force, accounting for 30 percent of the total number of labor days. At the time public dining halls were few, and only 6 million children were in nurseries. The table shows that, in 1958, 55 million more women joined the work force, but women's labor still represented only 33 percent of the total number of agricultural days. Ninety percent of the villages operated public dining halls, and 67 million children were in nurseries (I think the jump took place in the cities more than in the villages). In 1959, women accounted for 40 to 45 percent of the total number of labor days; 20 million more rural women participated in collective work. Seventy percent of rural households ate in the public dining halls, which totalled 3,600,000. Seventy percent of the children in the rural areas were in nurseries. I am suspicious of the large percentages quoted, especially since the dividing line between rural and urban women is not clear in the data. The figures could be describing an urban phenomenon.

8. See also works by M. Wolf (1985), K. Johnson (1983), and Stacey (1983) on the "unfinished revolution" of Chinese women in general.

9. See "Guanyu renmin gongshe fenpei wenti de chuli yijian," in *Guanyu renmin gongshe fenpei wenti de diaocha*, by Zhonggong Guangdong Shengwei Nongcun Gongzuobu (1958). In the model, 45 percent of the commune's net income was to be set aside for a capital and welfare fund. Of the members' income, 20 to 30 percent was given to the brigades, while the rest was handed out by the commune. Moreover, though labor was graded, cash wages were to constitute only 35 to 40 percent of one's income, and the rest was to be distributed in the form of food and services.

10. See "Guanyu Huancheng Lile renmin gongshe fenpei wenti de diaocha" by Zhonggong Guangdong Shengwei Nongcun Gongzuobu (1958).

11. The plan was published in *Xinhui gongzuo* (October 1958:6–8).

12. *Xinhui gongzuo* (July 15, 1958): 1.

13. I was told about these mobilization campaigns by old cadres whom I interviewed in the late 1970s and early 1980s. Their accounts matched those in *Xinhui bao* (1957–60) and *Xinhui gongzuo* (1958–64).

14. See Guang (1966), a news article in *Zhongguo xinwen* (4585 [October 26, 1966]: 10). Exaggeration is to be expected, particularly in this period.

15. I obtained this information on a field trip in September 1977 and from *Xinhui qiaokan* (21 [1965]: 1–3).

16. See Xinhui Xian Zhengfu Tonqzhishi (1947, 4–7). However, statistical information from the Republican era should be treated with caution. I think the figures for the public schools may have been inflated so that the county government could manipulate their funds. The number of village schools, on the other hand, may have been understated.

17. See Pepper (1986) and Unger (1982) for general policies on education; see also Zhang (1981) on rural education in Doushan Commune, Taishan County, and Rosen (1982) on the educational structure and Red Guard factionalism in Guangzhou.

18. Again, these figures must be treated with some skepticism. Though the new government has a much more efficient system for recording data, the magazine is a propaganda piece put out by the county government to appeal to overseas Chinese.

19. See articles by He Zhiping and Yang Jianbai (1984) and by Yu Qinghe (1984). See also the debates on agrarian socialism and the dangers of small producers' adopting extreme egalitarian attitudes. A summary of these views is found in an article by Wang Xiaoqiang (1980).

20. Sobering statistics published by the government some twenty years later revealed the devastating social and economic consequences of the radical programs of the 1959–61 period. See Bernstein (1984) and Mu Fu (1984). It is difficult to estimate how many people died of famine-related diseases because the deaths occurred mostly in the rural areas. Mu Fu quotes figures that range from 15 million to 30 million. Even in the Pearl River delta, which was endowed with a mild climate and abundant rice fields, famine drove 60,000 refugees across the border into Hong Kong in May 1962, with a total of 200,000 for the year (Zhou 1980, 23).

21. See Li and Hong (1952, 19) on the closing of the major local newspapers in Huicheng and Jiangmen. See also an article on the *Minchuan bao* by Lun Haibin (1983).

22. Such tightening occurred at several levels of the economy. For example, the Guangdong Provincial Government issued a directive on March 10, 1957, which

placed live pigs in the category of state unified purchase (*Xinhui bao*, March 13, 1957). Private sales became illegal. Simultaneously, party officials in Xinhui County urged the collectives to set higher production standards for their teams. The county newspaper reported that after some collectives raised their standards, peasants "took production work more seriously" by working harder (*Xinhui bao*, March 13, 1957). In April the party committee of the county followed with an announcement that cadres should reclaim land that was unaccounted for or that had been lost in the records in the land swapping between collectives. Every inch of soil must be used for food production, the county party urged (*Xinhui bao*, April 22, 1957). In June, the county government started a campaign for the sale of government bonds in the rural units. Cadres at all levels were given quotas to fulfill, even though "the principle of voluntarism" was to be enforced.

Chapter 9. Complicity and Compliance

1. The Party Central Committee's conference at Lushan in July 1959 revealed strong opposition among the nation's leaders to Mao's programs. Mao himself admitted that local situations had gotten out of hand. See Selden (1979, 467—85) for his analysis and for translations of the exchanges among top party leaders such as Mao and Peng Dehuai. According to Selden, Peng Dehuai summarized his criticisms of the Great Leap Forward in his "Letter of Opinion." Mao's self-critical "Speech at the Lushan Conference" described the problems of "blowing the Communist winds." The decentralization of authority to allow team autonomy was discussed in the party document of the Central Committee for November 1960, "Urgent directives concerning present policy problems in the rural people's communes." Summing up their experiences, Mao drew up the "Regulations on the work of the rural people's communes" and later a revised draft known as "the Sixty Articles," which was approved by the Tenth Plenum of the Eighth Central Committee in September 1962. See Zhongguo Gongzhandang Zhongyang Weiyuanhui (1961, 1962).

2. The three contracts were *bao gong* (contracted work), *bao chengben* (contracted costs), and *bao chan* (contracted delivery).

3. See *Xinhui bao* (December 5, 1960) and *Xinhui gongzuo* (October 23, 1960): 1—3.

4. See *Xinhui gongzuo* (n.d., 1964:4—5) and *Xinhui xian nongye quhua baogaoji* (1983:289—98).

5. Baum (1975) provides a detailed account of the events preceding the Cultural Revolution; see also MacFarquhar (1975, 1985). Political scientists often maintain that Mao's radical associates used his political objectives to get rid of old cadres and to elevate themselves in the party hierarchy. For analyses of factional politics in China, see Nathan (1973), Tsou (1976), and Lee (n.d.).

6. See Selden (1979, 536—41) for a translation of the "First Ten Points." This is taken from *Ssu-Ch'ing—The Socialist Education Movement*, by Richard Baum and Frederick Teiwes (Berkeley: Center for Chinese Studies, 1968).

7. See *Xinhui gongzuo* (August 12, 1964): 1—6. I suspect that every brigade was told to investigate class differences in the villages around that time. I have been

shown reports listing class categories and details of the economic situations of each category similar to the ones published in *Xinhui gongzuo*.

8. An article in *Xinhui gongzuo* (January 1964:3–5) uses a case study to describe what the wages of brigade and team cadres should be. There were strict rules governing the members' responsibilities for the grain procurement quota and the number of work-points they could accumulate based on the time they spent in the fields. Many cadres were accused of taking work-points without laboring with the peasants. In the eyes of the Maoists, such cadres had detached themselves from the masses and were extracting the peasants' surplus through their positions as administrators.

9. According to Rosen (1982, 144–47), whose study focuses on middle-school student factions in Guangzhou during the Cultural Revolution, the university and middle-school student groups in Guangzhou emerged as Red Guard factions in mid-1966. Despite the waxing and waning of their power, depending on their alignment with student groups from Beijing and from other provinces, and on the interference of the military, the groups settled into two major factions. The Red Flag faction rebelled against the party committees and work teams in the initial period of the Cultural Revolution, and consisted of students from what were politically defined as "middle and bad class" backgrounds (that is, the children of intellectuals, overseas merchants, landlord and rich peasants, rightists, and counterrevolutionaries) and of young workers. The East Wind, or General, faction was a more united group centered on youths from "red class" backgrounds (children from the families of established party and military cadres and of workers). The movement of the Red Guards was important in provincial politics. They joined forces with the factions from outside the province in late 1966 to criticize Tao Zhu and brought him down in January 1967. An extremist rebel group (Shenggelian) seized power in January 22, 1967, but was dispersed by the military when Guangdong came under the Military Control Committee in March (Rosen 1982, 133). According to Rosen (1982, 197), the two factions remained rather stable from April 1967 to the autumn of 1968. Still, responding to the power struggles emanating from Beijing, the factions in Guangzhou underwent several other realignments. See also Hong Yung Lee (1978) for Red Guard factionalism, and Hai Feng (1971) on their activities in Guangzhou.

10. While reading the county papers of that period, I remember commenting to a teacher at the county library that I would go crazy if I had to read about the political frenzy for one more day. He gave me a bitter smile and said "If you feel that way from reading the material fifteen years after the episodes, just think of us in the midst of them."

11. The regular army troops at Niuguling sided with the General faction, whereas those in Huicheng sided with the Red Flag faction.

12. In a report in *Nanfang ribao* (October 22, 1979), it was estimated that 444 persons were given bad class labels. Many of the labels were given to landlords during the land reform. A friend who had been a landlord in a neighboring district told me that he had advised his daughter to marry "among her own kind" because mothers-in-law with revolutionary class status might use this advantage against their daughters-in-law during family squabbles. A young couple there also told me that if it had not been for the reforms in recent years, they could not have started

any relationship. The woman's father fell into one of the "black categories," whereas the man's father was a "revolutionary martyr."

13. For more detailed descriptions of village politics involving the young rebels during the radical decade in Guangdong villages, see Chan, Madsen, and Unger (1984) and Madsen (1984). On the specific language and politics of class in Chen Village, see Jonathan Unger, "The Class System in Rural China: A Case Study," in Watson (1984).

14. A similar situation was described to me in Hebei Brigade. In the chaotic years between 1966 and 1969, the party secretary was replaced by a member of the Poor Peasant League who was forty-three years old and had not joined the party until his position forced him to do so in 1969. Though the post of party secretary was given to a young rebel from 1970 to 1976, another friend of the old cadres (who joined the party in 1971 at the age of thirty-seven) afterward assumed the position.

15. The political dynamics described in *Chen Village* seem more turbulent. I suspect that the old cadres I interviewed downplayed the trauma and the importance of the mass meetings, whereas the former rebels of Chen Village over-dramatized the events.

16. In the commune, state cadres (*guojia ganbu*) served mainly as party secretaries and members of the commune revolutionary committee (such as Chen Sheyuan); a few cadres were sent either from the provincial government (such as Xu Wenqing) or from the county government (such as the present head of the Huancheng Zhen). The collective cadres (*jiti ganbu*) received some subsidies from the state, but their incomes were taken from the collective savings of their respective brigades. Until their transfer to the commune enterprises, Chen Mingfa, Xu Decheng, and Huang Tao were collective cadres, and their families were considered rural households entitled to a share of the grain distribution and income from their teams. The commune also had collective cadres who were supported by income from the commune enterprises. Their families were treated as market-town residents and were entitled to grain rations from the commune's quota.

17. According to Rosen (1982, 247), about 75 percent of the middle-school graduates in Guangzhou were dispatched to the countryside in the winter of 1968–69. I could not obtain a reliable figure for the number of youths sent down to the Huancheng area. However, cadres I interviewed acknowledged their presence. I interviewed some who worked in the brigade enterprises in Chengnan. Sancun Brigade used the connections of one student from Guzhen of Zhongshan County to obtain a contract for their twine factory. During my visit to Jiangzui Brigade in 1978, I saw rows of small sheds at one end of the village where the youths resided.

18. Lin Qing in Tianlu recalled that the party secretary was once accused in a mass meeting of having pulled strings to get an exit visa for a sick man who needed medical treatment in Hong Kong. The man died anyway, but unfortunately for the cadre, he was a relative of a former official of the Nationalist party. Rebel Red Guards accused him of being lenient toward class enemies and suspected him of having been bribed by spies. The party secretary could have sought protection from the county officials who actually issued the exit visa; but since they too had been purged, the attacks of the rebels were unmediated. The cadre was not dismissed, but the experience was extremely unpleasant for him.

19. For discussions of patron-client politics in China, see Oi (1985) and Shue

(1985, 1988). For discussions of the overarching structure of dependence in the state bureaucracy, see Lee (n.d.).

Chapter 10. The Paradox of Power

1. For descriptions of how the authority of Mao was perceived by the Red Guard factions, see a personal account by Gao (1987). For an account of the situation in Guangdong, see Hai Feng (1971). For an account of events in Guilin, see Hua (1987). See also Lee (1978).

2. See *Nongye xue Dazhai* (Learning from Dazhai), vols. 7–22, published by Nongye Chubanshe from 1972 to 1978. Dazhai, the model commune promoted by the Maoists during this period, emphasized self-reliant development, local initiative and ingenuity, boldness and persistence in changing the material environment, high collective spirits, egalitarian work-responsibility systems, and grain production.

3. I have searched through the issues of *Xinhui tongxun*, a publication of the county party committee (Zhonggong Xinhui Xian Weiyuanhui 1972–74) that commented on this problem during the anti-Lin Biao, anti-Confucius, and Basic Line Education campaigns, the latter a renewed effort to improve rural leadership.

4. Tianlu Brigade has over four thousand residents and its eight teams are larger than normal. The team leaders are party members.

5. According to Lin Qing, Tianlu had a brigade party committee of nine members in 1958. From the Cultural Revolution to the early 1980s, there were four elections.

6. The 2.3 percent figure seems much higher than the national average of 0.4 percent for the rural population. The figure was given to me by the cadre in charge of political work in the commune. The high figure could be due to the large number of nonagricultural residents in its market town. Even so, 1.4 percent for Tianlu (a total of eighty-eight party members out of a population of 5,927) is still higher than the national average. Sancun Brigade had twenty-six party members out of a population of 1,570 (1.6 percent). Hebei Brigade had twenty party members out of a population of 1,065 (1.9 percent).

7. At the county level, the overlapping of party and government organizations continued. I was told in 1982 that of the twenty members of the government committee of the county, eighteen were in the party committee.

8. Five work teams were sent to the brigades. The last group finished its work in May 1978. The teams consisted of cadres, Party Youth League members, activists in the commune enterprises, and student leaders.

9. The figures were given to me by a cadre in the political section of the commune administration in the summer of 1982.

10. I was able to read *Xinhui tongxun* and *Xinhui gongzuo* from 1958 to 1980. To supplement these documents, I interviewed former members of the work teams that "squatted" in the villages between 1974 and 1978.

11. One must of course allow for underreporting. However, many of these documents were compiled by the county party committee, whose radical members often tried to exaggerate delinquency in order to discredit political opponents who were patrons to rural cadres.

12. I was able to interview five young cadres groomed for leading positions in the commune and county. The first was Huang Youfen, a native of Chengjiao Brigade,

a graduate of the commune senior middle school, technician in the commune's agricultural machinery factory, and member of the Party Youth League. When I met him in 1978, he was twenty-five years old. Yuan Dewei, a native of Chakeng Brigade, recruited as a state cadre at the age of eighteen, former secretary of the commune's Party Youth League, graduated a year behind Huang from the senior middle school, was posted to the county legal department, and later transferred to the municipal legal department in Jiangmen, but asked to be transferred back to the commune as deputy party secretary in 1986. When we met in 1980, he was twenty-five years old. Zhang Deman, a classmate of Yuan's, graduate of the commune senior middle school, and a native of Huancheng, was recruited to the commune at nineteen, participated in the last work team in 1978, became party committee member in charge of political work in 1981, was sent to cadre college in 1985, and, upon finishing, was assigned to Hetang Commune as party secretary in 1986. I also met him in 1980. Li Jin, a native of Daze Commune, group leader in the Basic Line Education movement in 1974–75, became Party Youth League secretary of the county in 1980 at the age of twenty-eight. Zhang Yuanyi, lecturer in the cadre school in the county and former head of the county propaganda department, transferred to Sanjiang Commune as party secretary in 1981, and became first secretary of the county party committee in 1986 at the age of thirty-eight.

13. Xinhui Xian Nongye Quhua Bangongshi (1983).

14. Part of it was to be bought by the state as above-quota grain at a higher price. The procurement price was 11.9 yuan per picul. The above-quota price was around 13 yuan per picul until 1980, when it was raised to 18 yuan.

15. Li Chaolun of Chengnan and Chen Mingjian of Meijiang were identified as the two leading Maoists. I read an article published by Li in *Xinhui tongxun* in 1974 on the anti-Confucius campaigns. Both were purged in the early 1980s.

16. The system was similar to the one practiced by the nation's 50,000 communes. There were very few cases where brigades were the accounting units, but they were all models created by the Maoists.

17. For detailed descriptions of the labor management and incentive system of the communes in other parts of the country, see Yuan Ruofei (1981), *Nongcun renmin gongshe laodong guanli.* See also Jian Yusheng and Zhang Guozhong (1981), *Shengchandui ding'e guanli.*

18. The figures were quoted to me by the commune accountant and confirmed by the 1983 report (see Xinhui Xian Nongye Quhua Bangongshi 1983:279).

19. Among the brigades in Huancheng Commune, Jiangzui and Shagang had operated as the basic accounting unit since the mid-1960s. However, they did not go through the process of transition from team to brigade accounting. They were two isolated villages that could not be practically merged with other villages as part of a brigade, and were thus given independent brigade status.

20. An educated youth happened to have a brother in the Guzhen Commune of neighboring Zhongshan County, who secured contracts for the twine factory.

21. See Unger (1984, 129–34) for very similar arguments.

Chapter 11. The Paradox of Self-Reliance

1. The issue of the cellular development of Chinese agriculture in general is discussed by Donnithorne (1972), Lardy (1975, 1976), and Shue (1988).

2. The 43-million-yuan figure listed in the county records is smaller than the one in the commune accounts. The discrepancy is due in part to the fact that the commune's agricultural enterprises are not included in the county data.

3. It is worth noting that, unlike small-scale enterprises in other developing countries, whose operation fluctuates primarily according to market demands, commune enterprises in Huancheng are more sensitive to political climate.

4. Huancheng Commune went through drastic changes in the early 1980s. The commune was dismantled in the fall of 1983, but organizational changes had been taking place since 1981. I therefore use 1980 as my baseline.

5. Six leading cadres in the bureau supervised three sections and two cooperatives. The production section was responsible for ensuring the supply of raw materials contracted for the commune enterprises. The finance section estimated production costs and prices and kept records for all rural enterprises in the county. The administrative section supervised labor management, workers' welfare, and propaganda work. Its function was to make sure that the enterprises did not divert laborers from the fields. Because of a low level of mechanization, a multiple-cropping area like Huancheng faced serious labor shortages during summer harvest and planting. Not only were workers sent to the fields, but students from Huicheng were mobilized as well. It was not until 1978 that labor quotas for the enterprises ceased being a political issue.

6. Before the reforms in the 1980s, commune enterprises could not easily have contracts with foreign business because of strict foreign exchange control. The reforms radically altered the situation in the Pearl River delta; market-town and township enterprises have been given special "open-door" status, which translates into tax breaks, some autonomy in contracting with overseas clients, and the right to handle foreign exchange. See Qiu et al. (1986) on the special administrative favors.

7. The agricultural machinery station and the grain mill had all-male work forces except for their cooks.

8. For his experiences in Hong Kong, see Siu (1986b).

9. Agricultural machinery factories all over the county had been subsidized by the state (a policy of the Maoists) as a helpful gesture toward agriculture. Many factories survived on these "welfare contracts" reluctantly given by county factories. The brigades were also obliged to buy their products, however low in quality. When the contracts were withdrawn, these enterprises had a hard time surviving. Facing a period of liberalization, the factory managers realized that they needed to improve performance, but there were few resources they could draw on.

10. The brigade acted as the contractor for these labor groups. In 1980, there were 293 contracted laborers. In 1981, there were 485, and in 1982 there were 265.

11. From the brigade accounts, one can see that the difference between agricultural and enterprise wages was large. In 1976, when the average wage of a brigade enterprise worker was 318 yuan, the per capita agricultural income was 81 yuan (equivalent to 160 yuan per laborer). Brigade cadres said that the workers were strongly opposed to the idea of tying their wages to the value of work-points in the teams, but the policy was pushed for two years. The two wages were again separated in late 1979. From then till 1982, the enterprise wage increased to 389 yuan, 980 yuan, 1,024 yuan, and 1,099 yuan. Per capita agricultural income also rose, but at a much slower pace, to 105 yuan, 176 yuan, 163 yuan, and 282 yuan.

Chapter 12. State Involution

1. Policy debates and case studies are summarized in articles from *Nongye jingji wenti* (Problems in agricultural economy, 1980–86). A collection of essays by Du Runsheng, a key figure in the agricultural reforms, outlines the leadership's intentions and rationalizations from 1980 to 1984 (Du 1985). See also Lin (1983) for a summary of the responsibility systems.

2. For summaries of the consequences of the reforms on the urban-rural relationships in the Pearl River delta, see Xu (1987) and Siu (1989). For the government's promotion of the "open-door" policies, see Qiu et al. (1986). For comparative studies of southern Jiangsu, see Shen (1987), Jiangsu Sheng Xiao Chengzhen Xiaozu (1986), and Fei (1985). Party elections conducted in 1980 and in 1982 aimed at removing older cadres and replacing them with younger, better educated ones. The provincial government's ostensible reason for this move was to reduce obstacles in the decollectivization process to be pursued in the following year.

3. The district-level office is a unique feature of Guangdong Province. In other provinces, the township government often replaces that of the commune. In 1986, many of the rural districts in Guangdong that had nucleated, nonagricultural populations of over two thousand were converted into market towns (*zhen*), and their subordinate township government was given village status (*cun*) in an effort to integrate the activities of the nonagricultural population with those of the villagers. The measure was also intended to produce a better administrative alignment of the subcounty units in Guangdong with those of other provinces.

4. For the country in general, see Skinner (1985b) on the history of the regime's treatment of rural marketing, and Oi (1986a) on the strategies of peasants and cadres toward the new grain procurement policies.

5. The concept of involution originates with Clifford Geertz (1963), who describes Java's baroque rice cultivation within the traditional institutional context. Prasenjit Duara (1987) creatively adapted the concept for his analysis of state-society relations in Republican China and describes the powerful reach of the state as an extension of existing administrative means. He termed the phenomenon "state involution." I think the concept can be appropriately applied to postrevolutionary China to describe the reforms that took place in the shadow of the Marxist state bureaucracy built up over the previous three decades.

6. The Huancheng area is 111 kilometers southwest of Guangzhou. It is also a short distance away from the special economic zone of Zhuhai.

7. See Oi (1986b) and Latham (1985) on the plight of the rural cadres in the decade of reforms. Oi argues that the cadres were able to take advantage of the reforms to become the entrepreneurial elite. See also Zweig (1986) on social conflicts during the reforms.

8. See Party Document Number 1 from 1982 to 1985 on the different stages of liberalization in the rural and urban sectors. A good analysis of these documents can be found in Liu (1985).

9. They were renamed *xiang* in 1983 and then *cun* in 1986.

10. As a matter of fact, the whole commune was slow in adopting *da bao gan*. By the summer of 1982, 98 of 191 teams in the commune had distributed land to the households. Fewer than half practiced *da bao gan*.

11. Peasants all agreed that rice yields had already peaked in 1963 at 1,206 catties per mu and again in 1977 at 1,256 catties per mu.

12. A construction worker could earn 5 to 10 yuan a day, depending on his skills and the season.

13. A similar situation in a market town in neighboring Zhongshan County in the mid-1980s is described by Siu (1989).

14. A good indicator of the lack of growth in the market town is the fact that the nonagricultural population in Huancheng remained virtually the same for twenty years.

15. See Chan and Unger (1983) on the second economy in rural China.

Chapter 13. Agents and Victims

1. This quote is taken from Siu (1986a).

2. This idea derives from conversations with William Kelly. See Scott (1977b, 1985) for a discussion of resistance within a dominant cultural mode.

3. See Ru (1983, 371–72). In 1979, she wrote a piece entitled "A Badly Edited Story" to portray the history of rural transformation through the eyes of a clear-headed but powerless old peasant. This passage is part of an essay she later wrote to explain why she decided on the story.

4. There is a vast literature on the relationship between changing moral paradigms, state hegemony, and resistance. The issues of intentionality and inevitability in moral discourse continue to be debated. Applying the insights of Mikhail Bakhtin and French critical theorists on social hierarchies, Stallybrass and White (1986) use four centuries of European literary and cultural history to analyze symbolic domination and political change. The central issue they address is the degree to which rules of hierarchy and order are transgressed. Do people perpetuate cultural and political hegemony by actively internalizing what they perceive as inevitable, as Bourdieu would have it (1977), or do their actions suggest other ways of coming to terms with and challenging authority?

5. Cultural change and political economy can be fruitfully joined in scholarly analysis. Michael Taussig, for example, focuses on the process through which the symbolic, religious orders of the poor developed symbiotically with the spread of capitalism. In the folklore of contemporary plantation workers and miners in South America, the devil is "a stunningly apt symbol of the alienation experienced by peasants as they enter the ranks of the proletariat" (1980, xi). Another insightful example is provided by James Scott (1985), who analyzes the weapons of the weak in the moral discourse of a Malaysian village undergoing the green revolution. Similarly, Jean Comaroff investigates how the Tshidi of South Africa have transformed the signs and practices of their colonizers into a dynamic counterculture. In the development of their religious sects, the Tshidi demonstrate how a system of domination is reproduced and at the same time resisted (1985).

6. See Sangren (1987) for a recent revision of the works of both Skinner and Wolf. He focuses on the cultural reproduction of a community in Taiwan.

References

Abrams, Philip. 1982. *Historical Sociology*. Ithaca: Cornell University Press.

Ahern, Emily. 1973. *The Cult of the Dead in a Chinese Village*. Stanford: Stanford University Press.

———. 1976. "Segmentation in Chinese Lineages: A View through Written Genealogies." *American Ethnologist* 3:1–16.

———. 1981. *Chinese Rituals and Politics*. Cambridge: Cambridge University Press.

Alitto, Guy. 1979. "Rural Elites in Transition: China's Cultural Crisis and the Problem of Legitimacy." In *Select Papers from the Center for Far Eastern Studies*, ed. Susan Mann Jones, 218–75. Chicago: Center for Far Eastern Studies, University of Chicago.

American Rural Small-Scale Industry Delegation. 1977. *Rural Small-Scale Industry in the People's Republic of China*. Berkeley: University of California Press.

Anagnost, Ann. 1985. "The Beginning and End of an Emperor." *Modern China* 11, 2:147–76.

Asad, Talal. 1972. "Market Models, Class Structure and Consent: A Reconsideration of Swat Political Organization." *Man* 7, 1 (March): 74–94.

Baker, Hugh. 1966. "The Five Great Clans of the New Territories." *Journal of the Hong Kong Branch of the Royal Asiatic Society* 6:25–47.

———. 1968. *A Chinese Lineage: Sheung Shui*. London: Frank Cass.

Ba Lei. 1946. "Mianlin siwang de Xinhui nongmin" (Xinhui peasants on the verge of death). *Zhongguo nongcun banyuekan* 1, 1:22–27.

Bailey, F. G. 1969. *Stratagems and Spoils: A Social Anthropology of Politics*. New York: Schocken.

Balazs, Etienne. 1964. *Chinese Civilization and Bureaucracy*. New Haven: Yale University Press.

Barth, Fredrik. 1959. *Political Leadership among Swat Pathans*. London: Athlone Press.

Baum, Richard. 1975. *Prelude to Revolution*. New York: Columbia University Press.

Bendix, Reinhart. 1978. *Kings or People. Power and the Mandate To Rule*. Berkeley: University of California Press.

Bendix, Reinhart, et al., eds. 1968. *State and Society*. Berkeley: University of California Press.

Berger, Peter, and Thomas Luckmann. 1967. *The Social Construction of Reality*. New York: Doubleday.

Bernstein, Thomas. 1984. "Stalinism, Famine and the Chinese Peasant." *Theory and Society* 13, 3:339–77.

341

Blok, Anton. 1974. *The Mafia of a Sicilian Village, 1860–1960: A Study of Violent Peasant Entrepreneurs*. New York: Harper and Row.

Bourdieu, P. 1977. *Outline of a Theory of Practice*. Trans. R. Nice. Cambridge: Cambridge University Press.

Brewer, Anthony. 1979. *Marxist Theories of Imperialism*. London: Routledge & Kegan Paul.

Caizheng Jingji Chubanshe. 1955. "Nongcun liangshi tonggou tongxiao zanxing banfa" (Provisional measures for the unified purchase and sales of grain in the rural areas). In *Nongcun liangshi tonggou tongxiao he shizhen liangshi dingliang gongying*, 24–112. Beijing.

Chan, Anita, Richard Madsen, and Jonathan Unger. 1984. *Chen Village*. Berkeley: University of California Press.

Chan, Anita, and Jonathan Unger. 1983. "The Second Economy of Rural China." In *Studies in the Second Economy of the Communist Countries*, ed. Gregory Grossman. Berkeley: University of California Press.

Chan, Kam Wing, and Xueqiang Xu. 1985. "Urban Population Growth and Urbanization in China Since 1949: Reconstructing a Baseline." *China Quarterly* 104 (December): 583–613.

Chang, Chung-li. 1955. *The Chinese Gentry*. Seattle: Washington University Press.

Chang Gong, et al. 1950. *Guangdong de jiefang* (The liberation of Guangdong). Guangzhou.

Chao Lian. 1986. "Yimin qiao, Shenchong qiao, Zhongxin lu—jian da Mo shizhong tongzhi" (Yimin bridge, Shenchong bridge, Zhongxin road—a reply to comrade Mo Shizhong). In *Xinhui wenshi ziliao xuanji* 22:68–69, 73.

Chaolian xiangzhi (Chaolian township gazetteer). 1946.

Chen, Ch'i-nan. 1984. *Fang and chia-tsu: The Chinese Kinship System in Rural Taiwan*. Ph.D. diss., Yale University.

Chen Chunsheng. 1987. "Lun qingdai Guangdong de changpingcang" (On the state granaries of Guangdong in the Qing period). Paper presented at the International Conference on Qing Regional Social Economic History, December 1987, in Shenzhen, China.

Chen, Ta. 1940. *Emigrant Communities in South China*. New York: Institute of Pacific Relations.

Chen, Han-seng. 1936. *Agrarian Problems in Southernmost China*. Shanghai: Kelly & Walsh.

Chen Jiangtian. 1956. "Ba Xinhui jiancheng shehuizhuyi de Xinhui" (Build Xinhui into a socialist county). In *Zhongguo renmin zhengzhixieshang huiyi Guangdong sheng Xinhui xian weiyuanhui diyici quanti huiyi huikan*, 12–13. Huicheng: Zhongguo Renmin Zhengzhixieshang Huiyi, Guangdong Sheng Xinhui Xian Weiyuanhui, Mishuchu.

Chen Ruojin. 1964. "Chen Lin liangzu xiedou de qiyin" (The cause of the lineage feud between the Chen and the Lin). In *Wenshi ziliao xuanji* 2:16–21. Huicheng: Xinhui Xian Zhengxie Wenshi Ziliao Gongzuozu (abbreviated hereafter as Xinhui Xian Zhengxie).

Chen Xiangheng. 1963. "Chen Lin xiedou jishi" (An account of the lineage feud between the Chen and the Lin). In *Wenshi ziliao xuanji* 15:11–20. Huicheng: Xinhui Xian Zhengxie.

Chen Xujing. 1946. *Danmin de yanjiu* (A study of the Dan people). Shanghai.

Chen Yifeng. 1984. "Xinhui xian tugai xuanchuan gongzuodui huodong riji" (A diary of the activities of the land reform propaganda team in Xinhui). In *Xinhui wenshi ziliao xuanji* 16:36–47. Huicheng: Xinhui Xian Zhengxie.

Chen Yun. 1981. *Chen Yun tongzhi wengao xuanbian, 1956–1962* (The selected writings of Comrade Chen Yun, 1956–1962). Ed. Zhonggong, Zhongyang Shujichu, Yanjiushi. Beijing: Renmin Chubanshe.

———. 1982. *Chen Yun wengao xuanbian, 1949–1956* (The selected writings of Chen Yun, 1949–1956). Ed. Zhonggong, Zhongyang Shujichu. Beijing: Renmin Chubanshe.

Chen, Yung-fa. 1986. *Making Revolution: The Communist Movement in Eastern and Central China, 1937–1945.* Berkeley: University of California Press.

Chen Zhanbiao. 1984. "Liang Qichao jiating chushen de diaocha cailiao" (Investigation materials on the family background of Liang Qichao). In *Xinhui wenshi ziliao xuanji* 13:1–4. Huicheng: Xinhui Xian Zhengxie.

———. 1985. "Xinhai geminghou Jianghui diqu zhengju fasheng de shijian" (Political events in the Jiangmen-Xinhui Area after the 1911 Revolution). In *Xinhui wenshi ziliao xuanji* 17:23–29. Huicheng: Xinhui Xian Zhengxie.

Chen Zhengxiang. 1978. *Guangdong dizhi* (A geography of Guangdong). Hong Kong: Tiandi Tushu Gongsi.

Chen Zhongheng and He Dayun. 1984. "Kangzhan chuqi Huicheng de Qing Qing She" (The Qing Qing Association in Huicheng early in the war of resistance). In *Xinhui wenshi ziliao xuanji* 14:28–31. Huicheng: Xinhui Xian Zhengxie.

Chen Zhoutang. 1986. *Guangdong diqu Taiping Tianguo shiliao xuanbian* (A selection of historical materials on the Taipings in Guangdong). Guangzhou: Guangdong Renmin Chubanshe.

Chenzu shipu (Genealogy of the Chen lineage). 1923. Huicheng.

Choujian Xinhui shuyuan zhengxinlu (The public account of the planning for the Xinhui academy). 1927.

Ch'u, T'ung-Tsu. 1962. *Local Government under the Ch'ing.* Stanford: Stanford University Press.

Cohen, Myron L. 1969. "Agnatic Kinship in South Taiwan." *Ethnology* 8:167–82.

Comaroff, Jean. 1985. *Body of Power, Spirit of Resistance: The Culture and History of a South African People.* Chicago: University of Chicago Press.

Crook, David, and Isabel Crook. 1959. *Revolution in a Chinese Village: Ten Mile Inn.* London: Routledge & Kegan Paul.

Dang Xiangmin. 1956. "Diaodong yiqie liliang, ba Xinhui jianshe hao" (Mobilize every effort to build up Xinhui). In *Zhonguo renmin zhengzhixieshang huiyi Guangdong sheng Xinhui xian weiyuanhui diyici quanti huiyi huikan,* 3–8. Huicheng: Zhongguo Renmin Zhengzhixieshang Huiyi, Guangdong Shen Xinhui Xian Weiyuanhui, Mishuchu.

Davis, Natalie. 1965. *Society and Culture in Early Modern France.* Stanford: Stanford University Press.

Davis-Friedmann, Deborah. 1983. *Long Lives.* Cambridge, Mass.: Harvard University Press.

De Groot, J. J. M. 1892–1910. *The Religious Systems of China.* Leiden: E. J. Brill.

Deng Zihui. 1950. "Guanyu tudigaige de jige jiben wenti" (On some basic problems of the land reform). In *Zhonggong de tudigaige,* ed. Dong Fangwang 1953. Hong Kong: Nanfeng Chubanshe.

Dong Fangwang. 1953. *Zhonggong de tudigaige* (The land reform of the Chinese Communists). Hong Kong: Nanfeng Chubanshe.

Donnithorne, Audrey. 1972. "China's Cellular Economy: Some Economic Trends since the Cultural Revolution." *China Quarterly* 52:605–19.

Du Runsheng. 1985. *Zhongguo nongcun jingji gaige* (Rural economic reforms in China). Beijing: Zhongguo Shehui Kexue Chubanshe.

Duara, Prasenjit. 1987. "State Involution: A Study of Local Finances in North China, 1911–1935." *Comparative Studies in Society and History* 29, 1:132–61.

———. 1988. *Culture, Power, and the State: Rural North China, 1900–1942.* Stanford: Stanford University Press.

Eberhard, Wolfram. 1962. *Social Mobility in Traditional China.* Leiden: E. J. Brill.

———. 1968. *The Local Cultures of South and East China.* Leiden: E. J. Brill.

Ebrey, Patricia, and James Watson, eds. 1986. *Kinship Organization in Late Imperial China, 1000–1940.* Berkeley: University of California Press.

Eckstein, Alexander. 1977. *China's Economic Revolution.* Cambridge: Cambridge University Press.

Eisenstadt, S. N., and René Lemarchand, eds. *Political Clientelism, Patronage and Development.* Beverly Hills: Sage.

Eng, Robert. 1986. "Institutional and Secondary Landlordism in the Pearl River Delta, 1600–1949." *Modern China* 12, 1:3–37.

Evans, Peter, et al., eds. 1985. *Bringing the State Back In.* Cambridge: Cambridge University Press.

Fang Fang. 1950. "Fang Fang fuzhuxi zai Guangdong sheng diyijie gejie renmin daibiao huiyi shang guanyu Guangdong tudigaige wenti de baogao" (A report to the First Provincial People's Congress by vice chairman Fang Fang on land reform in Guangdong). In *Guangdong tudigaige faling huibian.* Guangzhou: Guangdong Sheng Tudigaige Weiyuanhui.

Faure, David. 1985. "The Plight of the Farmers." In *Modern China* 11, 1:3–37.

———. 1986. *The Structure of Chinese Rural Society: Lineage and Village in the Eastern New Territories, Hong Kong.* Hong Kong: Oxford University Press.

———. n.d.-1. "Economic Development and Lineage Growth in Ming-Qing Guangdong." Unpublished paper.

———. n.d.-2. "Tax or No Tax: Notes on the Origin Myths of the Yao and the Cantonese." Unpublished paper.

———. 1989. "Lineage as a Cultural Invention: The Case of the Pearl River Delta." *Modern China* 15, 1:4–36.

Fei Xiaotong. 1948. *Xiangtu chongjian* (Rebuilding community). Shanghai: Guanchashe.

———. 1985. *Xiao chengzhen siji* (Four chapters on market towns). Beijing: Xinhua Chubanshe.

Fei Xiaotong and Wu Han. 1948. *Huangquan yu shenquan* (Imperial authority and gentry authority). Shanghai: Guanchashe.

Feng Hefa, ed. 1962. *Zhongguo nongcun jingji ziliao* (Materials on the Chinese rural economy). Huashi Chubanshe.

Forster, Robert, and Orest Ranum. 1982. *Ritual, Religion and the Sacred.* Baltimore: Johns Hopkins University Press.

Foucault, Michel, 1977. *Discipline and Punishment: The Birth of the Prison.* London: Penguin.

Freedman, Maurice. 1958. *Lineage Organization in Southeastern China.* London: Athlone Press.

―――. 1966. *Chinese Lineage and Society: Fukien and Kwangtung.* London: Athlone Press.

―――. 1974. "On the Sociological Study of Chinese Religion." In *Religion and Ritual in Chinese Society,* ed. Arthur Wolf, 19–41. Stanford: Stanford University Press.

Friedman, Edward. 1974. *Backward Toward Revolution.* Berkeley: University of California Press.

Frolic, Michael. 1980. *Mao's People.* Cambridge, Mass.: Harvard University Press.

Fu Yiling. 1961. *Ming-Qing nongcun shehui jingji* (Rural society and economy during the Ming and Qing). Beijing: Sanlian Shudian.

Gallin, Bernard. 1966. "Matrilateral and Affinal Relationships in a Taiwanese Village." *American Anthropologist* 62:632–42.

Gan Weiguang. 1956. "Guanyu siying gongshangye de shehuizhuyi gaizao wenti de fayan" (Addressing the problem of the socialist transformation of private commerce). In *Zhongguo renmin zhengzhixieshang huiyi Guangdong sheng Xinhui xian weiyuanhui diyici quanti huiyi huikan,* 18–20. Huicheng: Zhongguo Renmin Zhengzhixieshang Huiyi, Guangdong Sheng Xinhui Xian Weiyuanhui, Mishuchu.

Geertz, Clifford. 1963. *Agricultural Involution.* Berkeley: University of California Press.

―――. 1973. *The Interpretation of Cultures.* New York: Basic Books.

―――. 1980. *Negara: The Theatre State in Nineteenth-Century Bali.* Princeton: Princeton University Press.

―――. 1983. *Local Knowledge.* New York: Basic.

―――. 1984. "Culture and Social Change: The Indonesian Case." *Man* 19:511–32.

Gellner, Ernest, and John Waterbury, eds. 1979. *Patrons and Clients.* London: Duckworth.

Giddens, Anthony. 1979. *Central Problems in Social Theory: Action, Structure and Contradiction in Social Analysis.* Cambridge: Cambridge University Press.

Gluckman, Max. 1956. *Custom and Conflict in Africa.* London: Basil Blackwell.

―――. 1963. *Order and Rebellion in Tribal Africa.* London: Cohen & West.

―――. 1969. "Interhierarchical Roles: Professional and Party Ethics in Tribal Areas in South Central Africa." In *Local-Level Politics,* ed. Marc Swartz, 69–94. London: University of London Press.

Granet, Marcel. 1922. *La religion des chinois.* Presses universitaires de France.

Grimm, Tilemann. 1977. "Academies and Urban Systems in Kwangtung." In *The City in Late Imperial China,* ed. G. William Skinner, 475–98. Stanford: Stanford University Press.

―――. 1985. "State and Power in Juxtaposition: An Assessment of Ming Despotism." In *The Scope of State Power in China,* ed. Stuart Schram, 27–50. London: School of Oriental and African Studies.

Guan Xiekuang. 1983. "Jiefangqian Xinhui kuiye jingying gaikuang" (The fan palm trade before the liberation). In *Xinhui wenshi ziliao xuanji* 12:1–28. Huicheng: Xinhui Xian Zhengxie. An earlier version appears in *Guangdong wenshi ziliao* (1980) 28:187–201.

Guang Xin. 1966. "Nongcun gongshe ban gongye de yige dianxing" (A typical example of commune industries). *Zhongguo xinwen* October 26. Guangzhou.

Guangdong Gangzhou shangfu zhangcheng quanjuan (The complete constitution of the Gangzhou commercial port in Guangdong). 1911.

Guangdong Gongshang Fudaochu Gongshangbu. 1948. *Liangguang gongshang jing-ji teji* (A special issue on the commerce of Guangdong and Guangxi). Guangzhou.

Guangdong Jiansheting Nonglinju Nongqing Baogaochu. 1936. *Xinhui kuiye diao-cha baogao* (An investigative report on Xinhui's fan palm industry). Guangzhou: Guangdong Jiansheting, Nonglinju, Jingjixi.

Guangdong Jingji Nianjian Bianzuan Weiyuanhui. 1941. *Guangdong jingji nianjian* (The economic yearbook of Guangdong). Guangzhou.

Guangdong Minzhengting. 1934. *Guangdong quansheng difang jiyao* (Local conditions in Guangdong Province). Guangzhou.

Guangdong Sheng Cehuiju. 1982. *Guangdong sheng xiantu ji* (County maps of Guangdong). Guangzhou: Guangdong Sheng Cehuiju.

Guangdong Sheng Lao Genjudi Jianshe Weiyuanhui Bangongshi. 1959. *Guangdong sheng geming lao genjudi jiben qingkuang tongji ziliao* [chugao] (Statistical material on the conditions of the old revolutionary bases of Guangdong). draft.

Guangdong Sheng Renmin Zhengfu. 1956. "Guangdong sheng 1956 nongcun liangshi tonggou tongxiao shishi xize" (Regulations on the unified purchase and sales of grain in Guangdong province for 1956). *Xinhui nongmin bao,* June 13.

Guangdong Sheng Renmin Zhengfu Minzu Shiwu Weiyuanhui. 1953. *Yangjiang yanhai ji Zhongshan gangkou shatian danmin yanjiu cailiao* (Materials on the Dan fishermen along the coast of Yangjiang and in the sands of Zhongshan). Guangzhou.

Guangdong Sheng Tudigaige Weiyuanhui. 1950a. *Guangdong tudigaige faling hui-bian* (Collected directives on land reform in Guangdong). Guangzhou.

———. 1950b. "Guangdong sheng tudigaige zhong huaqiao tudi chuli banfa" (Policies for handling the properties of overseas Chinese during land reform in Guangdong). In *Guangdong tudigaige faling huibian,* 16–17. Guangzhou.

———. 1950c. "Guangdong sheng tudigaige zhong shatian chuli banfa" (Policies on the sands during land reform in Guangdong). In *Guangdong tudigaige faling huibian,* 18–20. Guangzhou.

———. 1951. *Tuizu tuiya qingfei fanba yundong chubu zongjie yu jinhou renwu* (A preliminary summary of the campaign to retrieve rent and rental deposits and to struggle against local bosses, and its prospects). Guangzhou: Huanan Renmin Chubanshe.

Guangdong Sheng Yinhang Jingji Yanjiushi. 1941. *Guangdong gedi jingji diaocha* (Investigations of the local economies in Guangdong). Guangzhou.

Guangdong Sheng Zhengfu Caizhengting. 1929. *Guangdong caizheng yaolan* (A survey of financial administration in Guangdong). Guangzhou.

Guangdong Xinhui Shanghui. 1907. *Guangdong Xinhui Shanghui gonghuibao* (Regulations of the Xinhui Chamber of Commerce, Guangdong). n.p.

Guangzhou Xiangshan Gonghui. 1912. *Donghai Shiliusha wushiyunian zhi tongshi* (Over fifty years of sorrow in the Sixteen Sands area of Donghai). Guangzhou.

———. 1912. *Donghai Shiliusha jishi* (A verified account of the Sixteen Sands area of Donghai). Guangzhou.

Guoli Zhongshan Daxue Nongke Xueyuan. 1925. *Guangdong nongye gaikuang diao-cha* (A survey of general agricultural conditions in Guangdong). 2 vols. Guangzhou.

Hai Feng. 1971. *Guangzhou diqu wenge licheng shulüe* (An account of the Cultural Revolution in the Canton area). Hong Kong: Union Research Institute.

Harrison, James. 1968. *The Communists and Chinese Peasant Rebellions: A Study in the Rewriting of Chinese History.* New York: Atheneum.

Hayes, James. 1977. *The Hong Kong Region, 1850–1911.* Hamden: Archon Books.

He Bai. 1948. "Zhongzai Xinhui yihou Li Boqian" (Reprimanding the county head of Xinhui Li Boqian). *Guangdong siyi qiaobao,* 16, 4, 2:29–30. Hong Kong.

He Dayun. 1982. "Kangri zhanzheng chuqi de Xinhui qingnian shuqi xunlianying" (The summer youth-training camps in Xinhui at the beginning of the anti-Japanese war). In *Xinhui wenshi ziliao xuanji* 7:57–59. Huicheng: Xinhui Xian Zhengxie.

————. 1983. "Wo canjia Xinhui 'Jiemeng' gongzuo de gaikuang" (My participation in the Liberation Alliance of Xinhui). In *Xinhui wenshi ziliao xuanji* 10:8–11. Huicheng: Xinhui Xian Zhengxie.

He Dayun and Zhao Gongqing. 1981. "Kangzhan chuqi Huicheng de kangri jiuwang xuanchuan tuanti" (Anti-Japanese patriotic propaganda groups early in the anti-Japanese war). In *Xinhui wenshi ziliao xuanji* 4:10–16. Huicheng: Xinhui Xian Zhengxie.

He Jitang. 1985. "Wo suo zhidao de Gangzhou junhe malu" (The Gangzhou highway as I knew it). In *Xinhui wenshi ziliao xuanji* 20:14–22. Huicheng: Xinhui Xian Zhengxie.

————. 1986. "Wo suo zhidao de Zhao Qixiu" (Zhao Qixiu as I knew him). In *Xinhui wenshi ziliao xuanji* 22:24–29. Huicheng: Xinhui Xian Zhengxie.

He shi jiapu (Genealogy of the He lineage).1864. Reprinted in Huicheng, 1986.

He Zhiping, and Yang Jianbai. 1980. "Guanyu gaishan dang dui jitinongye lingdao de wenti" (On the party's effort to improve rural collective leadership). *Nongye jingji wenti* (April):2–9.

He Zhuojian. 1963. "Shangshufang He shi de fengjian zuzhi" (The feudal organization of the He lineage of Shangshufang). In *Wenshi ziliao xuanji* 1:51–56. Huicheng: Xinhui Xian Zhengxie.

————. 1965a. "Jiefangqian de Xinhui chenpiye"(The orange peel trade in Xinhui before the liberation). In *Guangdong wenshi ziliao* 20:111–21. Guangzhou: Zhongguo Renmin Zhengzhi Xieshang Huiyi, Guangdong Sheng Weiyuanhui, Wenshi Ziliao Yanjiu Weiyuanhui (Abbreviated hereafter as Guangdong Sheng Zhengxie).

————. 1965b. "Xinhui kuiye shilüe" (A brief history of the fan palm trade of Xinhui). In *Guangdong wenshi ziliao* 15:132–51. Guangzhou: Guangdong Sheng Zhengxie.

————. 1985. "Xinhui xian Xi'nan Xuetang ji Gangzhou Zongxue xiaoshi" (A brief history of the Xi'nan Academy and Gangzhou Middle School in Xinhui). In *Xinhui wenshi ziliao xuanji* 17:6–12. Huicheng: Xinhui Xian Zhengxie.

————. 1986. "Huicheng zhen siying gongshangye jieshou shehui zhuyi gaizao qianhou de huiyi" (Recollections of the socialist transformation of private enterprises in Huicheng). In *Xinhui wenshi ziliao xuanji* 22:44–52. Huicheng: Xinhui Xian Zhengxie.

Henderson, Gail E., and Myron S. Cohen. 1984. *The Chinese Hospital: A Socialist Work Unit.* New Haven: Yale University Press.

Hinton, William. 1966. *Fanshen: A Documentary of Revolution in a Chinese Village.* New York: Monthly Review Press.

Ho, Ping-ti. 1962. *The Ladder of Success in Imperial China: Aspects of Social Mobility, 1368–1911.* New York: Columbia University Press.

Hobsbawm, Eric. 1965. *Primitive Rebels: Studies in Archaic Forms of Social Movement in the Nineteenth and Twentieth Centuries.* New York: Norton.

Hobsbawm, Eric, and Terrence Ranger. 1983. *The Invention of Tradition.* Cambridge: Cambridge University Press.

Hsiao, Kung-chuan. 1960. *Rural China: Imperial Control in the Nineteenth Century.* Seattle: University of Washington Press.

Hsieh, Winston. 1974. "Peasant Insurrections and the Marketing Hierarchy in the Canton Delta, 1911." In *The Chinese City Between Two Worlds,* ed. Mark Elvin and G. William Skinner, 119–142. Stanford: Stanford University Press.

Hu Erren. 1982. "Bayi nongmin dangjia zouzhu" (Eight hundred million peasants are their own masters). *Renmin ribao,* December 27.

Hua, Linshan. 1987. *Les Années rouges.* Translated from Chinese by Henri Leuwen and Isabelle Thireau. Paris: Editions du Seuil.

Huanan Chengxiang Wuzijiaoliu Zhidao Weiyuanhui. 1952. *Guangdong tutechan jieshao* (Introducing the local products of Guangdong). Guangzhou.

Huang Fa, Zhang Hou, and Xu Ji. 1983. "Huicheng cumihang he nianmiye de shengshuai" (The rise and decline of the grain trade and grain milling in Huicheng). In *Xinhui wenshi ziliao xuanji* 12:29–39. Huicheng: Xinhui Xian Zhengxie.

Huang Lun. 1983. "Xinning tielu kuahai luxian weihe shejin qiuyuan" (Why did Xinning railroad take the long route) In *Xinhui wenshi ziliao xuanji* 11:62. Huicheng: Xinhui Xian Zhengxie.

Huang, Philip. 1985. *The Peasant Economy and Social Change in North China.* Stanford: Stanford University Press.

Huang Yonghao, comp. 1987. *Xu Shu boshi suoji Guangdong zongzu qiju huilu* (Lineage land deeds from Guangdong collected by Dr. James Hayes). Tokyo: Tōyō bunka kenkyūjo.

Huang Zhaoxing. 1953. "Hezuoshe caiwugongzuo zhong sange wenti" (Three problems in the financial affairs of cooperatives). In *Gongfei tudizhengce yu nongminzuzhi zhi yanjiu,* 53. Taiwan: Zhongyang Weiyuanhui Shejikaohe Weiyuanhui.

Huicheng Zhen Gejie Renmin Fan Fengjianbao Chuban Weiyuanhui. 1952. *Fan fengjian* (Against feudalism). Nos. 4, 6, 12, and 19. Huicheng.

Ji Cheng. 1965. "Dongguan Mingluntang shilüe" (A brief history of the Mingluntang of Dongguan). In *Guangdong wenshi ziliao* 15:22–32. Guangzhou: Guangdong Sheng Zhengxie.

Jia Mu. 1964. "Liang Qichao guxiang shuwen" (Reflections on the native village of Liang Qichao). In *Guangdong wenshi ziliao* 12:126–29. Guangzhou: Guangdong Sheng Zhengxie.

Jian Yusheng and Zhang Guozhong. 1981. *Shenchandui ding'e guanli* (The management of piece rates in the production teams). Shenyang: Liaoning Renmin Chubanshe.

Jiangsu Sheng Xiaochengzhen Wenti Yanjiuzu. 1984. *Xiaochengzhen, dawenti* (Small towns, big issues). Jiangsu Renmin Chubanshe.

―――. 1986. *Xiaochengzhen, xinkaituo* (Small towns, new growth). Jiangsu Renmin Chubanshe.

Johnson, Chalmers. 1962. *Peasant Nationalism and Communist Power: The Emergence of Revolutionary China, 1937–1945*. Stanford: Stanford University Press.

Johnson, Kay. 1983. *Women, the Family, and Peasant Revolution in China*. Chicago: University of Chicago Press.

Katayama Tsuyoshi. 1982. "Shinmatsu Kōtōshō Shukō deruta no zukōsei ni tsuite—zeiro, koseki, dōzoku" (The local administration system of the Pearl River delta during the Qing—taxes, household registration and lineage). *Tōyō gakuhō* 63, nos. 3 and 4:1–34.

Kelly, William. 1985. *Deference and Defiance in Nineteenth-Century Japan*. Princeton: Princeton University Press.

Kertzer, David. 1988. *Ritual, Politics, and Power*. New Haven: Yale University Press.

Kraus, Richard. 1981. *Class Conflict in Chinese Socialism*. New York: Columbia University Press.

Kuhn, Philip. 1970. *Rebellion and Its Enemies in Late Imperial China*. Cambridge, Mass.: Harvard University Press.

―――. 1975. "Local Self-Government under the Republic: Problems of Control, Autonomy and Mobilization." In *Conflict and Control in Late Imperial China*, ed. Frederic Wakeman and Carolyn Grant, 257–98. Berkeley: University of California Press.

―――. 1979. "Local Taxation and Finance in Republican China." In *Select Papers from the Center for Far Eastern Studies*, ed. Susan Mann Jones, 100–136. Chicago: Center for Far Eastern Studies, University of Chicago.

Kuhn, Philip, and Susan Mann Jones. 1979. "Introduction." In *Select Papers from the Center for Far Eastern Studies*, ed. Susan Mann Jones, v–xix. Chicago: Center for Far Eastern Studies, University of Chicago.

Kuishanhang Heqinghui huigui (Regulations of the Heqing Association of the fan palm guild). 1885.

Kulp, Daniel. 1972. *Country Life in South China*. Taipei: Ch'eng Wen Publishing Company. Originally published in 1925 by the Bureau of Publications, Teachers' College, Columbia University.

Lardy, Nicholas. 1975. "Centralization and Decentralization in China's Fiscal Management." *China Quarterly* 61;25–60.

―――. 1976. "Reply to Audrey Donnithorne." *China Quarterly* 66:340–54.

―――. 1983. *Agriculture in China's Modern Economic Development*. Cambridge: Cambridge University Press.

―――. 1984. "Prices, Markets and the Chinese Peasant." In *Agricultural Development in the Third World*, ed. Carl Eicher and John Staatz, 420–35. Baltimore: Johns Hopkins University Press.

Lardy, Nicholas, and Kenneth Lieberthal. 1983. *Chen Yun's Strategy for China's Development*. New York: M. E. Sharpe.

Latham, Richard. 1985. "The Implications of Rural Reforms for Grass-root Cadres." In *The Political Economy of Reform in Post-Mao China*, ed. Elizabeth Perry and Christine Wong, 157–74. Cambridge, Mass.: Harvard University Press.

Lau, Siu-kai. 1975. "Monism, Pluralism and Segmental Coordination: Toward an Alternative Theory of Elite, Power and Social Stability." *Journal of the Chinese University of Hong Kong* 3, 1:187–206.

Law, Joan, and Barbara Ward. 1982. *Chinese Festivals*. Hong Kong: South China Morning Post.

Lee, Hong Yung. 1978. *The History of the Cultural Revolution: A Case Study*. Berkeley: University of California Press.

———. n.d. *The Socialist State, Political Elites, and Reforms in China*. Unpublished manuscript.

Lei Tongqun, ed. 1941. *Siyi bingzai fenxiang tachaji* (An on-the-ground investigation of the ravages of war in the Siyi). Hong Kong: Siyi Bingzai Tachatuan.

Le Roy Ladurie, Emmanuel. 1979. *Carnival of Romans*. New York: George Braziller.

Li Anzhi. 1982a. "Huicheng lunxian de huiyi pianduan" (Brief recollections on Huicheng during the Japanese occupation). In *Xinhui wenshi ziliao xuanji* 5:27–31. Huicheng: Xinhui Xian Zhengxie.

———. 1982b. "Guoqu shinian yijie de Delintang dahuijing" (The once-in-ten-years temple festival of Dilintang in the past). In *Xinhui wenshi ziliao xuanji* 6:55–58. Huicheng: Xinhui Xian Zhengxie.

Li Jian, and Hong Tao. 1952. *Xinhui Zhonggong baoxing shilu* (A verified account of the atrocities of the Communists in Xinhui). Hong Kong: Qiaosheng Tongxun Chubanshe.

Li Jinbo. 1982. "Jiangmen Huicheng liming qianhou" (At liberation in Jiangmen and Huicheng). In *Xinhui wenshi ziliao xuanji* 5:5–8. Huicheng: Xinhui Xian Zhengxie.

Li Langru and Lu Man. 1962. "Zhujiang sanjiaozhou de lülin haojie he datianer" (The heroes in the greenwoods and the local bosses of the Pearl River delta). In *Guangdong wenshi ziliao* 5:1–19. Guangzhou: Guangdong Sheng Zhengxie.

Li Mubai. 1954. *Zhongong zenyang shougou minjian wuzi* (How the Communists procure the people's resources). Hong Kong: Youlian Chubanshe.

Li Muzi. 1985. "'Jiangmen shijian' yu 'Chenggong Xiaozu'" (The Jiangmen incident and the City Work Small Group). In *Xinhui wenshi ziliao xuanji* 20:45–53. Huicheng: Xinhui Xian Zhengxie.

Li Rui. 1952. "Hunan nongcun de zhuangkuang he tedian" (Conditions and special features of rural areas in Hunan). In *Xinqu tudigaigeqian de nongcun*, 58–68. Beijing: Renmin Chubanshe.

Li Ruizi Tang zhengli changchan weihui yian bu (The minutes of the committee to sort and retrieve the ancestral estates of the Li Ruizi trust). 1946. Huicheng.

Li Yuncheng Tang. 1905. *Zhiqing zuci luocheng gongding cigui fu zhengxinlu* (Regulations of the newly established Zhiqing ancestral hall and the accounts). Huicheng.

Li Zhichen. 1921. *Li zu Shaoyin taizuci changye guanli guitiao* (Regulations for managing the estate of Shaoyin focal ancestral hall of the Li). Guangzhou.

Liang Zaoquan. 1919. *Xinhui Xi'nanfang shenshi renminglu* (Membership directory of the Xi'nan Academy). Huicheng: Wenming Shuju.

Liao Gailong. 1980. "Dang zai shehuizhuyi jieduan de lishi jingyan" (The historical experience of the party in the socialist stage). *Dangshi yanjiu* 6 (December).

Lin Datian. 1984. "Sanjiang Longquan xiedou de qianyin" (Factors leading to the feud between Sanjiang and Longquan). In *Xinhui wenshi ziliao xuanji* 13:39–40. Huicheng: Xinhui Xian Zhengxie.

———. 1986. "Huiyi Xinhui zhanshi xiangcun gongzuo xunlianban" (Reflections on the rural work training classes during the war in Xinhui). In *Xinhui wenshi ziliao xuanji* 22:36–37.

Lin Man Shu, Hai Feng, and Chen Hai, eds. 1978. *Histoire de la littérature en Ré-*

publique Populaire de Chine, 1949–1965. Paris: Centre de Publication Asie Orientale.

Lin Qichang. 1985. "Gangzhou malu de yixie huiyi" (Recollections of the Gangzhou road). In *Xinhui wenshi ziliao xuanji* 20:25–28. Huicheng: Xinhui Xian Zhengxie.

Lin Shidan. 1977. "Guangdong quansheng tianfu zhi yanjiu" (A study of the land tax in Guangdong). In *Minguo ershi niandai Zhongguo dalu tudi wenti ziliao,* ed. Xiao Zheng, Taipei: Zhongguo Dizheng Yanjiushuo Congshu.

Lin Zili. 1983. *Lun lianchang chenbaozhi* (On production responsibility systems). Shanghai: Shanghai Renmin Chubanshe.

Lippit, Victor, and Mark Selden, eds. 1979. *The Transition to Socialism in China.* New York: M. E. Sharpe.

Liu Airu. 1957. *Zhonggong zhengquan xia de nongmin wenti* (The peasant problem under the Chinese Communist regime). Hong Kong: Ziyou Chubanshe.

Liu Bogao. 1963a. "San Long xiedou" (The feud between Sanjiang and Longquan). In *Wenshi ziliao xuanji* 1:21–26. Huicheng: Xinhui Xian Zhengxie.

———. 1963b. "Riren ruqin Huicheng zhen lunxian gaikuang" (Huicheng under the Japanese occupation). In *Wenshi ziliao xuanji* 1:29–34. Huicheng: Xinhui Xian Zhengxie.

———. 1983. "Xinning Tielu xingjian shi zai Xinhui yudao de difang fengjian shili de zunao ji qita" (The obstructions by feudal powers over the construction of the Xinning Railroad). In *Xinhui wenshi ziliao xuanji* 9:9–11. Huicheng: Xinhui Xian Zhengxie.

Liu Bang. 1985. *Xueshi Zhongyang yihao wenjian zhengce jieda yibai ti* (A hundred answers to study the number one documents of the Party Central Committee). Beijing: Xinhua Chubanshe.

Liu Maochu, ed. 1934. *Guangdong jingji jishi* (A verified account of the economy of Guangdong). n.p.

Liu Maofeng wei zhengju zongbu (A collection of the records of the Liu Maofeng polder). 1932. Macao.

Liu Yousheng. 1981. "Huicheng lunxianhou jianwen huiyi" (Recollections of Huicheng during the Japanese Occupation). In *Xinhui wenshi ziliao xuanji* 4:35–42. Huicheng: Xinhui Xian Zhengxie.

Liu Zhiliang. 1948. "Shatian zhi chugao" (A draft gazetteer on the Sands). In *Zhongshan wenxian* 2:75–88. Zhongshan.

Liu Zhiwei. n.d. "Lun Qingdai Zhujiang sanjiaozhou diqu tujia zhong de 'hu' " (On the "tax account" in the tujia administrative divisions of the Pearl River delta). Unpublished paper.

Long Qingzhong, et al. 1985. *Nanhai shengmiao* (The temple of the Nanhai deity). Guangzhou: Guangzhou Shi Wenhuaju.

Lu Wen. 1965. "Hengxing Siyi de Zhou Hanling he Zhao Qixiu datianer jituan" (The local bosses of the Siyi—Zhou Hanling and Zhao Qixiu). In *Guangdong wenshi ziliao* 15:48–65. Guangzhou: Guangdong Sheng Zhengxie.

Lujiang He shi shiyuan (The genealogy of the He lineage of Lujiang). 1870. Vols. 1 and 3.

Lun Haibin. 1981. "Huicheng lunxian shiqi de canju" (The horrors in Huicheng during occupation). In *Xinhui wenshi ziliao xuanji* 4:43–45.

———. 1982. "Mani ren daohui 'Minquan bao' " (The attack on Minquan bao by the people of Mani). In *Xinhui wenshi ziliao xuanji* 6:47–50. Huicheng: Xinhui Xian Zhengxie.

————. 1983. "Cong fukan dao tingkan—kangzhan shenglihou de 'Minquan bao'" (From reopening to closingdown—The Minquan bao after the Japanese war). In *Xinhui wenshi ziliao xuanji* 10:36–46. Huicheng: Xinhui Xian Zhengxie.

MacFarquhar, Roderick. 1974, 1983. *The Origins of the Cultural Revolution.* Vols. 1 and 2. New York: Columbia University Press.

Madsen, Richard. 1984. *Morality and Power in a Chinese Village.* Berkeley: University of California Press.

Mai Bingkun and Huang Xiaonan. 1965. "Xinhui cheng shangtuan shimo" (An account of the merchant militia of Xinhui). In *Wenshi ziliao xuanji* 3:1–19. Huicheng: Xinhui Xian Zhengxie.

Mann, Susan. 1987. *Local Merchants and the Chinese Bureaucracy. 1750–1950.* Stanford: Stanford University Press.

Marks, Robert. 1984. *Rural Revolution in South China.* Wisconsin: University of Wisconsin Press.

Matsuda Yoshiro. 1981. "Minmatsu Shinsho Kanton deruta no shadan kaihatsu to kyōshin shihai no kesei katei" (Rural gentry control and the development of the sands in the Pearl River delta in the late Ming and the early Qing). *Shakai keizai shigaku* 46, 6:55–81.

Mao Zedong. 1982. *Mao Zedong nongcun diaocha wenji* (Collected rural investigations by Mao Zedong). Ed. Zhonggong, Zhongyang, Wenxian Yanjiushi. Beijing: Renmin Chubanshe. Originally published in 1941.

Meisner, Maurice. 1967. *Li Ta-Chao and the Origins of Chinese Marxism.* Cambridge, Mass.: Harvard University Press.

————. 1986. *Mao's China and After.* New York: Free Press.

Meskill, Johanna. 1979. *A Chinese Pioneer Family: The Lins of Wu-feng, Taiwan, 1729–1895.* Princeton: Princeton University Press.

Michael, Franz. 1964. "State and Society in Nineteenth-Century China." *World Politics* 7, 3:419–33.

Mo Rongfang and Xu Zhongtao. 1964. "Xinhui xian chaicheng zhulu de jingguo" (An account of tearing down the city walls to build a road in Xinhui county). In *Wenshi ziliao xuanji* 2:20–29. Huicheng: Xinhui Xian Zhengxie.

Mo Shizhong. 1986. "'Aimen lu jieming kao' zhiyi" (A query on the name of Aimen road). In *Xinhui wenshi ziliao xuanji* 22:65–67.

Mori Masao. 1986. "Weirao 'xiangzu' wenti" (On the question of lineage community). *Zhongguo shehui jingjishi yanjiu* 2:1–8.

Mu Fu. 1984. "Zhonggong zhiguo de sanci dacuobai" (The three political failures of the Chinese Communists). *Jiushi niandai* 177:41–48.

Muramatsu, Yuji. 1966. "A Documentary Study of Chinese Landlordism in Late Qing and Early Republican Jiangnan." *Bulletin of the School of Oriental and African Studies* 29, 3:566–99.

Nanmen Mo shi zupu (The genealogy of the Mo lineage). 1921.

Nanzhong Tongxunshe Ziliaoshi. 1947. *Guangdong fengyun* (The volatile political scene of Guangdong). Hong Kong: Yinshua Gongye Hezuoshe.

Nathan, Andrew. 1973. "A Factional Model for Chinese Politics." *China Quarterly* 53:34–66.

Nee, Victor, and David Mozingo, eds. 1983. *State and Society in Contemporary China.* Ithaca: Cornell University Press.

Nie Erkang. 1867. *Gangzhou gongdu* (Public pronouncements while in office in Gangzhou).

Ning Ke. 1985. "Shu 'sheyi'" (On community shrines). *Beijing shifan xueyuan xuebao* 1:12–24.

Nishikawa Kikuko. 1985. "Qingdai Zhujiang sanjiaozhou shatian kao" (A study of the sands of the Pearl River delta). Trans. Cao Lei. *Lingnan wenshi* 2:11–22. Originally published in *Tōyō gakuho* 63, 1, 2 (1981): 93–136.

Nongye Chubanshe. 1971–78. *Nongye xue Dazhai* (Learn from Dazhai in agriculture). Vols. 7–22. Beijing.

Nongyezhi. See *Zhujiang Sanjiaozhou nongyezhi.*

Oi, Jean. 1983. *State and Peasant in Contemporary China: The Politics of Grain Procurement.* Ph.D. diss., University of Michigan.

———. 1985. "Communism and Clientelism: Rural Politics in China." *World Politics* 37, 2 (January): 238–66.

———. 1986a. "Peasant Grain Marketing and State Procurement: China's Grain Contracting System." *China Quarterly* 106 (June): 272–90.

———. 1986b. "Commercializing China's Rural Cadres." *Problems of Communism* (September–October): 1–15.

Ortner, Sherry. 1984. "Theory in Anthropology since the Sixties." *Comparative Studies in Society and History* 26, 1:126–66.

Ouyang Jianmei zuci jichang lunchangbu (Records of the rotating ritual estate of the Ouyang Jianmei ancestral hall). 1930. Huicheng.

Pan Guangdan and Quan Weitian. 1952. *Sunan tudigaige fangwenji* (A study tour of land reform in southern Jiangsu). Beijing: Sanlian Shudian.

Parish, William, and Martin Whyte. 1978. *Village and Family in Contemporary China.* Chicago: University of Chicago Press.

Pasternak, Burton. 1969. "The Role of the Frontier in Chinese Lineage Development." *Journal of Asian Studies* 28:551–61.

Peng Qiuping. 1980. "Huigu Luiyi qiyi" (Recollections of the insurrection in the six counties). In *Guangdong wenshi ziliao* 26:229–42. Guangzhou: Guangdong Sheng Zhengxie.

Pepper, Suzanne. 1986. "Post-Mao Reforms in Chinese Education." University Field Staff International Reports, no. 10. Indiana: UFSI.

Perry, Elizabeth. 1980. *Rebels and Revolutionaries in North China, 1845–1945.* Stanford: Stanford University Press.

———. 1984. "Collective Violence in China, 1880–1980." *Theory and Society* 13, 3:427–54.

———. 1985. "Rural Violence in Socialist China." *China Quarterly* 103 (September): 414–40.

Perry, Elizabeth, and Christine Wong, eds. 1985. *The Political Economy of the Reform in Post-Mao China.* Cambridge, Mass.: Harvard University Press.

Potter, Jack. 1970. "Land and Lineage in Traditional China." In *Family and Kinship in Chinese Society,* ed. Maurice Freedman, 121–38. Stanford: Stanford University Press.

Qi Jiu. 1964. "Dongguan datianer Liu Faru" (The local boss Liu Faru of Dongguan). In *Guangdong wenshi ziliao* 16: 66–86. Guangzhou: Guangdong Sheng Zhengxie.

Qin Qingjun. 1983. "Minguo shiqi Guangdong caizheng shiliao, 1911–1949" (A history of the financial administration in Guangdong, 1911–1949). In *Guangzhou wenshi ziliao* 29:1–115. Guangzhou: Guangdong Sheng Zhengxie.

Qiu Bincun. 1941. *Guangdong shatian* (The sands of Guangdong). Qujiang: Diyi Zhanqu Bianzuan Weiyuanhui.

Qiu Zuohua et al., eds. 1986. *Zhujiang sanjiaozhou jingji kaifangqu touzi zhinan* (An investment guide for the open economic zones of the Pearl River delta). Hong Kong: Xinhua Chubanshe.

Qu Dajun. [1700] 1985. *Guangdong xinyu* (New items relating to Guangdong). Reprint. Beijing: Zhonghua Shuju, 1985.

Rankin, Mary. 1986. *Elite Activism and Political Transformation in China, Zhejiang Province, 1865–1911.* Stanford: Stanford University Press.

Ren, Bishi. [1948] 1949. "Tudigaige zhong de jige wenti" (Several problems arising from the land reform). In *Tugai zhengdang dianxing jingyan*, ed. Liu Shaoqi, 43–60. Hong Kong: Zhongguo Chubanshe.

Renmin Chubanshe. 1952. *Xinqu tudigaigeqian de nongcun* (The newly liberated countryside before the land reform). Beijing: Renmin Chubanshe.

Renmin ribao. 1953a. "Jiaqiang liangshi shougou zhong de jingji gongzuo" (Strengthen the economic work in the procurement of grain) November 30 editorial. In *Nongye shehuizhuyi gaizao wenji* (1955) 1:219–24. Beijing: Caizheng Jingji Chubanshe.

———. 1953b. "Jiaqiang liangshi shougou zhong de zhengzhi gongzuo" (Strengthen the political work in the procurement of grain) November 23 editorial. In *Nongye shehuizhuyi gaizao wenji* (1955) 1:225–29. Beijing: Caizheng Jingji Chubanshe.

———. 1954a. "Gongxiaohezuoshe bixu guanche wei nongye shengchan fuwu de fangzhen" (The supply and marketing cooperatives must implement the goal of serving agricultural production). July 26 editorial. In *Nongye shehuizhuyi gaizao wenti* (1955) 1:273–78. Beijing: Caizheng Jingji Chubanshe.

———. 1954b. "Liangshi gongzuo dangqian de zhongyao renwu" (The important goal of the present grain policies). February 10 editorial. In *Nongye shehuizhuyi gaizao wenji* (1955) 1:201–6. Beijing: Caizheng Jingji Chubanshe.

———. 1954c. "Liangshi jihua shougou he jihua gongying shi zongluxian de yige zhongyao zucheng bufen" (The planned purchase and supply of grain is an important component of the general policy line). March 1 editorial.

———. 1954d. "Liangshi tonggou tongxiao dui nongmin de haochu" (The benefits of unified purchase and sale of grain for the peasants). November 17 editorial. In *Nongye shehuizhuyi gaizao wenji* (1955) 1:230–36. Beijing: Caizheng Jingji Chubanshe.

Riskin, Carl. 1978. "Rural Industry: Self-Reliant Systems or Independent Kingdoms." *China Quarterly* 73:77–98.

Rosen, Stanley. 1982. *Red Guard Factionalism and the Cultural Revolution in Guangzhou (Canton).* Boulder: Westview Press.

Rowe, William. 1985. *Hankow: Commerce and Society in a Chinese City, 1796–1889.* Stanford: Stanford University Press.

Ru Zhijuan. 1983. "Wo dui chuangzuo de yidian kanfa" (My views on creative writing). In *Ru Zhijuan xiaoshuo xuan.* Chengdu: Sichuan Renmin Chubanshe.

Sabean, David. 1984. *Power in the Blood: Popular Culture and Village Discourse in Early Modern Germany.* Cambridge: Cambridge University Press.

Sangren, Steven. 1987. *History and Magical Power in a Chinese Community.* Stanford: Stanford University Press.

Schmidt, Steffen, et al., eds. 1977. *Friends, Followers and Factions.* Berkeley: University of California Press.

Schoppa, Keith. 1982. *Chinese Elite and Political Change: Zhejiang Province in the Early Twentieth Century.* Cambridge: Harvard University Press.

Schram, Stuart. 1969. *The Political Thought of Mao Tse-tung.* New York: Praeger.
———. ed. 1985. *The Scope of State Power in China.* London: School of Oriental and African Studies.
Schurmann, Franz. 1968. *Ideology and Organization in Communist China.* Berkeley: University of California Press.
Scott, James. 1976. *The Moral Economy of the Peasant.* New Haven: Yale University Press.
———. 1977a. "Political Clientelism: A Bibliographical Essay." In *Friends, Followers and Factions,* ed. Steffen Schmidt et al., 483–505. Berkeley: University of California Press.
———. 1977b. "Protests and Profanation." *Theory and Society* 4, 1:1–38.
———. 1985. *Weapons of the Weak: Everyday Forms of Ideological Struggle.* New Haven: Yale University Press.
Selden, Mark. 1971. *The Yenan Way in Revolutionary China.* Cambridge, Mass.: Harvard University Press.
———. 1979. *The People's Republic of China: A Documentary History of Revolutionary Change.* New York: Monthly Review Press.
Shangyebu. See Shangyebu Shangye Jingji Yanjiusuo 1984.
Shangyebu Shangye Jingji Yanjiusuo. 1984. *Xin Zhongguo shangye shigao, 1949–1982* (A history of commerce in new China, 1949–1982). Beijing: Caizheng Jingji Chubanshe.
Shen, Guanbao. "Town Systems and Chinese Urbanization." Unpublished paper.
Shi Jingtang et al., eds. 1957. *Zhongguo nongye hezuohua yundong shiliao* (Historical materials on the cooperative movement in China). Vol. 1. Beijing: Sanlian.
Shue, Vivienne. 1980. *Peasant China in Transition: The Dynamics of Development Toward Socialism, 1949–1956.* Berkeley: University of California Press.
———. 1985. "The Reach of the State: Modernization and the Reform of Local Government in China." Unpublished paper.
———. 1988. *The Reach of the State.* Stanford: Stanford University Press.
Sigurdson, Jon. 1977. *Rural Industrialization in China.* Cambridge, Mass.: Harvard University Press.
Silverman, Sydel. 1979. "On the Uses of History in Anthropology: The Palio of Siena." *American Ethnologist* 6, 3:413–36.
Siu, Helen. 1986a. "Collective Economy, Authority and Political Power in Rural China." In *Political Anthropology, vol. 5: The Frailty of Authority,* ed. Myron Aronoff, 9–50. New Brunswick: Transaction.
———. 1986b. "Emigrants and Social Ethos: Hong Kong in the 1980s." *Journal of the Hong Kong Branch of the Royal Asiatic Society* 26:1–16. Hong Kong.
———. 1987. "Reforming Tradition: Politics and Popular Rituals in Contemporary Rural China." Paper presented at the Conference on Popular Thought in Contemporary China, October 1987, San Diego
———. 1988. "Recycling Tradition: Culture, History, and Political Economy in the Chrysanthemum Festivals of South China." Paper presented at Ethnohistory Seminar, October 1988, at The University of Pennsylvania.
———. 1989. "Socialist Peddlers and Princes in a Chinese Market Town." *American Ethnologist* 16, 2 (May).
Siu, Helen, and Zelda Stern, eds. 1983. *Mao's Harvest: Voices from China's New Generation.* New York: Oxford University Press.

Skinner, G. William. 1964, 1965. "Marketing and Social Structure in Rural China." *Journal of Asian Studies* 24, 1:3–43; 24, 2:195–228; 24, 3:363–99.

———. 1971. "Chinese Peasants and the Closed Community: An Open and Shut Case." *Comparative Studies in Society and History* 13, 3:270–81.

———. 1977. *The City in Late Imperial China.* Stanford: Stanford University Press.

———. 1985a. "Presidential Address: The Structure of Chinese History." *Journal of Asian Studies* 104, 2:271–92.

———. 1985b. "Rural Marketing in China: Repression and Revival." *China Quarterly* 103 (September): 393–413.

Solinger, Dorothy. 1984. *Chinese Business under Socialism.* Berkeley: University of California Press.

Stacey, Judith. 1983. *Patriarchy and Socialist Revolution in China.* Berkeley: University of California Press.

Stallybrass, Peter, and Allon White. 1986. *The Politics and Poetics of Transgression.* Ithaca: Cornell University Press.

Starr, John. 1979. *Continuing the Revolution: The Political Thought of Mao.* Princeton: Princeton University Press.

Strauch, Judith. 1983. "Community and Kinship in Southeastern China: The View of the Multi-Lineage Villages of Hong Kong." *Journal of Asian Studies* 103, 1:21–50.

Sun Jingzhi et al., eds. 1959. *Huanan diqu jingjidili* (An economic geography of south China). Beijing: Kexue Chubanshe.

Sun Longji. 1983. *Zhongguo wenhua de shenceng jiegou* (The deep structure of Chinese culture). Hong Kong: I-shan Publishers.

Swartz, Marc. 1969. Introduction. In *Local-Level Politics,* ed. Marc Swartz, 1–46. London: University of London Press.

Taiwan Sōtoku-fu, Gaiji-bu, Taikuku. 1943. *Minami Shina Soran* (Outline of South China). Taiwan: Taiwan Sōtoku-fu.

Tambiah, Stanley. 1985. *Culture, Thought, and Social Action.* Cambridge, Mass.: Harvard University Press.

Tan Xingyue. 1956. "Guanyu nongye shengchan hezuo wenti de fayan" (An address on the problems of agricultural cooperativization). In *Zhongguo renmin zhengzhixieshang huiyi guangdong sheng Xinhui xian weiyuanhui diyici quanti huiyi huikan,* 23–28. Huicheng: Zhongguo Renmin Zhengzhixieshang Huiyi, Guangdong Sheng Xinhui Xian Weiyuanhui, Mishuchu.

Tanaka Issei. 1981. *Chūgoku saishi engeki kenkyū* (A study of Chinese ritual and theater). Tokyo: Institute of Oriental Culture, University of Tokyo.

Tang, Jianzhong, and Laurence Ma. 1985. "Evolution of Urban Collective Enterprises." *China Quarterly* 104 (December): 614–40.

Tangang xiang zazhi (The Tangang township magazine). 1938. Huicheng: Guangdong Xinhui Xian Tangang Xiang Zazhishe.

Tangang (Xinhui) xingzu jijuhui guizhang (The regulations of the Tangang Association for the restoration of the lineage). 1916.

Tao Zhu. 1953. *Guanyu wunianjihua jingji jianshe zhong Huanan dang de renwu* (The party's targets in South China for economic construction during the First Five-Year Plan). Guangzhou: Huanan Renmin Chubanshe.

Taussig, Michael. 1980. *The Devil and Commodity Fetishism in South America.* Chapel Hill: University of North Carolina Press.

Thaxton, Ralph. 1983. *China Turned Rightside Up: Revolutionary Legitimacy in the Peasant World.* New Haven: Yale University Press.

Thomas, R. D. 1903. *A Trip on the West River*. Canton: China Baptist Publication Society.

Thompson, E. P. 1974. "Patrician Society, Plebeian Culture." *Journal of Social History* 7, 4: 382–405.

Thompson, Roger. 1988. "Statecraft and Self-Government: Competing Visions of Community and State in Late Qing China." *Modern China* 14, 2:188–221.

Thurston, Ann, and Burton Pasternak, eds. 1984. *The Social Sciences and Fieldwork in China*. Boulder: AAAS and Westview Press.

Tongren Hao. 1887. *Shanhehang Tongren Hao jinzhisu nianjielu* (Annual accounts of the Tongren Enterprises of the Fan-Making Guild).

Tsou, Tang. 1976. "Prolegomenon to the Study of Informal Groups in ccp Politics." *China Quarterly* 65:98–113.

Tsou, Tang, ed. 1981. *Select Papers from the Center for Far Eastern Studies*. Chicago: Center for Far Eastern Studies, University of Chicago.

Turner, Victor. 1969. *The Ritual Process*. Chicago: Aldine.

Unger, Jonathan. 1982. *Education under Mao: Class and Competition in Canton Schools, 1960–1980*. New York: Columbia University Press.

———. 1984. "The Class System in Rural China: A Case Study." In *Class and Social Stratification in Post-Revolution China*, ed. James Watson, 121–41. Cambridge: Cambridge University Press.

Vincent, Joan. 1971. *The African Elite: The Big Man of the Small Town*. New York: Columbia University Press.

———. 1978. "Political Anthropology: Manipulative Strategies." *Annual Review of Anthropology* 7:175–94.

Vogel, Ezra. 1969. *Canton under Communism: Programs and Politics in a Provincial Capital, 1949–1968*. Cambridge, Mass.: Harvard University Press.

Wakeman, Frederic. 1966. *Strangers at the Gate: Social Disorder in South China, 1839–1861*. Berkeley: University of California Press.

———. 1973. *History and Will: Philosophical Perspectives of Mao Tse-tung's Thought*. Berkeley: University of California Press.

———. 1975a. "The Evolution of Local Control in Late Imperial China." In *Conflict and Control in Late Imperial China*, ed. Frederic Wakeman and Carolyn Grant, 1–25. Berkeley: University of California Press.

———. 1975b. *The Fall of Imperial China*. New York: Free Press.

Wan Nong. 1956. *Tantan nongye hezuohua yundong jieji zhengce de jige wenti* (A discussion of several problems with class policies in agricultural cooperativization). Beijing: Zhongguo Qingnian Chubanshe.

Wang Xiaoqiang. 1980. "Nongye shehuizhuyi pipan" (A critique of agrarian socialism). *Nongye jingji wenti* (February): 9–19.

Wang Xizhe. 1981. "Mao Zedong yu Wenhua Dageming" (Mao Zedong and the Cultural Revolution). In *Wang Xizhe lunwenji* (A collection of essays of Wang Xizhe). Hong Kong: Qishi niandai.

Ward, Barbara. 1979. "Not Merely Players: Dramas, Art and Ritual in Traditional China." *Man* 14:18–39.

———. 1985. *Through Other Eyes*. Hong Kong: Chinese University Press.

Watson, James. 1975. *Emigration and the Chinese Lineage*. Berkeley: University of California Press.

———. 1976. "Chattel Slavery in Chinese Peasant Society: A Comparative Analysis." *Ethnology* 15:361–75.

———. 1977. "Hereditary Tenancy and Corporate Landlordism in Traditional China." *Modern Asian Studies* 11:161–82.

———. 1982. "Chinese Kinship Reconsidered: Anthropological Perspectives on Historical Research." *China Quarterly* 92:589–627.

———, ed. 1984. *Class and Social Stratification in Post-Revolution China.* Cambridge: Cambridge University Press.

———. 1985. "Standardizing the Gods: The Promotion of T'ien Hou ("Empress of Heaven") along the South China Coast, 960–1960." In *Popular Culture in Late Imperial China,* ed. David Johnson, Andrew Nathan, and Evelyn Rawski, 292–324. Berkeley: University of California Press.

Watson, Rubie. 1985. *Inequality Among Brothers: Class and Kinship in South China.* Cambridge: Cambridge University Press.

Wechsler, Howard. 1985. *Offerings of Jade and Silk: Ritual and Symbol in the Legitimation of the T'ang Dynasty.* New Haven: Yale University Press.

Wen Zhiyu. 1983. "Jiefangzhanzheng qianxi Minmeng zai Jianghui diqu de huodong qingkuang" (The activities of the Democratic Alliance in the Jiangmen-Huicheng area on the eve of the liberation). In *Jiangmen wenshi ziliao* 9:83–93. Jiangmen: Jiangmenshi Zhengxie.

Wenshi Ziliao Bianjizu. 1964. "Xingjian Xinhui Shuyuan de jingguo" (An account of the establishment of the Xinhui Academy). In *Wenshi ziliao xuanji* 2:30–36. Huicheng: Xinhui Zhengxie.

Whyte, Martin. 1974. *Small Groups and Political Rituals in China.* Berkeley: University of California Press.

Whyte, Martin, and William Parish. 1984. *Urban Life in Contemporary China.* Chicago: University of Chicago Press.

Wilson, Dick, ed. 1977. *Mao Tse-tung in the Scales of History.* Cambridge: Cambridge University Press.

Wolf, Arthur, ed. 1974. *Religion and Ritual in Chinese Society.* Stanford: Stanford University Press.

Wolf, Margery. 1985. *Revolution Postponed.* Stanford: Stanford University Press.

Wong, Christine. 1985. "Material Allocation and Decentralization of the Local Sector on Industrial Reforms." In *The Political Economy of Reform in Post-Mao China,* ed. Elizabeth Perry and Christine Wong, 253–80. Cambridge, Mass.: Harvard University Press.

Wu Han. 1948. *Zhu Yuanzhang zhuan* (Biography of Zhu Yuanzhang). Hong Kong: Zhuanji Wenxueshe. Reprint.

Wu Qingshi. 1962. "Guangdong shatian zhi yimian" (An aspect of the sands in Guangdong). In *Guangdong wenshi ziliao* 5:72–89. Guangzhou: Guangdong Sheng Zhengxie.

Wu Ruilin and Huang Enlian. 1935. "Jiu Fenghuangcun diaocha baogao" (A field report on Old Phoenix Village). *Lingnan xuebao* 4, 3:93–162.

Wu Shangshi and Zeng Shaoxuan. 1947. "Zhujiang sanjiaozhou" (The Pearl River delta). *Lingnan Xuebao* 8, 1.

Wu Shaoquan. 1947. *Dao nongcun qu* (To the countryside). Shanghai: Shenghuo Shudian.

Wu Wanli, ed. 1947. *Guangdong gongye* (The industries of Guangdong). Guangzhou: Guangdong Shiyegongsi.

Xiao I-shan. [1935] 1986. *Jindai mimi shehui shiliao* (Historical materials on the secret societies of the early modern period). Changsha, Hunan: Yuelu Shushe.

Xiao Zheng, ed. 1977. *Minguo ershi niandai zhongguo dalu tudi wenti ziliao* (Data on Chinese land problems in the 1930s). Taipei: Zhongguo Dizheng Yanjiusuo.

Xie Yingming. 1980. "Chen Jitang zhuyue shiqi shengying gongye gaikuang zayi" (Recollections of provincial industries during the era of Chen Jitang). In *Guangdong wenshi ziliao* 28:110–42. Guangzhou: Guangdong Sheng Zhengxie.

Xi'nan Shuyuan quantu (A comprehensive map and account of the Xi'nan Academy). The first preface is dated 1847; this edition was compiled in 1921.

Xinhui Aiqun Shanyuan zhengxinlu (A public account of the Aiqun Charity Association of Xinhui). 1931.

Xinhui cheng Tongshan Shantang Renji Yihui Taoze Yihui Zequn Yihui xizi shicha zhimai baigu ershiwu qi zhengxinlu (A public account of the activities of the Tongshan, Renyi, Taoze, and Zequn Charity Associations in Huicheng). 1936.

Xinhui Cheng Yanhe Shanghu Weichituan. 1924. *Chenghui Huihe liang'an puwei shimoji* (An account of redeeming the land attached to shops along the banks of Huicheng). Xinhui.

Xinhui Shuyuan gongding changji ji guanli zhangcheng (The estate rituals of the Xinhui Academy and its operating regulations). Preface dated 1928.

Xinhui Xian Chengxiang Weiyuanhui Lianluochu. 1952. *Xinhui xian chengxiang lianluochu sangeyuelai gongzuo qingkuang he yixie zhuyao jingyan* (Some important experiences of the Urban-Rural League of Xinhui in the last three months). Huicheng.

Xinhui Xian Dang'anguan. 1984. *Xinhui xian xingzheng quyu yange cankao ziliao (chugao)* (A draft of the reference materials for the history of administrative regions in Xinhui county). Huicheng.

Xinhui Xian Gongshangye Lianhehui, ed. 1957. *Zhengming kuaibao* (Debate express). Vols. 12, 13, and 15–22). Huicheng.

Xinhui Xian Kuishan Shangye Tongye Gonghui. 1948. *Benhui huiyuan shanghao damai cewei yezhu sanqi changbing sheng shan boli shengbi laokui yi lan biao* (A list of the contracted amounts of the different types of fan palm between member enterprises of the guild and growers). Xinhui.

Xinhui Xian Nongye Quhua Bangongshi. 1983. *Xinhui xian nongye quhua baogaoji*. Huicheng.

Xinhui Xian Renmin Weiyuanhui. 1956. "Guanyu fangkuan shichang guanli de gexiang cuoshi" (On the measures to relax market administration). *Xinhui nongmin bao,* November 4.

Xinhui Xian Renwei Bangongshi. 1958. *Xinhui xian caimao gongzuo jingyan huibian* (A collection on finances and trade in Xinhui). Huicheng.

Xinhui Xian Shedui Qiye Guanliju. 1980. *Xinhui xian sheban qiye jingyan xuanji* (Selected experiences of commune enterprises in Xinhui county). Huicheng.

Xinhui Xian Siqu Tugaidui. 1952. *Siqu tugai jianxun* (Dispatches on the land reform in the Fourth District). Huicheng.

Xinhui Xian Xinhui Shuyuan Xi'nan Shuyuan Dongbei Ju Changchan Zhengli Weiyuanhui. 1946. *Xinhui xian Xinhui Shuyuan, Xi'nan Shuyuan, Dongbei Ju Changtian cehuitu* (A map of the landed estates of the Xinhui Academy, Xi'nan Academy, and Dongbei Public Bureau in Xinhui county). Xinhui.

Xinhui Xian Zhengfu Tongjishi. 1947. *Xinhui xian xianzheng tongji ziliao shouce.* (A pamphlet for the statistical materials of Xinhui county). Huicheng.

Xinhui xiancheng nanbiantang Xu xing zugang (The lineage rules of the Xu surname in Nanbiantang of Huicheng). 1936. Huicheng.

Xinhui xiancheng zuixin xiangxi jiedaotu (The most recent street map of Huicheng). 1925. Huicheng: Wenming Shuju.

Xinhui Xiangcun Gongzuo Xiehui. 1938. *Zhanshi xiangcun gongzuo renyuan xunlianban jiniance* (A pamphlet To commemorate the training classes for rural cadres during the war). Huicheng: Wenming Shuju.

Xinhui xiangtuzhi (Xinhui local gazetteer). [1908] 1970. Hong Kong: Gangzhou Xuehui.

Xinhui xianzhi (Xinhui county gazetteer). Editions of 1690, 1751, 1840, and 1870.

Xu Xing. 1987. *Mao Zedong shenquan shidai* (Mao's holy empire). Hong Kong: Pioneer Publishers.

Yang, C. K. 1959. *Chinese Communist Society: The Family and the Village.* Cambridge, Mass: MIT Press.

————. 1961. *Religion in Chinese Society.* Berkeley: University of California Press.

Ye Shaohua. 1965. "Wo suo zhidaode Dongguan Mingluntang" (The Mingluntang of Dongguan as I knew it). In *Guangdong wenshi ziliao* 15:1–21. Guangzhou: Guangdong Sheng Zhengxie.

Ye Shaolin. 1965. "Xinhai, tao-Long liangyi Zhujiang sanjiaozhou xiwuxian datianer de huodong" (The activities of the local bosses in the five western counties of the Pearl River delta during the political upheavals of 1911 and the campaign against Long). In *Guangdong wenshi ziliao* 15:33–47. Guangzhou: Guangdong Sheng Zhengxie.

Ye Wenwei and Xu Zhongtao. 1963. "Xinhui kuiye lüetan" (A brief account of the fan Palm trade of Xinhui). In *Wenshi ziliao xuanji* 1:1–5. Huicheng: Xinhui Xian Zhengxie.

Ye Xian'en. 1983. *Ming-Qing Huizhou nongcun shehui yu dianpuzhi* (Rural society and bond servants in Huizhou during the Ming and Qing). Hefei: Anhui Renmin Chubanshe.

————. 1985. "Lüe lun Zhujiang sanjiaozhou de nongye shangyehua" (A brief discussion of the agricultural commercialization of the Pearl River delta). *Zhongguoshi Yanjiu* 3:16–29.

Ye Xian'en and Tan Dihua. 1984. "Ming Qing Zhujiang sanjiaozhou nongye shangyehua yu xushi de fazhan" (The agricultural commercialization of the Pearl River delta and the development of market towns). *Guangdong shehui kexue* 2:73–90.

————. 1985a. "Lun Guangdong Zhujiang sanjiaozhou de zutian" (On the ancestral estates of the Pearl River delta). In *Ming Qing Guangdong shehui jingji xingtai yanjiu* (A study of the socioeconomic conditions of Guangdong during the Ming and Qing dynasties), ed. by Guangdong Lishi Xuehui, 22–64. Guangzhou: Guangdong Renmin Chubanshe.

————. 1985b. "Guanyu Qing zhongyehou Zhujiang sanjiaozhou haozu de fuyi zhengshou wenti" (Problems related to the levying and collection of taxes and corvée by the lineages in the Pearl River delta after the mid-Qing). *Qingshi yanjiu tongxun* 2:1–4.

Yu Qiaozi. 1985. "Jiefang qian Xinhui laokui hengye gaikuang" (The palm residue products trade in Xinhui before the liberation). In *Xinhui wenshi ziliao xuanji* 20:30–39. Huicheng: Xinhui Xian Zhengxie.

Yu Qinghe. 1984. "Buweishang yu tong dangzhongyang baochiyizhi" (On not blindly following superiors and being in agreement with the Party central). *Fendou* (June): 13–14.

Yu Yingshi. 1982. *Shixue yu chuantong* (Historiography and tradition). Taipei: Shibao Wenhua Chubanshiye Youxiangongsi.

Yu Ziliang. 1982. "Huicheng lunxian de huiyi" (Recollections of Huicheng during the Japanese occupation). In *Xinhui wenshi ziliao xuanji* 5:14–26. Huicheng: Xinhui Xian Zhengxie.

———. 1986. "Xiri Huicheng xiangdu" (The ferries of yesteryear in the Huicheng area). In *Xinhui wenshi ziliao xuanji*, vol. 22, 63–64. Huicheng: Xinhui Xian Zhengxie.

Yuan Ruofei. 1981. *Nongcun renmingongshe laodong guanli* (The labor management in rural communes). Beijing: Nongye Chubanshe.

Yuexiqu Dangwei Zhengce Yanjiushi. 1952. *Jianchi fadong qunzhong guanche helihefa douzheng dedaole shengli* (A victory for insisting on the reasonable and legal ways of struggle among the masses). Guangdong.

Yuezhongqu Tuweihui Xijiang Tugai Gongzuozu. 1953. *Tugai fucha gongzuo cankao ziliao* (Reference materials for review work on the land reform). Guangdong.

Yun Han. 1980. "Guangdong zanbian dier zongdui zai Jiangmen Xinhui diqu qiyi jingguo" (The insurrection of the Guangdong Number Two Army Corps in the Jiangmen-Huicheng area). In *Guangdong wenshi ziliao* 26:216–28. Guangzhou: Guangdong Sheng Zhengxie.

Zeng Qiqing. 1962. "Guomindang tongzhi shiqi de Guangdong bingyi" (The military draft in Guangdong during the rule of the Nationalists). In *Guangdong wenshi ziliao* 5:146–58. Guangzhou: Guangdong Sheng Zhengxie.

Zeng Zhongmou. 1942. *Guangdong jingji fazhanshi* (A history of economic development in Guangdong). Qujiang: Guangdong Sheng Yinhang Jingji Yanjiushi.

Zha Ke'en. 1962. "Guomindang fandong zhengfu de bingyi yu bingyi chuzhang Cheng Zerun zhi si" (The military draft of the reactionary Nationalists and the death of the head of the conscription office, Cheng Zerun). In *Guangdong wenshi ziliao* 5:159–71. Guangzhou: Guangdong Sheng Zhengxie.

Zhang Desheng. "Xuexiao jiaoyu" (School Education). In *Renmin gongshe yu nongcun fazhan: Taishan xian Doushan gongshe jingyan*, ed. Rance Lee and S. K. Lau. Hong Kong: Chinese University Press.

Zhang Yang. 1948. "San-Long zhi zhan" (The feud between Sanjiang and Longquan). In *Guangdong siyi qiaobao* 16, 4, 3(September): 15–17. Hong Kong.

Zhao Gongqing. 1983. "Kangri zhanzheng Xinhui cheng lunxian shiqi de mijia" (Grain prices during the Japanese occupation of Huicheng). In *Xinhui wenshi ziliao xuanji* 9:17–22. Huicheng: Xinhui Xian Zhengxie.

———. 1986. "Jiu shehui zhengshou shuijuan zafei de zhongzhong" (The taxes and surcharges of the old society). In *Xinhui wenshi ziliao xuanji* 22:58–62. Huicheng: Xinhui Xian Zhengxie.

Zhao shi zupu (Genealogy of the Zhao lineage). 1937. Hong Kong.

Zhonggong Guangdong Shengwei Nongcun Gongzuobu. 1958. "Guanyu renmin gongshe fenpei wenti de chuli yijian" (Opinions on how to handle income distribution in the people's communes). In *Guanyu renmin gongshe fenpei wenti de diaocha*, 2–3. Guangzhou: Guangdong Renmin Chubanshe.

Zhonggong Xinhui Xian Weiyuanhui. 1955–80. *Xinhui gongzuo* (Political work in Xinhui).

———. 1958–80. *Xinhui tongxun* (Communications in Xinhui).

Zhonggong Xinhui Xianwei Hezuobu. 1958. "Guanyu Huancheng, Lile renmin gongshe fenpei wenti de diaocha" (On the distribution policies of Huancheng and Lile communes). In *Guanyu renmin gongshe fenpei wenti de diaocha* 4–11. Guangzhou: Guangdong Renmin Chubanshe.

Zhonggong Xinhui Xianwei Xuanchuanbu. 1960. *Xinhui xian tugai yundong ziliao huibian* (A collection of materials on land reform campaigns in Xinhui county). 2 vols. Huicheng.

Zhonggong Zhongyang Bangongting, ed. 1956. *Zhongguo nongcun de shehui zhuyi gaochao* (The high tide of socialism in the Chinese countryside). 3 vols. Beijing: Renmin Chubanshe.

Zhonggong Zhongyang Huanan Fenju Zhengce Yanjiushi. 1950. *Guangdong qingkuang huibian* (Materials on conditions in Guangdong).

Zhonggong Zhongyang Weiyuanhui. 1964. *Guanyu nongcun shehuizhuyi jiaoyu yundong zhong yixie juti zhengce de guiding* (Regulations on some concrete policies of the rural socialist education campaign).

Zhongguo Gongchandang Zhongyang Weiyuanhui. 1953. "Guanyu fazhan nongye shengchan hezuoshe de jueyi" (Decisions on developing agricultural cooperatives). Reprinted in *Zhongguo Gongchandang Zhongyang Weiyuanhui guanyu fazhan nongye shengchan hezuoshe de jueyi jiqi youguan wenti* (1955), 13–31. Beijing: Renmin Chubanshe.

————. 1961. "Nongcun renmin gongshe gongzuo tiaoli caoan" (A draft of the regulations of the people's communes). Commonly referred to as The Sixty Articles.

————. 1962. "Nongcun renmin gongshe gongzuo tiaoli xiuzheng caoan" (A revised draft of the regulations on the people's communes).

————. 1963. "Guanyu muqian nongcun gongzuo zhong ruogan wenti de jueding" (Decisions on some of the current issues in rural work).

Zhongguo Kexueyuan Jingji Yanjiusuo, ed. 1957. *Guomin jingji huifushiqi nongye shengchan hezuoshe ziliao huibian* (Source materials on agricultural cooperation during the recovery period of the national economy). Vols. 1 and 2. Beijing: Kexue Chubanshe.

Zhongguo Kexueyuan Jingji Yanjiusuo Shougongyezu. 1957. "1954 nian quanguo geti shougongye diaocha ziliao" (The 1954 national investigation materials on individual handicrafts). Beijing: Sanlian.

Zhongguo Nongye Nianjian Bianji Weiyuanhui. 1982–84. *Zhongguo nongye nianjian.* Beijing: Nongye Chubanshe.

Zhongguo Renmin Zhengzhi Xieshang Huiyi Quanguo Weiyuanhui Mishuchu. 1951. *Tudigaige cankao ziliao xuanbian* (Reference materials on the land reform). Beijing.

Zhongguo Shehuikexueyuan Lishi Yanjiusuo. 1981. *Zhongguoshi yanjiu* (Chinese historical study). Vol. 3.

Zhongnan Junzheng Weiyuanhui Tudigaige Weiyuanhui Diaocha Yanjiuchu. 1953. *Zhongnanqu yibaige xiang diaocha tongji biao* (A statistical collection of investigations of 100 townships in the south central district). Wuhan.

Zhongxin Guomin Xuexiao Chuban Weiyuanhui. 1948. *Xinhui xian Tianma xiang Zhongxin Guomin Xuexiao sizhounian jinian tekan* (A special publication to commemorate the fourth anniversary of the Zhongxin Guomin School of the Tianma township). Xinhui.

Zhongyang Renmin Zhengfu Zhengwuyuan. [1950] 1965. "Zhongyang Renmin Zhengfu, Zhengwuyuan guanyu huafen nongcun jieji chengfen de jueding" (Decision of the State Council of the Chinese People's Government on the differentiation of classes). Reprinted in *Zenyang fenxi nongcun jieji*, 1–2. Beijing: Renmin Chubanshe.

————. [1953]. 1955. "Zhongyang Renmin Zhengfu, Zhengwuyuan guanyu shixing liangshi de jihua shougou he jihua gongying de mingling" (Directives from the State Council of the Chinese People's Government on the planned purchase and supply of grain). In *Nongye shehuizhuyi gaizao wenti* 1:190–93. Beijing: Caizheng Jingji Chubanshe.

Zhongyang Weiyuanhui Shejikaohe Weiyuanhui. 1953. *Gongfei tudi zhengce yu nongmin zuzhi zhi yanjiu mulu* (A bibliography of the land policies and peasant organizations of the Communist bandits). Taipei, Taiwan.

Zhou Siming. 1962. "Wushi nianlai de Guangdong jinrong gaikuang" (The general state of Guangdong's finances in the last fifty years). In *Guangdong wenshi ziliao* 5:20–41. Guangzhou: Guangdong Sheng Zhengxie.

Zhou Yongxin. 1980. Xiang Gang mianlin renkou baozha" (Hong Kong faces a population explosion). *Qishi niandai* (November): 23–26.

Zhujiang sanjiaozhou nongyezhi (Agricultural gazetteer of the Pearl River delta). Vols. 1–6. Foshan: Foshan Diqu Geming Weiyuanhui, 1976.

Zweig, David. 1986. "Prosperity and Conflict in Post-Mao Rural China." *China Quarterly* 105 (March): 1–18.

In preparing this book, I consulted the following Chinese newspapers and serials:
Fan fengjian (1952)
Gangzhou xingqibao (1920s)
Gongshe caiwu (after June 1983 renamed *Nongcun caiwu kuaiji*)
Guangdong Siyi qiaobao (1940s, Hong Kong)
Minzong shibao (1930s, Xinhui)
Nanfang ribao
Nongye jingji wenti
Qishi niandai (renamed *Jiushi niandai* after March 1984)
Siyi huaqiao daobao (1940s)
Xinhui nongmin bao (renamed *Xinhui bao* in 1957)
Xinhui qiaokan (1960s)
Xinhui wenshi ziliao xuanji (vols. 1–22; vols. 1–3 are referred to as *Wenshi Ziliao Xuanji*)

Glossary

babao 八包
Baiqing Sha 百頃沙
bao 保
Bao Qing Tian 包青天
baodian 包佃
baogong tou 包工頭
baolianghui 保良會
Beidi 北帝
bopo 伯婆
boxue shouru 剝削收入
Cao Cao 曹操
Changni 長薿
changpingcang 常平倉
chaogeng 炒更
Chaolian 潮蓮
Chen Jitang 陳濟棠
Chen Kao 陳考
Chenghuang 城隍
chengzhe weiwang, baizhe weikou 成者為王, 敗者為寇
chenhuo dajie 趁火打刼
chenpi 陳皮
citang 祠堂
citang baiyi 祠堂白蟻
cun 村
da bao gan 大包幹
da enren 大恩人
da gan chu da bian 大幹出大變
Da Gubu 大穀埗
da hepiao 打禾票
Da Sha 大沙
da tian er 大天二
da xiang 大鄉
da zongci 大宗祠
dai maozi 戴帽子
Dan 蛋
dang quan pai 當權派
danjia 蛋家

danmin 蛋民
danwei 單位
Dawang 大王
Daze 大澤
Dazhai 大寨
Deng Zihui 鄧子恢
diaogeng 釣耕
dibao 地保
difang 地方
Dilintang 帝臨堂
dingti 頂替
ditoushe 地頭蛇
dizi 娣仔
Dongbei Gongju 東北公局
Dongguan 東莞
Donghai Shiliusha 東海十六沙
Doumen 斗門
douzheng guoshi 斗爭果實
du 都
duikou danwei 對口單位
dun dian 蹲點
enqing 恩情
fang 坊
fang 房
Fang Fang 方方
fangeng 翻耕
fen 分
fengjian boxue 封建剝削
fengjian wangguo 封建王國
Foshan 佛山
fulao 父老
Gangzhou Gongdu 岡州公牘
Gangzhou Shuyuan 岡州書院
geqinghe 割青禾
gong chang 公嘗
Gonglu Dawei 公路大圍
Gong-Shang-Lian 工商聯
gongsheng 貢生
gongsuo 公所
gongxiao she 供銷社
Gu Dacun 古大存
guan ka ya 管卡壓
Guandi 關帝
Guangdong Huiguan 廣東會館
guangrong gan 光榮感
Guangshun Tang 廣順堂
Guang-Zhao Gongsuo 廣肇公所
guanli qu 管理區

guanmen dagou 關門打狗
Guanyin 觀音
Gugang Zhan 古岡棧
Guifeng 圭峰
Gujing 古井
Guo Podai 郭婆帶
guoji yutang 果基魚塘
guojia ganbu 國家幹部
Guzhen 古鎮
hangdi 行底
hangzong 行總
Hanlin 翰林
haomen 豪門
haomin 豪民
He Wenyi Gong Tang 何文懿公堂
hepiao 禾票
heping fentian 和平分田
Heqing Hui 合慶會
Hetang 荷塘
Hongsheng 洪聖
hu 戶
Huaguang 華光
huajuan 花捐
Huancheng 環城
Huicheng 會城
jia 甲
Jiang Jieshi (Chiang Kai-shek) 蔣介石
Jiangmen 江門
Jiangmen Chenggong Xiaozu 江門城工小組
Jiangmen-Xinhui Dongtai 江門新會動態
jiao 醮
jiashou 甲首
Jinniutou 金牛頭
jinshi di 進士第
jishu gugan 技術骨幹
jiti ganbu 集體幹部
Jiujingtang 久敬堂
Jiuzisha 九子沙
jizhen 集鎮
juren 舉人
jushen 局紳
kaichu chushe 開除出社
kaifang hu 開放戶
Kaiping 開平
Kangwang 康王
Kejia (Hakka) 客家
kou liang tian 口糧田
Kuishan Huiguan 葵扇會館

kuiwei 葵圍
kuiye 葵業
lao dage 老大哥
laosha weitian 老沙圍田
leng re bing 冷熱病
lian 連
lian chan dao hu 聯產到戶
lian chan dao zu 聯產到組
lianfang 聯防
liang 兩
Liang Yue Guang Yi Tang 兩粵廣義堂
Lianhe Tang 聯和堂
Lianhu Tang 聯護堂
Lianxing Gongzhan 聯興公棧
Lianyi Tang 聯益堂
Lianzhu Tang 聯珠堂
lijin (likin) 釐金
Lile 禮樂
Lingnan 嶺南
lingxiu 領袖
litu bulixiang 離土不離鄉
Liu Yiji 劉怡記
Long Jiguang 龍濟光
longmai 龍脈
Longmu 龍母
Longquan 龍泉
Lu Man 陸滿
Luokeng 羅坑
mai chan zu 埋產組
man tang hong 滿堂紅
Mani 馬熊
meiyou ganqing 沒有感情
mihang gonghui 米行公會
min jun 民軍
minban jiaoshi 民辦教師
Ming 明
mingluntang 明倫堂
Minhui bao 民會報
Minmeng 民盟
mintian 民田
minzhu pingfen 民主評分
mu 畝
Nanhai 南海
Nanhai Hongsheng Guangli Zhaoming Longwang 南海洪聖廣利昭明
Niuguling 牛牯嶺
nong-gong-shang zonggongsi 農工商總公司
pai 排

panming qu gan 拚命去幹
Panyu 番禺
pi Lin pi Kong 批林批孔
pin xia zhong nong 貧下中農
pinnong xiaozu 貧農小組
qiang huapao 搶花炮
qiangge 搶割
Qibao 七堡
Qin Zheng 秦政
qing 頃
Qing 清
qu 區
qu gongsuo 區公所
quan 全
qunzhong daibiao 羣眾代表
Renji Yihui 仁濟義會
san bao 三包
san bao yi jiang 三包一獎
san ding 三定
san guang didai 三光地帶
san jiehe 三結合
san pa 三怕
san zi yi bao 三自一包
Sanbao 三寶
sangji yutang 桑基魚塘
Sanjiang 三江
Sanhe 三和
sanmian hongqi 三面紅旗
Sanyaying 三丫營
saodi chumen 掃地出門
sha 沙
shafu 沙夫
shagu 沙骨
shaji jinghou 殺雞儆猴
shajuan 沙捐
shamin 沙民
Shanghengsha 上橫沙
Shangshu Fang 尚書坊
shangtian haili 傷天害理
shangtuan 商團
shatian 沙田
she 社
shehui zhuyi jingsai 社會主義競賽
shenggelian 省革聯
shi 石
shidian 試點
shoushi hangzong 首事行總
Shuangshui 瀧水

Shui Hu Zhuan 水滸傳
Shunde 順德
Shuni 鼠熊
Shushan 鼠山
shushi 書室
shuyuan 書院
si guding 四固定
sifen huoping 死分活評
Siyi (Sze Yap) 四邑
Song Ziwen 宋子文
Sun Yixian (Sun Yat-Sen) 孫逸仙
Taishan 台山
tang 堂
Tangang 潭岡
Tangxia 棠下
Tao Zhu 陶鑄
Tianhou 天后
tianshi dili renhe 天時地利人和
ting 亭
Tongren Hao 同仁號
Tongshan Tang 同善堂
tu 圖
tuanlian 團練
tugai ganbu 土改幹部
tuhao 土豪
tuizu tuiya qingfei fanba 退租退押清匪反霸
tujuan 屠捐
Wanqingsha 萬頃沙
weichihui 維持會
weiguan 圍館
weihai zuotian 圍海造田
weisuo 衛所
weitian 圍田
Wenwu 文武
wu da lingxiu 五大領袖
Wubentang 務本堂
wujinshi 武進士
wujuren 武舉人
Wutu 五圖
wuxiucai 武秀才
xiafang 下放
xiahu 下戶
xiang 鄉
xiangbao 鄉保
xiangdu 鄉渡
Xiangshan 香山
xiangyue 鄉約
xiangzu 鄉族

Xianxian Xiang 仙賢鄉
Xiao Gubu 小穀埠
Xiao Siqing 小四清
xiao yao pai 逍遙派
Xiaogang 小岡
Xiaolan 小欖
Xihai Shibasha 西海十八沙
Xi'nan Shuyuan 西南書院
Xinhui 新會
Xinhui Shuyuan 新會書院
Xinhui Yiyong Youji Dadui 新會義勇游擊大隊
Xinkuijiao 新魁滘
Xinsha 新沙
xiucai 秀才
xu 墟
xuezhai 血債
xunjian si 巡檢司
Ya Men 厓門
Yao 瑤
yicang 義倉
yi tian er niu san poniang 一田二牛三婆娘
yigong yinong 亦工亦農
ying 營
Yinzhouhu 銀州湖
yonggan fenzi 勇敢份子
you renqing 有人情
Yu Hanmou 余漢謀
Yuan Dai 袁帶
Yuanqing Xiang 源清鄉
Yuecheng 悅城
Yuezhong 粵中
Yuqing Tang 余慶堂
zeren tian 責任田
Zhang Bao 張保
Zhang Fagui 張發圭
zhansha 佔沙
zhao an 招安
Zhao Qixiu 趙其休
zhen 鎮
zhenggao 掙槀
zhinong zhuangui 支農轉軌
zhong zi wu 忠字舞
Zhongshan 中山
Zhou Hanling 周漢玲
Zhoujia bing 周家兵
Zhu Yuanzhang 朱元璋
Zhuhai 珠海
Zhujiang sanjiaozhou 珠江三角州

zhuxi tuan 主席團
zhuyao laodong 主要勞動
zong luxian 總路線
zong pai 總派
zongdian 總佃
zou zi pai 走資派
zu 祖
zuchang 祖嘗
zuci 祖祠
zuosheng 座聖

Index

Academies, 7, 55, 57, 67–71, 77, 294, 310n4, 316n21, 316n23. *See also individual academies*

Accounting: brigade-level, 238–40, 271; team-level, 229–30, 282

Activists, 86, 108–10, 118–24, 131–42, 167, 213–15, 327n32; peasant, 135–40, 144, 157, 162, 180, 193, 264, 291; rebel, 206–11; women, 174, 209–10

Agricultural enterprises, 26–27, 179, 250, 252; experiment station, 179, 180, 250, 258; farms (duck) 28, 219, (lumber) 179, 251, 258; fish (hatcheries) 179, 250, 258, (ponds) 24, 25, 225, 275; machinery factory, 179, 252, 253, 254, 260–66, 286, 338n9; machinery station, 179, 238, 252, 254, 258, 286; orchards, 156, 179, 251, 258, 268, 274; veterinary station, 251, 258

Agricultural producers' cooperatives, 155–59, 163, 188

Agriculture: commodities, 279–80, 329n17, 333–34n22; crop diversification, 192, 275; farmers (fruit) 162, (migrant) 4, 25, 36, 45, 134, (tenant) 60–61; mulberry, 24, 25. *See also* Cash crops; Citrus fruits; Fan palm

Ahern, Emily, 10, 42, 299, 314n25, 318n42

Alitto, Guy, 310n2, 321n13

Ancestors: graves, 49; tablets, 57, 67, 77, 81, 243, 319n49. *See also* Ritual practices

Ancestral halls, 15, 49, 53, 57–58, 303n4, 314n33, 315n4; apical, 42, 50, 303n4, 312n16; focal, 42, 43, 49, 54, 290, 298, 312n17; study chamber type, 43, 313n17. *See also* Wubentang

Ancestral trusts, 4–5, 43, 49, 53, 59, 62; as contractors, 54; managers of, 25, 36, 54, 59, 86, 128–29. *See also* Estates

Anti-bully campaigns, 115, 141

Authority, 292, 294; defined, 304n1

Baker, Hugh, 304n7, 311n12, 312n16

Bandits, 61, 88, 111

Baum, Richard, 333n5

Beidi Temple, 53, 54, 290, 314n27

Bernstein, Thomas, 332n20

Bond servants, 48

Bosses, local. *See* Strongmen, local

"Brave elements," 132, 135, 142, 326n26

Brigades, 143, 171, 173, 196–97; accounting, 238–40, 271; class differentiation, 198–201; economy, 194, 266; income, 248, 278, 282; workshops, 268. *See also* Enterprises; Work teams

Brotherhood associations, 95, 320n12

Bureaucratization, 146, 255

Cadres, xvii, xviii, xix–xx, 121, 124–25, 160–61, 167, 189, 192–93, 195, 304n5, 324n15, 334n8, 335n18, 339n7; brigade, 173, 190, 203, 216–18, 226–29, 237, 240, 270, 276, 305n9; commune, 175, 184–86, 201–03, 212–13, 217–18, 252, 253, 256, 258, 259; compliance of, 176–77; conflict of interests, 128–29, 159, 164–65, 166, 305n14; enterprise, 178–80; generations of, 87, 140, 203–04, 339n2; party, 7, 8, 9, 118, 146, 330n30; political leverage of, 246, 249; rural, xvii, 2, 4, 9–10, 162, 167–69, 171, 188, 203, 211, 213–15, 219, 241–44, 273, 288, 291, 294, 300, 304n8 (prologue); salaried, 140, 144–45, 335n16. *See also* Collectives; Cooperatives; Land reform

Cash crops, 49, 62, 99, 221, 224, 225; household responsibility for, 280–81; state control of, 153–55, 226, 274–75, 309n33. *See also* Agriculture

Chan, Anita, 331n4, 335n13, 340n15

Chaolian Hongsheng Temple, 16, 306n5

Chen Hansheng, 309n32

Chen Kao Temple, 50, 53, 54

Chen Yun, 329*n*19

Citrus fruits, 35, 49, 62, 98, 225, 275; mandarin oranges, 30–31; tangerines, 228, 279; trade in, 31; production, 29–30, 152; revival of industry, 121–22, 192; state control of, 151, 154

Class: composition, 126, 199, 200; Mao Zedong's understanding of, 118; politics, 120, 125; status, 134, 135, 324*n*7, 324*n*9, 334*n*12

Cohen, Myron L., 3, 304*n*4, 311*n*12

Collectives, 160–66, 175–76; agricultural, 155–56, 329*n*20

Collectivization, 2, 144, 149, 164–65, 169, 292; cadres, role of, 146, 155–59, 165, 335*n*16; personal autonomy decreased, 168, 330*n*31. *See also* Decollectivization

Comaroff, Jean, 318*n*42, 340*n*5

Commodity: grain, 286; taxes, 63, 74

Communes, xvi, 175, 177, 192, 248, 274, 336*n*6; leadership, 174, 215–18, 257–58; management model, 175, 332*n*9; *vs.* Red Guards, 206

Communities: building and development, 36–40, 45–48, 55–56, 82–83, 143. *See also* Towns; Villages

Communization, 116–17, 175–76, 187, 188, 292, 330*n*2

Compliance and complicity, xviii, xxi, 11, 13, 192–93, 204, 211, 212, 226, 240, 242, 294

Compounds, enclosed, 27, 39–40

Conscription, 106, 107, 322*n*36

Construction: projects, 178; team, 252, 258

Contractors, 27, 28, 38, 43, 49, 66; *vs.* gentry, 60, 62, 75–76; *vs.* landlords, 39, 75, 318*n*39; temples as, 47

Cooperatives, 147, 155–59, 163, 188, 328*n*7; cadres, role of, 158; competition among, 160

Corruption, xviii, 88, 105

County MCBE Bureau, 255–57, 338*n*5

Crook, David and Isabel, 323*n*2

Cultural Revolution, 2, 206, 213, 240–44, 300, 301. *See also* Mao Zedong

Dan fishermen, 36, 44, 46–47, 51–53, 297–98, 309*n*1. *See also* Tianhou Temple

Davis-Friedmann, Deborah, 304*n*4, 318*n*42

Dawang Temple, 50

Daze Commune, 99, 273

Dazhai model, 212, 235, 238, 303*n*6, 336*n*2

Decollectivization, 3, 273, 277–81; failure at Dongjia, 281–84; reactions to, 274, 275–77; success at Huancheng, 275–76

Deities, 11, 64, 78, 79

Democratic Alliance, 109–10, 187

Deng Zihui, 329*n*18

Dikes, xviii, 24, 323–35, 236, 307*n*10

Dilintang Temple, 58, 79, 84

Disarmament of townships, 112–13

Dongbei Public Bureau, 37, 59, 71, 94, 310*n*4, 316*n*19

Dongjia Brigade, 270, 277, 281–84

Du Runsheng, 339*n*1

Duara, Prasenjit, 304*n*1, 310*n*2, 319*n*52

Eberhard, Wolfram, 313*n*18

Ebrey, Patricia, 311*n*12, 312*n*16

Economic liberalization, 287–88

Elites, 67–71, 85–86, 90, 294; managerial, 5, 84, 87; merchant, 67

Emigration, 33, 127, 276, 287, 324*n*12, 325*n*21

Eng, Robert, 311*n*5

Enterprises, 179, 245–72; brigade, 235–37, 266–70; cadres, profiles of, 178–80; collectivization of, 148; commune, 247, 250, 254, 257–60, 286; development of, 246, 266–67, 271; leadership, 271–72; managers, xvii, 72–73, 317*n*32; performance of Sancun Brigade, 241, 246, 271; small-scale, xvi, 173, 178, 245; *vs.* state, 147–48. *See also individual enterprises*; Workers

Entrepreneurship, 1, 292

Estates: ancestral, 37, 58, 59, 129–30, 310*n*3; corporate, 5, 60, 62, 304*n*8 (chap. 1)

Executions, 94–95

Factionalism, 204–06, 210, 212, 220, 240, 254

Famine, 65, 332*n*20

Fan palm, 49, 62, 225, 274, 275, 280, 307*n*22; drying field, 179, 268; enterprises, 129, 286, 308*n*24; handicraft factory, 179, 249, 251, 252, 258, 260; production of, 31, 33, 35, 153–54; trade of, 32–33

Fan Palm Guild, 33, 58, 59, 62–65, 102, 316n15; economic power of, 64, 66, 74; militia, use.of, 64, 100; patron deities, 64

Faure, David, 42, 44, 297, 304n7, 307n12, 312n14, 312n16, 313n17, 314n26, 317n31, 317n36, 318n44, 319n51

Fei Xiaotong, 284

Feng Hefa, 317n37

Ferries, river, 16, 306n3

Fertilizer, 26, 199

Festivals, 5, 16, 64, 168, 304n9, 311n10

Feudal exploitation, 128, 129, 137

Feuds, 44, 50–51, 72, 103, 105–06, 114–15, 161–62, 313n21, 317n30

"Five anti" campaigns, 147–48, 187

Flour mills, 28, 62, 238, 253

Food shortages, 100, 170, 184–87, 321n20

Formalist conception model, 296

"Four fixed" allocations, 190–91, 229

Four Small Cleanups campaign, 201

Freedman, Maurice, 41, 42, 55, 56, 295–300 passim, 304n7, 312n15, 312n16

Freeholders, 54

Frolic, Michael, 4

Fu Yiling, 312n13

Gallin, Bernard, 311n12

Gang of Four, 212, 218, 238

Gangzhou, Port of, 72

Gangzhou Academy, 57, 67

Geertz, Clifford, 306n12, 318n42, 318n43, 339n5

Genealogical ties, 42, 54, 162–63, 203–04, 315n8

Gentry, xviii, 8, 36, 49, 56, 85–87, 294, 315n1; vs. contractors, 60, 62; vs. local bosses, 102; vs. merchant activists and militarists, 87; profile, 45–47

Grain, 24, 221–22, 225, 273, 275, 282; commodity, 286; consumption of, 223; double–cropping, 26, 152, 161, 307n14; mills, 28, 62, 238, 253; policies, 328n11; procurement, 150–53, 220–21, 223, 226; production goals, 183, 184–85, 218–19; production systems, 229–30, 279; production teams, 160, 203; quotas, 164, 191, 224, 226–29, 243; tickets, 65, 91, 96; trade, 28, 150; yields, 196

Granet, Marcel, 299

Great Leap Forward, 170, 187, 245

Grower-entrepreneurs, 36

Guangdong, government of, 120, 339n3

Guangzhou Xiangshan Gonghui, 311n5

Guerrillas, Communist, 97–99

Hai Feng, 208, 212, 334n9

Handicrafts, 98, 149, 252–53, 260

Haomen, 37. See also Strongmen, local

"Harvesting green shoots," 61

Health care, 180, 182, 292

Henderson, Gail, 3

"High tide of socialism," 160, 163

Highway-dike project, xviii, 232–35, 236

Hinton, William, 323n2

Hongsheng Temple, 78–83 passim, 289, 300, 307n19

Households, 156, 158, 273, 275, 280–81, 283–84, 324n31; mean, 46, 48; peasant, 26, 129, 177, 191–92; registration of, 7, 143, 211

Hua Linshan, 208, 212

Huaguang Temple, 50

Huancheng, 18–24, 36; commune, xvi, 171–73; enterprises, 251–52

Huang, Philip, 89, 114

Huicheng, 19, 41, 57–59, 118, 321n15; fall of, 97–100

Immigration, 54

Income, per capita, 175, 183–84, 186, 194, 199, 241, 279; distribution policy, 162, 189–90, 229, 231; grain quotas and, 228

Industrial enterprises, xvii, 33–34, 129, 179, 249–51, 292, 308n28; small-scale, xvii. See also individual industries; Wages; Workers

Industry-Commerce League, 143, 148

Intellectuals, 108–10, 323n45

Japanese occupation, 31, 51, 97–104 passim, 321n17, 321n20

Jiangmen City Work Group, 110

Jingxian Academy, 67

Jinniutou Flood Prevention Gate, 178, 179, 232

Johnson, Kay, 324n9, 331n8

Katayama Tsuyoshi, 6, 37, 317n34

Kinship. See Genealogical ties; Lineages

Kraus, Richard, 324n8
Kuhn, Philip, 90, 309n2, 315n1

Labor. See Workers
Land: reclamation, 24–26, 49; reform,
    120–21, 125, 128–29, 132–40 passim,
    167, 292; registration, 307n13; swap-
    ping, 331n4; tenure, 49, 53, 54, 59–60,
    61, 315n9. See also Peasant claims; Sands
Landlords, xxi, 125–28, 199, 206, 325n18;
    vs. contractors, 39, 75, 318n39; defined,
    133; profile of, 101–02
Lardy, Nicholas, 4, 285, 327n3, 329n19
Law, Joan, 319n51
Lee, Hong Yung, 9, 323n45, 334n9
Li Dazhao, 117
Liang Qichao, 45–47, 313n22
Lieberthal, Kenneth, 327n3, 329n19
Lineage, 1, 4, 311n12, 319n50; communi-
    ties, 5, 43–45, 119, 211, 296–97,
    312n13; paradigm, 41, 296–98; segmen-
    tation, 42, 298, 312n15
Lippit, Victor, 327n3
Literati, 5, 8, 36, 39, 57, 86, 315n1
Liu Shaoqi, 195
Liu Xinwu, xxi
Liuist movement, 201–03, 333n5
Longmu Temple of Yuecheng, 78
Loyalty parade, 206
Lu Wen, 82

MacFarquhar, Roderick, 333n5
Macroregions, 295–96
Madsen, Richard, 4, 14, 193, 304n5,
    331n4, 335n9
Mann, Susan, 310n2, 317n36
Mao Zedong, Maoists, 7, 116, 136, 195,
    240, 291, 333n5; policies, 8, 246, 253;
    revolution, 170, 292
Market towns, 4, 34, 274, 284–85
Markets, 4, 15, 34–35, 47, 168, 192; dur-
    ing Japanese occupation, 99, 102; sched-
    ules of, 309n33, 321n18; rural, 329n18;
    state control of, 146–50
Marks, Robert, 323n2
Matsuda Yoshiro, 5, 37, 40
Meisner, Maurice, 324n9
Merchants, 5, 36, 71; activism, 72–73, 87;
    associations, 83; militia, use of, 110,
    316n15; strongmen, 85
Migrant workers, 41, 134, 285–86

Migration myth, 43–44, 313n18
Militarization of social life, 330n1
Militia, 64, 206, 207; "107 militia," 208;
    colonies, 4, 25, 307n11; defections from,
    110–12; vs. Red Guards, 208
Moonlighting, 286–87

Nationalists, 95, 97–99, 103–05, 107,
    111–12
Newspapers. See Tabloids and newspapers
Ningyang railroad project, 71
Nishikawa Kikuko, 4, 25, 26, 37–40 pas-
    sim, 307n17, 314n32

Oi, Jean, 2, 327n3, 335n19, 339n4, 339n7
Operas, 64, 78, 82, 83–84, 243, 310n2
Oranges. See Citrus fruits

Pacification campaign, 94, 97, 104–06
Palm. See Fan palm
Paper-making factory, 253, 256, 260, 264,
    286
Parish, William, 3, 4, 304n4, 327n3,
    327n4, 330n31, 331n5
Party Youth League, 144, 157, 203, 204,
    206
Pasternak, Burton, 311n12
Pearl River delta, 20–24, 292, 306n9,
    308n25
Peasants, 87, 99, 126, 198–200, 293; activ-
    ists, 135–40, 144, 157, 162, 180, 193,
    264, 291; associations, 112, 131, 135–
    39, 327n2; vs. cadres, 130–33, 141, 211,
    242; categories of, 198–200, 206,
    324n12; claims, 129–30; collectives,
    165–66, 211; complaints, 165, 183–84,
    329n15; cooperatives, 158, 159, 329n22;
    decollectivization era, 200, 275; disillu-
    sioned, 243–44; households, 26, 158,
    192; march on Huicheng, 130; vs. pro-
    curement agents, 322n38; in revolution-
    ary movement, 116, 117–18, 141;
    settlement rights, 325n19; workers, 259–
    60
People's Liberation Army, 111–12, 118–19
Perry, Elizabeth, 4, 330n27
Pilgrimages, 78, 289
Piracy, 107
Polder, 24–26
Police, 92, 93, 101, 106, 107, 160, 322n30

Political brokers, 12, 85–86, 101, 293, 294. *See also* Cadres; Strongmen, local

Poor Peasant League, 123, 131, 138, 207, 305n15

Population, 4, 194, 308n25; rural, 133, 326n29

Potter, Jack, 304n7, 311n12

Power, 62, 77, 84, 187, 292, 294; cultural nexus of, 87, 144, 305n9; defined, 304n1; paradox of, 212–44, 293

Qu Dajun, 312n17

Qu leadership, 288

Red Guards, 2, 205–06, 208, 212, 282, 335n18; *vs.* cadres, 211; *vs.* communes, 206; damage to ancestral tablets, 319n49; factions, 334n9; in periurban areas, 207

Red Turbans, 46, 68

Regional economic systems, 12, 295–96

Rent, 27, 49, 54; cash, 62, 316n13, 316n18; collectors, 66; deposits, 60, 315n10; fluctuations in, 65–66

Rentiers, 126, 127, 325n20

Republican era, 76, 83–84, 87, 90, 319n4

Revolutionary committees, 207, 208–10

Revolutionary movement, 117–18. *See also* Cultural Revolution; Mao Zedong

Rice. *See* Grain

Ritual practices, 1, 5, 10, 11, 292, 299–300, 318n42; community, 48, 50, 63, 77; kinship, 46, 49, 58, 77; and politics, 49, 77, 79, 318n43, 318n47; revival of, xxi, 10–11, 295, 300. *See also* Deities; Festivals; Operas; Shrines, earth; Temples; Theatrical troupes

Rosen, Stanley, 332n17, 334n9, 335n17

Rural areas: leadership, 135–40; population, 34–35, 89

Sancun, 241, 246, 271; brigade accounting, 238–40

Sands, 4, 20, 68; cultivation of, 24; development of, 4–6, 24, 36–39, 40; harvests from, 27; management of, 38; political economy of, 43–45, 60, 307n17, 315n11; revenue from, 26–29, 91, 315n8; Sands for the Ninth Son, 59; set-

tlement of, 39, 46, 311n11; taxation of, 26, 307n13. *See also* Land: reclamation; Shamin

Sangren, Steven, 340n6

Schools, 110, 180–83, 292, 316n23

Schram, Stuart, 2, 324n8

Schurmann, Franz, 10, 193, 324n9

Scott, James, 305n12, 340n2, 340n5

Secret societies, 88–89, 93, 94, 320n9

Seldon, Mark, 323n2, 327n3, 330n2, 331n7, 333n1, 333n6

Self-defense corps, 88, 91, 101, 107, 111, 112, 131, 323n49

Settlement: early stages, 44; rights, 42, 54, 77, 127, 299, 312n14

Shamin, 46, 48, 51, 61

Shangshu Fang, 57, 59

Shangtuan, 63, 64

Shangyebu, 328n7

She, 78

Shrines, earth, 50, 77, 78, 318n44

Shue, Vivienne, 2, 4, 193, 304n1, 304n5, 304n6, 327n3, 335n19

Siqing movement, 189, 201–03, 213

Skinner, G. William, 4, 12, 89, 114, 284, 295, 296, 300, 306n4, 307n12, 308n25, 317n36, 339n4

Smuggling, 53, 88, 102, 106

Solinger, Dorothy, 327n3

Spence, Jonathan, xxii

State: agents of, 6, 7–10, 13, 46, 150, 154, 213, 274, 292; defined, 304n1; purchasing stations of, 151

Strongmen, local, 34, 40–41, 55, 75–76, 83–84, 87, 97, 281; local bosses, 88–115, 130–33, 284–85, 291, 300, 321n21; merchant, 85; military, 70, 87, 91, 96, 114, 317n33. *See also* Anti-bully campaigns

Surname groups, 50–51. *See also* Feuds

Tabloids and newspapers, xx, 109, 121, 187, 204, 205, 243

Tan Dihua, 4, 6, 37, 310n3, 315n7, 315n8, 315n10, 316n13, 317n34, 317n35

Tanaka Issei, 319n48

Tangang Xingzuhui, 72

Tax farming, 73–76, 90, 310n2

Taxes, 26, 44, 74–76, 92–93, 194, 307n13, 320n5; collection of, 6, 90–91, 107, 148, 317n34; commodity, 63, 74; evasion of, 37–38; exemptions from, 26; land, 73–

Taxes (*continued*)
74; payments of, 54; resistance to, 71; skeletal levy, 27, 106, 313*n*21

Teams, 192; autonomy, 190, 333*n*1; construction, 252, 258; income of, 186, 278, 282; mutual aid, 155, 156; output of, 248; production, 160, 173, 203; transport, 173, 179, 252, 253, 258; work, 131, 133–34, 137, 158, 167, 201, 218–19

Temples: celebration rules, 81–82; at Chakeng, 47–48; cults, 79; festivals, 78, 83, 168, 315*n*5; merchant participation in rituals, 82, 84. *See also individual temples*; Ritual practices

Tenant claims, 129

Thaxton, Ralph, 323*n*2, 323*n*3

Theatrical troupes, 53, 64, 108

Third Plenum of the Party Central Committee, 273

Thomas, R. D., 16

"Three anti" campaigns, 147–48, 187

"Three bare zones," 98

"Three fixed" policy of procurement, 150, 231, 239

"Three red flags," 177, 188, 301

Three-tiered ownership system, 229–30

Tianhou Temple, 47, 53, 314*n*26, 314*n*35

Tianlu Xiang, 48, 51, 277–81

Towns: market, 4, 34, 274, 284–85; townships, 143–46, 229, 305*n*14, 306*n*8

Trade, 5, 16, 17, 99–100; of citrus, 31; export, 16, 29, 32, 64, 269, 338*n*6; of fan palms, 32–33; of grain, 28, 150

Training classes and camps, 108, 177, 178, 201, 264, 330*n*24

Transport team, 173, 179, 252, 253, 258

Unger, Jonathan, 332*n*17, 335*n*13

Urban areas: periurban communities, 89, 97, 99, 207, 251, 270; residency, 264, 278, 282, 283, 285, 331*n*5; work in, 276, 277, 281

Village Defense League, 78

Villages, 5, 6, 189, 292, 300; militia, 107; temples, 16, 54; trade, 99–100

Wages, 237, 268, 338*n*11; piece-rate, 230–31

Wakeman, Frederic, 309*n*2, 313*n*24, 315*n*1, 318*n*46, 320*n*9, 324*n*8

Ward, Barbara, 319*n*51

Warlords, 69, 73, 91, 94–97, 115, 318*n*46; regime of, 89, 115, 117

Waterways, in Huancheng, 20

Watson, James, 300, 304*n*7, 311*n*12, 312*n*12, 312*n*16, 314*n*25, 318*n*42, 318*n*47, 335*n*13

Watson, Rubie, 304*n*7

Wen Zhiyu, 112, 121, 323*n*44, 323*n*45

Wenwu Temple, 50

Whyte, Martin, 3, 4, 7, 304*n*4, 327*n*3, 327*n*4, 330*n*31, 331*n*5

Winter wheat, 221, 224

Wolf, Arthur, 10, 78, 295, 299, 300, 318*n*42

Wolf, Margery, 331*n*8

Women's League, 209

Work teams, 131, 133–34, 137, 158, 167, 201, 218–19, 228

Work-points, 199, 229–30, 237, 239, 270, 334*n*8

Workers, xxi, 33, 241, 247, 252–53, 266; in enterprises, 261–63, 269, 271, 272; labor management, 230–32, 235, 237, 260–64; migrant, 41, 134, 285–86; peasant, 259–60; profiles of, 264–66; recruitment of, xviii, 237; seasonal, 61; temporary, 283; women, 269, 331*n*7

Wu Qingshi, 307*n*17

Wubentang, 53, 100, 298

Xiang. *See* Townships

Xiao Zheng, 309*n*32

Xi'nan Academy, 37, 57, 59, 67–69

Xinhui Academy, 37, 59, 69–71, 317*n*27

Xinhui Chamber of Commerce, 72

Xinhui County, 15–18, 21, 22, 160

Yao, 36, 44

Ye Xian'en, 4, 6, 37, 310*n*3, 315*n*7, 315*n*8, 315*n*10, 316*n*13, 317*n*34, 317*n*35

Zhang Bao, 80

Zhongguo Gongzhandang Zhongyang Weiyuanhui, 333*n*1

Zhou Enlai, 176